TODAY'S GOLFER COMPANION

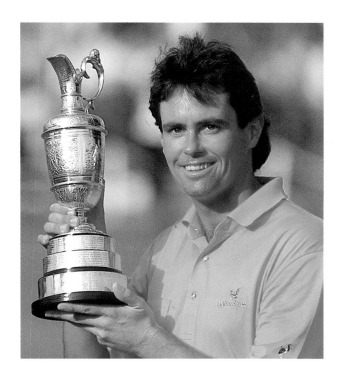

EDITED BY   FOREWORD

BILL ROBERTSON   JOSE MARIA OLAZABAL

Published in association with *Today's Golfer* magazine

ANAYA
PUBLISHERS LTD

First published in Great Britain in 1992
by Anaya Publishers Ltd, Strode House 44-50 Osnaburgh Street,
London, NW1 3ND
in association with *Today's Golfer* magazine

Text Editor: Mike Johnstone
Design by Design 23

BRITISH CATALOGUING-IN-PUBLICATION DATA

Today's Golfer Companion - (Today's Golfer series)
1. Robertson, Bill 11. Series
796.352
ISBN 1 85470 121 5

Typesetting by Design23
Colour origination by Columbia Offset, Singapore
Printed and bound in Great Britain by
Butler & Tanner Ltd, Frome and London

CONTENTS

FOREWORD

Jose Maria Olazabal

As a regular contributor to *Today's Golfer* magazine, I am delighted to provide the foreword to this exciting book. It covers all the main golfing events, along with a host of other fascinating golfing subjects which all contribute to making the game enjoyable for everyone who plays and also so interesting to the thousands who take the game up every year. As well as reviewing the four Major championships, both in words and superb pictures, there are also pages of practical playing advice, for both the high-handicapper as well as the more experienced golfer.

I'm confident that this first issue of the *Today's Golfer Companion* will not only give you many hours of interesting reading, but also provide a great deal of useful information which will help to make your golfing year more enjoyable.

As a youngster, I was lucky enough to grow up living on a golf course and I spent every spare minute practising and dreaming of the day when I would have the opportunity to play some of the fine courses featured in the course strategy section.

I have yet to meet a golfer who has reached the top through natural ability alone. To be successful, especially in the tough world of professional golf, takes dedication and hard work and lots of practice, a sentiment which I'm sure would be echoed by my five fellow tournament professionals featured in the section showing them, and me, in action.

Winning a Major championship is high on my list of priorities for 1992 and that is why I was particularly interested to read the features on the courses which will host the four Major championships in 1992. Some, like Augusta National, I have been fortunate enough to have played several times; however this year will be my first experience of playing at the

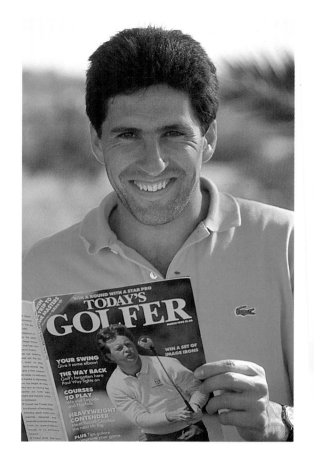

spectacular Pebble Beach course in the US Open championship. I am also looking forward to the British Open at Muirfield which is certainly one of the best championship venues in the world. And while eager to win my first Major title, I'm only too well aware that I have to be patient, have that little bit of luck that every winner needs and also be playing at the top of my form at just the right time.

INTRODUCTION

Bill Robertson

Golf has become so popular that a recent report commissioned by the Royal & Ancient golf club, the game's governing body, highlighted the need for literally hundreds of new courses to be built throughout Great Britain to meet the ever-growing demand, in both the private and public sectors.

Golf is booming and it is from this surge in popularity that new and innovative ideas such as Family Golf Centres, have evolved and flourished, offering the ideal introduction to the game for the keen beginner, while at the same time fulfilling the needs for the more accomplished and experienced player.

Today's Golfer Companion features many of the most prestigious courses of England, Scotland, Ireland and Wales, with a personal guide by the local club professional, to playing the key holes on each course. And the comprehensive Course Directory, listing almost two thousand golf courses in Great Britain and Ireland, reveals a wonderful variety of golfing locations to visit and explore, including one of the new Family Golf Centres at Chesfield Downs.

As well as providing an in-depth guide on where and when to play, *Today's Golfer Companion* also includes a special section under the

heading, 'All about Golf' specifically to help those who may be new to the game, and which covers such things as how to get started, what you need in the way of equipment and how much it will cost.

The more accomplished golfers will be keen to study the swing analyses section featuring six of the world's top tournament stars, each demonstrating his individual skill in different departments of the game: Ian Woosnam on long driving; Bernhard Langer and Payne Stewart on iron shots: how to chip close to the green with Seve Ballesteros: how to improve bunker play with Jose Maria Olazabal: and how to improve putting skills with Nick Faldo.

While the dedicated devotees of the fairway would claim that golf is a year-round sport, for the armchair golfer, the season usually tees-off in April when the US Masters championship, played at the

Ian Woosnam takes you through the stages of power driving.

stunningly beautiful Augusta National course, in Georgia, heralds the arrival of Spring. The first Major championship of the year brings together the cream of world golf, and it was here in 1991 that Ian Woosnam finally joined that elite band of golfers who have captured Major titles. And 'Woosie's' dramatic Masters victory, introduces a review of the four Major championships.

Lanark, which offers some of the best heathland golf in Scotland, is one of the sixteen top courses discussed in the Strategies section.

John Daly exploded onto the golfing scene by winning the 1991 USPGA.

Today's Golfer Companion recalls how close Nick Faldo came to forcing his way into the play-off for the 1991 US Open championship and details how Payne Stewart battled his way to the second major title of his career in an eighteen-holes play-off with fellow American, Scott Simpson at Hazeltine. In July, Royal Birkdale was the venue for the 1991 British Open championship, which saw the popular and talented Australian, Ian Baker-Finch spreadeagle a world-class field by playing the first nine holes of the final round in a remarkable 29 strokes, to join Ian Woosnam as a first-time Major championship winner.

Shoal Creek, venue of the USPGA championship in August was considered by many to be the most demanding course of the four Major championship venues of 1991. Unfortunately, someone forgot to mention that fact to John Daly and the unknown from Texas, who

had been ninth reserve before receiving a dramatic last-minute entry into the championship, proceeded to write his name into golfing folklore.

One of the longest hitters the game has ever seen, 'Long John' not only brought one of the world's most difficult courses to its knees, he also did the same to the rest of the world-class field and in the process, joined Woosnam and Baker-Finch as first-time Major champions in 1991. And looking ahead, *Today's Golfer Companion* features Augusta National, Muirfield, Pebble Beach and Bellerive golf courses, the venues which will host the Major championships of 1992.

The highlight of the 1991 amateur season was the Walker Cup match between America and Great Britain and Ireland at the spectacular Portmarnock course in Ireland. Despite making a dreadful start by losing all the matches in the first round of the foursomes matches, the home team fought back bravely and looked as if they might just be able to snatch victory from the jaws of defeat. In the end however,

the Americans, led by Phil Mickelson, one of golf's potential superstars of the 90s steered his team to victory in the final day's singles.

From the very start of the 1991 season, top professionals on both the American and European PGA Tours had their sights set on making their respective Ryder Cup teams for the match at Kiawah Island in South Carolina at the end of September. And by the time the teams finally met at the controversial new seaside course designed by Pete Dye to do battle for the famous trophy donated by Sam Ryder, there had been so much hype in the media that the contest was being described as 'Desert Storm 2'.

Like the Great Britain and Ireland Walker Cup team, Europe made a disastrous start to the first series of foursomes matches, and the only point gained came from the Spanish duo of Seve Ballesteros and Jose Maria Olazabal. Yet despite gloomy predictions that the five Ryder Cup newcomers in the European team would be overcome by the pressure and tension, the new boys more than held their own in three of the most exciting days of Ryder Cup golf ever seen.

Sadly for Europe, who had won the past three Ryder Cup matches, a six-foot putt by Bernhard Langer to half the match and retain the trophy, slipped agonizingly past the hole allowing America to claim the narrowest of victories. However, the Americans will have their work cut out to retain the Ryder Cup when the contest returns to The Belfry, venue for the 1985 and 1989 matches when Europe emerged victorious.

THE MAJORS

A player who wins any of the competitions discussed in this section is guaranteed a place in the golfers' hall of fame. We look back at the play on the 1991 circuit and preview the courses where the Major competitions will be played in 1992.

THE US MASTERS

The 1991 US Masters was, as in other years, unique among golf's four Major championships for two reasons. First because it is played at the same venue each year and secondly, unless you are a past defending champion, entry is by invitation only.

There is another aspect of the Masters which sets it aside from the other major events and that is the fact that the golf course is probably more famous than the majority of the field. With its superbly manicured fairways, lightning-fast greens and infamous Amen Corner, it is not exaggerating to suggest that the Augusta National course is the real star of the show which takes place each April in Georgia and which, for many impatient followers, signals that the golf season is well and truly under way.

The story of Augusta National began in 1930 when the legendary Bobby Jones retired from competitive golf after becoming the only man ever to win golf's Grand Slam. Jones had always had an interest in golf-course design and his ambition was some day to put all the knowledge and experience he had gained in his remarkable career into building a course which was a little different from the conventional type of layout being built in the United States at that time.

During the Great Depression of the 1930s, land was selling cheaply, and a 350-acre site came on the market which appeared to be ideal for what Jones had in mind. Along with a number of his friends, he purchased the land and the famous Scottish architect, Dr Alistair Mackenzie, was engaged to design the course. Construction work began in

The par-five, 465-yard 13th hole, one of the four holes that make up the infamous Amen Corner and one of the most treacherous holes at the Augusta National, has spelt disaster for many contenders for the title.

1931 and although the land was ideal for building a golf course, Jones and Mackenzie spent months planning every detail of the layout. When their labours were completed, Augusta National was immediately recognised as one of America's and the world's finest new courses.

Even today, although there have been many subtle alterations to the original layout, Augusta National continues not only to reflect the talent and vision of Jones and Mackenzie, but also serves as a living monument to both men. Once described as, 'a cathedral among the pines', Augusta is probably as close as you can get to perfection in golf-course design. Towering pine trees, beautifully rolling terrain and a great variety of plants, shrubs and flowering plants, including dogwood and rosebud, line the superbly manicured fairways in colourful profusion.

First impressions tend to suggest that as well as being stunningly beautiful, Augusta National should be a walk in the park for the seasoned tour professionals. However, nothing could be further from the truth, for the heavily contoured and lightning-fast greens place the kind of premium on accuracy and course management that only the best players in the world can meet.

To play well at Augusta requires a sound swing, a cool head and a deft touch. To win not only requires all the aforementioned, but also the ability to cope with the unique pressures that prevail at a Major championship. And the more intense the pressure, the more the subtleties of Augusta National come into play; no more so than over the four holes from the tenth to the thirteenth, which make up Augusta National's infamous Amen Corner on the final afternoon of the championship.

Augusta reflects Bobby Jones's own attitude to the game of golf. The course demands precision rather than power, a cool head and a steady hand and, above all, patience. Players who attempt to force birdies from the course inevitably make bogey; let concentration wander for an instant and a shot will be gone and with it, perhaps, the chance of winning the tournament.

On a sunny Sunday evening in early April, Ian Woosnam stood over the most important putt of his career. The only thing between the Welshman and his first major title was six feet of green. The green in question was the eighteenth at Augusta National and the occasion, the 72nd hole of the 1991 US Masters championship.

Woosnam's destiny was in his own trembling hands: hole the putt and he was the champion; miss and he would face a sudden-death play-off, where one bad bounce or the slightest miss-hit could decide the outcome. The Welshman composed himself then sent the ball rolling across the frighteningly-fast

putting surface on a line which was just outside the right edge of the hole.

The golfing world held its breath as the ball slowed and started to turn towards the hole. It seemed to pause for what must have felt like an eternity to Woosnam, before finally disappearing into the cup to give him the game.

Woosnam barely had time to punch the air with delight before being swept off his feet by his caddie in an impromptu victory jig.

Later, as the awareness of what he had just achieved began to sink in, Woosnam said, "You dream of holing a putt on the final green to win the Masters. In the Majors in the past, I've got worked up and put myself under too much pressure. I'm surprised that a 72 today has been good enough to win, but that shows how much pressure there is on everyone."

Prior to the Masters, Woosnam had won two out of the three events he had entered and after his victory

in the New Orleans Classic he said, "I came over here to win and right now I think I'm the best player in the world. I'm at the age now when I should be in my prime and I really feel that I've been underestimated."

In the past, Woosnam's Achilles' heel has been his putting. Not that he is a bad putter; you don't get to be number one in the world unless you hole your fair share of putts. Nevertheless, in previous Major championships a lacklustre performance on the greens meant that Woosnam was unable to capitalise on the strength of his long game and the accuracy of his iron shots.

However, the combination of a ladies' putter and a grip which had been put on incorrectly, produced a magic formula on the greens throughout the second half of the 1990 season. And although that specific putter was no longer in his bag when he arrived at Augusta, it had played a vital role in

The 10th hole, a tough par four, is the first hole to be played in the event of a play-off. The green slopes severely as Scott Hoch found to his cost in 1989 when he hit his putt past the hole and missed the little one coming back down the slope.

helping to build the kind of confidence on the greens which is essential for any aspiring Major champion.

After a steady, rather than spectacular opening round of 72, Woosnam served notice of his intentions, with a superb, six-under-par 66 that left him just two shots behind the half way leader, Tom Watson and one ahead of fellow European and world number two, Jose Maria Olazabal.

Two 68s by the five-time Open winner and former Masters champion Watson, set the target for the lowest 36-hole cut at Augusta in recent years. It was a score which saw Scotland's Sandy Lyle, the 1986 champion, and Australian Greg Norman, one of the pre-tournament favourites, heading for home, with defending champion Nick Faldo, and former Masters winner, Seve Ballesteros narrowly avoiding the same fate.

The pairing which drew the largest gallery on the second day, was that of Jack Nicklaus and Tom Watson.

It was Nicklaus who started the gallery buzzing when he took a three-over-par seven, at the dangerous twelfth hole. But in typical Nicklaus style, Jack promptly birdied the next four holes to save the day. Watson returned a second consecutive 68 which was four shots better than Nicklaus's level par 72 and two shots ahead of the field.

Leading the chasing group in the third round were Americans Lanny Wadkins, Mark McCumber and Mark Calcavecchia, with Ian Woosnam joining that group, just to remind them that there was a European presence within striking distance of the lead. The Welshman's 66 in the second round must have

Two eagles on the back nine of the last round put Tom Watson level with Woosnam and Olazabal after the fifteenth.

looked extremely ominous to the American contingent.

Woosie's position as number one in the world appeared to be resting easily on his broad shoulders, and a third-round 67 hoisted the Welshman to the top of the leader-board by the end of an exciting day's play. Tom Watson had weathered Woosie's birdie barrage and finished the day with a two-under-par 70, which left him just one shot off the lead. And a 69 from Spain's Jose Maria Olazabal, to add to his previous rounds of 68 and 71, reinforced Europe's bid for an unprecedented fourth consecutive Masters victory. Like Woosnam, the young Spaniard was seeking his first Major title, and had eased into the ideal position from which to launch his own challenge for the famous Green Jacket.

Defending champion Nick Faldo had been desperately short of match practice prior

to the Masters and it had showed in two lacklustre opening rounds of 72 and 73. Faldo's normally sharp short game had been the main culprit. However he revived his flagging spirits with a sparkling 67 in the third round to start the final round at four under par, seven shots behind Woosnam. On most championship courses this would have been too much of a deficit to make up, but at Augusta National on the final day of the Masters, a player of Faldo's pedigree was still very much in contention.

Woosnam made a steady start over the first few holes of the final day and although American Steve Pate was in the process of mounting a final round charge, it was Olazabal who was proving to be the major threat. And when the Spaniard recorded his third birdie of the round at the seventh, he shared the lead with Woosnam at eleven under par.

No sooner had the Spaniard grabbed a share of the lead however, than he promptly threw it away again, thanks to errant drives at the next two holes which dropped him back to nine under par, Woosnam on the other hand, was showing admirable control and patience, reaching the turn in 35 to establish a precious two-shot lead over the field.

It has often been said that the real battle for the Masters title does not really get under way until the leaders reach the tenth tee on Sunday afternoon.

As the leaders entered the stretch of holes which make up Augusta National's infamous Amen Corner, American Steve Pate was completing his final day's work. Rounds of 72, 73, 69 and a sizzling last-day 65, had set a nine-under-par target for the players still in contention to beat. And with the fearsome holes of Amen Corner still to negotiate, the men at the top of the leader-board were only too well aware, that there was now very little margin left for any error whatsoever.

While a wayward driver was still making life difficult for Olazabal, Woosnam was attempting to play his way cautiously through Amen Corner. A bogey five at the tenth was not exactly the kind of start he wanted to make on what could well turn out to be the most important nine holes of his life. However a par at the eleventh and a solid par five at the potentially-disastrous thirteenth, looked to have put the Welshman back in control of the championship.

Meanwhile, Watson had birdied the tenth but a dropped shot at the next, and a demoralising double bogey at the thirteenth temporarily halted his charge. A long wait on the tee at the par-five fourteenth, followed by a hooked tee shot, left Woosnam swallowing hard and settling for a one-over-par six, at a hole which even under the pressure of leading the Masters, he would have expected to birdie.

Woosie's lapse provided a much-needed and immediate

Nick Faldo and Phil Mickelson at the short, par-three 16th hole. Both Faldo, in 1990, and Sandy Lyle, in 1989, sank long, curly putts at this hole before going on to win the championship.

spur to Tom Watson, who hit two superb shots to the heart of the thirteenth green and then rolled home a fifteen-footer for a three. Up ahead Olazabal was also taking advantage of a wobbly Woosnam, and three consecutive birdies from the thirteenth took him to the top of the leader-board for the first time in the championship.

Woosnam drew level with Olazabal after a birdie at the fifteenth, but a rampant Watson went one better, with his second eagle of the back nine to join the two Europeans at the top of the leader-board on 11 under par.

All three men made hard work of the short sixteenth, with Olazabal saving his par from a greenside bunker and both Watson and Woosnam having to hole lengthy putts for threes.

Olazabal's nerve and skill redeemed his par at the next hole after yet another

wayward drive, while Woosnam and Watson played the hole by the more conventional route for the same result.

Golf can be a cruel game, and after hitting what he thought for once that week was a perfect drive, Olazabal could only watch in horror as his ball took an uncharitable bounce from the centre of the manicured eighteenth fairway and into the one place he had been desperate to avoid, the large bunker which guards the left side of the hole.

Unlike Sandy Lyle, who three years earlier had produced a seven-iron recovery shot from the same bunker which was eventually to win him the Masters and with it a place in golfing folklore, the Spaniard's ball was lying poorly. With the pin at the back of the final green and forced to take an eight iron rather than the seven he would have preferred to hit,

Olazabal's chances of emulating Lyle's feat were considerably less than even money. Although his recovery shot did reach the front of the eighteenth green, the ball spun back into the bunker which guards the front left of the putting surface.

Even for a brilliant bunker player like Olazabal, it was asking for a miracle to get down in two from this position. Sadly no miracle was forthcoming. A one-over-par five gave Olazabal a 72-hole total of 278 – ten under par.

It was Watson to play first. Taking a three wood from the tee for accuracy, he attempted to hit a fade but failed; his ball sliced to the right and landed in the tall trees which run all the way along the right side of the eighteenth hole.

Waiting to tee-off with Ian Woosnam is his caddie, whose curious gait has earned him the nickname, "Wobbly".

Ian Woosnam holed his putt at the eighteenth to become the 53rd US Masters champion and the third successive British winner.

which has never held much appeal for Tom Watson, and the American went boldly for the hole in a last-ditch attempt to make his four. The ball slid by the cup and ran some five feet past the hole.

Woosnam's moment of truth had finally arrived, and he embraced it like a true champion by bravely holing the putt and claiming his first Major title and the fourth consecutive Masters victory for European players.

On Friday, after his stunning 66, Woosnam had cheekily said that his coat size was 40 short. Now, on Sunday, he got to wear his green jacket, the size perfect, the colour clashing terribly with his tartan trews.

It was a smashing sight, the view of Nick Faldo bending to help his pal into the most coveted coat in sport. Everyone smiled, no one more than Woosnam. He'd done it at last.

Now it was Woosnam's turn to hit. The experts debated which shot he would choose to play, Woosnam surprised everyone by taking his driver, aiming directly at the bunkers and then unleashing every ounce of his awesome power at the ball. The gallery gasped in amazement as the ball carried 268 yards, uphill and over the bunker, returning to earth on the wide, grassy area of ground which lies between the eighteenth and ninth fairways.

Watson attempted a do-or-die escape shot from the trees, and died; his ball finishing in the same bunker that had sealed Olazabal's fate a few minutes earlier. After his enormous drive, Woosnam punched an eight iron on to the front left corner of the putting surface. Watson's recovery shot almost pitched in the hole before running some 25 feet past, while Woosnam's approach putt slid to the right of the hole, leaving him six feet still to negotiate for the most important par of his life.

Second place is something

Two masters champions, Nick Faldo and Ian Woosnam, proudly sport their Green Jackets, the exclusive privilege of members of Augusta National and winners of the US Masters.

1991 US MASTERS RESULTS

Position	Name	Rd1	Rd2	Rd3	Rd4	Total		Prize Money £
1	I Woosnam	72	66	67	72	**277**	(−11)	**135,000**
2	J M Olazabal	68	71	69	70	**278**	(−10)	**81,000**
3	T Watson	68	68	70	73	**279**	(−9)	**36,000**
	S Pate	72	73	69	65	**279**	(−9)	**36,000**
	B Crenshaw	70	73	68	68	**279**	(−9)	**36,000**
	L Wadkins	67	71	70	71	**279**	(−9)	**36,000**
7	J Mudd	70	70	71	69	**280**	(−8)	**23,388**
	I Baker-Finch	71	70	69	70	**280**	(−8)	**23,388**
	A Magee	70	72	68	70	**280**	(−8)	**23,388**
10	H Irwin	70	70	75	66	**281**	(−7)	**19,527**
	T Nakajima	74	71	67	69	**281**	(−7)	**19,527**
12	B Mayfair	72	72	72	66	**282**	(−6)	**14,722**
	M Calcavecchia	70	68	77	67	**282**	(−6)	**14,722**
	F Zoeller	70	70	75	67	**282**	(−6)	**14,722**
	C Stadler	70	72	71	69	**282**	(−6)	**14,722**
	N Faldo	72	73	67	70	**282**	(−6)	**14,722**
17	J Gallagher Jnr	67	74	71	71	**283**	(−5)	**10,511**
	M McCumber	67	71	73	72	**283**	(−5)	**10,511**
	P Jacobsen	73	70	68	72	**283**	(−5)	**10,511**
	R Floyd	71	68	71	73	**283**	(−5)	**10,511**
	L Mize	72	71	66	74	**283**	(−5)	**10,511**
22	S Ballesteros	75	70	69	70	**284**	(−4)	**7,200**
	S Elkington	72	69	74	69	**284**	(−4)	**7,200**
	R Mediate	72	69	71	72	**284**	(−4)	**7,200**
	C Pavin	73	70	69	72	**284**	(−4)	**7,200**
	S Simpson	69	73	69	73	**284**	(−4)	**7,200**
27	M O'Meara	74	68	72	71	**285**	(−3)	**5,666**
	J D Blake	74	72	68	71	**285**	(−3)	**5,666**
29	J Sluman	71	71	72	72	**286**	(−2)	**5,111**
	J Huston	73	72	71	70	**286**	(−2)	**5,111**
	M Hatalsky	71	72	70	73	**286**	(−2)	**5,111**
32	D Frost	71	73	71	72	**287**	(−1)	**4,444**
	B Langer	71	68	74	74	**287**	(−1)	**4,444**
	W Levi	69	73	70	75	**287**	(−1)	**4,444**
35	M McNulty	72	74	75	67	**288**	(Level)	**3,539**
	M Brooks	69	72	74	73	**288**	(Level)	**3,539**
	S Hoch	72	70	73	73	**288**	(Level)	**3,539**
	K Green	70	74	71	73	**288**	(Level)	**3,539**
	M Ozaki	68	77	69	74	**288**	(Level)	**3,539**
	F Couples	68	73	72	75	**288**	(Level)	**3,539**
	J Nicklaus	68	72	72	76	**288**	(Level)	**3,539**
42	J Hammond	72	73	73	71	**289**	(+1)	**2,708**
	D Love III	72	71	74	72	**289**	(+1)	**2,708**
	C Strange	72	74	72	71	**289**	(+1)	**2,708**
	B R Brown	74	65	77	73	**289**	(+1)	**2,708**
46	P Mickelson (a)	69	73	74	74	**290**	(+2)	**(am)**
	J Sindelar	72	70	70	78	**290**	(+2)	**2,250**
	D Pooley	72	71	69	78	**290**	(+2)	**2,250**
49	L Trevino	71	72	77	71	**291**	(+3)	**1,962**
	T Aaron	70	74	74	74	**291**	(+3)	**1,962**
	N Price	72	73	72	74	**291**	(+3)	**1,962**
52	P Azinger	73	67	80	72	**291**	(+4)	**1,833**
53	B Tennyson	78	67	75	73	**293**	(+5)	**1,777**
	N Henke	73	71	72	77	**293**	(+5)	**1,777**
55	L Nelson	74	69	76	75	**294**	(+6)	**1,722**
56	T Kite	71	75	78	71	**295**	(+7)	**1,722**
57	M Zerman (a)	71	71	77	80	**299**	(+11)	**(am)**

Missed cut (36 holes): 147 – **G Norman** 78, 69; **J Cook** 77, 70; **B Britten** 72, 75; **G Player** 72, 75; 148 – **B Casper** 77, 71; **M Donald** 73, 75; **S Jones** 73, 75; **T Sieckmann** 72, 76; 149 – **R Rafferty** 73, 76; **R Gamez** 72, 77; **L Roberts** 72, 77; 150 – **B Tway** 75, 75; **C Beck** 74, 76; **W Grady** 74, 76; 151 – **T Simpson** 73, 78; **K Knox** 72, 79; 152 – **J Benepe** 78, 74; **G Brewer** 78, 74; **T Schulz** 74, 78; 153 – **J P Stuart** (am) 81, 72; **F Minoza** 78, 75; **G Morgan** 77, 76; **S Lyle** 77, 76; 154 – **C Coody** 77, 77; 155 – **M S Combs** (am) 81, 74; **A Palmer** 78, 77; **R Muntz** 80, 75; **J Inman** 75, 80; **G Archer** 73; **D Ford** 90.

ROLL OF HONOUR

Venue — Augusta National Golf Course, Augusta, Georgia

Year	Winner	Score
1934	Horton Smith	284
1935	Gene Sarazen	282
1936	Horton Smith	285
1937	Byron Nelson	283
1938	Henry Picard	285
1939	Ralph Guldahl	279
1940	Jimmy Demaret	280
1941	Craig Wood	280
1942	Byron Nelson	280
1946	Herman Keiser	282
1947	Jimmy Demaret	281
1948	Claude Harmon	279
1949	Sam Snead	283
1950	Jimmy Demaret	282
1951	Ben Hogan	280
1952	Sam Snead	286
1953	Ben Hogan	274
1954	Sam Snead	289
1955	Cary Middlecoff	279
1956	Jackie Burke	289
1957	Doug Ford	283
1958	Arnold Palmer	284
1959	A Wall	284
1960	Arnold Palmer	282
1961	GJ Player (SA)	280
1962	Arnold Palmer	280
1963	JW Nicklaus	286
1964	Arnold Palmer	276
1965	JW Nicklaus	271
1966	JW Nicklaus	288
1967	G Brewer	280
1968	R Goalby	277
1969	G Archer	281
1970	W Casper	279
1971	C Coody	279
1972	JW Nicklaus	286
1973	T Aaron	283
1974	GJ Player (SA)	278
1975	JW Nicklaus	276
1976	R Floyd	271
1977	T Watson	276
1978	GJ Player (SA)	277
1979	F Zoeller	280
1980	S Ballesteros (Sp)	275
1981	T Watson	280
1982	C Stadler	284
1983	S Ballesteros (Sp)	280
1984	B Crenshaw	277
1985	B Langer (WG)	282
1986	JW Nicklaus	279
1987	L Mize	285
(After a tie)		
1988	AWB Lyle	281
1989	N Faldo	283
1990	N Faldo	278

1991 Ian Woosnam
277

US OPEN CHAMPIONSHIP

After his dramatic play-off victory at the US Open at Hazeltine which gave him his second Major title in two years, Payne Stewart looks to be the next American golfing great.

The real test of a true champion is not, as many would claim, winning a Major title: it is winning a *second* Major title. This was something that Payne Stewart was discovering the hard way as the eighteen-hole play-off for the 1991 US Open championship approached its climax at Hazeltine.

With only three holes left to play, it looked as though Scott Simpson, winner of the 1987 US Open at California's Olympic Club, would complete a US Open double and join that elite group of golfers who have won the same Major title on more than one occasion.

For most of the regulation 72 holes, Simpson's solid if unspectacular game had been tailor-made for the revamped, demanding and, on this occasion, fair Hazeltine course. Then he reached the sixteenth hole, a notoriously treacherous par four.

Formerly a par three, the hole had been rebuilt as a par four especially for the championship, and had created enough excitement and drama during the US-Open week to establish it alongside the thirteenth at Augusta National and the seventeenth at St. Andrews' Old Course as the holes you would least like to have to par to save your life.

The final three holes of the new Hazeltine had already proved expensive for Simpson, costing him his two-shot lead in both the third and fourth rounds; surely, with the winning-post finally in sight, he would not falter again at the last hurdle.

As the players reached the sixteenth tee, it seemed that Stewart's only hope was to believe the old adage, everything happens in threes.

Once again, the old-wives' tale proved to be right, for when Simpson again dropped a shot at the sixteenth, Stewart answered by picking up a birdie. Simpson's precious two-shot lead had vanished; the scores were level with two holes to play.

Stewart edged one shot ahead with a par at the seventeenth. And when the crestfallen Simpson completed his hat trick of

Scott Simpson missed a birdie opportunity at the sixth hole in the play-off for the title.

dropped shots with a bogey five at the eighteenth, Stewart rolled home a short putt for the par four that gave him his first US Open by two shots.

Even before the first ball had been hit, there had been much debate regarding the quality of the field. Not the field of players but the field over which the competition was to be played. When Hazeltine had last hosted the event, in 1970, the American Dave Hill had likened the course to a cow pasture. And although he was the only player to voice his concerns publicly, the majority of the players that year privately seemed to share his sentiments about both the design and quality of the Hazeltine course which is laid out around the shores of Lake Chaska in Minnesota.

Twenty-one years and seven million dollars later, Hazeltine presented the field for the US Open with a very different picture. The course had been almost totally revamped. Prior to the start of the championship, course architect Rees Jones said, "I feel like a student who has just finished a difficult test. I think I did well and answered all the questions. But now I'm waiting for the players to give me my grade."

Both he and the USPGA must have heaved a collective sigh of relief when the competitors were unanimous in their praise for the new course.The ghosts of 1970 had been well and truly laid.

Before the competition started, much had been written about the strength of the European challenge. So strong was the conviction that 1991 would see the first European winner since Tony Jacklin in 1970, that the speculation was not if a

Fuzzy Zoeller, the gallery's favourite, tied for fifth position. His scorecard contained an ace, made at the 184-yard fourth hole with his four iron.

European would win, but which European would win.

The expectation of European victory was well founded, for with Ian Woosnam newly crowned as US Masters champion, Seve Ballesteros in sparkling form after a spectacular play-off victory in the PGA championship at Wentworth and European players dominating the top spots of the Sony World Rankings, the odds on a European US Open champion were the best they had been since the days of Vardon, Taylor and Braid.

Sadly, the reality did not live up to the pre-tournament expectations. The thunder storms which sadly claimed the life of one spectator seemed to dampen the fires that had burned so brightly in the European camp. The rain-soaked fairways may have seemed made-to-measure for the attacking style of play we have come to expect from Woosnam, Olazabal and Ballesteros, but none of them was able to make any

impact in the opening round. There were 23 sub-par scores in the first round. Only at Medinah in 1990 had this figure been topped.

Nick Faldo was making his usual cautious start, but he, too, ended the day five shots adrift of the first-round leaders, Payne Stewart and Nolan Hinkle who both carded 68s. The surprise opening-round performance from among the European challengers came from Sandy Lyle who had spent the past two years in the golfing doldrums. His ability to soldier on through difficult times without losing his sense of humour has won him the admiration of many and he must have allowed himself a wry smile when he ended the day with a 72, alongside Nick Faldo as top European.

If the opening round had left many top names trailing back in the pack, the second sent quite a few of them packing. Ballesteros, Norman, Azinger, Langer and Strange all failed to make the 36-hole cut.

The poor weather of the first two days did nothing to dampen the players' enthusiasm for the new-look Hazeltine and even at this stage the sixteenth was acquiring a reputation.

As the championship progressed, the Americans were slowly but surely once again gaining a stranglehold on the competition. While Fred Couples, Scott Simpson and Payne Stewart were consolidating their position at the top of the leader-board, the European challenge was spluttering to a halt. Woosnam and Olazabal improved on their opening rounds, but both seemed ill at ease with their games and were struggling to find their touch on the greens. Faldo was suffering more than most in this department and when he returned a second-day 74 it was difficult to see where the European challenge would come from. It was surprising and refreshing to find that the only European who seemed to feel he could win was Sandy Lyle. It may have seemed that the fact that he had made the cut for the first time in umpteen events was making the big Scot euphoric, but he was genuinely enjoying life again and was eager to build on his good work in the opening two rounds.

Faldo's usually meticulous planning had been wrecked by injury and a curtailed early season schedule. With only eight pre-Hazeltine events under his belt, the double Masters and reigning Open champion was lacking the vital match practice he required to hone his game to the degree required to compete at the highest level. He turned in a hard-earned but frustrating 73 but spectators and commentators could sense that he was now playing mainly for pride and that he knew his dreams of adding a US Open title to his other Major honours would have to wait for another year.

Things had started to look a little brighter for Ian Woosnam after an excellent second-round 68 had propelled him up the leader-board and briefly into contention. But a disastrous third-round 79 sent him sliding back down again into the pack where he remained for the rest of the championship.

The third round produced the most difficult playing conditions of the week with the strong wind whipping in off the lakes whipping up the scores, too. Payne Stewart and Scott Simpson were the only leaders who seemed able to cope with the elements and by the end of the day they had established a four-stroke lead over the rest of the field going into the final round.

Woosnam, going for broke in the last round, carded an 80. Afterwards he said, "At the end I was just trying to break 80. My swing seems to get tangled up now and again. Maybe it will come back in the next few weeks after I have some time off." Lyle emerged from the rough weather with a third round 74. His final round of 75 gave him a total of 291 and a tied sixteenth place with Tom Watson and Nick Faldo who ended as he started with a 72.

Leading the pack of players chasing Simpson and Stewart was Fred Couples who had scored 70, 70 and 75 going in to the last round. Although he has won several USPGA competitions, Couples has yet to capture a Major title. Well-known for hitting the ball huge distances, his ability to hole more long putts for pars than short ones for birdies was once again evident. For although he hit some

---

Tragedy marred the first day's play when lightning hit this tree that stands between the eleventh and sixteenth holes, killing one of the spectators sheltering under it.

spectacular shots in his closing round of 70, he was unable to capitalize enough on the birdie opportunities he created to close the gap on the leaders.

Larry Nelson, the veteran USPGA and US Open winner had also tip-toed up throughout the final day. Still one of the most stylish players on the professional tour, Nelson returned a stylish 68 for a total of 258 and a tied third place with his fellow American, Fred Couples.

Jose Maria Olazabal returned to something like his old form with a closing round of 70 for a place in the top ten and the honour of being highest-placed European.

As the final round reached its conclusion, it became clear that the battle for the title was now between Simpson and Stewart. When the leaders of a stroke play championship are paired in the final round and find themselves well clear of the rest of the field, the contest takes on the character of a match-play head-to-head encounter with, more often than not, the outcome decided by which player has the greater desire to win.

Simpson, probably wary of the water which guards the right side of the sixteenth hole, pulled his one-iron tee shot into the heavy rough on the left from which he was fortunate to escape in the end with a one-over-par five. Stewart took full advantage of Simpson's mistake and played the hole to perfection only to suffer the agonies of watching his ten-foot birdie putt slide by the hole.

Both men made par three at the seventeenth, with a shaky Simpson having to save his with a chip and single putt, while Stewart once again narrowly missed the birdie which would have put him on level terms with Simpson still one shot ahead going in to the 72nd hole. It looked as though Stewart had allowed his opportunity to slip away, but Simpson promptly opened the door again by missing the fairway and finding the rough with his drive and consequently unable to make his par. This time Stewart made no mistake in grabbing his last-minute reprieve and although his approach shot finished just through the back of the green, a cautious two putts gave him the par four he needed to force the second play-off in the US Open in the past three years which gave Payne Stewart his well-deserved victory.

There is a strong body of opinion in the United States that believes that the day of the eighteen-hole play-off is long since past and that the championship should be decided on the same day as the final round. The most popular alternative is the format now used at the British Open whereby golfers who have tied over 72 holes return to the course on the same day and play four extra holes of stroke play. If the championship is not decided at the end of these four holes, it is decided on a sudden-death basis.

However, the USGA has never taken much notice of this lobby and there was a rumour circulating at

Payne Stewart jigs for joy after his last putt gave him the championship.

Hazeltine that the authorities were not only determined to continue the eighteen-hole play-off but that they were also considering turning the clock back even further and asking the competitors to play 36 holes on the final day at Pebble Beach where the 1992 US Open will be played.

The last time the competition was played here, in 1982, it looked, as it entered its final stages like Jack Nicklaus would collect his fifth US Open title.

He had surged through the field over the closing stages and his final-round 69 looked certain to give him victory. The one man who could spoil Nicklaus' day was Tom Watson. Throughout the final round, these two giants of the game had battled for the lead, but when Watson who was chasing his first Open title missed the green at the difficult par-three seventeenth, it looked as if Nicklaus was going to edge home for his third title.

Although he was within six feet of the putting surface, Watson had what, to all intents and purposes, was an impossible shot. His ball had come to rest in ankle-deep rough. With the green running away from him and the pin perched on the top of the slope, it looked as though Watson would drop a shot, even though he was noted for his brilliant short game. Always a brisk player, Watson settled quickly over the ball, picked the club up quickly and chopped the ball up and out of the rough. It bounced once on the fringe of the green and ran down the slippery slope and straight into the hole for a miraculous birdie two.

Although Watson now had a one-shot lead, the

The eighth hole at Pebble Beach is a testing par four.

championship was not over as he still had to negotiate the treacherous final hole which is a long par five with the ocean running all the way down the left side. Watson hit a perfect drive, followed by a long iron which finished about one hundred yards short of the green. From here he pitched past the flag and then rolled the putt home for an audacious, but popular, two-shot victory.

Nicklaus and Watson may no longer feature among the world's top golfers, but Pebble Beach remains one of the world's top courses. It runs along the spectacular Monterey Peninsula in California and is considered the finest 'ocean' course in the United States. Its distance from a major city – San Francisco is 120 miles away – is probably the main reason why it has only hosted the US Open twice: once in 1982 and the first time in 1972 when Jack Nicklaus won, hitting the pin with his tee shot at the seventeenth in the final round giving him a tap-in birdie which virtually assured him of the US Open title.

Golf was first played here in 1911 when Samuel Morse,

nephew of the inventor of Morse Code and the telegraph, acquired the land from the Southern Pacific Railway Company and engaged Jack Neville to build the course at Pebble Beach.

Neville was a real estate salesman with no previous experience of building golf courses, but he created a magnificent course. A par 72, it measures 6,799 yards and takes in some breathtaking clifftop views of the Pacific while other holes wind their way along the edges of the Del Monte Forest.

Pebble Beach hosted the 1977 USPGA, won that year by Lanny Wadkins, and is the venue of the annual National Pro-Am previously known as 'The Crosby' after the late Bing Crosby. The event, sponsored by AT&T has raised millions of dollars for charity in America.

Despite its high standing, Pebble Beach is open to the public, at least to those who can afford its understandably high green fees.

1991 US OPEN RESULTS

	Position	Score	Total	Prize Money
PAYNE STEWART	1	67—70—73—72	282	$235,000.00
SCOTT SIMPSON	2	70—68—72—72	282	$117,500.00
FRED COUPLES	3	70—70—75—70	285	$62,574.00
LARRY NELSON	3	73—72—72—68	285	$62,574.00
FUZZY ZOELLER	5	72—73—74—67	286	$41,542.00
SCOTT HOCH	6	69—71—74—73	287	$36,090.00
NOLAN HENKE	7	67—71—77—73	288	$32,176.00
RAY FLOYD	8	73—72—76—68	289	$26,958.34
JOSE MARIA OLAZABAL	8	73—71—75—70	289	$26,958.33
COREY PAVIN	8	71—67—79—72	289	$26,958.33
JIM GALLAGHER, JR	11	70—72—75—73	290	$20,909.20
HALE IRWIN	11	71—75—70—74	290	$20,909.20
DAVIS LOVE III	11	70—76—73—71	290	$20,909.20
CRAIG PARRY	11	70—73—73—74	290	$20,909.20
D.A. WEIBRING	11	76—71—75—68	290	$20,909.20
NICK FALDO	16	72—74—73—72	291	$17,186.00
SANDY LYLE	16	72—70—74—75	291	$17,186.00
TOM WATSON	16	73—71—77—70	291	$17,186.00
BILLY RAY BROWN	19	73—71—77—71	292	$14,166.58
MARK BROOKS	19	73—73—73—73	292	$14,166.57
JOHN COOK	19	76—70—72—74	292	$14,166.57
PETER PERSONS	19	70—75—75—72	292	$14,166.57
NICK PRICE	19	74—69—71—78	292	$14,166.57
TOM SIECKMANN	19	74—70—74—74	292	$14,166.57
CRAIG STADLER	19	71—69—77—75	292	$14,166.57
RICK FEHR	26	74—69—73—77	293	$11,711.60
JODIE MUDD	26	71—70—77—75	293	$11,711.60
MIKE REID	26	74—72—74—73	293	$11,711.60
TIM SIMPSON	26	73—72—76—72	293	$11,711.60
BOB TWAY	26	75—69—74—75	293	$11,711.60
ED HUMENIK	31	72—70—78—74	294	$10,133.17
PETER JACOBSEN	31	72—73—74—75	294	$10,133.17
BRIAN KAMM	31	69—73—73—79	294	$10,133.17
CHRIS PERRY	31	72—73—75—74	294	$10,133.17
DAVE RUMMELLS	31	72—73—77—72	294	$10,133.16
LANCE TEN BROECK	31	72—73—74—75	294	$10,133.16
MARK CALCAVECCHIA	37	69—74—78—74	295	$8,560.43
KEITH CLEARWATER	37	70—76—74—75	295	$8,560.43
BUDDY GARDNER	37	74—72—74—75	295	$8,560.43
TOM KITE	37	71—75—74—75	295	$8,560.43
ANDY NORTH	37	71—71—77—76	295	$8,560.43
TOM PURTZER	37	77—68—77—73	295	$8,560.43
BILLY MAYFAIR	37	72—73—76—74	295	$8,560.42
IAN BAKER-FINCH	44	77—70—75—74	296	$7,477.50
JIM HALLET	44	72—74—73—77	296	$7,477.50
RODGER DAVIS	46	74—68—81—74	297	$6,875.67
JACK NICKLAUS	46	70—76—77—74	297	$6,875.67
BLAINE MCCALLISTER	46	72—72—76—77	297	$6,875.66
MIKE HARWOOD	49	71—74—77—76	298	$6,033.75
WAYNE LEVI	49	72—72—76—78	298	$6,033.75
STEVE PATE	49	72—75—77—74	298	$6,033.75
LOREN ROBERTS	49	75—70—74—79	298	$6,033.75
JOHN INMAN	53	72—72—77—78	299	$5,389.00
LARRY RINKER	53	72—72—77—78	299	$5,389.00
STEVE ELKINGTON	55	77—69—76—78	300	$5,164.50
STEVE GOTSCHE	55	72—75—76—77	300	$5,164.50
LARRY MIZE	55	73—73—79—75	300	$5,164.50
IAN WOOSNAM	55	73—68—79—80	300	$5,164.50
PHIL MICKELSON	55	73—72—80—75	300	Amateur
DAVID GRAHAM	60	74—71—80—77	302	$5,008.00
STAN UTLEY	61	73—71—81—78	303	$4,958.00
JOHN ADAMS	62	72—75—78—79	304	$4,958.00
WAYNE GRADY	63	73—74—78—80	305	$4,958.00
TERRY SNODGRASS	63	74—73—80—78	305	$4,958.00
LANNY WADKINS	63	76—70—80—79	305	$4,958.00

THE FOLLOWING PLAYERS MISSED THE CUT

Paul Azinger 148, Tom Byrum 148, Bob Estes 148, Lee Janzen 148, Eric Johnson 148, Jeff Sluman 148, Mitch Adcock 149, Fulton Allem 149, Seve Ballesteros 149, Jon Chaffee 149, Jay Delsing 149, Frank Dobbs 149, Tom Eubank 149, David Frost 149, John Huston 149, Bernhard Langer 149, Mark McCumber 149, Gil Morgan, 149 Mark O'Meara 149, Timothy Robyn 149, Lee Trevino 149, Dave Barr 150, Jim Benepe 150, Bob Boyd 150, Mike Donald 150, Allen Doyle 150, Scott Gump 150, Robert Meyer 150, Brad Sherfy 150, Hal Sutton 150, Kirk Triplett 150, John Wilson 150, Billy Andrade 151, Bill Britton 151, Fred Funk 151, Chris Gorgone 151, Dan Halldorson 151, David Jackson 151, Rocco Mediate 151, Rick Price 151, Curtis Strange 151, Thomas Tolles 151, Billy Tuten 151, Bobby Wadkins 151, Dennis Zinkon 151, Chip Beck 152, Steve Jones 152, Jumbo Ozaki 152, Jerry Pate 152, Rocky Walcher 152, Phil Blackmar 153, Jerry Foltz 153, Jon Hough 153, Andrew Magee 153, Ray Stewart 153, Robert Gamez 154, Jim McGovern 154, Rick Osberg 154, Jay Overton 154, Dicky Thompson 154, Bruce Zabriski 154, Eric Booker 155, Ed Dougherty 155, Brad Faxon 155, Bob Lasken 155, Bryan Norton 155, Cary Hungate 156, John Ross 156, Brian Tennyson 156, Jacob Ferenz 157, Jay Gunning 157, John Paesani 157, Jeb Stuart 157, Scott Beaugureau 158, Jeff Lee 158, Sam Randolph 159, Rick Vershure 159, Michael Weeks 159, James Detrixhe 160, Louie Garcia 161, Terry Dear 161, Darrell Kestner 161, Clay Devers 162, Jack Kay Jr. 163, Joe Hajduch 163, Chris Endres 165, George Daves 167, Paul Oglesby 167, Greg Norman WD, Ronan Rafferty WD, Ken Green WD.

ROLL OF HONOUR

Year	Winner	Runner-up Venue		By
1894	Willie Dunn	W Campbell St Andrews, NY		2 holes
After 1894 decided by medal play				

Year	Winner	Country	Venue	Score
1894	HJ Rawlins	USA	Newport	173
1896	J Foulis	USA	Southampton	152
1897	J Lloyd	USA	Wheaton, III	162
1898	F Herd	USA	Shinnecock Hills	328
72 holes played from 1898				
1899	W Smith	USA	Baltimore	315
1900	H Vardon	England	Wheaton, III	313
1901	W Anderson	USA	Myopia, Mass	315
1902	L Auchterlonie	USA	Garden City	305
1903	W Anderson	USA	Baltusrol	307
1904	W Anderson	USA	Glenview	304
1905	W Anderson	USA	Myopia	335
1906	A Smith	USA	Onwentsia	291
1907	A Ross	USA	Chestnut Hill, PA	302
1908	F McLeod	USA	Myopia, Mass	322
1909	G Sargent	USA	Englewood, NJ	290
1910	A Smith	USA	Philadelphia	289
1911	JJ McDermot	USA	Wheaton, III	307
1912	JJ McDermot	USA	Buffalo, NY	294
1913	F Ouimet(Am)	USA	Brookline, Mass	304
(After a tie with H Vardon and E Ray)				
1914	W Hagen	USA	Midlothian	297
1915	JD Travers(Am)	USA	Baltusrol	290
1916	C Evans(Am)	USA	Minneapolis	286
1917-18	No Championship			
1919	W Hagen	USA	Braeburn	301
1920	E Ray	England	Inverness	295
1921	J Barnes	USA	Washington	289
1922	G Sarazen	USA	Glencoe	288
1923	RT Jones, jun(AM)	USA	Inwood, LI	295
1924	C Walker	USA	Oakland Hills	297
1925	W MacFarlane	USA	Worcester	291
1926	RT Jones, jun(AM)	USA	Scioto	293
1927	TD Armour	USA	Oakmont	301
1928	J Farrell	USA	Olympia Fields	294
1929	RT Jones, jun(AM)	USA	Winged Foot, NY	294
1930	RT Jones, jun(AM)	USA	Interlachen	287
1931	B Burke	USA	Inverness	292
1932	G Sarazen	USA	Fresh Meadow	286
1933	J Goodman(Am)	USA	North Shore	287
1934	O Dutra	USA	Menon	293
1935	S Parks	USA	Oakmont	299
1936	T Manero	USA	Springfield	282
1937	R Guldahl	USA	Oakland Hills	281
1938	R Guldahl	USA	Cherry Hills	284
1939	Byron Nelson	USA	Philadelphia	284
1940	W Lawson Little	USA	Canterbury, Ohio	287
1941	Craig Wood	USA	Fort Worth, Texas	284
1942-45	No Championship			
1946	Lloyd Mangrum	USA	Canterbury	284
1947	Lew Worsham	USA	St Louis	282
1948*	Ben Hogan	USA	Log Angeles	276
1949	Dr Cary Middlecoff	USA	Medinah, III	286
1950	Ben Hogan	USA	Merion, PA	287
1951	Ben Hogan	USA	Oakland Hills, Mich	287
1952	Julius Boros	USA	Dallas, Texas	281
1953	Ben Hogan	USA	Oakmont	283
1954	Ed Furgol	USA	Baltusrol	284
1955	J Fleck	USA	San Francisco	287

Year	Winner	Country	Venue	Score
1956	Dr Cary Middlecoff	USA	Rochester	281
1957	Dick Mayer	USA	Inverness	282
1958	Tommy Bolt	USA	Tulsa, Okla	283
1959	W Casper	USA	Winged Foot, NY	282
1960	Arnold Palmer	USA	Denver, Col	280
1961	Gene Littler	USA	Birmingham, Mich	281
1962	JW Nicklaus	USA	Oakmont	283
1963	Julius Boros	USA	Brookline, Mass	293
1964	Ken Venturi	USA	Washington	278
1965	Gary Player	SAfrica	St Louis, Mo	282
1966	W Casper	USA	San Franciso	278
1967	JW Nicklaus	USA	Baltusrol	275
1968	Lee Trevino	USA	Rochester	275
1969	Orville Moody	USA	Houston, Texas	281
1970	A Jacklin	England	Chaska, Minn	281
1971	L Trevino	USA	Merion, PA	280
1972	JW Nicklaus	USA	Pebble Beach	290
1973	J Miller	USA	Oakmont, PA	279
1974	H Irwin	USA	Winged Foot, NY	287
1975	L Graham	USA	Medinah, III	287
1976	J Pate	USA	Atlanta, Georgia	277
1977	H Green	USA	Southenr Hills, Tulsa	278
1978	A North	USA	Cherry Hills	285
1979	H Irwin	USA	Inverness, Ohio	284
1980	JW Nicklaus	USA	Baltusrol	272
1981	D Graham	Aus	Merion, PA	273
1982	T Watson	USA	Pebble Beach	282
1983	L Nelson	USA	Oakmont, PA	280
1984	F Zoeller	USA	Winged Foot	276
1985	A North	USA	Oakland Hills, Mich	279
1986	R Floyd	USA	Shinnecock Hills, NY	279
1987	S Simpson	USA	Olympic, SF, Cal	277
1988	C Strange	USA	Brookline, Mass	278
1989	C Strange	USA	Oak Hill	278
1990	H Irwin	USA	Medinah, III	280

1991 Payne Stewart usa Hazeltine 282

THE BRITISH OPEN

Ian Baker-Finch's record-breaking 64 in the third round of the 1991 British Open was ample notice that the young Australian was serious in his challenge for what is probably the most prestigious of the four Major titles.

With just one round left to play in the 1991 Open championship at Royal Birkdale, everything looked to be going exactly to plan for Seve Ballesteros. His sparkling opening round of 66 had been slightly tempered by a not-so-sparkling 73 on the second day, but once the wind had dropped from hurricane to mere gale force, a third round of 69 had left Ballesteros just where he wanted to be – just behind the leaders going into the final round.

Ballesteros was reasonably sure that as the players ahead of him had precious little experience of what it is like to lead a Major championship on the final day, one by one, they would crack and play themselves out of contention.

There would be no need for the Spaniard to produce any fireworks. Instead, a steady closing round would be all that was required to win him his fifth Open. A closer look at the leaders would have seemed to lend credence to this scenario. There was Ian Baker-Finch who had twice been close to winning the Open in recent years only to falter badly in the final round on both occasions.

He had a good swing but obviously lacked the necessary temperament.

Then there was Mark O'Meara. He had won at Birkdale before when he came first in the now-defunct Lawrence Batley tour. But he had been nursing a rib

injury all week and, although he had played impressively in the first three rounds, he never really looked to be the stuff of champions.

Also ahead of Ballesteros were the Australian, Mike Harwood and Ireland's Eamonn Darcy. Harwood had proved that he could handle pressure when he won the PGA championship at Wentworth in 1990, but he was untested in a Major. Darcy had started the season by openly airing his fears that if he was selected for the Ryder Cup he was afraid that his nerves may not have been up to it! If Ryder Cup selection was giving him nightmares, what must have been going through his mind as he stepped on to the first tee to start his final round in the Open Championship one shot in the lead.

On the eve of the final round, Ballesteros said, "Tomorrow I don't have to attack. I wait for them to fall.

The thing they are afraid of is the trophy."

A combination of strong winds and bumpy greens had led to a log-jam at the top of the leader-board after two rounds. The big names were no doubt frustrated by this, but many of the lesser lights in the professional golf world enjoyed the television coverage they got as a result. Among them was Martin Gale who no doubt impressed would-be sponsors with an opening round of 67 that took him to the top of the board for a brief moment of glory. It was soon over when Ballesteros eagled the seventeenth and birdied the eighteenth to come home in 66!

The second round conditions meant that no one player had broken away from the rest of the field to build a commanding lead: this lead to the biggest field for the final two rounds in the history of the championship.

Two past Open champions, Sandy Lyle and America's Mark Calcavecchia, failed to make the 36-hole cut. Lyle opened with a 79 and did not bother to return a card at the end of the second round which saw Calcavecchia so disgusted with his performance that he gave his clubs to a member of the public.

There was little to be seen of the men who had won

Mark O'Meara finished with a stylish 69 to give him tied third place with Fred Couples who finished with a barnstorming 64.

Major titles and thus proved that they could stand the pressure. Neither defending champion Nick Faldo, nor Masters victor, Ian Woosnam were at ease with their game throughout the championship. Jose Maria Olazabal produced only a glimpse of his undoubted genius with a second round of 67 before the malaise that has plagued his game since the narrow defeat in the US Masters returned, yet again, in the shape of two ugly closing 72s.

Among the new breed of home players, Colin Montgomerie, Roger Chapman, Mark Mouland and Richard Boxall all acquitted themselves well, in Boxall's case until he suffered a stress fracture of his left leg while hitting his tee shot at the ninth. But no matter how well they were playing, there was a consensus that at this stage of their careers, the Open was still part of the learning curve and their role at Birkdale was supporting players to Seve Ballesteros' starring role.

1991 had seen the re-emergence of Ballesteros and he had shown that he was still a force to be reckoned with by notching up impressive back-to-back victories in the PGA championship and the Dunlop Masters. Now, the stage was set for another triumph. But if that was to be the case, someone forgot to tell Ian Baker-Finch.

On the eve of the final round someone asked the 30-year-old Australian, nick-named 'The Dark Shark' if, in the light of his two previous, last-day failures at the Open, he was ready to make the giant leap from good tournament professional to Major champion. "In 1984 (at

Mike Harwood plays a delicate chip shot on his way to a final round 67 and second place.

St. Andrews) I was a 23-year-old kid with starry eyes. Last year I learned a lot from the guy that won (Nick Faldo). Now I'm tougher, stronger and better prepared."

Like Faldo, Baker-Finch had undergone a major change to his swing and the long hours of hard work had started to bear fruit so that his form coming into the 1991 Open had never been better.

Two opening 71s, followed by a course record of 64 on the third day had elevated the tall, thin Queenslander to joint leader. While the rest of the field had been struggling with the controversial Birkdale greens, Baker-Finch had been sinking putts as though the hole was as big as a bucket.

The scores from some of the early starters on the final day indicated that the conditions for good scoring were the best they had been all week. This was confirmed by a record-breaking 63 from America's Jodie Mudd, followed by a 66 from Greg Norman who could have been seriously in the running had it not been for a four-over-par opening round of 74.

Things started to go wrong for Ballesteros at the very first hole on the final day when he elected to hit a one-iron from the tee for position, and promptly carved the ball into the deep rough on the right.

Unable to reach the green with his recovery shot, a tense-looking Ballesteros hit his third shot well short of the flag and then two-putted for a bogey five. Not the start that the scenario of the previous evening had called for, but no need for any immediate concern. However, when the great man dropped another shot at the third, it seemed that the pressure which he had predicted would cause the leaders to wilt, was getting to him.

Eamonn Darcy and Mike Harwood each began steadily, but Baker-Finch made a start which was reminiscent of Ben Jonson's explosion from the blocks in the 1990 Olympics 100-metres final. He parred the first and then went on to birdie five of the next seven holes. Pars at the eighth and ninth took him to the turn in a blistering 29, creating an Open record for the first nine holes on a final day, and at the same time virtually put an end to the championship as a contest.

1991 (120th) OPEN CHAMPIONSHIP RESULTS

	Position	Score	Total	Prize Money
IAN BAKER-FINCH	1	71–71–64–66	272	£90,000.00
MIKE HARWOOD	2	68–70–69–67	274	£70,000.00
FRED COUPLES	3	72–69–70–64	275	£55,000.00
MARK O'MEARA	3	71–68–67–69	275	£55,000.00
JODIE MUDD	5	72–70–72–63	277	£34,166.67
BOB TWAY	5	75–66–70–66	277	£34,166.67
EAMONN DARCY	5	73–68–66–70	277	£34,166.67
CRAIG PARRY	8	71–70–69–68	278	£27,500.00
GREG NORMAN	9	74–68–71–66	279	£22,833.33
BERNHARD LANGER	9	71–71–70–67	279	£22,833.33
SEVE BALLESTEROS	9	66–73–69–71	279	£22,833.33
RODGER DAVIS	12	70–71–73–66	280	£17,100.00
MAGNUS SUNESSON	12	72–73–68–67	280	£17,100.00
DAVID WILLIAMS	12	74–71–68–67	280	£17,100.00
ROGER CHAPMAN	12	74–66–71–69	280	£17,100.00
VIJAY SINGH	12	71–69–69–71	280	£17,100.00
CHIP BECK	17	67–78–70–66	281	£10,055.56
LEE TREVINO	17	71–72–71–67	281	£10,055.56
NICK FALDO	17	68–75–70–68	281	£10,055.56
PETER SENIOR	17	74–67–71–69	281	£10,055.56
PAUL BROADHURST	17	71–73–68–69	281	£10,055.56
BARRY LANE	17	68–72–71–70	281	£10,055.56
IAN WOOSNAM	17	70–72–69–70	281	£10,055.56
ANDREW SHERBORNE	17	73–70–68–70	281	£10,055.56
MARK MOULAND	17	68–74–68–71	281	£10,055.56
TOM WATSON	26	69–72–72–69	282	£6,750.00
WAYNE GRADY	26	69–70–73–70	282	£6,750.00
COLIN MONTGOMERIE	26	71–69–71–71	282	£6,750.00
EDUARDO ROMERO	26	70–73–68–71	282	£6,750.00
MARK JAMES	26	72–68–70–72	282	£6,750.00
MIKE REID	26	68–71–70–73	282	£6,750.00
STEVEN RICHARDSON	32	74–70–72–67	283	£5,633.33
PAYNE STEWART	32	72–72–71–68	283	£5,633.33
CHRISTY O'CONNOR JNR	32	72–71–71–69	283	£5,633.33
MIKE MILLER	32	73–74–67–69	283	£5,633.33
GORDON BRAND, JNR	32	71–72–69–71	283	£5,633.33
GARY HALLBERG	32	68–70–73–72	283	£5,633.33
ANDERS FORSBRAND	32	71–72–73–68	284	£4,980.00
JIM PAYNE (A)	32	72–72–70–70	284	
NOLAN HENKE	32	77–71–66–70	284	£4,980.00
PETER O'MALLEY	32	72–71–70–71	284	£4,980.00
CURTIS STRANGE	32	70–73–69–72	284	£4,980.00
MARTIN POXON	32	71–72–67–74	284	£4,980.00
SAM TORRANCE	44	72–76–70–67	285	£4,234.62
DES SMYTH	44	71–73–73–68	285	£4,234.62
TOM KITE	44	77–71–68–69	285	£4,234.62
STEVE ELKINGTON	44	71–68–76–70	285	£4,234.62
ROBERT GAMEZ	44	71–72–72–70	285	£4,234.62
NICK PRICE	44	69–72–73–71	285	£4,234.62
GRAHAM MARSH	44	69–73–72–71	285	£4,234.62
JACK NICKLAUS	44	70–75–69–71	285	£4,234.62
FULTON ALLEM	44	70–72–71–72	285	£4,234.62
JAMIE SPENCE	44	70–73–70–72	285	£4,234.62
DAVIS LOVE III	44	71–72–69–73	285	£4,234.62
DONNIE HAMMOND	44	70–75–67–73	285	£4,234.62
COSTANTINO ROCCA	44	68–73–70–74	285	£4,234.62
GAVIN LEVENSON	57	72–73–73–68	286	£3,550.00
HALE IRWIN	57	74–70–73–69	286	£3,550.00
TIM SIMPSON	57	72–72–72–70	286	£3,550.00
SCOTT SIMPSON	57	74–72–70–70	286	£3,550.00
GARY PLAYER	57	75–71–69–71	286	£3,550.00
JOSE RIVERO	57	74–73–68–71	286	£3,550.00
ANDREW MAGEE	57	71–74–69–72	286	£3,550.00
GIL MORGAN	64	72–74–74–67	287	£3,155.56
JAY DON BLAKE	64	75–73–72–67	287	£3,155.56
STEVE PATE	64	73–72–74–68	287	£3,155.56
MICHAEL McLEAN	64	71–75–72–69	287	£3,155.56
STEVE JONES	64	70–77–71–69	287	£3,155.56
MIGUEL MARTIN	64	71–75–71–70	287	£3,155.56
MARK McNULTY	64	76–71–70–70	287	£3,155.56
ANDY OLDCORN	64	71–67–72–72	287	£3,155.56
DARREN CLARKE	64	79–67–68–73	287	£3,155.56
FRANK NOBILO	73	74–74–71–69	288	£3,000.00
PHIL MICKELSON (A)	73	77–67–73–71	288	
LANNY WADKINS	73	71–75–71–71	288	£3,000.00
MARTIN GATES	73	67–75–73–73	288	£3,000.00
PETER JACOBSEN	73	75–72–68–73	288	£3,000.00
TONY JOHNSTONE	73	69–74–71–74	288	£3,000.00
BRETT OGLE	73	73–75–66–74	288	£3,000.00
MIGUEL A. JIMENEZ	80	74–74–72–69	289	£3,000.00
FUZZY ZOELLER	80	72–72–75–70	289	£3,000.00
DANIEL SILVA	80	73–71–75–70	289	£3,000.00
MALCOLM MACKENZIE	80	71–73–74–71	289	£3,000.00
BEN CRENSHAW	80	71–75–72–71	289	£3,000.00
JOHN BLAND	80	71–76–71–71	289	£3,000.00
MARK BROOKS	80	73–74–70–72	289	£3,000.00
SANTIAGO LUNA	80	67–77–72–73	289	£3,000.00
DANNY MIJOVIC	80	70–72–74–73	289	£3,000.00
JOSE-MARIA OLAZABAL	80	74–67–74–74	289	£3,000.00
HOWARD CLARK	80	71–69–73–76	289	£3,000.00
DAVID GILFORD	80	72–67–73–77	289	£3,000.00
BRIAN MARCHBANK	92	72–73–75–70	290	£3,000.00
RICK GIBSON	92	73–75–70–72	290	£3,000.00
PETER TERAVAINEN	92	71–72–72–75	290	£3,000.00
PATRICK HALL	95	77–71–72–71	291	£3,000.00
JOHN HOSKISON	96	74–73–74–71	292	£3,000.00
PETER HEDBLOM	96	74–74–73–71	292	£3,000.00
ALASTAIR WEBSTER	96	73–74–73–72	292	£3,000.00
PETER ALLAN	96	70–71–75–76	292	£3,000.00
CARL SUNESON	96	69–77–69–77	292	£3,000.00
CHRIS MOODY	101	74–71–78–71	294	£3,000.00
MAGNUS PERSSON	101	77–71–74–72	294	£3,000.00
CRAIG STADLER	101	77–71–74–72	294	£3,000.00
JOHN MORSE	101	73–71–77–73	294	£3,000.00
TOM WEISKOPF	101	74–74–73–73	294	£3,000.00
JEFF SLUMAN	101	71–71–75–77	294	£3,000.00
STEPHEN McALLISTER	107	79–69–70–77	295	£3,000.00
ROBIN MANN	108	73–74–75–75	297	£3,000.00
EOGHAN O'CONNELL	108	74–74–74–75	297	£3,000.00
JOHN OATES	110	77–71–76–75	299	£3,000.00
PAUL MAYO	110	71–74–71–83	299	£3,000.00
NEAL BRIGGS	112	73–74–77–76	300	£3,000.00
RICHARD BOXALL	Ret	71–69–WD		£3,000.00

ROUND-BY-ROUND ANALYSIS

Missed cut:- 149: Corey Pavin 74, 75; **Tony Charnley** 75, 74; **Robert Allenby (A)** 73. 76; **Kenny Perry** 73, 76: **150:** Jose-Maria Canizares 77, 73; **Jimmy Heggarty** 74, 76; **Larry Mize** 75, 75; **Philip Walton** 74, 76; **David Frost** 76, 74; **Simon Townend** 78, 72; **John Hawksworth** 77, 73; **Marc Farry** 75, 75; **Mark Calcavecchia** 71, 79; **Jim Rutledge** 74, 76; **Adam J Hunter** 75, 75; **Jean Van de Velde** 73, 77; **151:** **Massy Kuramoto** 71, 80; **Rocco Mediate** 76, 75; **Henry Roblin (A)** 71, 80; **152: Peter Smith** 78, 74; **Lucien Tinkler** 75, 77; **Ricky Kawagishi** 71, 81; **Greg Turner** 77, 75; **153:** Andrew J Coltart 73, 80; **David Graham** 75, 78; **Yago Beamonte** 72, 81; **Gary Evans (A)** 77, 76; **Glyn Krause** 75, 78; **Manuel Pinero** 79, 74; **154: Sandy Stephen** 75, 79; **Rolf Muntz (A)** 75, 79; **Johnny Miller** 74, 80; **Miguel Fernandez** 81, 73; **David Feherty** 79, 75; **155: Jonathan Wilshire (A)** 76, 79; **Fredrik Lindgren** 79, 76; **Mark Roe** 73, 82; **156: Mikael Hogberg** 78, 78; **Craig Corrigan** 76, 80; **158: Raymond Floyd** 80, 78; **166: Ronald Gregan** 79, 87; **Retired: Sandy Lyle** 79 WD.

ROLL OF HONOUR

The Belt

Year	Winner	Venue	Score
1860	W Park, Musselburgh	Prestwick	174
1861	Tom Morris, sen, Prestwick	Prestwick	163
1862	Tom Morris, sen, Prestwick	Prestwick	163
1863	W Park, Musselburg	Prestwick	168
1864	Tom Morris, sen, Prestwick	Prestwick	167
1865	A Strath, St Andrews	Prestwick	162
1866	W Park, Musselburgh	Prestwick	169
1867	Tom Morris, sen, St Andrews	Prestwick	170
1868	Tom Morris, jun, St Andrews	Prestwick	157
1869	Tom Morris, jun, St Andrews	Prestwick	154
1879	Tom Morris, jun, St Andrews	Prestwick	149

The Cup

Year	Winner	Venue	Score
1872	Tom Morris, jun, St Andrews	Prestwick	166
1873	Tom Kidd, St Andrews	St Andrews	179
1874	Mungo Park, Musselburgh	Musselburgh	159
1875	Willie Park, Musselburgh	Prestwick	166
1876	Bob Martin, St Andrews	St Andrews	176
1877	Jamie Anderson, St Andrews	Musselburgh	160
1878	Jamie Anderson, St Andrews	Prestwick	157
1879	Jamie Anderson, St Andrews	St Andrews	169
1880	Bob Ferguson, Musselburgh	Musselburgh	162
1881	Bob Ferguson, Musselburgh	Prestwick	170
1882	Bob Ferguson, Musselburgh	St Andrews	171
1883	W. Fernie, Dumfries	Musselburgh	159
1884	Jack Simpson, Carnoustie	Prestwick	160
1885	Bob Martin, St Andrews	St Andrews	171
1886	D Brown, Musselburgh	Musselburgh	157
1887	W. Park, jun, Musselburgh	Prestwick	161
1888	Jack Burns, Warwick	St Andrews	171
1889	W. Park, jun, Musselburgh	Musselburgh	155
1890	John Ball, Royal Liverpool(Am)	Prestwick	164
1891	Hugh Kirkaldy, St Andrews	St Andrews	166

(After 1891 the competition was extended to 72 holes and for the first time entry money was imposed).

Year	Winner	Venue	Score
1892	HH Hilton, Royal Liverpool(Am)	Muirfield	305
1893	W Auchterlonie, St Andrews	Prestwick	322
1894	JH Taylor, Winchester	Sandwich	326
1895	JH Taylor, Winchester	St Andrews	322
1896	H Vardon, Ganton	Muirfield	316
1897	HH Hilton, Royal Liverpool(Am)	Hoylake	314
1898	H Vardon, Ganton	Prestwick	307
1899	H Vardon, Gaton	Sandwich	310
1900	JH Taylor, Mid Surrey	St Andrews	309
1901	James Braid, Romford	Muirfield	309
1902	Alex Herd, Huddersfield	Hoylake	307
1903	H Vardon, Totteridge	Prestwick	300
1904	Jack White, Sunningdale	Sandwich	296
1905	James Braid, Walton Heath	St Andrews	318
1906	James Braid, Walton Heath	Muirfield	300
1907	Arnaud Massy, La Boulie	Hoylake	312
1908	James Braid, Walton Heath	Prestwick	291
1909	JH Taylor, Mid Surrey	Deal	295
1910	James Briad, Walton Heath	St Andrews	299
1911	Harry Vardon, Totteridge	Sandwich	303
1912	E Ray, Oxhey	Muirfield	295
1913	JH Taylor, Mid Surrey	Hoylake	304
1914	Harry Vardon, Totteridge	Prestwick	306
1915-19	No Championship owing to the Great War		
1920	George Duncan, Hanger Hill	Deal	303
1921	Jock Hutchison,Glenview,Chicago	St Andrews	296
1922	Walter Hagen, Detroit, USA	Sandwich	300
1923	AG Havers, Coombe Hill	Troon	295
1924	Walter Hagen, Detroit, USA	Hoylake	301

Year	Winner	Venue	Score
1925	Jim Barnes, USA	Prestwick	300
1926	RT Jones, USA(Am)	Lytham	291
1927	RT Jones, USA(Am)	St Andrews	285
1928	Walter Hagen, USA	Sandwich	292
1929	Walter Hagen, USA	Muirfield	292
1930	RT Jones, USA(Am)	Hoylake	291
1931	TD Armour, USA	Carnoustie	296
1932	G Sarazen, USA	Prince's Sandwich	283
1933	D Shute, USA	St Andrews	292
1934	TH Cotton, Waterloo, Belgium	Sandwich	283
1935	A Perry, Leatherhead	Muirfield	283
1936	AH Padgham, Sundridge Park	Hoylake	287
1937	TH Cotton, Ashridge	Carnoustie	290
1938	RA Whitcombe, Parkstone	Sandwich	295
1939	R Burton, Sale	St Andrews	290
1940-45	No Championship owing to Second World War		
1946	S Snead, USA	St Andrews	290
1947	Fred Daly, Balmoral	Hoylake	293
1948	TH Cotton, Royal Mid Surrey	Muirfield	284
1949	AD Locke, South Africa	Sandwich	283
1950	AD Locke, South Africa	Troon	279
1951	M Faulkner, GB	Portrush	285
1952	AD Locke, South Africa	Lytham	287
1953	Ben Hogan, USA	Carnoustie	282
1954	PW Thomson, Australia		283
1955	PW Thomson, Australia	St Andrews	281
1956	PW Thomson, Australia	Hoylake	286
1957	AD Locke, South Africa	St Andrews	279
1958	PW Thomson, Australia	Lytham	278
1959	GJ Player, South Africa	Muirfield	284
1960	KDG Nagle, Australia	St Andrews	278
1961	Arnold Palmer, USA	Birkdale	284
1962	Arnold Palmer, USA	Troon	276
1963	RJ Charles, New Zealand	Lytham	277
1964	Tony Lema, USA	St Andrews	279
1965	PW Thomson, Australia	Birkdale	285
1966	J Nicklaus, USA	Muirfield	282
1967	R De Vicenzo, Argentina	Hoylake	278
1968	GJ Player, South Africa	Carnoustie	289
1969	A Jacklin, GB	Lytham	280
1970	J Nicklaus, USA	St Andrews	283
1971	L Trevino, USA	Birkdale	278
1972	L Trevino, USA	Muirfield	278
1973	T Weiskopf, USA	Troon	276
1974	G Player, South Africa	Lytham	282
1975	T Watson, USA	Carnoustie	279
1976	J Miller, USA	Birkdale	279
1977	T Watson, USA	Turnberry	268
1978	J Nicklaus, USA	St Andrews	281
1979	S Ballesteros, Spain	Lytham	283
1980	T Watson, USA	Muirfield	271
1981	B Rogers, USA	Sandwich	276
1982	T Watson, USA	Troon	284
1983	T Watson, USA	Birkdale	275
1984	S Ballesteros, Spain	St Andrews	276
1985	A Lyle, GB	Sandwich	282
1986	G Norman, Australia	Turnberry	280
1987	N Faldo, GB	Muirfield	279
1988	S Ballesteros, Spain	Lytham	273
1989	M Calcavecchia, USA	Troon	275
1990	N Faldo, GB	St Andrews	275

1991 Ian Baker-Finch AUS Birkdale 272

Although he did drop a shot to par at the tenth, he was so far ahead of the other players that the only thing left for them to play for was second place.

While Baker-Finch flourished, Ballesteros floundered and it was left to Mark O'Meara and Fred Couples to battle it out with Mike Harwood. The rock-steady Harwood remarked, "I'm not one of the greatest players, I'm just a grinder," He ground round in a very creditable closing round of 67 to take second place by one shot from the fast-finishing Mark O'Meara and the ever-popular Couples.

There was a brief spell in the middle of his last round when the long-hitting Couples seemed unable to miss the hole from anywhere around the twenty-foot mark. But as has happened so often in the past, Couples was unable to make the short putts when they really mattered. The downs in Eamonn Darcy's up-and-down final round finally got the better of the ups, especially at the long fifteenth where he took a seven that took the edge of what had otherwise been a brave, closing 70 which gave him fifth place, £34,000 and what he thought was a virtual guarantee of a place in the European Ryder Cup team.

Ballesteros never recovered from the two dropped shots in the final round and a day which had started with such high hopes ended with a disappointing one-over-par 71 and a tied eighth place with Greg Norman and Bernhard Langer. Many of Ballesteros's vast army of fans were left wondering what had happened to change one of the game's most exciting and aggressive players into a man whose game-plan for victory

had rested solely on the mistakes of others.

The winner of the medal for leading amateur was Jim Payne whose closing round of 70 denied American Phil Mickelson, who was leading amateur in the US Masters and US Open, a unique Grand Slam.

Meanwhile, Baker-Finch continued his cautious march to victory, concentrating on landing his tee shots on the fairway, hitting his approach shots into the middle of the green and then nursing his first putts close enough to the hole to make pars a formality. He reached the eighteenth tee still three shots clear of the field and permitted himself the luxury of completing his round with a one-over-par five for a 72-hole total of 272.

After realizing his childhood dreams and actually raising the famous claret jug aloft to the acclaim of the thousands of fans packed into the huge stand around the eighteenth green, Baker-Finch said, "There have been a lot of Saturday afternoons when I've gone into Sunday with a chance of winning and haven't made it. Today erases those memories. All the times I didn't go on to win made

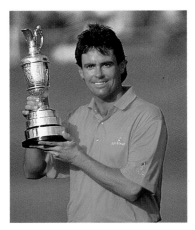

Ian Baker-Finch holds the famous claret jug and joins the elite of golf's great as Britsh Open champion.

me stronger." He finished by saying, "The Open championship is the most special event in my life. Just to play in it is fantastic: to win it is just a dream. I feel like I'm on top of the world."

Whoever stands on the eighteenth green at the end of the last round of this year's Open holding the same, silver jug will, no doubt, share Baker-Finch's emotions, for to

The cheers drowned the cameras' clicks as Ian Baker-FInch sank his final putt to take the Open.

win the Open is one of the jewels in the golfing crown, especially when played over a course that is itself a golfing jewel, Muirfield, on Scotland's Firth of Forth coastline.

The course is the home of the Honourable Company of Edinburgh Golfers who originally played at Leith and Musselborough and who moved to their present location in 1891. It has hosted the Amateur Championship on eight occasions, the Ryder Cup in 1973, the Walker Cup in 1959 as well as the Curtis Cup in 1952, and the Home Internationals three times. It is considered by many to be the best and fairest of all the courses which currently host the British Open.

Jack Nicklaus rates it as the best 'shot value' course in the world, meaning the more accurate the first shot, the easier the second shot becomes. One of the course's greatest strengths is the way in which the holes change direction: only the third, fourth and fifth run consecutively in the same direction. Although the course does not run directly along the shore line of the Firth of Forth, there are very few days when wind is not a factor when playing Muirfield, so whoever wins this year's open will have to be constantly aware of the way the wind is blowing.

The first hole is a 447-yard par four. The opening drive in any championship is testing: the first drive at Muirfield is more daunting than most. A partially-hidden large bunker about 230 yards out on the left-hand side is the first hazard. Very long hitters are faced with a landing area that narrows as it stretches from the tee until it gets to about 300 yards out.

An approach shot pulled to the left will probably find one of the two bunkers set in the rough about 90 yards short of the putting surface which is reasonably flat but guarded by a large bunker in the front with two more on the left and right. This is such a difficult hole that, no doubt, many of the contenders for this year's title will tee-off at the second one or two over par – hardly the best start for the campaign for the championship.

There will also be those whose dreams of holding the claret jug aloft in a victory salute will come to grief at the thirteenth, a 152-yard, par three. It is one of the world's truly great short holes. The 50-yard long green is cut into a high ridge and the tee shot is played from well below the level of the putting surface. Fearsome bunkers are positioned close to the putting surface, all set into large sand hills surrounding the green.

Golfing fans with long memories will no doubt recall that Lee Trevino dashed Tony Jacklin's hopes of victory in the 1972 Open when he holed an outrageous chip shot at the seventeenth. The

The wide-open spaces and blowing wind will make choice of club an important factor at Muirfield.

hole is the last and most demanding of Muirfield's par fives. A player who aims to stand on the eighteenth tee with the championship in his grasp will probably have flirted with the nest of bunkers which guard the left side of the seventeenth fairway to land their ball in the middle, for the further right the tee shot lands, the longer the hole plays. That achieved, he will then have to cope with a large area of humps and hollows and three large bunkers. The choice is simple, either carry the area or lay up short for there is no way past on either right or left. If the wind is behind the player, aiming short leaves a fairly straightforward shot of around 150 yards to the green, carrying the hazards leaves a short pitch to the green which slopes from back to front and which is guarded by two large bunkers on either side.

USPGA CHAMPIONSHIP

On the eve of the 1991 USPGA, few had heard of John Daly. Four rounds later he had played his way into the record books, with a display of golf at its best.

After the final putt had been holed at the 1991 USPGA, someone joked that NASA, the American Space Agency, were evaluating a new and extremely cost-effective way of putting payloads into space. The plan was simple: all they had to do was put the object on a tee peg and get the 1991 USPGA champion, John Daly, to launch it into orbit with his drive!

Over four amazing days in August, Daly had powered his way from obscurity to the brink of golfing immortality and in the process had brutalised and overpowered one of the world's longest and most difficult golf courses. The 25-year-old unknown from Memphis, Tennessee had gained a last-minute entry to the competition: now he found himself standing on the 72nd hole of the championship with a three-shot lead over the rest of the star-studded international field.

Given that he had never been even remotely close to this kind of situation before in his short career as a tournament professional, and that he was facing the most difficult hole on the course with possible disaster lurking only a slice away, it might have been prudent, even sound course management to hit an iron from the tee and try to tiptoe his way cautiously to victory. Caution, however, is not a word in John Daly's golfing vocabulary. Instead of choosing the safe shot, he kept faith with the positive, attitude which had been the cornerstone of his game over the seventy-one holes, and pounded yet another huge drive down the centre of the fairway: This was followed by a towering eight-iron shot into the middle of the green from where he rapped his approach putt six-feet past the hole. He then drilled the return putt straight into the centre of the cup for a three-shot victory and an outstanding chance of winning 'the most remarkable sporting victory of the decade' award.

There are long hitters: there are monster hitters: and now there is John Daly. For four rounds he literally beat the living daylights out of one of the world's most difficult courses with a display of aggressive power-hitting and

John Daly cracks another of his enormous drives away - this one at the ninth hole.

in the process completely dominated a world-class field.

Daly's four rounds of 69, 67, 69 and 71 gave him a twelve-under-par total of 276 and a three-shot victory over fellow American, Bruce Lietzke.

The best-placed European was Stephen Richardson who tied for fifth place in his first American Major. Ireland's David Feherty claimed seventh place: a welcome return to form from Sandy Lyle whose four-round total of 286 gave him joint sixteenth place: so there was some consolation for a lacklustre performance by the more established European trio of Woosnam, Ballesteros and Nick Faldo.

The record books will show a three-shot win for Daly but his victory was far more emphatic than even that margin suggests. Not since the days when Jack Nicklaus was at the very pinnacle of his powers, has any golfer so completely dominated a world-class field in a Major championship.

However Daly's victory in his first appearance in a Major championship cannot be solely attributed to hitting the ball prodigious distances. Before the start of the tournament, 'Big John' had headed the US Tour statistics for driving. His distance average was 286 yards, but in the driving accuracy stakes he was 174th. But for those four magical days at Crooked Stick, Daly was able to combine power with accuracy: no mean feat on a course reckoned to be among the most difficult driving courses in the world. The ability to drive a ball long and straight coupled with a refreshing and very positive mental attitude to the game created the perfect platform

Bruce Lietzke's steady 68, 69, 72 and 70 earned him second place and a cheque for $200,000.

from which to mount what at first may have seemed an unlikely challenge for the final Major championship of the season. While the established stars were playing percentage golf by hitting irons from the tee and aiming their approach shots at the middle of the green, Daly was pounding out huge drives, hammering iron shots straight at the flag and ramming putts firmly into the centre of the hole for pars and birdies.

Newcomers had lead Major championships before only to crumble under final-day pressure. When Daly dropped a shot at the first hole in the final round, some thought that he, too, might be about to crack. John Daly, however, promptly responded with a birdie at the very next hole, and from that point on he virtually took the championship by the throat and refused to let go his stranglehold on the rest of the field, until the USPGA was well and truly won.

Talking emotionally after his remarkable victory, Daly said, "This is a dream come true. I'm just glad an American won another Major. It's just the greatest feeling in the world. I told myself before the start of the round not to think of it as a Major but just as another tournament. But I realized I couldn't tell myself that anymore when I got to the sixteenth. I just knew it was a Major and told myself, 'Hey! You can win this!' I felt comfortable until I got to the sixteenth, then I felt the pressure. I never got nervous until I got to three holes from the finish."

Before the start of the 1991 USPGA championship, the man most people were talking about was called Dye, not Daly. Pete Dye is one of America's foremost tournament and most controversial golf course architects. Crooked Stick is reckoned to be among his most demanding, some say diabolical, creations to date.

The general consensus was that victory at this venue would take long, straight hitting, sound course management, a silky touch on the greens and, above all, experience in handling the unique pressures of a Major championship. With golfers of the calibre of Seve Ballesteros, Nick Faldo and Ian Woosnam, the US Masters champion, all seemingly well qualified to meet these criteria, it looked as if the European contingent had its best chance to date of capturing the one Major title that has so far eluded them.

Enter John Daly! Although his 69 was among the best scores of the day, the initial interest was in the way Daly had gained entry to the championship. Having failed to pre-qualify for the event and in the position of ninth alternate, 'Big John' was at home in Memphis as the top stars were putting the final touches to their preparation. When he was informed that he was first alternate, he jumped in his car and drove all the way back to Crooked Stick. When he arrived in the small hours of the morning, he discovered that as Nick Price's wife was on the point of going into labour, Price had withdrawn and Daly was in the field.

He set about the course with the kind of controlled aggression that had not been seen in a Major championship, certainly in America, since the days of Arnold Palmer and, more recently, Johnny Miller.

Daly stuck to his 'go-for-broke' game plan on the second day and half-way through the second round he found himself in the lead.

Several of the pre-tournament favourites including Ballesteros, Faldo and Woosnam, were in touch with the leader, but all three were hanging on by their fingernails, rather than challenging for the lead on the tight and demanding Crooked Stick layout.

On the third day it was business as usual for John Daly and another power-packed, fearless display of shot-making took him three shots clear of the field with only one round to play. It looked as if his powerhouse display of golf had left the rest of the field so shell-shocked and dazed that any change in the leadership would come not from a late dash to glory from the trailing pack, but through Daly crumbling under the pressure of leading the field in a final

Craig Stadler's (ABOVE) putt for a birdie at the sixteenth stopped an inch or two short of the hole. He finished in joint seventh position.

round of a Major.

Despite the momentary hiccup at the opening hole, John Daly never gave the rest of the field even the slightest glimmer of hope. With a final round of 71, John Daly finished the 1991 USPGA championship at Crooked Stick as he had started – going for his shots and playing at full throttle.

Only a week before, John Daly (BELOW) would never have dreamed that he would be posing for the world's press alongside the splendid USPGA trophy.

Bellerive Country Club in St. Louis, Missouri, site of the 1992 USPGA Championship to be played from August 10 to August 16, has a long and honourable history of supporting golf and providing outstanding facilities for it.

It was founded in 1897 as the Field Club of St. Louis and built its first, nine-hole course only ten years after the first golf course in the United States had been built, at St. Andrews in Yonkers, north of New York City.

In 1909, the club moved to a larger site in northwest St. Louis County and changed its name to Bellerive Club in honour of Captain Louis Ange de Bellerive, the last French commander in North America and the first governor of St. Louis. A new, eighteen-hole golf course was designed by the club's new golf professional, Robert Foulis, a native of St. Andrews in Scotland. Foulis remained as the club's professional for 35 years but designed or helped design several other fine courses in the Midwest.

By the mid-1950s, several developments made it almost inevitable that Bellerive would have to move.

The new club was opened on Memorial Day 1960 with course designer Trent Jones playing in the foursome that officially opened the course.

Although it is a country club in every sense of the word with tennis, swimming and even croquet facilities, Bellerive is and always has been first and foremost a golf club. This became clear when the members decided, successfully, to go after the US Open which the club hosted in 1965. The event was the first US Open to be televised in colour and also the first to be sold out on a season ticket

A classic golf course such as Bellerive deserves an imposing and classical clubhouse.

basis. Bellerive broke the Open attendance record and held it for almost 25 years.

The United States Golf Association was impressed with Bellerive's ability to handle a large tournament and selected the club to host the USGA Mid-amateur Championship in 1981. The tournament is designed to feature outstanding amateurs of 25 and over who do not want to turn professional. The organizers wanted the competition, now an annual event, as a showcase for great golfers who play purely for the love of the game.

In 1989, the USPGA of America, selected Bellerive to host the PGA Junior championship for boys and

girls aged seventeen and under. Many of the competitors at Bellerive have gone on to turn professional, others are established stars on the amateur circuit.

When Bellerive was voted as the site for the PGA Championship, extensive modernization and improvement of the golf course was decided upon. Trent Jones was retained to supervise the work. The third and thirteenth greens were reconstructed, tees on several other holes were either reconstructed or remodelled and a number of low-water bridges were built. These and other changes combined to make Bellerive one of the most testing courses on the US circuit.

From the back tees, Bellerive plays 7,305 yards, one of the longest courses in the United States. The course, rated at 75.1, is so tough that players in the 1965 US Open dubbed it 'The Green Monster of Ladus Road.' Not even the winner, Gary Player, finished with a total score under par!

In 1992, whoever wins the USPGA Championship will have the satisfaction of knowing he has conquered one of the world's finest and most demanding golf courses.

Every golfer's dream of paradise, Bellerive's testing bunkers, one of the beautifully manicured greens, perfectly clipped fairways – and not another player in sight to spoil the idyll.

1991 USPGA CHAMPIONSHIP RESULTS

Name	Position	Scores	Total	Prize Money
JOHN DALY	1	69–67–69–71	276	£230,000.00
BRUCE LIETZKE	2	68–69–72–70	279	£140,000.00
JIM GALLAGHER, JR	3	70–72–72–67	281	£95,000.00
KENNY KNOX	4	67–71–70–74	282	£75,000.00
BOB GILDER	5	73–70–67–73	283	£60,000.00
STEVE RICHARDSON	5	70–72–72–69	283	£60,000.00
DAVID FEHERTY	7	71–74–71–68	284	£38,000.00
RAY FLOYD	7	69–74–72–69	284	£38,000.00
JOHN HUSTON	7	70–72–70–72	284	£38,000.00
STEVE PATE	7	70–75–70–69	284	£38,000.00
CRAIG STADLER	7	68–71–69–76	284	£38,000.00
HAL SUTTON	7	74–67–72–71	284	£38,000.00
JAY DON BLAKE	13	75–70–72–68	285	£24,000.00
ANDREW MAGEE	13	69–73–68–75	285	£24,000.00
PAYNE STEWART	13	74–70–71–70	285	£24,000.00
NICK FALDO	16	70–69–71–76	286	£17,000.00
KEN GREEN	16	68–73–71–74	286	£17,000.00
WAYNE LEVI	16	73–71–72–70	286	£17,000.00
SANDY LYLE	16	68–75–71–72	286	£17,000.00
ROCCO MEDIATE	16	71–71–73–71	286	£17,000.00
GIL MORGAN	16	70–71–74–71	286	£17,000.00
HOWARD TWITTY	16	70–71–75–70	286	£17,000.00
SEVE BALLESTEROS	23	71–72–71–73	287	£11,500.00
CHIP BECK	23	73–73–70–71	287	£11,500.00
MIKE HULBERT	23	72–72–73–70	287	£11,500.00
JACK NICKLAUS	23	71–72–73–71	287	£11,500.00
FRED COUPLES	27	74–67–76–71	288	£8,150.00
RICK FEHR	27	70–73–71–74	288	£8,150.00
JIM HALLET	27	69–74–73–72	288	£8,150.00
MARK McNULTY	27	75–71–69–73	288	£8,150.00
LOREN ROBERTS	27	72–74–72–70	288	£8,150.00
BILLY ANDRADE	32	73–74–68–74	289	£6,000.00
MARK CALCAVECCHIA	32	70–74–73–72	289	£6,000.00
DAVID EDWARDS	32	71–75–71–72	289	£6,000.00
STEVE ELKINGTON	32	74–68–74–73	289	£6,000.00
DAN FORSMAN	32	73–74–68–74	289	£6,000.00
DAVIS LOVE III	32	72–72–72–73	289	£6,000.00
JODIE MUDD	32	74–71–74–70	289	£6,000.00
GREG NORMAN	32	70–74–72–73	289	£6,000.00
COREY PAVIN	32	72–73–71–73	289	£6,000.00
TOM PURTZER	32	69–76–71–73	289	£6,000.00
DOUG TEWELL	32	75–72–74–68	289	£6,000.00
ED DOUGHERTY	43	75–70–69–76	290	£4,030.00
WAYNE GRADY	43	72–70–71–77	290	£4,030.00
SCOTT HOCH	43	71–75–72–72	290	£4,030.00
CRAIG PARRY	43	73–70–76–71	290	£4,030.00
LANNY WADKINS	43	71–74–72–73	290	£4,030.00
KEITH CLEARWATER	48	72–72–76–71	291	£3,175.00
BRAD FAXON	48	72–71–76–72	291	£3,175.00
DAVID FROST	48	74–70–75–72	291	£3,175.00
IAN WOOSNAM	48	67–72–76–76	291	£3,175.00
DAVID GRAHAM	52	72–73–73–74	292	£2,725.00
TOM KITE	52	73–72–75–72	292	£2,725.00
MARK McCUMBER	52	74–72–71–75	292	£2,725.00
EDUARDO ROMERO	52	72–75–73–72	292	£2,725.00
TOM SIECKMANN	52	68–76–74–74	292	£2,725.00
FRED FUNK	57	71–69–72–81	293	£2,537.50
NOLAN HENKE	57	74–70–75–74	293	£2,537.50
BLAINE McCALLISTER	57	71–76–77–69	293	£2,537.50
LINDY MILLER	57	72–72–77–72	293	£2,437.50
DAVE BARR	61	75–72–76–71	294	£2,462.50
JEFF SLUMAN	61	73–73–74–74	294	£2,462.50
GENE SAUERS	63	75–71–70–79	295	£2,400.00
JOEY SINDELAR	63	74–73–71–77	295	£2,400.00
BOB WOLCOTT	63	73–71–79–72	295	£2,400.00
DILLARD PRUITT	66	72–75–73–76	296	£2,312.50
BOB TWAY	66	73–71–78–74	296	£2,312.50
MARK WIEBE	66	72–73–73–78	296	£2,312.50
SCOTT WILLIAMS	66	70–77–76–73	296	£2,312.50
DENNY HEPLER	70	71–75–75–76	297	£2,225.00
LONNIE NIELSON	70	74–71–74–78	297	£2,225.00
DAVID PEOPLES	70	74–73–75–75	297	£2,225.00
PHIL BLACKMAR	73	73–72–82–71	298	£2,137.50
BILLY RAY BROWN	73	69–75–79–75	298	£2,137.50
HALE IRWIN	73	70–76–74–78	298	£2,137.50
DON POOLEY	73	72–74–72–80	298	£2,137.50
KENNY PERRY	72	77–73–79–76	300	£2,075.00

The following players missed the cut: **148: Bill Britton** 71, 77; **Mark Brooks** 73, 75; **Brian Claar** 76, 72; **Russ Cochran** 73, 75; **John Cook** 74, 74; **Bob Lohr** 78, 70; **Tommy Nakajima** 72, 76; **Peter Persons** 73, 75; **Peter Senior** 74, 74; **Dave Stockton** 71, 77; **Fuzzy Zoeller** 72, 76; **149: Scott Bentley** 75, 74; **Jay Delsing** 70, 79; **Terry Florence** 75, 74; **Ricky Kawagishi** 75, 74; **Bernhard Langer** 75, 74; **Larry Mize** 72, 77; **Lee Rinker** 73, 76; **Ken Schall** 74, 75; **Bobby Wadkins** 77, 72; **Tom Watson** 74, 75; **150: Ian Baker-Finch** 74, 76; **Billy Mayfair** 73, 77; **Jose-Maria Olazabal** 77, 73; **Ted Schulz** 75, 75; **Tim Simpson** 74, 76; **151: Hubert Green** 73, 78; **Morris Hatalsky** 74, 77; **Stu Ingraham** 73, 78; **John Mahaffey** 77, 74; **Scott Simpson** 72, 79; **152: Greg Farrow** 74, 78; **Larry Gilbert** 79, 73; **Mike Kallam** 74, 78; **Darrell Kestner** 74, 78; **Larry Nelson** 75, 77; **Sam Torrance** 74, 78; **Gary Trivisonno** 77, 75; **153: Jim Masserio** 74, 79; **Brett Upper** 74, 79; **154: Bruce Fleisher** 76, 78; **Buddy Gardner** 74, 80; **Gary Hallberg** 72, 82; **Mark O'Meara** 75, 79; **Stan Utley** 77, 77; **Tom Wargo** 76, 78; **155: Mel Baum** 78, 77; **Fran Marrello** 75, 80; **Arnold Palmer** 77, 78; **Milan Swilor** 77, 78; **Kim Thompson** 79, 76; **156: Bob Borowicz** 80, 76; **Dave Rummells** 77, 79; **157: Andy Bean** 80, 77; **Brent Buckman** 79, 78; **Terry Dear** 74, 83; **158: Mike Harwood** 73, 85; **Jeff Roth** 80, 78; **Brad Sherfy** 76, 82; **159: Bob Lendzion** 76, 83; **Brian Tennyson** 76, 83; **Brent Veenstra** 77, 82; **160: Robert Wilkin** 76, 84; **Tom Woodard** 84, 76; **161: Mike Lawrence** 82, 79; **162: Benny Passons** 85, 77; **Steve Veriato** 82, 80; **Gregg Wolff** 81, 81; **163: John Hendricks** 83, 80; **Shawn McEntee** 81, 82; **Jim White** 76, 87; **168: Jim Dickson** 83, 85; **Withdrew: Ben Crenshaw** 81; **Curtis Strange** 81.

ROLL OF HONOUR

Matchplay

Year	Winner	Runner-up	Venue	By
1916	Jim Barnes	Jock Hutchison	Siwanoy	1 hole
1919	Jim Barnes	Fred McLeod	Engineers' Club	6 and 5
1920	Jock Hutchison	Douglas Edgar	Floosmoor	1 hole
1921	Walter Hagen	Jim Barnes	Inwood Club	3 and 2
1922	Gene Sarazen	Emmet French	Oakmont	4 and 3
1923	Gene Sarazen	Walter Hagen	Pelham	38th hole
1924	Walter Hagen	Jim Barnes	French Lick	2 holes
1925	Walter Hagen	WE Mehlhorn	Olympic Fields	6 and 4
1926	Walter Hagen	Leo Diegel	Salisbury	4 and 3
1927	Walter Hagen	Joe Turnesa	Dallas, Texas	1 hole
1928	Leo Diegel	Al Espinosa	Five Farms	6 and 5
1929	Leo Diegel	J Farrell	Hill Crest	6 and 4
1930	TD Armour	G Sarazen	Fresh Meadow	1 hole
1931	T Creavy	D Shute	Wannamoisett	2 and 1
1932	O Dutra	F Walsh	St Paul, Minnesota	4 and 3
1933	G Sarazen	W Goggin	Milwaukee	5 and 4
1934	P Runyan	Criag Wood	Buffalo	38th hole
1935	J Revolta	TD Armour	Oklahoma	5 and 4
1936	D Shute	J Thomson	Pinehurst	3 and 2
1937	D Shute	H McSpaden	Pittsburg	37th hole
1938	P Runyan	S Snead	Shawnee	8 and 7
1939	H Picard	B Nelson	Pomonok	37th hole
1940	Byron Nelson	Sam Snead	Hershey, Pa	1 hole
1941	Vic Ghezzie	Byron Nelson	Denver, Colo	38th hole
1942	Sam Snead	Jim Turnesa	Atlantic City	2 and 1
1943	No Championship			
1944	Bob Hamilton	Byron Nelson	Spokane, Wash	1 hole
1945	Byron Nelson	Sam Byrd	Dayton, Ohio	4 and 3
1946	Ben Hogan	Ed Oliver	Portland	6 and 4
1947	Jim Ferrier	Chick Harbert	Detroit	2 and 1
1948	Ben Hogan	Mike Turnesa	Norwood Hills	7 and 6
1949	Sam Snead	Johnny Palmer	Richmond, Va	3 and 2
1950	Chandler Harper	Henry Williams	Scioto, Ohio	4 and 3
1951	Sam Snead	Walter Burkemo	Oakmont, Pa	7 and 6
1952	Jim Turnesa	Chick Harbert	Big Spring, Louisville	1 hole
1953	Walter Burkemo	Felice Lorza	Birmingham, Michigan	2 and 1
1954	Chick Harbert	Walter Burkemo	St Paul, Minnesota	4 and 3
1955	D Ford	C Middlecoff	Detroit	4 and 3
1956	J Burke	T Kroll	Boston	3 and 2
1957	L Herbert	D Finsterwald	Miami Valley, Dayton	3 and 1

Changed to Strokeplay

Strokeplay

Year	Winner	Venue	Score
1958	D Finsterwald	Llanerch, PA	276
1959	Bob Rosburg	Minneapolis, MN	277
1960	Jay Herbert	Firestone, Akron, OH	281
1961	Jerry Barber*	Olympia Fields, IL	277
1962	GJ Player	Aronimink, PA	278
1963	JW Nicklaus	Dallas, TX	279
1964	Bobby Nichols	Columbus, OH	271
1965	D Marr	Laurel Valley, PA	280
1966	Al Geiberger	Firestone, Akron, OH	280
1967	Don January*	Columbine, CO	281
1968	Julius Boros	Pecan Valley, TX	281
1969	Ray Floyd	Dayton, OH	276
1970	Dave Stockton	Southern Hills, OK	279
1971	JW Nicklaus	PGA National, FL	281
1972	GJ Player	Oakland Hills, MI	281
1973	JW Nicklaus	Canterbury, OH	277
1974	L Trevino	Tanglewood, NC	276
1975	JW Nicklaus	Firestone, Akron, OH	276
1976	D Stockton	Congressional, MD	281
1977	L Wadkins*	Pebble Beach, CA	287
1978	J Mahaffey*	Oakmont, PA	276
1979	D Graham*	Oakland Hills, MI	272
1980	JW Nicklaus	Oak Hill, NY	274
1981	L Nelson	Atlanta, GA	273
1982	R Floyd	Southern Hills, OK	272
1983	H Sutton	Pacific Palisades, CA	274
1984	L Trevino	Shoal Creek	273
1985	H Green	Cherry Hills, Denver, CO	278
1986	R Tway	Inverness, Toledo, OH	276
1987	L Nelson*	PGA National, FL	287
1988	J Sluman	Oaktree, OK	272
1989	P Stewart	Kemper Lakes	276
1990	W Grady	Shoal Creek	282

*(*After a tie)*

1991 John Daly Crooked Stick   276

THE RYDER CUP

Europe came within inches of retaining the Ryder Cup in a dramatic final-day battle at Kiawah Island.

For German Bernhard Langer, the situation which he found himself facing on the eighteenth green, in the final match of the 1991 Ryder Cup, must have been his worst nightmare come true; standing over a six-foot putt for par, which would decide the outcome of the competition.

On the two previous holes, the German who has battled with, and overcome three bouts of the putting yips, had dug deep into his well of courage and determination and come up with two life-saving putts at the sixteenth and seventeenth holes which had hauled the European cause back from the very brink of defeat to a position where winning or losing the Ryder Cup lay in his hands.

Sadly, at the third time of asking, Langer found that the well had run dry and the putt, which would have given Europe the vital point required to retain the trophy, slid agonisingly past the right edge of the hole. Langer bowed his head in anguish, and every chant of "USA, USA" from the gallery that heralded an American victory, must have felt like a stab to his heart. Thankfully the true spirit of the Ryder Cup, which at times over the previous three days had become strained, came to the fore as Hale Irwin, Langer's opponent in the last-day's singles match, was the first person to console him.

The American had gone through his own misery, knowing that he was the man who had allowed the Ryder Cup to all but slip from American hands. After playing four shots, his ball was still above ground and apart from praying, there was nothing Irwin could do to affect the outcome of the Ryder Cup. Irwin said, "I know how bad he must be feeling, I was expecting to feel the same way myself." And although the American team then let

The first day saw Faldo and Woosnam beaten in both the foursomes, by Payne Stewart and Mark Calcavecchia, and in the fourballs, by Ray Floyd and Fred Couples.

David Feberty jumps for joy on the seventeenth green having beaten Payne Stewart two and one in the singles.

their hair down and began to celebrate a victory which overall, they probably just deserved, the festivities may have been slightly tempered by the sobering knowledge that when it came to the crunch, victory was by courtesy of a missed European putt rather than a winning American one.

Despite all the hype, in the end, the seeds of the American victory may well have been sown by golf-course architect Pete Dye, rather than the American captain Dave Stockton, when the former decided to use Bermuda grass on the greens at the spectacular Kiawah Island course off the coast of South Carolina.

The difference between the teams, and also the main factor in the narrow America victory, was the home team's ability to read the greens and sink the putts that mattered, none more so than on the last green in the final match.

The first two days of foursomes and fourball matches had been a story of give and take, with the Europeans giving the Americans a head start in the morning foursomes and then clawing their way back in the afternoon fourball matches. The teams had begun the final series of singles matches all square with $8^1/2$ points each, and early in the day it seemed that Bernard Gallacher's plan to try to get early points on the board had paid off as a rejuvenated Nick Faldo held off a late challenge from Raymond Floyd to win the lead match on the final green. Another

vital point followed from Ryder Cup newcomer David Feherty, who claimed the scalp of US Open champion, Payne Stewart.

The magical number for the European team was fourteen points, the minimum they required to draw the matches and retain the Cup and when Scotland's Colin Montgomerie staged the comeback of the year by clawing his way back from four down with four to play, to half his match with a shell-shocked Mark Calcavecchia, it seemed as if fortune was indeed favouring the Cup-holders. But just as swiftly the tide turned in favour of the Americans, as Paul Azinger just edged through against Jose Maria Olazabal and then Corey Pavin, thanks to a miraculous bunker shot at the seventeenth, closed out Ian Richardson two and one.

Out on the course, fortunes ebbed and flowed as the players from both sides battled with both the pressure of the occasion and a strong

wind which was threatening to turn architect Pete Dye's ocean-side creation into an unplayable monster. The tension was electric and nerves became frayed even among battle-hardened Ryder Cup veterans.

Jose Maria Olazabal won both his first-day foursomes and fourballs with Seve Ballesteros. The pair won their second-day foursome against Fred Couples and Ray Floyd, halved their fourball with Couples and Payne Stewart, but whereas Ballesteros beat Wayne Levi in the Singles, Olazabal lost in a close match to Paul Azinger.

Holes were won with sevens and matches with rounds in the high seventies. There was no such thing as par golf. The only thing that mattered was taking one shot less than the opposition and trying to build up a big enough lead to ensure that the match would be over before it reached that dreaded seventeenth hole.

Just as the Americans were threatening to take control, back bounced Europe with wins by an inspired Seve Ballesteros and the impressive Paul Broadhurst. Then the Americans to counter once again, by claiming three more precious points through Chip Beck over Ian Woosnam, Fred Couples over Sam Torrance and Lanny Wadkins over Mark James. The tension had become almost unbearable and the intensity of the contest was reflected in the drawn and ashen face of America's toughest team member, Lanny Wadkins who was close to tears and unable to speak, after his win over Mark James.

Bringing up the rear in the final singles match of the day, were Bernhard Langer and Hale Irwin. And although both men are know for their cool nerve and steely determination, past Ryder Cup experience provided no antidote for the pressures now being brought to bear on both men. One down playing the sixteenth, Langer holed a downhill six-footer to prevent the American going two ahead. And another brave effort from the same distance at the seventeenth, squared the match.

With one hole left to play, Europe needed a win for victory while a half would secure the Ryder Cup for America. Both players were just off the putting surface in

two and when Irwin underhit his third shot leaving his ball more than twenty feet from the hole it seemed that the pendulum had finally swung in Europe's favour. Langer elected to putt from just off the green and his ball ran agonizingly past the hole, coming to rest six-feet beyond the pin.

Irwin, with the air of a Christian about to be fed to the lions, could only nudge his ball down to within a foot of the hole, leaving Langer with a putt for the Ryder Cup. Few of the players could bare to look and, to a man, they must have silently offered up thanks that it was Langer and not them standing over that nerve-shattering putt.

History will record that

Langer missed, the hole was halved and America won the Ryder Cup by a one point margin, $14^{1}/_{2}$ –$13^{1}/_{2}$.

The first two days had found Nick Faldo and Ian Woosnam sadly out of form, so it was left to the Spanish pairing of Seve Ballesteros and Jose Maria Olazabal to bear the brunt of the American challenge. And how magnificently they picked up the gauntlet.

Olazabal grew in stature with every shot he hit and

Paul Broadhurst had an excellent Ryder Cup debut winning both games in which he played. He and Woosnam beat Azinger and Hale Irwin in the second day fourballs: in the singles he beat Mark O'Meara three and one.

Ballesteros played the kind of inspired golf that made him the most exciting player of his generation, as they saw off whatever combination the Americans lined up against them. For those first two days this dynamic duo provided a life-line for the European team, keeping their heads above water and providing a source of inspiration to the five Ryder Cup novices. Having survived the initial phase the newcomers played their part, especially in the fourball matches. Although as

Paul Azinger congratulates Seve Ballesteros after the Europeans had beaten the Americans two and one to record Europe's first point.

David Feherty, talking about the fact that the players don't get paid for playing in the Ryder Cup, commented, "There must be easier ways of not making a living." The best performances from the Ryder Cup first-timers came from Steven Richardson and Paul Broadhurst, whose two points from two matches left some wondering why he had not been called upon until the fourball matches on the second day. David Gilford on the other hand may well want to put the memory of his first Ryder Cup appearance behind him. Mauled by seasoned American campaigners in both foursomes matches, he was then denied the opportunity to redress the balance when

he was asked to step down for the singles to match the withdrawal of American Steve Pate through injury.

As for the golf course, it might be said that there is sufficient pressure generated by a Ryder Cup match without staging the event on a layout which clearly added to that pressure. Ian Woosnam compared it to something from Mars.

However, in defence of Pete Dye's creation, it must be said that it certainly provided the stage for one of the most exciting contests in the history of the event.

For a long time the seventeenth hole looked like becoming the downfall of the United States, in much the same way as the eighteenth at

The Belfry was three years ago at the 1989 Ryder Cup.

Not once in ten attempts, during the first two days, did the Americans win the hole. It was only when Nick Faldo three-putted in the singles, that they achieved this feat. And before the day was over Paul Azinger and Corey Pavin followed suit. But over the three days, three wins out of eighteen was the most they could muster.

When it came to the singles, many players commented on how they would hate to play the Ocean Course with a scorecard in their hand and this was reflected in some of their totals.

In Colin Montgomerie's singles with Mark Calcavecchia, even allowing for a generous concession at the fourteenth, neither could break 80 and the American came home in 44, at best.

Fred Couples, a comfortable three and two winner over Sam Torrance, was four over par when the match

finished on the sixteenth. Two pars would have given him a 76, with a 79 for Torrance.

The best individual scoring on the final day belonged to Seve Ballesteros who, despite a seven at the second hole – which he still won – was level for the sixteen holes played. The best scoring of the entire match came in the thrilling fourball encounter between Seve Ballesteros and Jose Maria Olazabal, and Payne Stewart and Fred Couples, both pairs returning a 68. But at this level, normal better-ball scores are in the low 60s, which best illustrates the difficulty the course presented.

No doubt over the coming month and years, golfers will flock, almost leaming-like, to test both their nerve and skill at that infamous seventeenth hole. And just as many will be keen to try that six-foot putt on the eighteenth green that decided the 1991 matches.

Sadly Bernhard Langer will

Seve Ballesteros and Jose Maria Olazabal on the eighteenth green having halved their second-day fourball with Fred Couples and Payne Stewart.

Anguish for Bernhard Langer (TOP RIGHT) as the putt that would have kept the cup in Europe slips by.

US Team captain Dave Stockton (RIGHT) hugs Hale Irwin after his match with Bernhard Langer.

be remembered for the six-foot putt that he missed to retain the Ryder Cup, rather than for the two heroic putts he holed to keep the European challenge alive to the very last shot of a truly magnificent contest. That miss is something which Langer will have to learn to live with, at least until 1993 when the sides meet once again at The Belfry, at which time the unique demands and pressures of playing for team and country will pitch some other poor soul into the glare of the spotlight.

1991 RYDER CUP RESULTS

Individual records of the players showing matches played, holes won, halved or lost.

UNITED STATES

	Pld	W	H	L	Pts	Holes (+or-)
Paul Azinger	5	2	0	3	2	+3
Chip Beck	3	1	0	2	1	-1
Mark Calcavecchia	4	2	1	1	2^1/$_2$	-3
Fred Couples	5	3	1	1	3^1/$_2$	+7
Ray Floyd	4	2	0	2	2	+2
Hale Irwin	4	2	1	1	2^1/$_2$	+6
Wayne Levi	2	0	0	2	0	-6
Mark O'Meara	3	1	1	1	1^1/$_2$	+4
Steve Pate	1	0	0	1	0	-2
Corey Pavin	3	1	0	2	1	-5
Payne Stewart	4	2	1	1	2^1/$_2$	0
Lanny Wadkins	5	3	1	1	3^1/$_2$	+8
					Total	**+13**

EUROPE

	Pld	W	H	L	Pts	Holes (+or-)
Seve Ballesteros	5	4	1	0	4^1/$_2$	+10
Paul Broadhurst	2	2	0	0	2	+5
Nick Faldo	4	1	0	3	1	-11
David Feherty	3	1	1	1	1^1/$_2$	-2
David Gilford	2	0	0	2	0	-11
Mark Jame	5	2	0	3	2	+2
Bernhard Langer	3	1	1	1	1^1/$_2$	0
Colin Montgomerie	3	1	1	1	1^1/$_2$	-2
Jose Maria Olazabal	5	3	1	1	3^1/$_2$	+5
Steve Richardson	4	2	0	2	2	+5
Sam Torrance	3	0	1	2	^{1}/$_2$	-7
Ian Woosnam	4	1	0	3	1	-7
					Total	**-13**

NB: Figures do not include the Pate v Gilford fixture that was granted a half when the American withdrew with an injury.

All smiles now! The victorious US team show off The Ryder Cup on the beach at Kiawha Island. Top from left: Lanny Wadkins, Fred Couples, Paul Azinger, Raymond Floyd, Hale Irwin, Dave Stockton, Payne Stewart, Mark Calcavecchia. Bottom: Chip Beck, Mark O'Meara, Steve Pate, Corey Pavin, Wayne Levi.

First Day Foursomes
Ballesteros/Olazabal beat Azinger/Beck 2&1
Langer/James lost to Floyd/Couples 2&1
Gilford/Montgomerie lost to Wadkins/Irwin 4&2
Faldo/Woosnam lost to Stewart/Calcavecchia 1 hole

First day Fourballs
Torrance/Feherty halved with Wadkins/O'Meara
Ballesteros/Olazabal beat Azinger/Beck 2&1
Richardson/James beat Pavin/Calcavecchia 5&4
Faldo/Woosnam lost to Floyd/Couples 5&3

Second day Foursomes
Torrance/Feherty lost to Irwin/Wadkins 4&2
James/Richardson lost to Calcavecchia/Stewart 1 hole
Faldo/Gilford lost to Azinger/O'Meara 7&6
Ballesteros/Olazabal beat Couples/Floyd 3&2

Second day Fourballs
Woosnam/Broadhurst beat Azinger/Irwin 2&1
Langer/Montgomerie beat Pate/Pavin 2&1
James/Richardson beat Wadkins/Levi 3&1
Ballesteros/Olazabal halved with Couples/Stewart

Third day Singles
Faldo beat Floyd 2 holes.
Feherty beat Stewart 2&1.
Montgomerie halved with Calcavecchia.
Olazabal lost to Azinger 2 holes.
Richardson lost to Pavin 2&1.
Ballesteros beat Levi.
Woosnam lost to Beck 3&1.
Broadhurst beat O'Meara 3&1.
Torrance lost to Couples 3&2.
James lost to Wadkins 3 &2.
Langer halved with Irwin

ROLL OF HONOUR

1927	Worcester, Mass. US won $9^1/_2$ - $2^1/_2$
1929	Moortown, Yorkshire. GB&I won 7 - 5
1933	Southport & Ainsdale. GB&I won $6^1/_2$ & $5^1/_2$
1935	Ridgewood, New Jersey. US won 9 - 3
1937	Southport & Ainsdale, Lancashire. US won 8 - 4
1947	Portland, Oregan. US won 11 - 1
1949	Ganton, Yorkshire. US won 7 - 5
1951	Pinehurst, North Carolina. US won $9^1/_2$ - $2^1/_2$
1953	Wentworth, Surrey. US won $6^1/_2$ - $5^1/_2$
1955	Thunderbird Ranch, California. US won 8 - 4
1957	Lindrick, Yorkshire. GB&I won $7^1/_2$ - $4^1/_2$
1959	Eldorado, California. US won $8^1/_2$ - $3^1/_2$
1961	Royal Lytham, Lancashire. US won $14^1/_2$ - $9^1/_2$
1963	East Lake, Georgia. US won 23 - 9
1965	Royal Birkdale, Lancashire. US won $19^1/_2$ - $12^1/_2$
1967	Champions, Texas. US won $23^1/_2$ - $8^1/_2$

1969	Royal Birkdale, Lancashire. Match Drawn 16 - 16.
1971	Old Warson, St Louis. US won $18^1/_2$ - $13^1/_2$
1973	Muirfield, Scotland. US won 19 - 13.
1975	Laural Valley, Pennsylvania. US won 21 - 11.
1977	Royal Lytham, Lancashire. US won $12^1/_2$ - $7^1/_2$
1979	Greenbrier, West Virginia. US won 17 - 11
1981	Walton Heath, Surrey. US won $18^1/_2$ - $9^1/_2$
1983	PGA National, Florida - US won $14^1/_2$ - $13^1/_2$
1985	The Belfry, West Midlands - Europe won $16^1/_2$ - $11^1/_2$
1987	Muirfield Village, Ohio, Europe won 15 - 13
1989	The Belfry, West Midlands. Match Drawn 14 - 14.

1991   Kiawah Island, South Carolina, US won $14^1/_2$ - $13^1/_2$

THE WALKER CUP

In the 1991 Walker Cup, the man who many tip as golf's next superstar halted a brave fightback by the home team to inspire the USA to an exciting Walker Cup victory.

In the final-day's singles matches of the 1989 Walker Cup at Peachtree Golf Club in Atlanta, Jim Milligan stood behind the fifteenth green staring defeat in the face.

Like his fellow British team mates, Milligan was feeling the backlash of an American revival and what at one time had looked a stroll to victory for Britain was rapidly turning into a nightmare. Playing his third shot from just off the green, Milligan's task was clear; hole the chip or go to the next tee three down with three to play in his match against America's most experienced and tenacious team member, Jay Sigel.

The record books show that is exactly what Jim Milligan did. He then won the next hole with a birdie and went on to half his match and gain that elusive half point that assured an historic Great Britain and Ireland victory.

Two years later, Jim Milligan once again found himself at the sharp end of a vital Walker Cup singles match. On this occasion the venue was the superb Portmarnock course in Ireland and it was Great Britain and Ireland who were desperately trying to claw their way back into a match which had been all but lost when the home team were whitewashed four-nil in the foursomes that opened the competition on the first day.

Milligan, playing in the lead singles in the final series of matches, had just birdied the sixteenth hole to get back to all-square but unfortunately for the Scot, he was facing probably the hottest property in golf at the present time, Phil Mickelson.

Already a winner of a US-Tour event, Mickelson had been on the losing side at Peachtree in 1989 and did not want to repeat the experience. The stylish left-hander powered a huge drive down the middle of the fairway, stroked an eight-iron to within two feet of the hole for a tap-in birdie that took him one ahead with one hole left to play.

Milligan refused to give up and hit a great second shot close to the flag on the final hole. But when his opponent conjured up a miraculous third shot from the rough that left his ball almost stone dead, the match was over, and with it, went Great Britain and Ireland's hold on the Walker Cup.

Although there were still seven more singles matches out on the course, there was to be no dramatic fight-back as the American team cruised to a comfortable fourteen points to ten victory. After the match, George Macgregor, non-playing captain of the home team said, "It all seemed to change from that point,"

Phil Mickelson, the man who many consider will be the next great US golfer.

The US team pose for a victory photo with the cup, named after George Walker, USGA president in 1920.

1991 WALKER CUP RESULTS

Day One:

FOURSOMES

Milligan & Hay lost to Mickelson & B.May 5 & 3

Payne & G.Evans lost to Duval and Sposa 1 hole.

McGimpsey & R.Willinson lost to Voges & Egar 1 hole

MGinley & Harrington lost to Sigel & Doyle 2 & 1

SINGLES

Coltart lost to Mickelson 4 & 3
Payne bt, Langham 2 & 1
Evans bt. Duval 2 & 1
Willison lost to May 2 & 1
McGimpsey bt. Sposa 1 hole
McGinley lost to Doyal 6 & 4
Hay bt Scherrer 1 hole
White lost to Sigel 4 & 3

Day Two :

FOURSOMES

Milligan & McGimpsey bt Voges & Eger 2 & 1

Payne & Willison lost to Duval & Sposa 1 hole

Evans & Coltart bt Langham & Scherrer 4 & 3

White & McGinley bt Mickelson & May 1 hole.

SINGLES

Milligan lost to Mickelson 1 hole
Payne bt Doyle 3 & 1
Evans lost to Langham 4 & 2
Coltart bt Sigel 1 hole
Willison bt Scherrer 3 & 2
Harrington lost to Egar 3 & 2
McGimpsey lost to May 4 & 3
Hay lost to Voges 3 & 2

GB&I 10 USA 14

referring to the Mickelson/Milligan match. "It was like the domino effect and it all seemed to go against us from that point on." he added sadly.

The key to the outcome of what was a much more closely contested match than the margin of victory might suggest was the opening-morning foursomes matches. For although America won all four points, two of the games went to the final green.

In one match, the Great Britain and Ireland pairing of Garth McGimpsy and Ricky Willison were two up at the fourteenth but then tragically three-putted the final green to lose the match. In the other Mike Sposa holed a monster putt across the final green for a birdie three that clinched the match for the Americans.

Although they must have felt demoralized by their rout in the foursomes, the home team fought back bravely to half the afternoon singles series. And when they claimed the honours with a three matches to one victory in the second-day's foursomes, the gap was reduced to only two points and hopes were raised that Great Britain and Ireland could still snatch victory from the jaws of defeat.

Cheered on by huge crowds of supporters, the home team gave their all but to no avail. On this occation the American team, inspired by Mickelson was just too strong and had more experience in depth when it came to competing under the unique pressures that these matches exert on players.

Despite losing, the home team were able to draw some comfort from the fact that for one and a half days, they matched the Americans point for point. There were also excellent individual performances from the home team, the best from Jim Payne who notched up two excellent singles victories and who a month earlier had won the Amateur Medal in the Open championship at Royal Birkdale in the process, preventing Phil Mickelson from recording an amateur Grand Slam in the Majors.

THE 1991 EURO TOUR

One thing dominated the1991 European Tour – the Ryder Cup. All the top players wanted to do well and earn a place in the European team.

In Ryder Cup year, the European season is extended by a month-and-a half to beyond the USPGA championship. Events such as the Catalan Open and the Jersey Open take on added significance as the final qualifying deadline for selection approaches and by late August the atmosphere on the tour becomes electric. The spotlight turns from likely winners to the performances of those in contention for a place in the Ryder Cup team, and who the captain will choose as his wild cards.

In total, 26 players occupied the all-important top-nine positions in the Ryder Cup table at some stage during the year. Being there on August 25 was all that really mattered. As Des Smythe pointed out, "There's more pressure in Ryder Cup year. People say, 'You're in; you're not in; you're in; you're not in'. It all adds to the pressure."

The only player who occupied a place in the 'Club Nine' throughout the season was Steve Richardson on only his second season on the tour. At the other end of the spectrum was Paul Broadhurst who came second in the German Open, the final qualifying competition, and just squeezed into the team.

If Seve Ballesteros, Ian Woosnam and Bernhard Langer achieved their places by the quality of their performances on the Tour, Broadhurst, Gilford and Torrance achieved theirs by quantity, playing in almost every qualifying event. Steve Richardson, Colin Montgomerie and David Feherty came somewhere in between.

Eamonn Darcy who was lying in seventh place before the German Open figured that his place was quite secure and didn't play in the event. Three players overtook

Colin Montgomerie was £279,335 better off at the end of the 1991 Euro Tour thanks to his winnings in the 23 competitions in which he played.

him and he lost his place. The ninth place was claimed by Gilford who was just £58.26 ahead of Darcy who must have regretted his third round 78 at the NM English Open, and the lost play-off against Zimbabwe's Tony Johnstone in the Murphy's Cup. Johnstone finished with a birdie, birdie and an eagle to force a play-off which he won with another eagle.

Steve Richardson won his place on May 27 after the Volvo PGA. Seve Ballesteros went to the top of the table after the Dunhill British Masters and stayed there. The Monte Carlo Open saw Ian Woosnam's place secured and the Dutch Open a couple of weeks later saw Bernhard Langer home and dry. The Scandinavian Masters secured the places of Colin Montgomerie and David Feherty, and Torrance, Broadhurst and Gilford scraped into the team with their winnings in the German Open tournament.

Ballesteros played in ten events to top the table with prize money totalling £333,069 (and 63 pence!) while David Gilford played in 21 tournaments on the Tour to win £182,203. Colin Montgomerie, who won £279,335, was the busiest man to make the team playing in 23 tournaments, one more event than both Steven Richardson and Paul Broadhurst. Ian Woosnam (£246,851) and Bernhard Langer (£191,913) both played ten tournaments.

Sam Torrance played in the same number of tournaments as David Gilford but won almost £12,000 more in prize money.

One player who did not occupy a place in the top nine was Per-Ulrik Johansson, but he will undoubtedly play

for Europe one day. The 24-year-old Swede, straight from Arizona University, earned his place on the European Tour by finishing nineteenth in the 1990 Qualifying School at Montpellier in France.

In his debut at the Girona

1991 saw the debut of Per-Ulrik Johansson who looks set to have a long, successful career on the professional circuit.

Paul Broadhurst's second place in the German Open, the last competition of the 1991 Euro Tour, gave him a last-gasp place in the European Ryder Cup team.

Open, the Tour's opening event, he shot a last-round 68 to come home fourth. In the Belgian Open, his last round score of 68 included an eagle at the 71st hole and earned him a play-off for the title against Paul Broadhurst which he won with a five at the first.

At the Dutch Open, the cool Swede beat Fred Couples and Jose Maria Olazabal to share second place with Bernard Langer, behind the winner Payne Stewart.

Johansson, with winnings of £150,000, was twelfth on Ryder Cup deadline day. He was ahead of Nick Faldo and Mark James, but Bernard Gallacher chose them as his wild cards, no doubt knowing that if the Swede maintains the form that he showed on his first European Tour, he will probably be playing for Europe at The Belfry in 1993.

THE 1991 US TOUR

By 1938, there was $158,000 to be won on the US Tour; there is now more than $20 million. But to the top Americans playing the 1990-1991 Tour, national pride meant more than dollars.

As in Europe, Ryder Cup selection was one of the major aims of the native Americans who played the US tour in 1991. But unlike the Europeans who selected their team on the basis of prize money won between mid-February and the end of August, the American team was picked on the number of times players had featured in the top ten in US Tour events over two seasons on the US Tour—with performances in the Major competitions carrying more weight than those at regular US Tour events. The top ten players automatically qualify with the Captain being allowed two wild-card selections.

Wayne Levi's 1991 form was not up to the standard he achieved the previous year when he led the US Order of Merit.

Wayne Levi, the leading American in the 1990 US Order of Merit with four victories, was virtually guaranteed his place before he teed-up in the new year and, as it transpired, needed only 80 points from the first seven months of 1991 to secure his place. He made it with fifteen points to spare, but was hardly the man on form as the US team headed for Kiawah Island.

Lanny Wadkins, Corey Pavin and Steve Pate moved up the table as they played the US Tour. Pate finished seventh in the final event, the USPGA championship at Crooked Stick to earn his place, elbowing out Tim Simpson by thirteen points. Had he not got down in two on the 72nd green, he would not have qualified and Simpson would have made his Ryder Cup debut at Kiawah Island.

RIGHT: Fred Couples who topped the list of contenders for the US Ryder Cup team at the end of the US Tour. BELOW: Mark Calcavecchia had a disappointing 1991 Tour finishing twelfth in the US Masters, 32nd in the USPGA and 37th in the US Open.

The top ten players were Fred Couples with 721 points Payne Stewart with 546, Larry Wadkins on 525, Hale Irwin who had 517, Paul Azinger on 501, Corey Pavin with 498, Mark O'Meara 435, Mark Calcavecchia and Wayne Levi who both finished on 407 and Steve Pate on 405.

It is the first time in a Ryder Cup team for Pavin, Levi and Pate. Interestingly, had the Americans adopted the European system for selection, seven of the US team would have been making their debut.

AUSSIE RULES

Ian Baker-Finch's victory at the 1991 British Open confirmed what many golfing fans had come to realize: Australia looks set to become a golfing superpower again.

The 1990s has seen the re-emergence of Australia as a power in world golf. Not only have they won two Majors in the new decade—Wayne Grady won the 1990 USPGA championship and Ian Baker-Finch took the 1991 British Open—they have also claimed many prestigious titles and currently have more players in the top 100 of the Order of Merit than any other nation apart from the United States.

And while they probably don't have the strength in depth to beat either Europe or the United States in Ryder Cup-style matches of twelve-player sides, they would certainly hold their own in a six-against-six competition. This was illustrated last year when, even without their number one, Greg Norman, they won the Four-Tours Championship in Japan against a European Team boasting Ian Woosnam, Nick Faldo and Bernhard Langer, and a US side consisting of Fred Couples, Payne Stewart and Mark Calcavecchia.

The magnitude of their achievement is best understood when it is realized that Australia has a population of just sixteen million people. With eight players in the world's top fifty, Australia ties for second place with Britain and Ireland who have a combined population almost four times that of Australia. The United States boasts 27 of the top fifty players, but it has a

Mike Harwood (ABOVE) and Ian Baker-Finch, the two Australians who crowned their 1991 seasons by coming second and first respectively in the British Open.

population of almost 250 million.

The top-ranking Australian players are Greg Norman, ranked number four, Ian Baker-Finch at number eleven, Craig Parry, the number eighteen, Rodger Davis at nineteen, Mike Harwood who comes in at 23, Steve Elkington at 46, Wayne Grady and Peter Senior who rate 49th and 50th respectively.

With players of that calibre and others waiting in the wings, Australia has served notice that more and more of its golfers will be up there, challenging for the Major titles and the other tournaments in the European and US Tours as the decade progresses towards the new millenium.

SWING TECHNIQUES OF THE STARS

*There is no such thing as 'the perfect golfer'
but there are such things as the perfect strokes.
Each of the players featured in this section
exemplifies one of these strokes.
And the one thing they all have in
common is that practice makes perfect.*

Six world-class golfers are featured here demonstrating how to play six different types of shot. While they each have their own, individual method of swinging the club, they all have three things in common: practice, more practice and even more practice.
The time spent playing four rounds of a tournament is just the tip of the iceberg, for throughout their careers they all have spent, and still spend, many more hours refining and polishing the skills which have helped to make them the great players they are today.

POWER DRIVING
with Ian Woosnam

There are few more exciting sights in golf than watching Ian Woosnam pull his driver from the bag and crunch a drive miles down the middle of the fairway. Most club golfers find it a mystery how someone of Woosnam's build is able to hit the ball such huge distances.

Strength is certainly a factor, but the real key to hitting the ball a long way is rhythm and timing. By studying the Woosnam swing sequence you can gain a valuable insight into how to improve this aspect of your game and add some much-needed extra yards from the tee.

PLAYING LONG IRONS
with Payne Stewart

This is one area of the game which most weekend golfers find extremely difficult to master. Help is at hand in the shape of 1991 US Open champion, Payne Stewart.

Stewart is recognized as one of the best long-iron players in the modern game. An analysis of his superb action reveals some of the most important aspects of long-iron play – a smooth backswing and retaining good balance throughout the whole swing sequence to follow through.

MIDDLE IRON SHOTS
with Bernhard Langer

When he is on form, there is no more accurate medium-iron player than the German ace, Bernhard Langer.

The swing analysis of the former US Masters champion and European Ryder Cup regular explains how his very individual grip is a major factor in his ability consistently to hit the ball close to the hole with the middle irons. Another important feature of the Langer swing is his left-side dominance, something which many weekend golfers could benefit from adopting.

Payne Stewart shows his long-iron style at the 1991 US Open.

Nick Faldo showing typical exactness in lining up a putt.

APPROACH SHOTS
with Severiano Ballesteros

Unquestionably the most natural talent to appear on the golfing scene in the past twenty years, nowhere does Seve Ballesteros bring his deft touch and imagination more into play than from anywhere around the green.

The swing sequence demonstrates just one of the many different ways that the Spaniard has perfected of rolling three shots into two from just off the putting surface. The sequence also demonstrates the similarities between the chip-and-run shot and the putting action, and also the importance of choosing the right club for specific types of shot.

BUNKER BASICS
with Jose Maria Olazabal

Renowned as being one of the hardest workers on the Volvo European tour, Jose Maria Olazabal has reaped the reward from countless hours of practice which have made him one of the top bunker players in the game.

The young Spaniard demonstrates the basic bunker shot and shows how, with a sound grasp of the basics and a better understanding of technique, the weekend golfer can become more proficient at mastering the important art of sand play.

PERFECT PUTTING
with Nick Faldo

Putting is a skill which requires a sound, yet uncomplicated technique that will continue to work smoothly under pressure. And when it comes to holing putts under pressure, few can match Nick Faldo.

The double US Masters and British Open champion is featured in a swing sequence which reveals an extremely reliable method of swinging the putter smoothly with the absolute minimum amount of moving actions.

POWER DRIVING
with **IAN WOOSNAM**

*"Ian Woosnam has one of the best golf swings
of all time."*

SEVE BALLESTEROS

In the final-day singles of the Ryder Cup at Muirfield Village in the United States, Ian Woosnam was matched against Andy Bean. With Woosnam standing at just a fraction over five feet four inches, and Bean at least a foot taller, the American commentators were soon comparing the match with the biblical confrontation between David and Goliath.

When the television cameras picked up the two players on the final hole, both men had driven their tee shots onto the fairway – one twenty yards ahead of the other. Given the height and weight difference between the two men, it was hardly surprising when one of the commentators suggested to viewers that it would probably be Woosnam to play first.

However, as the two men approached the first ball, Woosnam marched straight on to the other one – some twenty yards ahead.

After Bean won the match by the skin of his

1

2

teeth, he told reporters that he had been consistently outdriven by the little Welshman. He then went on to say what most of the tour professionals on the European circuit could have told him – pound for pound, Ian Woosnam is undoubtedly the longest hitter in the game.

Although stories of the Welshman's prodigious hitting have become widely told, millions of golf fans around the world are still puzzled as to how such a small man is able to generate so much power from what appears to be such an effortless swing.

WOOSNAM'S DRIVING TECHNIQUE

The address. Woosnam's address position is perfect; arms hanging almost vertically down from the shoulders, body relaxed, legs flexed and ready to set the swing in motion. From a superb setup, lacking in any tension, Ian can bring all the separate components of his swing smoothly into play with the arms, hands, shoulders and legs all starting the club back together from the ball.

The backswing. At the start of the backswing, (1) Ian keeps the clubhead low to the ground for as long as possible. This not only allows him to create as wide an arc as possible, but also helps to get his weight moving across to the right side As the weight becomes established (2) on the right leg, the hips continue to resist the turning action of the shoulders in the backswing. This creates an ever-increasing coiling, or stretching action in the upper body which, in turn, starts to pull his right heel up off the ground. With the club approaching the top of the backswing (3) the hips are pulled further to the right as Ian virtually turns his back to the target, completing his shoulder-turn. Note, too, how the back of Ian's left hand is perfectly in plane and his grip has remained firm, with no hint of the club coming loose.

The downswing. Ian starts down to the ball by planting his left foot firmly on the ground, while he starts the club back to the ball by pulling down with his left hand. One of the keys to long hitting is to attack the ball on a line which travels through the hitting area from slightly inside to square, and then inside again. The club is now below waist level (5) in the downswing, yet there is still no sign of an attempt to hit at the ball with his right hand. Thanks to his strong leg drive, Ian's weight is now fully established back on his left side.

3

4

As the left hip continues to turn to the left, it clears a direct path down the target line for the club. Only then does Ian release his right hand to create that extra clubhead speed and deliver the face of the club squarely into the back of the ball (5). It is in this critical area of the swing that Ian's great strength comes into play. Because he is able to resist the effect of centrifugal force until the last possible moment, he ensures that the power generated in the swing is released at exactly the right instant to produce the maximum clubhead speed at impact.

The follow through. Although the ball is now well on its way towards the target, (6) Ian continues to accelerate the club through. Another strength of Woosnam's superb swing is his head position which has remained perfectly still from address and through impact to target. Even after the hit, his eyes are still firmly fixed on the spot where the ball was at impact. The true test of a full swing is how well-balanced it remains throughout the stroke. Even after hitting a full drive, you can see how Woosnam has moved through to complete his swing with his navel now facing directly at the target, (7) his shoulders level and his hands high. A superb example to follow.

He may be small in physical stature, but Ian Woosnam is immensely strong, partly as a result of spending hour after hour hitting thousands of practice balls, and partly because of the years he spent as a boy working on his parents' farm in Wales. Although strength is a great asset when it comes to hitting the ball a long way, without the correct grip, setup and posture, sheer strength can often be more of a hindrance than a help.

To the untrained eye, it looks as though Woosnam simply swings the club back and through at an easy, even lazy pace. However, there is plenty of power in the Woosnam swing, created from a superb setup and an enviable full shoulder-turn in the backswing. One of the reasons his swing always looks so effortless is that the power is always kept under control until it reaches the hitting area: then it is fully released into the back of the ball sending it zooming on its way.

5

6

PLAYING LONG IRONS
with **PAYNE STEWART**

*"Payne Stewart's swing is almost a throwback to the
free-wheeling style of the 1930s."*
ALEX HAY

When he first appeared on the professional golf scene in 1979, it was Payne Stewart's dress sense rather than his golf, that made an impact with the golfing public.

The image of this elegant American striding the fairways in plus twos and flat cap, conjured up images of the game of golf as it was played in the early 30s and it is also true to say that Payne Stewart's classic swing

would not have looked out of place alongside some of the great players of that bygone era.

In 1985 Stewart demonstrated to British fans that he could play every bit as well as he dressed, by finishing second behind Sandy Lyle in the 1985 British Open at Sandwich. However, that was the closest Stewart would come to winning a Major until he made a spectacular breakthrough in 1989 when he

produced a storming back nine to claim the USPGA title at Kemper Lakes.

Stewart came close to winning his second Major title with a brave final round at St. Andrews in 1990, finishing tied for second place with Mark McNulty behind the winner, Nick Faldo.

1991 proved to be Payne's year when his four-round total of 282 left him level with Scott Simpson to force a play-off – the second in three years in the US Open – which the stylish American won.

The weather during the tournament was dreadful. On the first day, a spectator was killed by lightning: during the third round, the wind whipped in off the lakes, sending the scores soaring. Stewart proved himself a true champion overcoming the opposition and the elements to assume the mantle of America's next great golf star – helped, needless to say, by his superb long-iron play for which he has become respected by his fellow professionals.

STEWART'S LONG IRON TECHNIQUE

The address. For a tall man, Payne Stewart looks remarkably well balanced and comfortable as he addresses the ball (1). His feet are positioned at shoulder width and there is no sign of any tension in his set-up: his legs are flexed and his arms hang well clear of his body.

The backswing. The key to hitting good long iron shots is to create a wide, shallow swing plane and Stewart makes the perfect start to his backswing by taking the club back in one piece (2), with the shoulders and arms working together as a single unit. Unlike many club golfers who pick the club up too steeply by breaking the wrists early in the backswing, there is no hint of any wrist break in Payne's swing until the club reaches almost waist level. The body weight is now fully established over Stewart's right leg (3) as the shoulders continue to create a full coil by winding against the resistance of the hips. Stewart's superb shoulder turn has finally pulled his hips round and carried the club past the horizontal position at the top of the backswing (4). The coil which Payne has built up in the backswing is now fully wound and ready to be released through the ball in the downswing.

3

4

The downswing. Exceptionally good footwork is one of the outstanding features of Payne Stewart's swing, and nowhere is this better illustrated than at the start of his downswing. The move back to the ball is instigated by a smooth, but positive move towards the target, getting the weight back over to the left side to build up momentum in the downswing and also provide a stable platform from which to swing the club down the target line (5). The positive action of the left arm pulling the club down towards the ball, ensures that the right shoulder stays on the inside to encourage the club to travel on a slightly in-to-out path through the impact area. As the clubhead approaches impact, the left hip is clearing to allow the arms to swing the club along the target line, and although Stewart's weight is now almost fully established on his left side, the head his remained well behind the ball.

The follow through. From this well-balanced position, Payne can now release the clubhead and apply maximum power to the shot. Thanks to the width which he created in the backswing, the club is now travelling back through impact on a shallow path, which will allow what little loft there is on the club to be used to its full effect, sweeping the ball away off the top of the turf. The ball is now well on its way towards the target, however Payne has retained his head position through impact and only allows it to rise as his arms sweep the club up and round (6) to a perfectly balanced follow through position (7). When the USPGA Tour decided to make a video of the tournament professionals demonstrating how to play the various clubs, they asked Payne Stewart to demonstrate the long irons. And looking at this superb long-iron sequence, it's clear to see why they chose him for the task.

5

6

MIDDLE IRON SHOTS
with **BERNHARD LANGER**

*"By developing a strong, left-sided swing Bernhard Langer has
become one of the most accurate middle iron players the game has ever seen."*

EDDIE BIRCHENOUGH

When he first appeared on the European golf scene in 1976, many people thought that unless he changed his very strong left-hand grip, Bernhard Langer would not last long in the tough and highly competitive world of professional golf.

Then as now, the bricklayer's son from Bavaria listened politely to what the critics had to say and then went about his business playing his own way.

One of the most dedicated workers in the game, Bernhard Langer has also become one of the most consistent golfers in the world. And his dedication and determination have helped him to develop the type of game which has so far brought him a US Masters

title, numerous international victories around the world and several close calls in other major championships, not to mention Ryder Cup honours. All this was achieved with the same strong grip with which he started his professional career!

LANGER'S MIDDLE IRON TECHNIQUE

The address. Like all great players, Bernhard Langer has an excellent address position (1). His posture is erect yet nicely relaxed with his legs flexed and his head well clear of his chest. There is no indication of any tension in the arms which hang almost vertically down from the shoulders. At address, Bernhard positions his hands slightly ahead of the ball to ensure that in the downswing, the hands will lead the club and that the clubhead will be striking down and through the ball. His feet are fractionally inside shoulder width with the legs flexed and the body weight slightly more towards the heels than the toes.

The backswing. As the club starts back (2), Langer's strong left-hand grip enables him to keep the clubface

pointing at the target. A player using a weaker left-hand grip would find this difficult and would be more likely to fan the clubface open much sooner in the backswing. The low, wide start to the backswing helps Bernhard to create width in his backswing, coupled with the resistance from the left shoulder, coupled with the resistance from the hips, starts to wind the upper half of his body as it begins to coil fully (3). As the shoulders reach the full extent of their turn, Langer's hips are pulled around to complete the backswing: the body weight is now established over his right leg and the back of the clubface and left arm are perfectly aligned, with the clubface pointing directly at the target.

The downswing. Bernhard starts his downswing with the weight moving back onto the left side and it is at this point in the downswing that he really reaps the reward of having strong left side. Whereas many weekend players would be tempted to hit at the ball with their right hand causing the right shoulder to be thrown forward and out of line, Langer pulls down hard with his left arm (4). This has the effect of bringing the club down to the ball on a slightly in-to-out swing path while still allowing him to store the power he is generating until exactly the right moment to release it through the ball.

3

4

Of course, there is much more to Bernhard Langer's success that just a strong grip and the capacity for hard work. He also has great natural talent, wonderful powers of concentration and an iron will to win – something he has shown time and time again by overcoming not one but three bouts of the dreaded putting yips. Not only has Bernhard overcome this soul-destroying golfing ailment, but he has also fought back to become one of the best putters on the European tour, topping the putting statistics on several occasions over the past ten years.

Taken in isolation, Langer's strong grip, with almost four knuckles showing on his left hand, could well have lead to his early demise as a tournament professional. However, allied to the strong left-side dominance in his swing, Bernhard's strong grip has proved to be a help, rather than a hindrance to his game as his record shows.

By developing a strong left-sided swing, Langer has been able to combine accuracy with power and this has undoubtedly been a major factor in his becoming not only one of the most successful players of the modern era,

5

6

but also one of the most accurate middle-iron players the game has ever seen and possibly the most successful German player of all time.

The follow through. Through impact (5), the hips have cleared well to the left creating a path on which the club can be swung down the ball-to-target line. The weight is established on the left leg and the club is being pulled rather than pushed through the ball. Once again Langer's strong left-hand grip and left-side dominance have helped him to resist releasing the clubhead until the optimum moment. This allows him to hold the face of the club square to the target for much longer than a player who tends to hit at the ball with his right hand. After impact Langer's hips have cleared to the left well ahead of the shoulders, a sure indication that the club has been pulled strongly through the impact area with the left arm and lower body action, rather than the hands hitting hard at the ball. And although Bernhard has hit a full shot, his head has remained beautifully still and well behind the ball at impact, in fact, the head only starts to rise as a result of the body being pulled through towards the follow through (6). As the stroke continues (7), the controlled power Langer generated pulls his weight round until it is completely on his left leg (8).

7

8

APPROACH SHOTS
with **SEVE BALLESTEROS**

*"When Seve is on song it's like matching a Cadillac
against a Model-T Ford."*
BEN CRENSHAW

At the 72nd hole of the 1976 Open
championship at Royal Birkdale, a young
Spanish golfer found himself in a tense battle
for a place in the top three, and facing what,
to all intents and purposes, was an impossible
shot even for an experienced professional.

His second shot to this long par-four hole
missed the green, landing to the left of the two
large bunkers that guard that side of the
putting surface. With the pin positioned almost
directly behind the bunkers, it looked as
though the direct shot to the hole was

blocked. The ground was baked hard after
weeks of scorching sunshine; the putting
surface was very fast and firm. It seemed that
the youngster's only option was to pitch the
ball high over the bunkers and allow it to roll
well beyond the flag from where he would
have to hole a long putt to save his par.

However, what may have appeared
impossible to most of the other competitors
was seen by the young Spaniard as simply
another challenge to be met and overcome.
He deliberated for a few moments before

1

2

playing an exquisite chip and run shot that had the gallery gasping in amazement and, a few seconds later, cheering in admiration.

Seemingly oblivious to the pressure of the occasion and with the calmness of a veteran, he threaded the ball through a tiny space between the bunkers, coaxing it gently over the thicker grass on the apron of the green, before it rolled towards the pin and finally came to rest a few feet from the hole.

SEVE'S CHIP AND RUN TECHNIQUE

When it comes to rolling three shots into two around the green, there are few players who can match the expertise of Seve Ballesteros.

While it is important to develop a sound technique for playing these little shots, it is equally important that you also develop a sense of feel and touch, along with the ability to visualise the shot you want to hit before you actually play it.

Club selection is very important too, and providing there are no bunkers between the ball and the hole, a simple rule of thumb to follow is the closer you are to the pin, the lower you should try to keep the ball to the

ground. If weekend golfers spent just one hour each week practising this type of shot, they could almost certainly save at least four or five strokes a round.

The address. With the ball coming to rest just off the putting surface, Seve has elected to play a chip and run shot with a fairly straight-faced club such as six – or seven – iron, His address position (1) is similar to that which he would adopt for putting, with the feet close together and the arms quite close to the body. Seve has also gripped down the handle of the club because the closer his hands are to the ball, the more feel and control he will have over the shot.

The backswing. Although this type of shot is played predominantly with the hands and arms, Seve has nevertheless taken care to position his body correctly. His knees are flexed and his stance slightly open which allows him to swing the club back almost in a straight line, while keeping the clubface low to the ground (2). Note that there is no quick wrist break or any attempt to lift the club up steeply in the backswing. Instead, the wrists remain firm and the swing is more like an extended putting stroke (3) with the clubface remaining square to the target on the backswing rather than fanning open as is often the case.

3

4

It was later called the shot that echoed around the world, and the young Spaniard who played it with such courage and skill was Severiano Ballesteros.

Since that memorable shot at Birkdale, Seve has continued to thrill golfing galleries all over the world with his aggressive style of play. His attacking attitude to the game has frequently landed him in some strange places on the golf course, but time after time his great natural talent and wonderful imagination have combined to save the day and win the tournament for the likeable Spaniard.

The closer you get to the green, the more you must rely on touch, feel and imagination. There is no golfer in the game today who has these qualities in greater abundance than Seve Ballesteros. Although blessed with a great natural talent, the years he spent as a boy perfecting a whole range of shots, using an old three-iron he had made himself, had honed that natural talent to the point where, given a decent lie anywhere around the green, including a bunker, he is looking not to get the ball close, but to knock it in the hole.

Learning to master the art of chipping is the fastest way to reduce your handicap and improve your scoring. Not only can a good short game help you save par when you miss the green, it can also help turn pars into birdies at all but the longest, par-five holes.

The downswing. Seve has maintained most of his weight on the left side throughout the backswing and because of this there is no need for him to use excessive weight-shift back to his left side in the downswing (4). (*previous page*) Instead, he can simply allow his arms to swing pendulum fashion back down the target line. At address, Seve positioned his hands fractionally ahead of the clubface and because there has been virtually no wrist action in the swing, that relationship has been maintained in the throughswing. There is no suggestion of the downswing being rushed: instead the club is accelerated smoothly into impact (5) with the hands continuing to lead the clubface.

The follow through. Because the arc of the swing is shallow, the follow through remains close to the ground. The ball flies low from the clubface (6) before landing on the green and then running like a putt. Throughout the swing, Ballesteros has kept his head perfectly still – a key factor in playing this type of shot successfully. And only when the ball is well on its way does he look up (7).

5

6

BUNKER BASICS
with JOSE MARIA OLAZABAL

*"He has the best short game in
the world – and nobody practises harder."*
GORDON BRAND JR.

There could hardly have been a finer example of the bunker-play brilliance of Jose Maria Olazabal than the stunning array of shots he produced over the final eighteen holes in the 1991 US Masters.

Plagued by an errant driver, time and time again the young Spaniard kept himself in contention for the famous Green Jacket by producing a number of miraculous bunker shots. The driver failed him yet again at the very last hole, leaving him stranded in a fairway bunker from where even a player of his immense talent could not save the day.

Olazabal is well known on the European Tour as one of the best bunker players in the game, and confidence born of long hours of practice is one of the keys to his ability to seemingly get the ball up and down in two on almost every occasion. 'Ollie', as he is affectionately known to his fellow professionals, believes that bunker play is one of the easier aspects of the game because it is the only stroke where the golfer does not actually have to hit the ball.

The Spaniard's technique for playing bunker shots is reasonably simple and in fact differs only slightly from the setup he adopts for playing chip shots. For normal bunker shots, Olazabal's stance is slightly open. However it is important to stress the word 'slightly', for many amateur golfers tend to exaggerate this position as they address the ball. By adopting a stance which is open to the target line it is easier to get the ball airborne quickly by sliding the clubhead through the sand and under the ball, throwing it up into the air.

At address, you can see how Olazabal has laid the face of the sand wedge open to the target line to ensure that the flange on the bottom of the club will bounce through the sand rather than dig into it. If you drew a line across Jose Maria's toes, you would find it pointing slightly left of the target, with the clubface aiming directly at the hole. Note that the ball is positioned farther forward in the stance than it would be for a conventional shot, and that his hands are slightly farther back.

OLAZABAL'S BUNKER TECHNIQUE

The stance. With his feet worked firmly down into the sand (1) Olazabal adopts a slightly open stance.

Aiming for the club to enter the sand about two inches behind the ball, he lowers his body (2) in order to slide the clubhead under the ball and lift it high into the air.

Although Olazabal breaks his wrists quickly at the start of his backswing, there is nothing rushed about the movement and as he has demonstrated so clearly on many occasions, the swing required to produce good bunker shots should be smooth and unhurried.

Players of Olazabal's standard always have a picture in their mind's eye of the type of shot they are about to play before they actually hit the ball. And Jose Maria will have visualised the club sliding down through the sand and under the ball, lifting it out of the bunker and high into the air.

Like all great players, Olazabal has the wonderful rhythm which is another key to good bunker play. After taking up his address position and working his feet firmly down into the sand to establish a firm base from which to swing, Olazabal will have picked a spot approximately two inches behind the ball where he wants the club to enter the sand.

The backswing. By making a good shoulder turn and a comparatively long backswing (3 – 3a) he compensates for the open clubface and stance.

3a

2

3

Too many amateur players look directly at the ball, which can often lead to the club striking the ball first instead of the sand. The mistake often leads to the ball being caught thin, either sending it flying over the green, or into the face of the bunker.

Although there is only a short distance between the ball and the hole, Jose Maria still makes a good shoulder-turn and a comparatively long backswing. Note how his weight has remained predominantly on the left side to help create a fairly steep backswing. Olazabal makes a long backswing in order to compensate for the open clubface and stance; both of which are designed to get the ball up quickly from the sand and flying on a high arc towards the hole.

Once again, rhythm is the key to starting the downswing. Whereas many weekend golfers

The downswing. Rhythm is the key to the start of the unhurried downswing (4) as he accelerates the clubhead through the sand behind and under the ball (5 –5a) in a shallow arc.

5a

4

5

stab the club down anxiously at the ball, Olazabal makes a smooth transition from the backswing to the downswing, accelerating the clubhead down through the sand and under the ball. Throughout the shot, he has kept his head beautifully still, his eyes firmly focused on the spot where he wants the leading edge of the sand wedge to slide into the sand.

Instead of employing a stabbing action, causing the club to dig down into the sand and stop, Jose Maria has slid it under the ball on a shallow arc and continued to keep it going onto at least waist height in the follow through. And the outcome is a typically fine bunker shot which takes the ball onto the putting surface. His talent for bunker play is a major factor in Olazabal's success.

The follow through. Olazabal makes a smooth transition from backswing to downswing, his weight still predominantly on his left side (6). Throughout the shot (7 – 7a) he keeps his head still and his eye firmly on the spot where he wants the club to strike the sand. The result is another fine bunker shot leaving the ball nestling well within putting distance of the hole.

7a

6

7

PERFECT PUTTING
with **NICK FALDO**

"There is no finer model to copy
than Nick Faldo."
DAVID LEADBETTER

Much has been made over the past few years about the changes Nick Faldo has made to his game in order to create the type of swing which will stand up to the pressures of competing successfully at the very top of the professional game. It certainly took great courage to abandon a swing which had already brought several tournament wins including the PGA championship. Nevertheless, Faldo was so determined to make the changes and start all over again almost from scratch, that he spent nearly two years in the wilderness building a swing which

he felt confident could win the world's major golfing championships.

Those long, hard and often frustrating hours spent on the practice ground have now paid off handsomely for Nick, but it would be wrong to believe that it is only the changes in

FALDO'S PUTTING TECHNIQUE

Although Nick uses the reverse overlap grip favoured by most tournament professionals, he does have one or two personal mannerisms worth examining more closely.

The address. Faldo's grip ensures that both palms are facing each other and also that they are square to the target line (1). Although a tall man, Nick still tilts his head well forward until it is almost in a horizontal position to ensure that his eyes are positioned directly over the ball and the line of the putt. His feet are around shoulder width and the ball is positioned just to the left of centre in his stance. Although bending from the waist, Nick's back remains straight with the arms hanging loosely and almost vertically down. There is no sign of tension in Faldo's setup with the legs also comfortably flexed,

The take away. The key to starting the backswing with the putter is the same as with all the other clubs: that is to ensure that all the elements of the stroke work together and not separately. The role of the shoulders is also a major factor as they actually swing the putter rather than the hands. This is because the smaller the muscles, the more difficult they are to control, although a certain amount of hand action, especially through the strike, is essential to help create some feel in the stroke. With his arms hanging down almost vertically and the elbows held firmly against his body, Nick has created a firm and steady platform to swing his putter back and through (2) with the pendulum action of the shoulders.

2

his swing that have carried him to the top of the golfing tree. Without an effective putting stroke, he would never have been able to reap the benefits that he has so justly deserved and which he now derives from a swing that has made him one of the most consistent and accurate ball-strikers in the modern game.

Although Faldo's three most recent Major victories are testament to his superb ball-striking and shot-making abilities, it was his putting that gave him that vital edge over the rest of the field in each competition. Who will ever forget that great six-footer he made for par at the first extra hole in the play-off for the 1989 Masters championship at Augusta National, followed at the next hole by a magnificent 25-footer for the winning birdie three?

A year later, playing the last nine holes at Augusta, Nick looked to be out of contention until he suddenly produced a string of birdie putts to force a play-off against Raymond Floyd of the United States which he went on to win – again at the second extra hole.

At St. Andrews in the 1990 Open championship, it was Faldo's putting that once again made the difference at the end of the day. On those huge greens where putts of 50 and 60 feet are commonplace, Faldo's judgment of line and pace was outstanding. And the fact that he three-putted only once during the four rounds of the championship, highlighted, yet again, just how good a putter he has trained himself to be.

Nick Faldo's approach to putting is exactly the same as his attitude to the rest of his game; he wants perfection.

The double Open and Masters champion is well known for his dedicated approach to the game and he spends almost as much time on the practice putting green as he does on the practice tee.

The superb rhythm that is one of the best features of Faldo's swing is evident in his putting stroke. Long or short, when he has his eye in Nick Faldo can knock them in from anywhere on the green.

3

4

The through swing. There is the slightest hint of a forward press which helps get the club started back (3) with a smooth, one-piece action with the wrists remaining firm and the rocking action of the shoulders providing the momentum to start the putter back. Just before this movement starts, Faldo lifts the putter fractionally off the ground. Notice how Nick's head has remained perfectly still and it will remain that way until the ball is well on its way towards the target.

Impact. As the putter approaches impact, the wrists (4) remain firm and the hands lead the putter back to the ball. Faldo accelerates the club smoothly through impact with the clubface striking the ball fractionally on the upswing, imparting a little top spin to help get the ball running smoothly towards the hole. In the backswing, Nick keeps the putter low to the ground, especially at the start of the stroke. He also swings the putter through low after impact, (5) almost pushing the face of the putter on down the target line.

TROUBLE SHOTS

The four situations looked at here are among the most common trouble shots in the game: and even the best players in the world land in trouble sometimes!

BALL ABOVE THE FEET

One of the main things to remember when playing with your feet well below the level of the ball is that you are almost certain to produce a shot that flies from right to left.

It is important therefore to compensate for this by aiming well to the right of your intended target line at address. With this type of shot, the arc of the swing is extremely shallow and the club feels as though it is turning around your waist.

This shallow arc can cause the clubface to make contact with the ground before it reaches the ball. Therefore, it is a good idea to grip down the handle of the club at address. This will not only help keep the spine as close to vertical as possible, but will also give more control over the club.

BALL BELOW THE FEET

This is one of the most awkward lies of all and you should try to avoid the mistake of sitting back too much on your heels at address. As the legs will be almost totally occupied keeping the body balanced, the shot will require more hand action to compensate.

Position your shoulders as far over the ball as possible without losing your balance and position the ball slightly forward in the stance. You will also find that shoulder turn is limited, but don't make the mistake of trying to create power with your arms and shoulders alone. If you are playing a long to medium iron, select an imaginary target well to the left of the primary target and try to hit the ball towards it.

DOWNHILL LIES

This is one of the most difficult shots in golf to play successfully. The downslope will have the effect of de-lofting the club which makes it extremely difficult to play a long iron. In fact, many professionals would recommend that most club golfers never hit anything less than a five-iron from a severe downslope. The good news is that playing from a downhill lie the ball will run farther when it lands.

At address, try to align your body as closely as possible to the slope without running the risk of losing your balance when you swing the club. The ball should be positioned farther back in your stance to ensure that it is struck before the turf. Balance is critical, therefore, do not attempt to make a full-blooded hit; settle instead for a three-quarter swing.

UPHILL LIES

The two main problems when it comes to playing from an uphill lie are trajectory and balance. The upslope will act like a launching pad with the result that the ball is likely to fly much higher than it would from a level lie.

Because of this, the ball will also stop much more quickly, something worth remembering when it comes to club selection. Because most of the weight is on the back foot at address, it is very difficult to get it onto the left side at impact. If you are determined to hit the ball a long way, there is a good chance that the shot will be pulled to the left.

When you find yourself playing from a severe upslope, it is vital to maintain your balance. Keep the knees flexed and try to mirror the slope as much as possible. Once again, position the ball more towards the centre of your stance. Don't try to hit the ball too hard: it is better to take one or even two clubs more than you need and then concentrate on making a smooth, well-balanced pass at the ball.

COURSE
STRATEGIES

*No two golf courses are alike: indeed, no one
golf course plays the same every day of the year.
In this section we look at sixteen courses
with the professional from each who selects
his favourite holes and gives tips on how
to play them.*

Not only are no two courses alike, no two holes are identical! And to add to the challenge very few holes play the same on two consecutive days. One round may find a player driving into the wind, the next he may be playing with it. A heavy shower can change the nature of the putting surface in a matter of minutes. It's all par for the course!

One of the unique aspects of golf is the almost infinite variety of geographical locations in which the game is played. From windswept, seaside links to manicured tree-lined avenues; through forest and in some cases, over the tops of mountains. Wherever there is a will, it seems there is also a way. Neil Armstrong even played golf on the moon, although the lunar surface may well have caused a few problems regarding the rule which covers a player grounding the club in a bunker.

The time has not yet come when we can play golf among the stars. However over the following pages, we will be visiting a variety of 'star' courses in Scotland, England, Ireland and Wales. And with the assistance and insight of the local professionals, highlighting some of the most spectacular and scenic holes in the world.

The first part of our journey through England takes us to the Lancashire coastland and the historic links of Royal Lytham; scene of so many exciting Open championship battles and a course which has one of the most testing closing stretches of all the Open venues.

Then we look at the Old Course at Sunningdale, unquestionably one of the most beautiful golf courses, not just in England, but the world. Sandy soil, silver birch trees, tight, firm fairways and fast greens are all the hallmarks of this golfing heaven less than an hour's drive from London. We then visit that avid golfing county of Yorkshire and the beautifully manicured greens and poplar-lined fairways of Fulford. Crossing the country, we pause at the impressive Hollinwell Club with its rolling fairways and

Lanark, an easy drive from both Glasgow and Edinburgh, is one of the best inland courses in Britain.

undulating greens, before returning to the south where we call in at the less demanding, but equally challenging, parkland course at Moor Park, which boasts perhaps the most impressive clubhouse in the world. Our last stop in England is in the Midlands, where we discover the secrets of playing that famous tenth hole on the Brabazon course at The Belfry which has become such an exciting focal point in recent battles between Europe and America for the Ryder Cup.

From Scotland we have selected four golfing gems that offer a variety and quality which would be difficult to surpass. We begin on the west coast, visiting the magnificent Open Championship course at Turnberry before turning east to call in at Lanark, a wonderful heathland layout which offers another aspect of Scotttish golf at its best.

Continuing east our path leads us to Edinburgh, Scotland's capital city and the location of the fine parkland course at Dalmahoy.

Turning north, we marvel at the magnificent scenery and admire the subtle challenge of Nairn before bidding farewell to Scotland.

Our travels then take us across the Irish Sea to explore the delights of Portmarnock with its demanding and challenging seaside layout. We pause at Killarney and Royal County Down, perhaps the toughest course in the British Isles, before returning to the coast it's on once more, to visit Royal Portrush.

Our final destination is Wales and we visit two very contrasting locations. To stand on the first tee at Royal Porthcawl on a fine summer's day watching the sun dancing on the waves of the Atlantic Ocean, is one of golf's truly memorable experiences. Our second stop in Wales is just over the Severn Bridge, at St. Pierre, home of the Epson Grand Prix, and where the long, par-three eighteenth hole, played over water, has provided so many exciting finishes to this unique event. Like fine wine, the two excellent courses at St. Pierre continue to improve with age. And the superb on-course hotel facilities complete an outstanding golfing location. These wonderful Welsh courses provide a fitting climax to this journey around sixteen of Britain and Ireland's memorable golf courses.

Dalmahoy, on the outskirts of Edinburgh, offers two excellent eighteen-hole courses and a range of other sports centred around the imposing clubhouse.

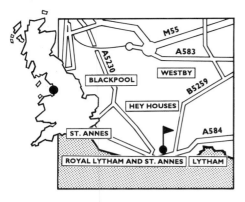

ROYAL LYTHAM and ST. ANNES

"A golf course which demands the very best from players, which is why only the very best have ever won here."

EDDIE BIRCHENOUGH: *Professional, Royal Lytham.*

As with all good courses, Royal Lytham sets the player a test which is demanding yet fair. Whether the golfer is a prospective Open champion, or simply a keen amateur making his first visit to the course, the criteria for success are the same.

The keys to winning here are accuracy from the tee, correct club selection from the fairway and a fair slice of good fortune on the greens.

However, in the case of a major championship such as the Open, several subtle changes are introduced to the characteristics of the course in order to create the ultimate test of skill and courage.

By allowing the rough to grow a little longer, narrowing the fairways in strategic areas and firming up the greens, the course can be prepared in such a way as to bring the very best out of the top players in what is generally accepted as the greatest championship in golf.

Royal Lytham differs in one significant way from the other courses currently on the Open championship rota because, in the words of Head Greenkeeper, Jim McDonald, "There are thirteen holes going out and five coming in." And as past Open championships at Royal Lytham have confirmed, those last five holes usually play a major role in deciding the outcome of the Open.

Yet if the last five holes determine where the Open is won, then the first three holes have also had a considerable influence on where the championship has been lost. That was certainly the case in 1979, when American Hale Irwin, leader after three rounds, found the cross-bunkers with his tee shot at the second hole. Irwin eventually took six on this par-four hole and from that point onward never really posed a serious threat to an inspired Severiano Ballesteros who went on to win his first Open championship.

As many famous names have discovered to their cost, the railway line and out of bounds that run alongside the second and third fairways, makes these opening holes formidable.

An aerial view of Royal Lytham showing the clubhouse and eighteenth green in the foreground, and on the right the railway line which parallels several of the holes on the first nine.

Although length is an obvious asset on any golf course, the numerous deep fairway bunkers at Royal Lytham, dictate that the premium should always be on accuracy from the tee, rather than distance. And as the greens are designed to accept running approach shots, there is no great penalty to pay for having to play a longer approach shot than might be desirable on an inland course.

Like all seaside courses, the wind is always a significant factor at Royal Lytham. For unless the conditions are flat calm, which is a rare occurrence on the Lancashire coast, the length of the last five holes will certainly demand outstanding golf from even the best players simply to match par, let alone better it.

The great American amateur Bobby Jones, won the first Open played at Royal Lytham in 1926 and since that time the list of winners has read like a 'Who's Who' of golf. For instance, who could

The clubhouse at Royal Lytham is big and hospitable – the perfect place to relax.

forget Tony Jacklin's historic win in 1969 when he became the first Briton to win the Open championship since Max Faulkner in 1953.

Seve Ballesteros returned again in 1988 and on this occasion held off a spirited challenge from South African Nick Price to become only the fifth man in the history of the Open to win consecutive Open championships at the same venue.

GOLFER'S VIEW

Unlike many top links courses, Royal Lytham is set well back from the sea, Nevertheless, the wind is still a major factor and good tactical fairway bunkering necessitates accuracy from the tee even when playing downwind.

With strong par threes and one of the most testing finishing stretches in golf, Royal Lytham is among the most demanding courses on the current Open championship rota.

The tee at the 356-yard sixteenth hole – a testing par-four but not impossible for the good amateur playing on form.

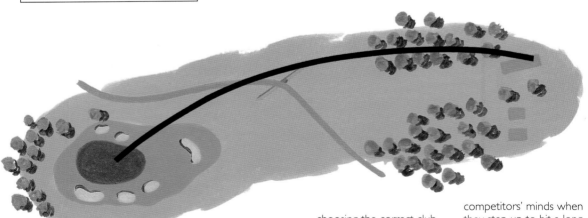

12th HOLE:
201 yards, par 3
This is a hole that catches everyone out. Like the first, the tee is set back in the trees and therefore it is difficult to detect the force and true direction of the wind.

Under normal conditions, it will come slightly from the left and against, and unless the players are certain of choosing the correct club, this hole could cost many of them dearly.

The first thing to avoid is the out-of-bounds area which runs down the right side of the hole. And although it is fairly far to the right, it will nevertheless be in the competitors' minds when they step up to hit a long iron, which must carry over the ridge in the green, to stand any chance of finishing close to the pin.

The putting surface itself is slightly raised and bunkered both front, left and right.

15th HOLE:
468 yards, par 4

This is probably the toughest hole on the course because it plays almost straight into the prevailing wind.

The hole is not terribly well defined from the tee and it is difficult to visualise exactly where you want to hit the tee shot. Many players like to line up with the bunker on the right of the fairway which is some 223 yards from the tee. Having said that, they will be hoping to draw the ball back into the centre of the fairway, because if they land in that bunker they could be looking at a double bogey, or worse.

There appears to be plenty of room down the left side but this is deceptive and many players choosing this line could find themselves in the rough when they thought they had hit the fairway. Even after a good drive, you will be looking at a second shot of over 200 yards which must also carry the cross bunkers approximately 75 yards from the green. The problem is further compounded by the fact that you cannot see either the bunkers or the green, but only the flag when playing the approach shot.

Once you have reached the green, your problems are not over, for the surface is sloping and very difficult to read.

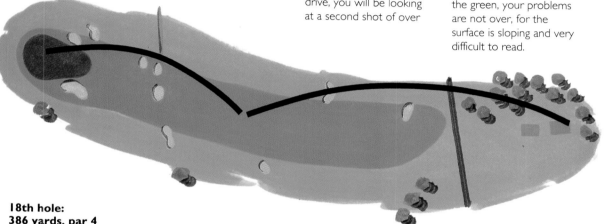

18th hole:
386 yards, par 4

It's not a particularly long hole, but it is one of the great finishing holes of all British golf courses. The number-one priority is to avoid the fairway bunkers which will almost certainly gather anything other than a long, straight tee shot probably with a driver as the hole normally plays into the wind. The green is some 45 yards long and very well bunkered, but should be within reach of a six- or seven-iron. However, clubbing might become a tricky problem if the wind gets up, with the size of the green and close proximity of the clubhouse to be considered in the equation. The putting surface is reasonably flat and if anything tends to gather the ball towards the centre unlike many of the other greens at Lytham which throw the ball to either side.

FACT FILE

The Open championship has been played at Royal Lytham on eight occasions; 1926, 1952, 1958, 1963, 1969, 1974, 1979, 1988.

No US tour player has ever won here and the only American winner was the legendary amateur Bobby Jones, who won in 1926.

Tony Jacklin became the first British player to win for almost fifty years when he captured the title in 1969.

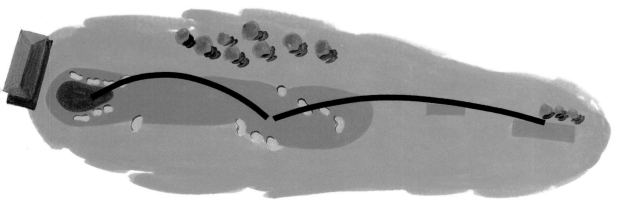

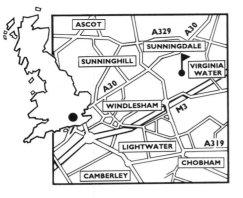

SUNNINGDALE

"It's a course that calls on most players to use every club in the bag – and there are not many courses like that any more."

KEITH MAXWELL: Professional, Sunningdale.

The clubhouse at Sunningdale - the home of two excellent eighteen-hole courses. The Old is a 6,341-yard par 70: the New is 300 yards longer and the same par.

When the increasing demand for golf first forced the game away from the coastal stretches where it was born to more accessible inland venues, there was considerable scepticism about the possibility of creating a worthwhile course on an area of heathland south of London.

The rather sour soil nevertheless supported an abundance of heather and a number of birch and pine trees. The great swathe of sandy soil which runs for miles through the region was an unexpected bonus for the foresighted men who laid out the first golf course here in the opening year of the twentieth century.

It was from such inauspicious beginnings that Sunningdale sprung to prominence as a course that captured the imagination of golfers from all parts of the world and became a model for heathland courses everywhere.

Opened in 1901 on largely open and windswept heath, the course was quickly and carefully transformed with the cultivation of thousands of trees now long-matured.

When Bobby Jones arrived to take part in the southern qualifying round for the 1926 Open Championship, the course had already taken on much of the tranquil, tree-shrouded appearance it has today. Jones's first round of 66

shattered all records at a time when good scores were still counted in the low 70s. He had 33 putts and 33 other shots: he missed only one green and the most he took for any hole was four!

Today's professionals average 28 or 29 putts a session, sometimes completing a four-round tournament with an average as low as 24. Think what Jones's score would have been had he putted with the precision of one of today's top pros.

Many years later, just after World War II, Norman von Nida of Australia won the

Dunlop Masters with an incredible final round of 63. That was in the days when the final two rounds of all tournaments were played on Fridays, with just enough time for a sandwich and a change of socks in between. Gary Player was to complete Sunningdale's Old Course in 64 on the way to his first victory in Britain in 1956.

Low scores are always possible on this, one of the earliest and greatest heathland courses. It is not long by modern standards and although most holes are now completely surrounded by trees, and fairways are flanked with great areas of heather, the challenge is subtle rather than punitive.

Sheer power will not get the job done at Sunningdale and even the shortest par fours need delicacy and precision with the little shots. The third, at 296 yards, is often in reach for the modern tournament pros – yet the green slopes infuriatingly away to back and right and a powerful tee shot can be on the green one moment and resting in a necklace of bunkers the next.

Even a 20-30 yard chip from short of the green must be meticulously judged to have any chance of a birdie.

There is a real links quality to the eleventh hole, where the second shot is to a slightly raised plateau green and the preferred approach is a low, running shot which must climb the bank and then stop on a slightly crowned green with a matching downslope at the back.

The seventeenth is a classic par four which needs precise placement of the tee shot in order to get the ball into the left half of a sloping green. This is a typical Sunningdale challenge – demanding a level of thought and planning which many longer courses

The seventeenth hole at Sunningdale Old Course is a 421-yard par four with a closely-bunkered green. Many golfers tend to fade their drives to avoid trees – and consequently find themselves trapped.

The Old Course at Sunningdale was laid out by Willie Park, Junior, in 1900. Many golfers find that the small expanse of water seen here becomes as wide as the Atlantic when their ball lands in it.

simply cannot offer.

In the 1920s a second course – the New – was added. It is not a copy of its older sister, but a more open and punishing challenge. Together they make as good a pair of inland courses as it is possible to find in Britain. Sunningdale professional Keith Maxwell rates the Old Course very highly. "It is a course which calls on most players to use every club in the bag and there are not many courses like that any more. If anything a slight fade is a useful weapon on the Old to work the ball into the best positions."

FACT FILE

The original course was designed by Willie Park, Junior and was first opened for play in 1901. It was subsequently redesigned by H. S. Colt.

In 1926, Bobby Jones scored 66 in the southern qualifying round for the Open.

The Prince of Wales, later Edward VIII, and his brother, the Duke of York, later George VI, were both captains of the club.

Gary Player won his first European tournament at Sunningdale, in 1956.

5th HOLE:
410 yards, par 4

This is one of those marvellous holes played from a raised tee with the full length of the challenge and all its hazards laid out in full view below. Great sweeps of heather fall away from the tee towards the fairway and while the trees on the right are well back from the playing line, those on the left are forced into the golfer's consciousness because two bunkers down the right edge, exactly at driving distance, mean that the tee shot must be aimed into the left half of the fairway.

The pond, which can look to be in range from the tee, is 50 yards past the farthest bunker and might occasionally trouble Seve Ballesteros, but club golfers need not worry.

From the flat perspective of the fairway the pond may seem to threaten the second shot, but the front of the green is 40 yards beyond its far edge so it really doesn't come into play.

What must be avoided with the second shot are the two bunkers which run tight against the left flank of the green. The two on the right are short of the putting surface and set wide of the green.

Keep the tee shot left of the bunkers and aim the approach into the right half of the green.

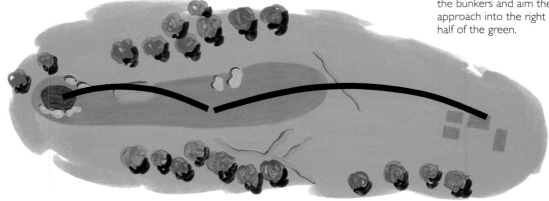

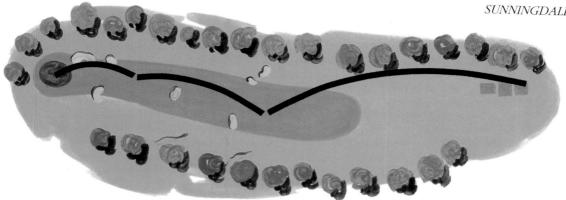

10th HOLE:
478 yards, par 5

This hole is a par five from the championship tee, but move forward a few yards and from the medal mark it becomes a long and difficult two-shotter. Yet, like the fifth, it is played from a tee perched high above the fairway with every hazard in clear view.

There is ample room out to the left of the fairway for shorter hitters, but lower handicap players must line up the drive on the far bunker in the centre of the fairway to keep away from the twin traps in the edge of the right rough and the large lone bunker which narrows the fairway from the other side.

In typical Sunningdale fashion the hole is completely enclosed by trees. While those on the left are set well back, anyone taking a very tight line directly at the pin, could be in trouble on the right.

The three bunkers that guard the green, two on the right, one on the left, are all short of the putting surface, the one on the left 30 yards in front of the green. Anyone in doubt about getting up in two should not risk aiming for the gap between the bunkers, but should lay up well short. This will leave a 60-70 yard pitch to a green which is 30 yards deep.

17th HOLE:
421 yards, par 4

This is an extremely tough driving hole which runs gently downhill and turns slightly to the right. Trees, thick rough and a bunker on the corner of the dog-leg at 240 yards make this a route only for the bigger hitting tournament pros - if they think it is worth the risk.

The opposite side of the dog-leg is marked by a copse of small trees. Too far left off the tee and the green is blocked out completely. The ideal tee shot it just to the right of the copse or a fade aimed at the trees and brought back into the fairway. The importance of having a clear sight of the green now becomes clear. Bunkered short and back left and front right, it slopes considerably from the left and the second shot must be aimed well up into the left half of the green.

This is not an easy shot to judge, with an area of dead ground short of the green making the approach seem shorter than it is in reality. Any shot short and on line for the centre of the green is almost certain to fall away into the bunkers on the right.

GOLFER'S VIEW

A wonderful setting for golf with its firm, fast fairways winding between banks of gorse and heather, in turn flanked by silver birch and pine trees, it requires precision rather than power to score well over one of the world's finest and most famous inland courses.

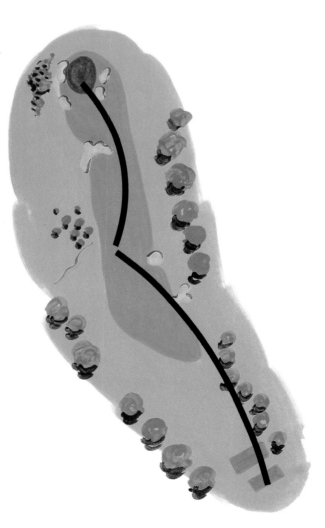

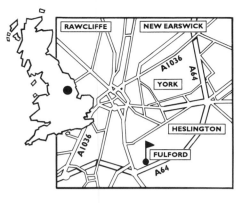

FULFORD

"The key to good scoring at Fulford is hitting the ball straight. I don't think you need a driver at all."

BRYAN HESSAY: *Professional, Fulford.*

There is a tree to the left of the seventeenth at this delightful Yorkshire club bearing a plaque that marks one of the most remarkable shots played during any championship round at any course in the world. During the 1984 Benson & Hedges Open championship which was played here until 1989, Bernhard Langer's approach shot finished up nestling in its branches: rather than lose a shot, the German climbed into the tree to chip his ball down onto the green!

Keeping the ball in play is a priority at Fulford. The club professional, Bryan Hessay, believes that the trouble with good amateurs is that they try to hit the ball too far and the farther they hit it, the farther off line they go! At Fulford, the errant shot is severely punished.

The first hole at this 6,299-yard course is a good one, wide and inviting – an excellent start to what should be a memorable day's golf. It introduces the player to the out-of-bounds fence which runs down the left side of every hole in the course, and the poplars which are such a

The seventeenth hole at Fulford is a 355-yard par four with a ditch on the left side of the fairway.

FROM THIS TREE BERNHARD LANGER PLAYED HIS THIRD SHOT DURING THE BENSON & HEDGES INTERNATIONAL OPEN AUGUST 1981

The last hole at Fulford has been the scene of many exciting finishes which have thrilled the spectators who crowd the grandstands.

GOLFER'S VIEW

Rated as one of the top half-dozen courses in Yorkshire, this delightful, tree-lined course on the outskirts of York is usually in top-class condition.

The opening holes are fairly gentle but once you get into the middle section of the course the layout becomes more testing.

At the height of summer the fairways are usually firm and the greens are fast. Fulford is not too tight from the tee, but the rough can be punishing and out-of-bound comes into play on several of the closing holes.

feature of Fulford. It also gives players a chance to get accustomed to the wind that usually blows from right to left for the first six holes and then, as they turn homeward on the twelfth, it blows from left to right.

The first real challenge is the 458-yard long, par-four fourth with its crevice that runs across the fairway 50 yards short of the green. The fairway is lined with trees and it calls for a near-perfect drive followed by a middle iron to the green to make par. Both Lee Trevino and Tom Weiskopf have holed two-iron shots at this hole to make eagle two!

After the fifth, you have to cross a bridge over a bypass to reach the sixth tee. When the road was built it cut

across the sixth and seventh holes which had to be altered to account for this intrusion of twentieth-century technology. The sixth was moved twenty yards farther on and became a 545-yard par five. The seventh was also moved – ten yards farther forward

From the seventh to the eleventh, the holes curl around the edge of a forest, the rough thickens and becomes an almost impenetrable tangle of purple heather, gorse and grasses. So long as you are not too distracted by the beauty of it all you should not drop too many strokes here. In fact, if you remember Bryan Hessay's words about hitting straight – preferably with an iron – you should make par.

Once you have come out of

The ground staff at Fulford work tirelessly to ensure that the greens are always in the same tip-top condition as the one seen here.

FACT FILE

Until recent years Fulford was the venue for the Benson & Hedges International Tournament.

In the 1982 Benson & Hedges Tournament, Bernhard Langer's approach shot at the seventeenth landed in a tree. about ten feet off the ground. Undaunted, he climbed the tree and hit a perfect shot up onto the edge of the green.

Since 1989, Fulford has been the venue for the Murphy's Cup, and the Stableford tournament, now a regular event on the European Tour.

the sylvan beauty of these five holes and have coped with the change of wind at the twelfth, you come to the thirteenth – a difficult par-four, 471-yarder. The usual out of bounds to the left coupled here with the copse to the right, necessitates a tight drive followed by a long iron shot to the green which has a very narrow entrance. This is definitely the toughest par four at Fulford, although the sixteenth, much shorter but also a par four, runs it a close second. The tee shot can't go too far to the right because of the copse there. Accurate iron shots,

the tee shot aimed to the left followed by a short iron to the green, should see you home, though.

At the seventeenth – another par four, 355-yards long – most players take a long iron off the tee and play safe, just short of the ditch on the left-hand side of the fairway to leave a relatively short chip to the green.

Once you have marked your card after the eighteenth, you can adjourn to the welcoming clubhouse which is the perfect place to calm your nerves after tackling the testing but individual course at Fulford.

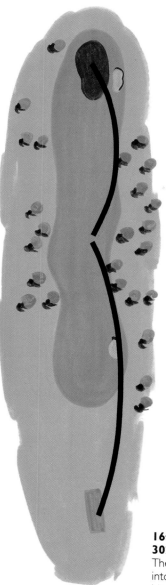

4th HOLE:
458 yards, par 4

Running across the fourth fairway about 50 yards short of the green is a crevice. If your ball hits it, it kicks left or right, you might think you've hit a good shot: then you don't get it on the green and you finish up in a little hollow. If the pin is on the left you don't have an easy shot to play for the green.

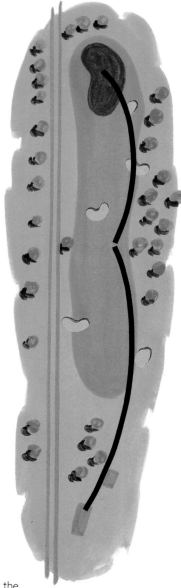

13th HOLE:
471 yards, par 4

The thirteenth is a difficult hole because of the out-of-bounds all the way down the left and the copse on the right. This is definitely the hardest par four on the course. You have a tight drive so it's probably best to use an iron and then you're left with a long iron to the green. There's a very narrow entrance as out-of-bounds is only fifteen yards from the green on the left.

16th HOLE:
302 yards, par 4

The sixteenth goes back into the trees so you can't hit it too far right because of the copse on the right and if you hook it you're in trouble. Usually you would take an iron off the tee aiming it towards the left side of the fairway then you will be left with a short iron into a narrow deep green.

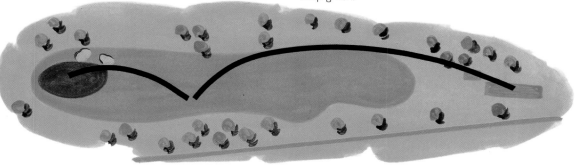

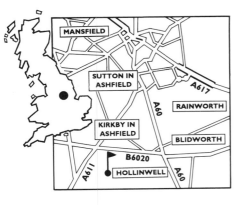

HOLLINWELL

"It's what I'd call an old-fashioned golf club with traditional ideas. When people come to Hollinwell they know what to expect."

BRIAN WAITES: *Professional, Hollinwell.*

At the end of the last century, Charles Robert Hemmingway, one of the leading railway engineers of his day, was surveying around Kirby Forest in Nottinghamshire for the Grand Central Railway. A keen golfer, Hemmingway played over the Notts Golf Club which was then situated on a stretch of common land at Bullwell Forest.

During the course of his work he found an area of gently-sloping, bracken-covered ground which he knew was ideal for a golf-course. He persuaded the club to commission Willie Park, Junior to lay out the course over the land. Later revised by John Henry Taylor, it has become one of Britain's top courses.

Many important championships have been played at Hollinwell which takes its name from the 'holy well' tucked away in the trees close to the eighth tee. Eric Brown shot a course record of 64 when playing the Dunlop Masters in 1957: the Brabazon trophy has been played here, the first time in 1975 when Sandy Lyle won his first important victory: the first John Player Classic was played at Hollinwell in 1970. Playing off the back tees, Hollinwell offers golfers a stern test of 7,020 yards: the

Hollinwell is in the top 100 courses in the world: it is also one of the most beautiful.

forward tees play 6,200 yards each one of which is still a challenge for the average amateur golfer.

The first hole, a fairly comfortable par four, prompted Henry Longhurst to say, "At any other point in the round it would be dull: as an opening hole it serves it purpose...no particular trouble, the early morning 'top' runs merrily along the fairway and nobody is delayed unnecessarily."

Longhurst described the second hole as a 'great one'. If you don't drive to the right you can't see the flag; if you go too far to the right you won't make the green with your second shot.

Next, there's a slightly downhill par five that offers some hope of a birdie as does the sixth, at 560 yards the longest on the course. The

ground at this hole encourages your ball to run once you have made it over the first crest.

The eighth is a right-hand dog-leg of 410 yards. The tee shot has to carry the water which stretches 160 yards from the tee and then carry the narrow gap through the trees. A good tee shot will give you a clear view of the green from the angle of the dog-leg, and perhaps the chance of a birdie. Many players opt for a three-wood rather than a driver, and then a five- or six-iron to the green which is guarded by a deep bunker to the right with out-of-bounds to the same side.

The twelfth is a real tester, playing as it does differently according to the wind direction. It is well over 400 yards long and the drive must be extremely well judged. It

The rough at Hollinwell is thick and heathery. The course meanders through a natural valley of trees.

has to clear a valley but not overshoot the mound beyond, for if it does, it tumbles away into another valley giving you a completely blind approach shot that is extremely difficult to judge.

GOLFER'S VIEW

Hollinwell is noted for its rolling landscape and tree-lined fairways. Playing from the competition tees, it is a fairly long and demanding course even if the fairways are generously wide and the rough is not too punishing. The often dramatic contours of the course call for correct club selection if you are to score well over this magnificent course.

The thirteenth hole at Hollinwell has been described as a great par three. Many players are happy to go one over here.

This is a most attractive hole. When you stand on the back tee you look to a green some 220 yards below. It gives any player a great thrill to see a well-struck ball sailing towards the pin and dropping down onto the green. Depending on the wind it can be a driver or a five-iron from the tee.

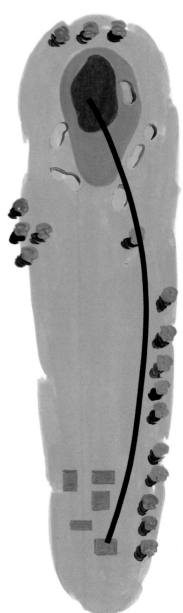

The thirteenth is an awe-inspiring par three. 236 yards long, it is played from a lofty tee through a steep-sided valley to the green. Both sides of the valley are lined with heather and gorse: there are bunkers both short left and right of the green – even household-name professionals have hit five here.

The fourteenth is a 403-yard par four, It's well bunkered and as you usually have to play into the wind, you need to hit your best tee and second shots if you are to have any chance of reaching the green in regulation.

The fifteenth is another par four. The tee shot is not a great problem here but the approach is critical as it has to be threaded through a narrow entrance to the green: miss it and you are liable to end up in an unplayable lie.

The par-four, 350-yard sixteenth offers another tight green – quite a small target to hit with the approach shot.

In the 1975 Brabazon, Geoff Marks holed a putt the length of a cricket pitch for an eagle three at the seventeenth. At 480 yards, it offers lesser talents the chance of a birdie which is more than can be said for the eighteenth – a testing 457-yard par four. Although the hole plays downhill, the wind is usually against you and the green can often be out of reach of two wood shots.

There's a hawthorn tree to the side of the green. During the 1982 Haig, Nick Faldo's ball bounced off it onto the putting surface. As he went on to win the championship, it is now called, 'Nick Faldo's Tree!' Those whom the Gods love can do no wrong.

Hollinwell offers lesser mortals eighteen superb holes which will demonstrate to anyone who plays them why the course (it lies within the bounds of Sherwood Forest) is always rated as one of the top 100 in the world.

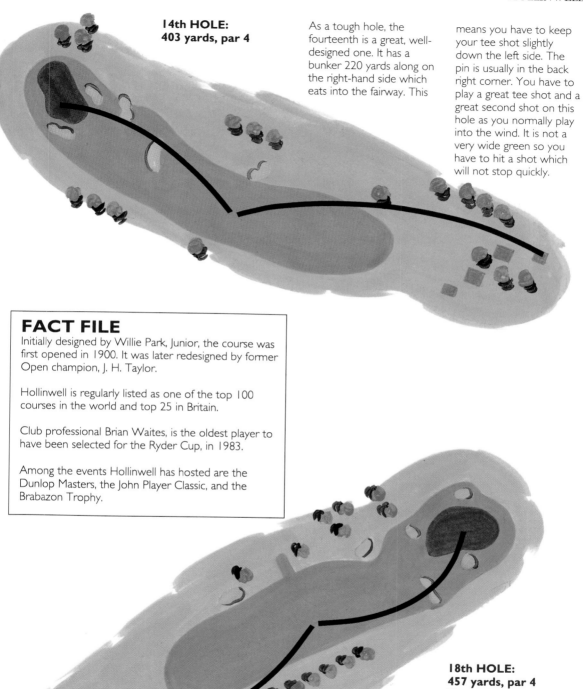

14th HOLE:
403 yards, par 4

As a tough hole, the fourteenth is a great, well-designed one. It has a bunker 220 yards along on the right-hand side which eats into the fairway. This means you have to keep your tee shot slightly down the left side. The pin is usually in the back right corner. You have to play a great tee shot and a great second shot on this hole as you normally play into the wind. It is not a very wide green so you have to hit a shot which will not stop quickly.

FACT FILE

Initially designed by Willie Park, Junior, the course was first opened in 1900. It was later redesigned by former Open champion, J. H. Taylor.

Hollinwell is regularly listed as one of the top 100 courses in the world and top 25 in Britain.

Club professional Brian Waites, is the oldest player to have been selected for the Ryder Cup, in 1983.

Among the events Hollinwell has hosted are the Dunlop Masters, the John Player Classic, and the Brabazon Trophy.

18th HOLE:
457 yards, par 4
The last hole is magnificent. There is no guarantee that you will make four here to win a championship. It normally plays slightly against the wind using probably a driver or a long iron and something like a three-iron to the green which is in front of the clubhouse.

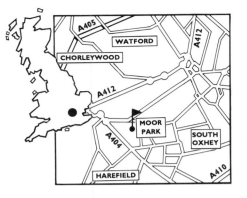

MOOR PARK

"Positional play is the key to a good round on the High Course. It is no longer as wide open as it used to be and you have to think about every shot."

ROSS WHITEHEAD: *Professional, Moor Park,*

For a beautifully peaceful golf course in the stately setting of a former deer park, Moor Park has had more than its share of tournament excitement in its history.

It was here in 1963 that young South African, Harold Henning, in the midst of a season of uncertain form and fluctuating fortune, holed in one in the Esso Golden Round Robin tournament. This novel event, which pitted fifteen leading professionals against each other in a series of fourteen matches, no longer exists. The first prize was won by Kel Nagle, the Australian who won the centenary Open at St. Andrews in 1960. He collected £750 for winning ten of his fourteen matches. Henning picked up £10,000 for his hole-in-one. That was in the days when a good salary was £1,000 a year and the average house cost less than £3,000.

House values had risen by a factor of about 40 when singer and comedian Jerry Stevens, a tireless fund-raiser through his interest in golf, holed his second shot at a par five to win a spectacular home for charity in the Four Stars pro-celebrity event which made its home at Moor Park for six years.

This popular event produced another hole-in-one, by Brian Barnes and

The clubhouse at Moor Park is a grade 1 listed building, once the home of Henry VIII and Catherine of Aragon.

another eagle, by Tony Johnstone. The amateur prize in 1988 went to Jimmy Tarbuck, one of the organisers and instigators of the tournament. It also saw the emergence of Jose Maria Olazabal, who finished in second place in his first season as a tournament professional in 1986.

Winners of the Four Stars have been Ken Brown, Antonio Garrido, Mark McNulty, Craig Parry – who beat Ian Woosnam in a sudden-death play-off in 1989

The West course at Moor Park is 800 yards shorter than the High course and a great deal easier.

– and Rodger Davis, who took the title twice in three years. When he won for the second time in 1990 his prize was £36,500 – a far cry from the £750 won by Kel Nagle in the early days of tournament golf at Moor Park.

On the very edge of Greater London, Moor Park is an ideal tournament venue and an excellent place for society golf, or just a good day out with a friendly fourball. The majestic manor house – surely one of the largest clubhouses in Britain – stands at the hub of the High and slightly shorter West Courses.

Golf was first played here in 1923 when the estate was owned by Lord Leverhulme, but there was a manor on the

Moor as far back as the thirteenth century. It became a private club in 1937.

The urban sprawl has long since engulfed the former deer park, but it was one of the earliest golf course and housing developments and, to a large extent, protected its own environment by developing attractive houses which bordered the course, but did not intrude.

In addition to the original beeches, oaks and willows which made the site such a promising proposition as a potential golf course, there has been an extensive programme of tree planting which has matured to such an extent that much of the unwelcome encroachment of

bricks and mortar has been successfully screened out. A game at Moor Park is still like playing in the country.

The undulating site gave original architect Harry Colt the opportunity to design some holes around the higher points and between the massive trees. He also created many memorable shots by playing other holes across valleys and lakes.

Although the tree cover has thickened dramatically in the 25 years that Ross Whitehead has been the club professional it has never been allowed to close in to the point where the fairways have become threateningly claustrophobic. But it has changed the playing lines in many cases, particularly on the dog-leg holes where taller trees now define the fairways and bold shots over the corner are no longer a sensible option. Ponds, lakes and drainage ditches all play their part in setting out the challenge of Moor Park. "Positional play is the key to a good round on the High Course," says Ross Whitehead. "It is no longer as wide open as it used to be and you have to think about every shot."

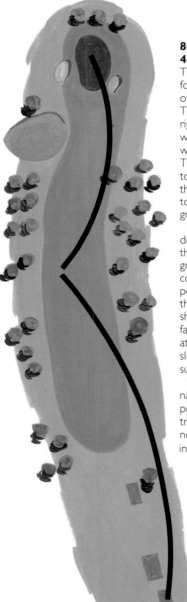

8th HOLE:
467 yards, par 4

This is a very strong par four, just a few yards short of becoming a par five. The hole turns to the right around a copse of willows and there is no way to cut the corner. This means it is essential to keep the tee shot in the left half of the fairway to get a line into the green.

For those who are doubtful about carrying the second shot to the green there is a further complication caused by a pond at the left edge of the fairway some 50 yards short of the green. The fairway drops fractionally at this point and then rises slightly to the putting surface.

Because the fairway narrows between the pond on the left and the trees on the right there is no percentage in aiming into the gap as the green is not in reach. The curious situation then arises of a player who cannot get the green with two woods, may only be hitting a seven-iron to lay up short of the pond - leaving a 90-yard pitch.

The green itself is severely contoured from the back and the left and is bunkered on either side. Any putt from above the hole is extremely difficult and the only safe solution is to hole it - or be faced with a difficult six-footer coming back.

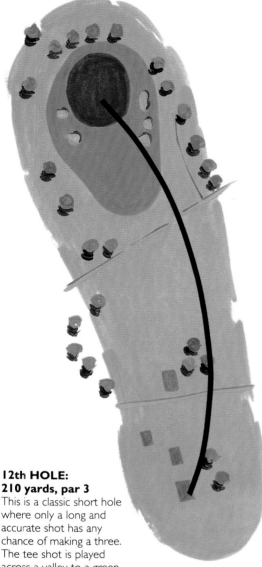

14th HOLE:
435 yards, par 4

There is no easy way to play this hole, which turns left around a spinney of trees at about 200 yard distance from the tee. In the right conditions big-hitters may fly the ball over the corner. Most often it is safer to draw the ball round the dog-leg. But pin placement is critical in positioning the tee shot.

The green is only some 20 yards deep, but 45 yards wide. With the pin tucked in close to the bunker on the left it is essential that the tee shot is played into the right half of the fairway. At the opposite end of the scale – with the pin at the right, where a hollow covers the approach – the second shot is ideally played from the left of the fairway.

Whatever the line of the approach, the second shot is demanding – uphill with a fairway wood or long-iron to a green with little depth, although the front left of the putting surface

is being reshaped to expand the possibilities for pin positions.

Just 90 yards short of the centre of the green a ditch crosses the fairway and causes problems for those who cannot get up in two. Laying up short of the ditch leaves a hard-to-judge pitch of more than 100 yards.

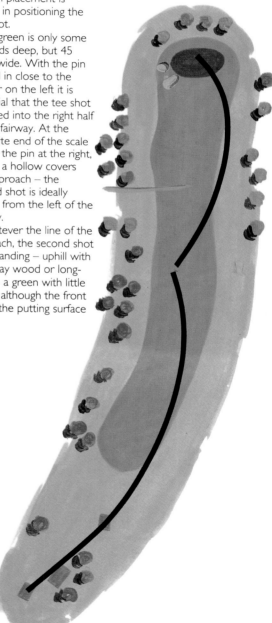

12th HOLE:
210 yards, par 3

This is a classic short hole where only a long and accurate shot has any chance of making a three. The tee shot is played across a valley to a green which is set slightly higher on the opposite slope. The green itself has two tiers with a steep incline between the two. The front section of the green is to be enlarged to extend the target area and give a greater variety of pin positions.

The ball has to be carried all the way to the green as there is a severe upslope short and bunkers on either side. Off to the right there are small trees and bushes and a line of oaks marches up the left.

Because the green is set higher than the tee the shot requires more club than normal. At 210 yards from the medal tee this does not leave many golfers with a choice.

Moor Park professional Ross Whitehead says the hole can be very deceptive. "I can get the lower tier with perhaps a one-iron, but if the pin is at the back it can be a full driver."

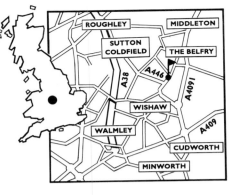

THE BELFRY

"Slowly but surely, The Belfry is writing itself into the history of the game."

CHRIS HART: Former Director of Operations, The Belfry.

"Accuracy is essential for low scoring at the Brabazon", said Chris Hart, former Golf Operations Director at The Belfry. "It doesn't matter if you're long off the tee, you've got to be straight."

The par 70, 6,077 yard-long Derby is three shots and 898 yards shorter than the Brabazon which is the more testing examination of your golfing skill. The lakes which are such a feature of the Brabazon are not part of the Derby although there are brooks at the second and sixteenth.

The courses are part of a multi-million pound leisure centre and were designed by former Ryder Cup players Peter Allis and David Thomas. The land they were given to work on was basically a flat open valley with very little character: a series of potato fields, featureless except for a smallish lake and a zigzagging stream.

It required extensive planning and much use of heavy machinery for it to begin to take shape. Even then, the weather played havoc: the long, hot summer of 1976 killed thousands of saplings: the rains that followed the virtual drought of the summer of 1977 washed away the fine American grasses.

Now, the Brabazon has water hazards at fifteen of its eighteen holes, trees galore and big greens and mounds

for the spectators who want to watch the games rather than enjoy the hospitality offered in the huge tented village that sprouts whenever there is an important competition at the course.

Both courses have been altered since they were opened. An extra two holes at the Derby allows the first and eighteenth to be used for the tented village during major events such as the Ryder Cup and the English Open, and also facilitates repairs enabling the ground-staff to take a hole out if necessary.

The tenth hole at the Brabazon has a new forward tee making it 275 yards instead of the original 301, to encourage the brave to go for the green. Several new bunkers have been put in to trap those who don't make it!

The Brabazon starts off with three par fours – the first 408

yards long, the second 340 and the third 455.

You usually have to drive into the wind at the fifth – a very long, 569-yard par five.

The fairway at the 386-yard, par-four sixth is only thirty yards wide, at a point where it snakes between two lakes. Accuracy is essential if you are to avoid the water, as the green is just ten feet from the lakeside where a watery fate awaits a loose second shot.

The seventh is 173 yards long and nicknamed, 'The Stockade'. When the course opened, the green was faced with split trunks. These have now been removed and the green is now surrounded by a large bunker, making it a testing par three.

The eighth stretches for 476 yards and is a short, but nevertheless testing, par five.

The green at the ninth – 390 yards – is elevated and tiered, with the lake cutting in on the right side. It's best to keep to the centre or left of the fairway from the tee to avoid having to pitch over the water onto the green to two putt for a par four. The green slopes from right to left and from back to front making

GOLFER'S VIEW

Although it is a little more open than it appears to be when seen on television, the Brabazon course at The Belfry is still an outstanding test of golf with water coming into play on many of the holes.

The course is always in good condition, especially the greens which are a joy to putt on. The Belfry, less than thirty minutes from Birmingham Airport, is the home of the PGA and host to the last two Ryder Cup matches.

The tenth hole at The Belfry was 301 yards long. Playing from the new forward tee it is now 26 yards shorter but still a testing par three.

putting difficult and sometimes expensive.

There are two plaques at the 301-yard, par-four tenth. One is dedicated to Seve Ballesteros, the other to Greg Norman. The sensible way to play this hole is to go for the middle of the fairway with a long to middle iron hoping you don't go to the right and into the water or to the left and into the bunker. A good lie, short of the water which runs along the right side and front of the green, will leave you with a wedge or a nine-iron shot, but too strong and you will be bunkered or tangled up in a grassy bank. The year after the course opened, in the 1978 Hennessey, Seve Ballesteros faded his drive to the centre of the green. Hence his plaque. Greg Norman got his for scoring an eagle at the hole! And England cricketer, Ian Botham was one of the first amateur golfers to drive the green.

The next seven holes are challenging – three par fours, two par threes at the twelfth

and fourteenth, and two mammoth par fives – the 540-yard fifteenth and the 555-yard seventeenth. And then the eighteenth – a hole that some consider the best closing hole of all British golf courses. Peter Allis writes that the best way to approach it is to drive over the water biting off as much as you dare to shorten the second shot, which is over the water, to the enormous three-tiered green. This may well be the best way for the professional to tackle this daunting hole. However, most amateur golfers would be advised to

play the hole as a par five: making sure of getting over the first lake from the tee, then playing short of the other lake that guards the front of the green.

The third shot, although having to carry the water, is comparatively short and a good pitch and two putts will produce a respectable one over par – and a single putt, the bonus of a memorable par four.

Water is a feature of fifteen holes at the Brabazon, designed by David Thomas and named after Lord Brabazon of Tara.

4th HOLE:
569 yards, par 5

I particularly like this par-five hole because a reasonable drive, followed by a well-struck fairway wood, can set up a good

birdie opportunity.

The drive needs to be accurate rather than long, to avoid the two fairway bunkers which pose a threat to the tee shot. It is also important to check

on the pin placement before hitting the second shot. The green is protected by two large bunkers, one on the left and one on the right and the location of the pin determines which side of the fairway you should

aim to hit with your second shot in order to leave the easiest line to the pin for the third shot.

The green is long and narrow therefore the third shot must be accurate, both in length and direction, to set up a possible single putt for a birdie.

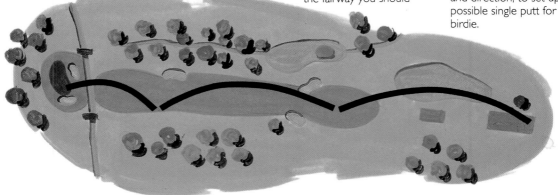

FACT FILE

There are two courses at The Belfry –
the Brabazon and the Derby.

It was at the Brabazon in 1985 that the
European team won the Ryder Cup for the
first time since 1957.

The Belfry is the home of The British
Professional Golfers Association.

7th HOLE:
173 yards, par 3

I chose the seventh as my
favourite short hole on
The Belfry because it is
not too long, which means
that the average golfer can
reach the green with a
middle iron.

As the green is almost
completely surrounded by
sand, tee premium is on
accuracy. However, the
putting surface at the
seventh is very receptive
and a well-struck tee shot
will stop quickly.

10th HOLE:
301 yards; par 4

This has become one of
the most famous par-four
holes in golf and I've
chosen it because it offers
the golfer several
alternative ways of
reaching the green.

Off the forward tee, the
long hitter can take the
risk and try to carry his
tee shot all the way over
the water to the green.
And even if the shot is
less than perfect, there is
still a chance to save par,
providing the ball finishes
to the right of the green
and can be successfully
threaded through the
trees and on to the
putting surface.

Alternatively, the shorter
hitter can hit an iron
down the fairway to the
left of the lake, from
where he should only
require a short iron to
reach the green. Before
hitting the tee shot it is a
good idea to check on the
pin placement. This is
because the farther down
the green the pin, the
shorter you should aim to
hit the tee shot. Like-
wise, when the pin is at
the back of the green it is
important to get your ball
well down the fairway, in
order to make the green
in regulation.

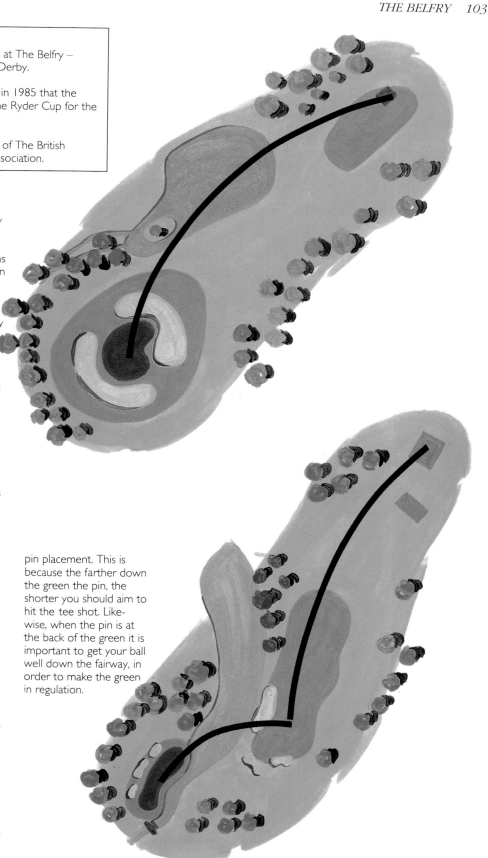

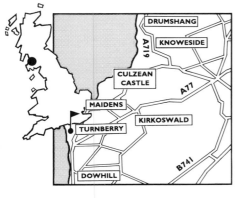

TURNBERRY

"If you can see Ailsa Craig, it's going to rain:
if you can't see it, it's raining."

LOCAL SAYING

Running alongside one of the most scenic stretches of coastline in the west of Scotland, the Ailsa course at Turnberry is among the most demanding and beautiful championship venues in the world.

Golf first began at Turnberry in 1906 when the legendary Open champion Willie Fernie was commissioned by the third Marquis of Ailsa to design a thirteen-hole course. The Marquis also leased land at Turnberry to the Glasgow & South Western Railway Company to build a hotel close by, thus creating probably the world's first golf hotel complex.

The amalgamation of the four major railway companies in 1926 led to the hotel and golf course becoming the property of the London, Midland & Scottish Railways and in those grand times, prior to Dr Beeching axing thousands of miles of railway lines and hundreds of small stations, it was possible to step aboard a sleeping car at Euston Station in London and awaken the next morning at the Turnberry hotel ready to step onto the first tee.

The course was still comparatively young when World War I started and a great deal of unintentional damage was done to the course by the Royal Flying Corps, who used the land as a pilot training station.

After the war, the Ailsa course, named after the Marquis, became the number-one course in the area and Major C. K. Hutchison, who had also worked on the course at Gleneagles, was engaged to lengthen and improve the existing layout. This work was completed in 1938 just a year prior to the outbreak of World War II.

This time the course became a base for RAF Coastal Command and the damage to the land, mainly through the laying of eighteen-inch-thick, concrete runways was thought by many at the time to have signalled the end of golf forever at Turnberry. Fortunately, one man who did not share the view was Frank Hole, Managing Director of British Transport Hotels Ltd, who by this time were the owners of Turnberry.

After a protracted but

The first hole at Turnberry is a 406-yard par four, named after Ailsa Craig, the volcanic plug that dominates the seascape at this stretch of the Ayrshire coastline.

The hotel at Turnberry stands on a clifftop overlooking the southern end of the Firth of Clyde.

eventually successful battle to extract financial compensation from the government to rebuild both the courses at Turnberry, Frank Hole brought in the celebrated golf-course architect, Mackenzie Ross to produce the superb links layout which is the Ailsa of the present day. The scars from World War II are still visible, but fading, in the shape of parts of the old runways, which lie between the Ailsa and the Arran course, which is slightly less testing and somewhat flatter than the Ailsa.

Since those early setbacks,

Turnberry has gone from strength to strength and the quality of the Ailsa course was recognised by the Royal & Ancient golf club in 1977, when Turnberry was chosen to host the 106th Open championship. The weather throughout the week of the tournament was glorious and the 1977 Open championship produced a finish which has seldom been equalled in the history of the competition and which is never likely to be surpassed.

Under unclouded blue skies, Jack Nicklaus and Tom Watson, two of the giants of the game, fought out what amounted to a 36-hole, head-to-head battle, that left the rest of the field trailing in their wake. At the end of an epic struggle, it was Watson who finally emerged

victorious by a single shot. And such was the quality of the golf played by both men, that Watson's four-round total of 268 still stands today as an Open championship record.

The Open returned to Turnberry again in 1986 but on this occasion the weather was less kind and a remarkable second-round 63 by Greg Norman, in very difficult conditions, laid the foundation for the talented Australian's first and only Major victory to date.

The Turnberry Hotel which sits majestically atop a hill overlooking the golf courses and the sweeping sands of Turnberry Bay, is one of the world's great golf hotels. And there is nowhere better on a warm summer evening to relax over a meal or a drink and reflect on the more memorable moments of your round. For spread out before you is a breathtaking vista which looks out across the Firth of Clyde and on past the great, granite bulk of the famous Ailsa Craig, to the soft purple hues which outline the distant hills and peaks of Kintyre.

There are times when the Ailsa course is at the mercy of the strong westerly winds which sweep in from the Atlantic and send huge waves crashing on to the rocky coast line which marks the western boundary of the course. On such days, par is meaningless and the challenge is simply to survive the encounter with the elements. However on a fine day, with a fresh breeze ruffling the flags, the Ailsa is a fair and challenging course which asks the best of the experienced player looking to play to his handicap, while at the same time, permitting the less accomplished player to stray occasionally from the straight and narrow, without extracting too harsh a penalty.

This lighthouse at Turnberry reminds golfers that the sea is just a few yards from where they are playing- should they need such a reminder.

FACT FILE

Turnberry has staged the Open championship twice, in 1977 when the winner was Tom Watson and 1986 the year Greg Norman became champion.

The course record on the Ailsa course is held by American Mark Hayes and was set in the 1977 Open championship.

The Arran course, which is laid out inside the Ailsa course, is shorter but runs between avenues of gorse and is still a fine test of golf.

8th HOLE:
427 yards, par 4

The key to success at this excellent par four, is avoiding the large fairway bunker which guards the right side of the fairway and dominates the tee shot. Situated some 250 yards from the medal tee, this perfectly-sited bunker tends to force the golfer to drive to the left. And although the fairway slopes slightly from left to right, it will require pin-point accuracy to thread your drive between the bunker and the heavy rough on the left side of a fairway. which also dog-legs slightly to the left.

The relief of avoiding the bunker can lure some golfers into believing that negotiating the rest of the hole is a comparatively simple task. However care should be taken in

selecting the right club for the approach shot played to a well-bunkered and elevated green, which visitors often tend to over-, rather than under-club with their approach shots.

Although the bunker guarding the right side of the fairway is some 250 yards from the tee, even high handicappers should be cautious rather than carefree, when deciding how to play this hole, especially downwind. A three wood from the tee to make sure of hitting the fairway, should also remove the threat posed by the fairway bunker. A second shot, played, again with a lofted wood or a long iron, into the valley short of the green, should then leave a full shot with a short iron and the possibility of a single putt for a well-earned par.

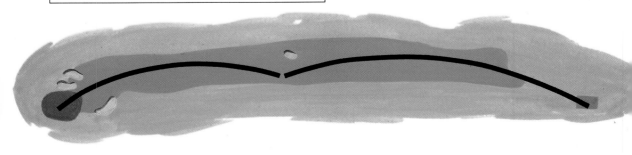

15th HOLE;
209 yards, par 3

Aptly named; 'Ca Canny', this is an outstanding short hole and one which demands accuracy and commitment from the golfer. Measuring over 200 yards and normally played into the prevailing wind, the tee shot calls for a long iron or on occasions, a wood.

The ball must be carried all the way to the putting surface, as anything which is short and a fraction right, will finish down a steep bank, from where the golfer will be faced with a blind shot to a green some thirty feet above him.

There is a bunker which also guards the front right of the green to catch the shot which although well struck, is still fractionally off line, along with three other bunkers that guard the left side of a putting surface with slopes from left to right. A ball finishing in any one of these bunkers, leaves the golfer facing the prospect of playing a delicate bunker shot which if slightly over-hit, could well run over the green and end up at the bottom of the steep bank.

In professional terms, there is; 'nowhere to miss' on this most demanding of short holes, and although it measures only 168 yards from the medal tee, the shot is every bit as demanding for the club golfer. The green measures some 35 yards from front to back, where it rises slightly to help hold the ball and prevent it from running through the back.

The philosophy for playing the fifteenth is simple; don't even think about missing the green, just stand up on the tee,

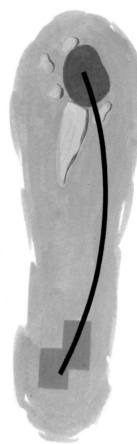

choose the right club and then pray that you hit one of your best shots of the day – or else.

GOLFER'S VIEW

Turnberry, one of the most spectacular links courses in the world, has a superb layout with each hole offering a challenge.

Many of the holes on the front nine run alongside the sea and the wind is usually a factor when playing this well-manicured course.

17th HOLE:
500 yards, par 5

The tee shot must carry just over 100 yards and also thread its way through a narrow gap in the giant dunes which continue all the way along the left side of the hole. Once the tee shot has negotiated this potential hazard, the fairway opens up to the right side which also features many large sand dunes and heavy rough.

Immediately in front of the tee, but not really posing a serious threat to the tee shot, is Wilson's Burn which winds it way on across the seventh fairway and on to the sea.

There is only one bunker guarding the right side of the fairway, but as it is positioned over 260 yards from the tee, it hardly poses a serious threat to the average golfer. However, as the hole continues, it starts to narrow and the second fairway bunker which is cut into a high ridge running across the whole width of the fairway some 100 yards short of the green, is certainly in play, either for the second shot of the long hitter, or the third shot after a poor drive.

Once past this bunker the only other problem facing the golfer is ensuring that he takes enough club for the third shot, in order to avoid coming up short of the green in the hollow in front of the putting surface, which over the years has become deeper and deeper.

The green is guarded by three bunkers; two on the left and one on the right, it is fairly narrow and measures some 35 yards from front to back.

Given calm conditions and hard, running fairways, the long hitters can get close to the green in two, provided they can keep their drive just left of centre and on the fairway. The higher handicapper should resist the

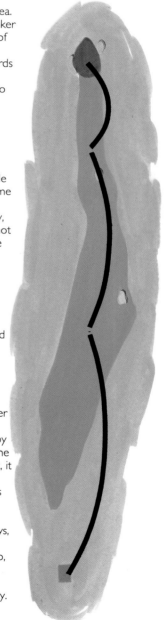

temptation to try to hit the tee shot too hard. Instead, the best they should hope for is to reach the level ground past the second bunker in two shots. From there the approach shot played with a short iron has a good chance of holding the green and with a little luck, and a smooth putting stroke, there is the chance of picking up a birdie.

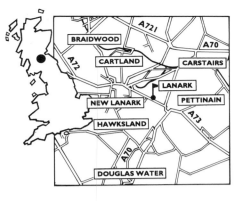

LANARK

*"It may not be the most famous golf course in Scotland,
but it is a challenge and a joy to play over."*

RON WALLACE: Professional, Lanark.

Anyone who enjoys a very challenging round on a course set among wonderful Scottish scenery should aim for Lanark and the delightful course there. Finding it can be just as testing an experience as the eighteen holes which cover 6,423 yards – a hard-to-match par 70.

One of the keys to success here is lining up putts accurately as the putting surfaces reflect the natural contours of the land and are normally fast and firm.

Straight putts are few and far between.

The first hole, a par four, 360 yards long, is a perfect opener – not too difficult and typically beautiful. Loch Lanark runs along the right side but is thankfully out of reach of even the most vicious slice. Two bunkers guard the green which is usually a fairly short iron shot even from a less than perfect drive from the tee.

The second is a monster 467-yard par four. You need

your best drive and an equally good fairway wood or long iron to make the putting surface in the regulation two shots – but don't be tempted to sacrifice accuracy for distance! A two-over-par six is not uncommon at this hole, even by the experts!

The third and fourth are also par fours –400 yards and 457

The twelfth green at Lanark is guarded by a trio of bunkers ready for short approach shots.

yards long respectively. The fourth is played from an elevated tee and the hole runs downhill through a series of humps and hollows that tend to gather a slightly wayward tee shot back into the fairway. The approach shot is played from the bottom of a small valley: choose your club well to make sure you carry the two bunkers that guard the front of the elevated green at this hole.

The 315-yard, par-four fifth may look as if it offers the opportunity to pick up a birdie. Short it may be: easy it is most definitely not. There's rough all the way up the right side of the fairway and out-of-bounds all along the left. Some players take a deep breath, reach for the driver and go for it. The more faint-hearted tee off with a long iron. Both are equally likely to to fall foul of the three bunkers guarding the green ready to trap any errant approach shots.

The green at the sixth hole – a 377-yard par four – is perched on a shelf cut into the side of a hill. If you are short with your second shot you may either land in the bunker that guards the green or simply stand helplessly watching your ball roll all the way back down the hill again!

The seventh is a short, 141 yards, par three – the only par three on the front nine. Played from an elevated tee, your tee shot must carry across a valley and avoid a string of deep bunkers which guard the green.

Few will make the putting surface at the eighth in two. It's 530 yards long with a well-placed bunker in the fairway ready to host your drive. Just short of the green, the land rises and falls, so your third shot has to carry

the ball onto the putting surface which is set in a small hollow that helps to gather the ball.

You can't see the putting surface from the ninth – it's over the brow of a hill. So, too, is a nasty spot on the right – not for nothing called 'The Golfer's Graveyard!' But a good, straight drive slightly to the left should leave you with a not-too-hard approach shot. The green is guarded by two bunkers: and a tree close to the edge of the green hinders an approach shot that has to be made from the right-hand rough.

The second par three is the tenth – only 152 yards long but as it can be played from two separate tees 50 yards apart, it's the luck of the draw, for from one, it is hard to hit the putting surface and from the other it's hard to miss!

The fairway at the par-four,

397-yard long eleventh is flanked by out-of-bounds all the way down the left side with a large bunker waiting to gather anything steered too far to the right! Avoid the out-of-bounds, miss the bunker and you could well land in the burn that flows across the fairway 270 yards from the tee with the hole playing downhill to the waiting water! And just to add to the fun, the second shot is blind - you can see the top of the flag but not the bottom. The domed green encourages any ball that is not exactly in the middle to roll off into the fringe.

The twelfth is a not-too-difficult 362-yard par four. If you hit a good drive and

On a sunny, summer day, Lanark is the perfect place to enjoy heathland golf at its best.

Lanark's postal address is, 'The Moor'. It is easy to see why from this view of part of the course.

FACT FILE

Founded in 1851, Lanark is the 25th oldest golf club in the world.

Lanark has been selected eight times as a qualifying course for the Open championship.

The superb silver claret jug, donated to the club in 1857 and on display in the clubhouse, predates the famous Open jug by five years.

avoid the three bunkers on the right of the fairway, a short iron should carry the trio of bunkers that guard the green and see you onto the putting surface for your par—with luck and a good putt maybe even a birdie. The thirteenth is much the same length as the twelfth and, again you have a reasonable chance of scoring a par here.

The fourteenth runs parallel to the thirteenth. It's one yard short of 400. Played uphill, a good straight drive is called for and an accurate second shot has to carry across a grassy hollow in front of the green if you are to make par.

And then we have the fifteenth. Only the longest hitters will make the green in the regulation two shots on this 470-yard par-four monster. Your drive needs to be over 200 yards if you are to carry the fairway bunker and the large mound that runs across the fairway. Bushes running along the right side of the hole wait to ensnare anyone who has gone for the big drive and come off the ball just a fraction. A bogey five feels like a well-earned par here. The sixteenth and seventeenth, Anstruther and Whitetrees, are both par fours at 337 and 308 yards respectively. Both are well bunkered from the tee and call for accurate clubbing at the second shot.

Ron Wallace, Lanark's professional, rates the par-three eighteenth the best hole on the course. At 216 yards, many players are tempted to use a wood which, if struck anything but accurately, can send the ball clattering into the clubhouse windows or fall away to the left into an area called the Cabbage Patch! The hole plays downhill with two bunkers situated short and to the right of the green.

The sandtrap thirty yards short is known to locals as 'The Par Five Bunker!': one shot from the tee, one to get out, one to get onto the green and then two putts!

The eighteenth encapsulates the character of the course – beautiful but demanding – a real golfing gem.

GOLFER'S VIEW

Lanark's rolling fairways, running over scenic, heathland terrain are a joy to play from. It is one of the finest inland courses in Britain and with the exception of three or four long and testing par-four holes, the course is not too demanding and from the member's tees gives average golfers the opportunity to play comfortably to their handicaps.

The final hole at Lanark is a beautiful par three, played from a high tee down to a green situated directly in front of the delightful clubhouse.

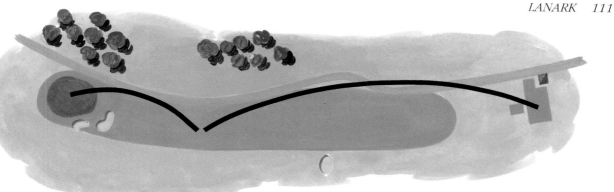

1st HOLE:
360 yards, par 4

This is not a long hole and the first thing the visitor will notice is the loch on the right of the hole: it is not in play but it is a real feature of the course. Also on the right is a road running the length of the hole and this is in play. A left-side fairway bunker will catch anything steered away from the road. Across the fairway is a fairly marked slope that the high handicapper will have trouble clearing from the tee. The green slopes quite severely from back to front and is a very difficult one on which to start a round.

11th HOLE:
397 yards, par 4

This has a very steep downhill slope from the tee with a burn at the bottom that is reachable in the summer for the good hitters. A bunker sits in the right of the fairway and a fence marks out of bounds all the way down the left.

The second shot is blind; the top of the flag is visible but not the bottom. The green is domed and very difficult to stay on — anything not exactly in the middle will roll off.

that sits to the right side of the green. To the left is a drop of about twenty feet and the road which featured on the first hole runs across the fairway, directly in front of the green. It is a fairly long hole for a par three so people can be hitting even wooden clubs here: facing the prospect of crashing into the clubhouse windows or falling away to the rough on the left.

18th HOLE:
216 yards, par 3

This is probably the best hole on the course. The hole is right below the windows of the clubhouse

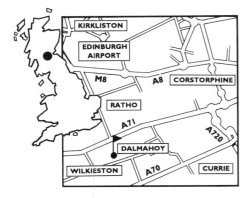

DALMAHOY

"There are two courses at Dalmahoy, both providing excellent parkland golf."

PETER ALLISS

It was recently reported that some of the potential US Ryder Cup players were opposed to 'older players' being selected as the youngsters believe that playing 36 holes is too arduous a task for anyone over forty!

Anyone who wants to prove the youthful Americans wrong should head for Dalmahoy, on the outskirts of Edinburgh, where the luxurious country club is centred around an elegant eighteenth-century mansion complete with restaurant, swimming pool, sauna and steam room, squash courts, tennis courts – and two challenging eighteen-hole courses, the East and the West: the perfect place for eighteen holes in the morning, a good lunch followed by a second round in the afternoon.

The 6,413-yard East Course is 1,165 yards longer than the West and with a par 71, two strokes more. Designed in 1927 by James Braid, it has hosted several tournaments, including the Senior Service Wills Open, the Sun Alliance and Haig Tournaments Players' Championships. It was during the final of the 1981 Haig that Brian Barnes shot a 62 coming home in a record-breaking 28 strokes.

One thing that Barnes did not have to contend with was

The clubhouse at Dalmahoy was designed in 1735 as a country house for the Earl of Morton.

the fickle wind which can exaggerate the merest push to the point of double or triple bogey! There have been a few changes to the East since Barnes played his astonishing round. The bunkers around the short fourth and fifteenth used to be flat and sharp-lipped at green level, often making recovery almost impossible. This has now been improved. As Brian Anderson, director of golf at Dalmahoy says, "I don't believe you've got an excuse if you are in a bunker because you have probably hit a bad shot. But I do believe you have a complaint if, when you are in there, you've got no shot." The new bunkers have steep, but soft rounded sides that throw the ball into the middle of the sand, so the golfer will always have a shot.

To return a good score at Dalmahoy's East Course, golfers have to master the twelve par fours, seven of which are over 400 yards long from the yellow tees. The opening holes in the outward and homeward halves are both par fives. The first plays uphill and is not particularly difficult: the tenth also plays uphill; to par this hole your drive must be positioned accurately as the slopes here can easily carry the ball into the rough, trees or bunkers.

As these slopes are common to several of the other holes at Dalmahoy, accurate driving is essential if you are to make your fair share of pars.

Brian Anderson advises players to take due note of the pin positions before contemplating their second shots. Many players tend to leave the ball short of the hole and risk catching the bunkers many of which are placed in the throat of the

greens. It's vitally important to make sure you get the ball up to the hole.

Most of the putting surfaces are large and because of this they appear flat but, as many golfers have discovered to their cost, they are very mature with subtle borrows. The course is built on a hill-side and the lie of the overall ground will tell astute players much about allowing a little more borrow on their putts.

The first hole, a not too testing 478-yard par five is followed by two par fours and then a short, 136-yard par three which is fairly straightforward. The eighth is a short, 347-yard par four and the ninth, a short par five measuring 480 yards. The drive is blind to a fairway that slopes severely from left to right. Heavy rough will gather anything too far to the right so it pays to aim your drive to the left and hopefully your reward will be a good lie and a clear view of the entrance to a green that sits in the shadow of the clubhouse.

The par-five tenth runs parallel to the first and then there is a quartet of par fours including the thirteenth which

Dalmahoy has developed into one of the East of Scotland's premier country clubs offering fishing, clay-pigeon shooting, squash, horse-riding, archery, dry-skiing and swimming facilities.

is one of Brian Anderson's favourites. The trees create the illusion that the green is nearer than it actually is and many an unsuspecting player has under-clubbed – and landed in the bunkers.

The fifteenth is a 139-yard par three. It may be short, but the bunkers are particularly well-placed here to catch anything other than a well-placed shot.

The sixteenth is reckoned by some to be the best hole on the course. A lake runs along the right but as there is a line of bunkers between the fairway and the lake, only a remarkably bad tee shot will land in the water. You must play to the right, though, because the ground is uneven to the left and the green is set at an angle that gives an easier line from the right: a broad gully that has to be carried adds an extra challenge.

Large bunkers are a feature of Dalmahoy. Many of them are designed so that the golfer who finds himself in one of them will always have a shot.

In 1981, Brian Barnes drove the green at the next – a par four, over 300 yards long – thus avoiding the danger that lurks left and right.

The eighteenth is yet another par four. At 290 yards it's not long, but the driving area is narrow and not only is the two-tier green well-protected, but with the majestic clubhouse behind it, it is easy to loose concentration when playing your approach shot.

The West Course is shorter but it's no pushover. There's one five and four threes in the par-69 eighteen holes. Accurate driving is essential and most holes are short enough to make a seven- or eight-iron the club to choose for the second shot. But if your drive strays there's typically doughty Scottish rough, water hazards, trees and, of course, bunkers to contend with.

9th HOLE: 480 yards, par 5

This hole dog-legs to the right and with the fairway also sloping in that direction, it is paramount that the tee shot be positioned down the left side of the fairway.

There is a large bunker or the right side of the hole where the fairway turns right, which catches many golfers who try to cut off the corner in the hope that they will reach the green with their second shot.

From the perfect position on the left side of the fairway, it is possible for the long hitters to reach the green in two, but to do so the ball must not only thread its way between trees on both sides of the fairway, it must also avoid two large bunkers that lie short of the green.

A more conservative approach would be to take a medium iron for accuracy which will stop short of the fairway bunkers, leaving a straight-forward third shot with a lofted iron to a fairly small green, guarded by a solitary bunker on the right side.

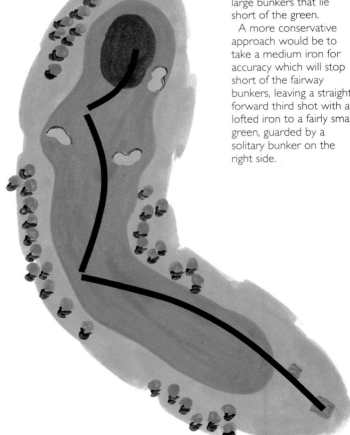

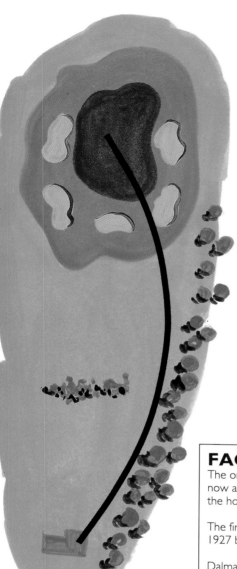

15th HOLE:
139 yards, par 3

This is a good, solid par three, which although not long, nevertheless demands correct club selection and pin-point accuracy with the tee shot.

The green is heavily bunkered and recent renovation work on the bunkers here have made it even more essential to make sure you hit the putting surface. Miss the green and you could be faced with an even tougher shot as the heavy rough makes it difficult to judge the recovery shot precisely.

Once you get to the green you will still face a few problems, for this is one of the more difficult putting surfaces on the course to read correctly.

GOLFER'S VIEW

Situated only seven miles from the centre of Edinburgh, Dalmahoy is a pleasant parkland course which also offers outstanding hotel and leisure facilities. The course, although not too demanding from the front tees, has many excellent holes, and when stretched to its full length Dalmahoy is long enough to have hosted several top professional tournaments.

Dalmahoy is currently developing its own golf academy and also offers a comprehensive range of leisure facilities.

16th HOLE:
416 yards, par 4

This is an outstanding par four where you cannot take the chance of hitting your tee shot too far for fear of the ball running into the deep quarry which is very much in play for the first shot.

The approach shot in perfect conditions is usually played with a medium iron, but if the wind gets up it can take a fairway wood or even a driver, to fly the ball all the way to the heart of the green.

The putting surface is well guarded by two large bunkers in front and the green also slopes quite considerably, making putting difficult.

FACT FILE

The original country house at Dalmahoy, now a country club, was built in 1735 as the home of the Earl of Morton.

The first golf course here was redesigned in 1927 by Open champion, James Braid.

Dalmahoy was the first British club to erect spectator stands and a tented village for a major competition, when it hosted the 1962 Senior Service tournament, won by Neil Coles.

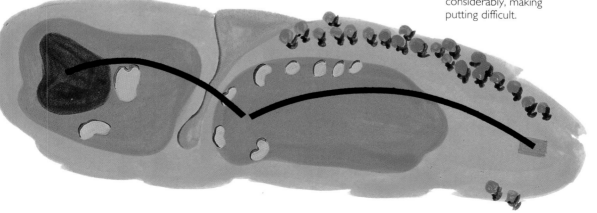

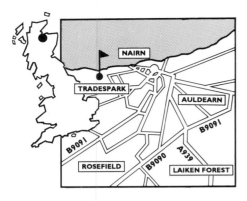

NAIRN

"Where else in the world is the line from the first tee to a mountain sixty miles away?"

SAM McKINLEY: Professional, Nairn.

Nairn is a genuine golf links built within sight and sound of the sea, thick with the heather, whins and burns golfers expect to find in such a location. There are few courses where the sea is a greater hazard. Willie Whitelaw, the politician whose 73 shot during a junior championship was not bettered for more than fifty years, has observed that it is possible to drive into the sea from the tees at each of the first seven holes. 'I know because I have!'

But it's not just the sea and the other typical hazards of a seaside links course that make Nairn such a challenge. It is not a long course – at 6,436 yards (a par 71) there are longer ones in Scotland, but the wind which is a law unto itself here can make a mockery of yardage. Golfers can battle against it for the front nine holes only to find that when they reach the turn, it has changed and they have to play into it on the way home!

It's a driver's course: good, long, straight hitting is one of the keys to conquering it. You line up your drive on the first tee with the extreme left peak of the Five Sisters of Kintail some 60 miles distant and usually visible! The sea runs alongside the right for most of the first nine holes.

The first hole, appropriately enough called, 'Sea' is a 400-yard par four. The second with its tee a few feet from the beach, is 74 yards longer. A dry ditch crosses the fairway and there are bunkers along the right of the driving area and around the green.

The third hole is a shortish 377-yard long par four: the fourth a 145-yard long par three. It's called 'Bunker'. Perhaps 'Sand' would be a better name because if you avoid one of the bunkers but land your mid-iron too far left of the green you will find yourself on the beach.

The 378-yard, par-four fifth hole is called 'Nets': you'll need one to fish your ball out of the sea if you drive too far to the right! Too far to the left and there's a bunker waiting to trap your ball. A short second shot is likely to land in a largish fairway cross bunker. There's also a semi-circle of sandtraps around the front of the two-tiered green. Good distance judgment is essential if you are to make par here.

The sixth is a difficult-to-make par-three. It's only 183 yards long but the heather and gorse bushes start to grow in profusion here, and the contour of the hole tends to throw off badly placed shots.

The seventh is a par five, a few yards short of 500 yards. With a typical dead-pan sense of humour the Scots have named the hole, 'Long!'

A par four may look on the cards for most golfers at the 330-yard eighth hole, but after driving onto a fairway of extravagant width, they are faced with a pitch over a cavernous bunker to a green that slopes down to the back from which the ball seems to gather speed as it heads for the long grass and the whins.

The ninth is a few yards longer than the one before but it's probably slightly easier to make a par four here.

GOLFER'S VIEW

Nairn is a superb seaside golf course situated some twenty miles to the east of Inverness. The course, laid out along the shoreline of the Moray Firth, is both scenically spectacular and an exciting challenge to play.

The opening six holes are all played close to the sea and many of the fairways at Nairn run between avenues of vibrant yellow gorse bushes which can intimidate the golfer from the tee.

Like all true links courses, the fairways here are firm and the greens fast, and well-positioned fairway bunkers are another outstanding feature of the course.

Two views of Nairn. Anyone who has coped with the wind at the 325-yard, par-four ninth hole at Nairn (bottom) will appreciate why it is called, 'The Icehouse'.

This is despite the fact that after a brief respite from the wind at the eighth, you are playing into it again here.

The 500-yard tenth is a par five called 'Cawdor'. It's not too hard to make a par here: and a par three at the 161-yard eleventh should be within the reach of most who aim for it.

The twelfth is a par four, 445 yards long. Good, straight, firm hitting is required here and assuming you miss the gorse bushes that avenue the fairway, and the bunker about 250 yards out, a nine-iron should see you onto the elevated green if the wind is with you.

There's an elevated green at the next hole, too, another par four a few yards shorter than the twelfth. Out-of-bounds bordered by bushes and heather is on both sides.

If your second shot is short, the ridge that runs across the green will send the ball back in your direction!

Another awkward ridge runs across the fourteenth green making a par three at this 206-yard hole quite a challenge to meet.

The next three holes are all par fours at 309 yards, 418 yards and 361 yards respectively. A dry ditch awaits a loose second shot at the sixteenth and at the seventeenth your approach shot is quite likely to plop into the Alton Burn meandering in front of the green.

The left side of the eighteenth fairway is thick with bunkers and there are more sandtraps cleverly arranged to catch those who play too far to the right. But with a decent wind, it is more than possible to get on the

putting surface in two and the chance of a birdie.

Nairn was one of the first towns to arrange a Golf Week when enthusiasts can pay to enjoy a week's accommodation, green fees and tuition from professionals. (Henry Cotton, Dai Rees and Max Faulkener have all coached here.) With two eighteen-hole courses (the other is Nairn Dunbar Golf Club) and a splendid nine-hole course (The Newton) to enjoy, the Golf Week offers those who do not have too many chances to play a typical links course the opportunity to do so.

Like most links courses, Nairn is flat, but on a clear day it offers breathtaking views as well as some of the best links golf in Scotland, if not the British Isles.

12th HOLE:
445 yards, par 4

There is trouble both on the left and right here. You have to hit the tee shot straight. There are gorse bushes along the fairway and a bunker on the left at 247 yards which can catch a well-struck tee shot. The second shot depends on the wind: downwind you can take a nine-iron but against the wind it is very difficult to reach the elevated green. You are above the green for your shot to it.

13th HOLE:
435 yards, par 4

There is trouble both left and right on this hole. You can go out-of-bounds on both sides. Just by the out-of-bounds there are bushes and heather. You need to take a driver from the tee. The green is in range of the second shot downwind. The green is elevated with a ridge across it and if you are short, your ball runs back down the hill.

FACT FILE

Nairn, long recognized as one of the finest seaside courses in the north of Scotland, was first laid out in 1887 and altered some years later by Old Tom Morris.

A feature of Nairn is the first six holes which all run alongside the sea, and the huge gorse bushes that avenue many of the fairways.

Both the Scottish Amateur and Professional championships have been played at Nairn, as have the Scottish Ladies', on seven occasions, and the British Ladies', once.

14th HOLE:
206 yards, par 3

This is an awkward green. It has a big ridge running right across it: it's four yards deep and drops into a gulley. Downwind, the tee shot can be a six-iron or against it, a driver. Most players would be delighted to make a par here and on the previous two holes.

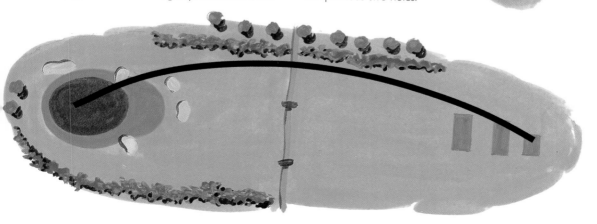

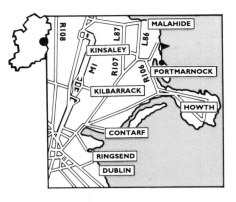

PORTMARNOCK

"You cannot fight the wind by trying to hold the ball up. You must play the wind by aiming off and letting the ball come back on line. Don't try to beat it."

JOEY PURCELL: *Professional, Portmarnock.*

Many of the finest links courses have only a fleeting acquaintance with the sea. Low-lying fairways are often shut out from a view of the water by giant sand hills. The quiet murmur of sea on sand on a still summer day or the persistent roar of breakers in the wilder days of spring and autumn is a constant reminder of the essential closeness of sea and links – but the golfer is often cocooned in a world of turf, sand and sky.

Not so at Portmarnock.

These famous links, which have played host to the Irish Open, the World Cup, the British Amateur and, most recently, the Walker Cup, are laid out on a peninsular of land that juts southwards into Dublin Bay. In its early days the course could only be reached by boat at high tide – now a finger of road offers a more conventional approach.

With the Irish Sea to the east, Dublin Bay to the west and the meeting of the two around its southern tip – just off the third and fourth fair-

ways Portmarnock is almost literally surrounded by water.

This not only improves the views, but leaves the course totally exposed to winds from all directions. And wind is the biggest threat to a good score at Portmarnock.

Although several holes run through shallow valleys between the dunes, they are not large enough to offer any real protection from the elements. Portmarnock is a wonderfully isolated natural golf course which nature does its best to protect.

With the prevailing south-westerly wind giving a helping hand it is possible to get up in two at the 586-yard sixth hole. But in a cold easterly breeze it takes three good woods – and often a little bit of something else – to reach the green.

The infamous long par-three fifteenth sometimes demands a tee shot starting out over the out-of-bounds beach to bring the ball back on target. The next day it can be a struggle to flight the ball far enough the other way to stop it being blown into the sea.

Set on a peninsula that juts into Dublin Bay, it is impossible for any golfer who plays Portmarnock not to know that he is playing a seaside links course. Not just any seaside links course, but one of the best on offer. The three pictures seen here show only a part of this beautiful, 7,100-yard course.

FACT FILE

Measuring over 7,000 yards from the championship tees, Portmarnock is one of the longest courses used to stage championship golf.

Within two years of its foundation in 1894, Portmarnock hosted the Irish Open Amateur championship, won that year by John Ball.

Portmarnock hosted the first Irish Open, won by George Duncan who received the first prize of £100, donated by members.

Because the championship course and its excellent back-up nine holes are laid out across, rather than along, the narrow peninsular, no more than two holes in succession play in the same direction – unlike many of the older links courses which have nine out and nine back.

The subtleties of tee shot line and angle of approach to greens are therefore enhanced, constantly changing and demanding of continuous thought in order to stay in touch with par.

Portmarnock professional Joey Purcell offers this advice: "It helps if you can punch the ball low, but the conditions here can be very strong. You cannot fight the wind by trying to hold the ball up. You must play the wind by aiming off and letting the ball come back on to line. Don't try to beat it."

The wind was the determining factor when the inaugural Irish Open was played at Portmarnock in 1927, members having donated the £100 prize fund. Competitors were severely battered by a force-nine gale in the final round. Only Scotsman George Duncan broke 80 and his incredible 72 earned him the title.

The championship has now become a major event on the European circuit, attracting top-class international fields. Recent winners at Portmarnock have been Ben Crenshaw, Seve Ballesteros, Bernhard Langer, Ian Woosnam and Jose Maria Olazabal. In 1987 Langer set a record unlikely to be equalled for many years. With an incredible display of precision golf he returned rounds of 67, 68, 66, 68 for a 19-under-par total of 269 to win by no less than ten shots.

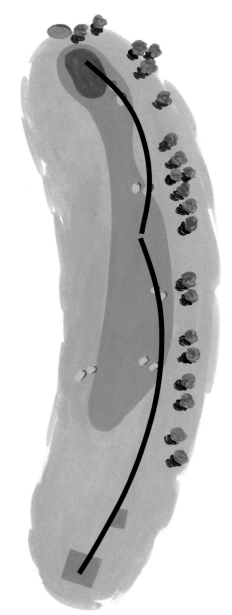

Ian Woosnam successfully defended his title in 1989 at the expense of Ireland's Philip Walton, who failed to hole a seven-foot putt on the final green which would have given him an outright win. He then had to endure a sudden-death decision and a few minutes later, as the two players again tackled the eighteenth as the first play-off hole, it was Woosnam's turn to hole from eighteen feet for a birdie to deny an Irish victory.

4th HOLE:
435 yards, par 4

This tough par four needs accurate, not just long hitting. The tee shot is aimed into a fairly generous fairway between two pairs of bunkers, but another matching pair on the right are very much in range.

Because the hole curves gently round to the left the ideal tee shot should be into the right half of the fairway – "a gentle fade," suggests Joey Purcell. "But don't overdo it, the rough down that side is fierce."

The second shot is usually a two-, three- or four-iron into a green protected by grassy mounds to the left and a couple of bunkers short and right. Getting the tee shot into the correct position on the fairway is critical in setting up the angle to the green. Even with a helping westerly breeze it is never an easy green to hit.

And although the putting surface itself looks flat it is full of little hollows and crowns and unexpected borrows. It is always a difficult green to read and from off the green it is hard to get a chip or pitch shot close enough to save par.

GOLFER'S VIEW

Portmarnock is one of the world's great courses. It combines wonderful scenery with some truly spectacular golf holes. Even from the front tees, when the wind blows the average golfer will be required to play his best golf to return a respectable score.

The bunkering, both in the fairways and around the greens, is fairly severe and it is often advisable to play short of the trouble from the tee, even if this means playing a longer second shot to reach the green.

8th HOLE:
368 yards, par 4

There is only one bunker on this hole, but it is positioned with such precision at the left entrance to the green that it determines both the tee shot and approach.

The hole turns left into the prevailing south-west wind and there are two good reasons for avoiding the left side of the fairway. A tee shot which successfully lands on the cut grass on this route means a second shot to the deep, narrow green must carry the lone bunker. And just off the fairway at driving distance is a large hollow covered in deep rough.

The perfect tee shot should be aimed as close to the right edge of the fairway as possible and this creates an angle from which to play the second shot down the length of the green, keeping the bunker as far out of play as possible.

The second shot can vary enormously depending on the strength and direction of the wind but it takes a firm, positive stroke to hold the ball on the slightly raised green, which falls away on all sides.

It is not easy to make controlled recovery shots up the slopes to the green at this seemingly innocent par four.

15th HOLE:
191 yards, par 3

This notorious par-three has tested the world's greatest players. In 1960, when the World Cup was still called the Canada Cup, Arnold Palmer hit one of the finest shots of his incredible career, flighting a three-iron across a strengthening wind to finish three feet from the hole. Yet such are the problems of putting on this exposed green that he failed to touch the hole with his putt. Nevertheless he and Sam Snead went on to win by eight clear shots.

The entrance to the green is flanked by bunkers and the ground drops away into rough on both sides, climbing again on the right to a small ridge before falling away steeply to the out-of-bounds beach.

The wind is almost always across the hole, either the prevailing southwesterly which pushes the ball towards the beach, or from the colder northeast in winter when it lashes waves against the shore. Professional Joey Purcell reckons the most effective shot is a punched long-iron under the wind aimed at the right half of the green – "the most dangerous side but the best angle to get the ball into the green."

The club golfer should aim for the back of the green. If he can hit it far enough, at least he has ruled out the bunkers at the front from this hole's list of dangers.

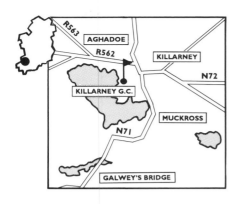

KILLARNEY

"As a place to play golf, Killarney must be the most beautiful in the world."

SIR PETER ALLEN

Golf has been played at Killarney since 1891 when a nine-hole course designed by former Open champions, Harry Vardon and Alex Herd was constructed on a site called Deer Park.

The land was owned by the Earl of Kenmare. And the fifth Earl, Valentine, Viscount of Castlerosse, then a famous Fleet Street gossip columnist for the London *Daily Express*, decided to move the club to another site, due to the growing popularity of golf in the area.

250 acres of land were found by the side of a lake, and this provided a superb setting for the new course and the Killarney Golf Club Ltd. was officially formed. Something of an eccentric in his later years, Lord Castlerosse hired Sir Guy Campbell to design the course, assisted by the late Henry Longhurst. However, the Earl insisted on contributing several of his own ideas to the design, including planting fully-grown trees in the middle of two greens.

It is also rumoured that His Lordship thought about inviting the Irish Air Force to use the site for bombing practice, in order to save money on digging bunkers.

Castlerosse succeeded his father in 1939, which was the same year that the course was opened for play. And despite the rumours about his eccentricity, it is said that by changing the design of several holes and building five new ones, he changed Killarney from a good golf

The tenth hole at Killarney's Killeen course is a par three, 170 yards long.

With vistas such as the one above, it is easy to see why so many golfers consider the Killeen and O'Mahoney's Point courses at Killarney as among the most beautiful in the world.

course, into a great one.

Sadly Castlerosse died in 1943 and never saw the full fruits of his labours. In 1971 Killarney was eventually developed into a superb 36-hole complex, when land purchased by the Irish Tourist Board in 1968 was combined with a stretch of reclaimed marsh land to create the second eighteen holes.

Today, Killarney is known throughout the world and some of the holes, on both the Killeen and O'Mahoney's courses have been listed among the best in the world. And although the late Castlerosse received much acclaim for his efforts, the work of Sir Guy Campbell has stood the test of time and the last few holes at O'Mahoney's Point are among the most delightful in the whole of Ireland. That great American golfing legend, Gene Saracen felt that the 18th in particular,

The par-four fourth hole is 355 yards long with the back tee sitting in the lake.

FACT FILE

A nine-hole course was first established at Killarney in 1891.

The club moved to Lough Leane in 1936, the new course being designed by Sir Guy Campbell and modified by Viscount Castlerosse.

The Irish Amateur Championship was first held at Killarney in 1949. Four years later the Home Internationals were played here for the first time.

The second eighteen-hole course at Killarney, O'Mahoney's Point, opened in 1971.

Killeen is 6,798 yards long: O'Mahoney's Point plays 6,667 yards.

was, "one of the most memorable holes in golf."

Scenic splendour apart, Killarney is also a fine test of golf. And the outstanding design means that while experienced golfers are tested to the limit of their skills, the high handicapper can also find a route around the course which although equally testing, is more within the scope of their more limited abilities.

Over the years, Killarney has attracted many top class events and the course hosted the Irish Amateur championship in 1949. The first two professional events held at Killarney were won by the late Eric Brown. And it was here that Gary Player made his first tournament appearance outside South Africa.

In more recent times, Killarney hosted the 1991 Carroll's Irish Open when the winner of this prestigious event was England's Nick Faldo.

3rd HOLE: 195 yards, par 3

This is a very difficult par three to meet so early in the round and with the water cutting so far into the front of the putting surface, the golfer faces additional pressure to ensure that he hits the green.

With a carry of 160 yards required to reach the front of the green it will take a solid four- or five-iron shot from the better player to fly the ball all the way to the heart of the green.

However when the prevailing right to left winds get up, it will take a long iron or in the case of the shorter hitter, a solid hit with a fairway wood to clear the water and find the fairly flat green protected on the left by a pot bunker.

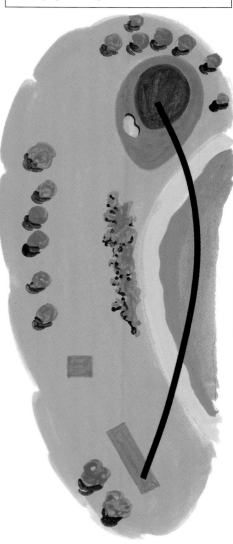

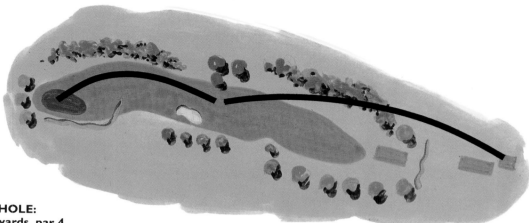

8th HOLE:
378 yards, par 4

This is the tightest driving hole on the course and the tee shot played from the high tee must find the fairway in order to give the golfer the best opportunity of reaching the green with a five- or six-iron approach shot.

A new bunker on the left side of the fairway narrows the landing area even more and another, built especially for the 1991 Irish Open, guards the front right side of a green that has water running alongside the left side and front.

The green is small but comparatively flat.

GOLFER'S VIEW

Several of the holes run around the famous lake at Killarney, one of Ireland's most beautiful inland courses where the lush green fairways and the velvet greens are a joy to play and putt on.

Although not as exposed to the winds as the links courses, Killarney is still a fine test of golf, calling for straight hitting from the tee and a sound judgment of distance on the approach shots to greens which are reasonably flat, but which are also well bunkered.

The short holes are excellent, with the 195-yard third the most demanding as the green is guarded in front by the waters of the lake.

16th HOLE:
550 yards, par 5

Played from the back tee, this testing three shotter requires a good drive and a long fairway wood second, to get anywhere near the green.

A new bunker on the right, at around driving range for the good player, ensures that the desire for length must be tempered with accuracy. And with large bunkers guarding the front of the green, anyone attempting to get home in two shots will have to fly the ball all the way to the putting surface.

There is also trouble short left of the green in the shape of trees which will catch a hooked second shot, Meanwhile if you miss the fairway on the right side then you have no chance of reaching the green.

This hole is a true three shotter, which even the top professionals must treat with the utmost respect.

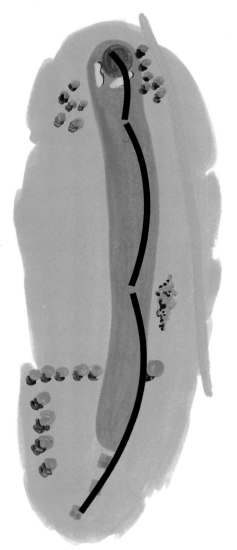

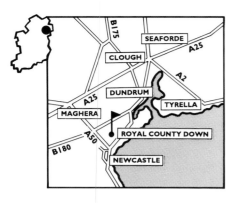

ROYAL COUNTY DOWN

"The toughest course in the British Isles and second only to Pine Valley as the severest golf course in the world."

SIR PETER ALLEN

Set against the backdrop of the Mountains of Mourne, Royal County Down is one of the most spectacular courses in a country which abounds with courses famous the world over for their unforgettable scenic beauty.

A true links course in every sense of the word, Royal County Down owes its evolution as much to the hand of nature, as it does to the endeavours of man. For if ever there was a natural site for a golf course, it is here, where the waters of Dundrum Bay meet the rolling, sandy links land that runs along this wonderful stretch of golfing territory on the east coast of Northern Ireland.

Royal County Down offers golfers not only spectacular scenery, but also a host of exhilarating challenges in the shape of holes which twist and turn, with the emerald green fairways often winding their way between huge sand dunes, many of which are covered in vivid yellow gorse bushes. These huge sand hills funnel the wind from the sea across the course, constantly changing the playing conditions and on certain occasions rendering the most accurate yardage charts obsolete.

On these occasions, it can take a full-blooded long iron, or even a wood, to reach the putting surface on a short par-

three, while a smooth drive and a lofted approach shot can put you through the green at a 400-yard plus, par-four hole when the wind is blowing from behind you.

The Mountains of Mourne offer a stunning backdrop to this wonderful links course.

Designed in 1898 by Old Tom Morris, the opening three holes at Royal County Down run hard against the shore line of Dundrum Bay, before turning inland. However there is not a single hole on the course where the wind is not a significant factor and to score well on this testing layout, requires a

sound long game and a deft touch, both on and from around the greens.

The first six holes at Royal County Down make up one of the most testing opening stretches you are likely to find anywhere the game is played. And if you can negotiate the deep fairway bunkers from the tee, flight your approach

One of the toughest
courses in the world,
Royal County Down
is a great test for the
golfer.

1st HOLE:
500 yards, par 5

This treacherous par five plays directly alongside the sea and must rate as one of the most testing opening holes in the Emerald Isle.

With gorse bushes on the left and a large sand hill guarding the right side of the fairway, it is essential to start your round at Royal County Down with a long, straight drive. Accuracy is again the key to the second shot, as the fairway narrows considerably around the landing area, with a large bunker waiting to gather any mis-hit second shot which leaks to the right.

The green at this opening hole, like all the other putting surfaces on the course, is fast and firm. In this instance it is also very narrow and measures over 40 yards from front to back, putting the onus on correct club selection and accurate ball striking.

shots on the wind, read the subtle borrows on the greens and find the deftness of touch required to roll thirty-foot approach putts stiff, you might just be able to match par over this demanding opening section, one of the most testing there is.

Although the course can be stretched to play at just under 7,000 yards from the championship tees, Royal County Down is no monster. And the fact that there are five blind tee shots and several approach shots where the green is virtually out of view, does not lessen in any way the enjoyment of playing this great seaside course. On the contrary, such shots only serve to heighten the anticipation for what lies ahead on this superb course.

Played from the members' tees, on a fine summer's day with just enough breeze to ruffle the flags, Royal County Down is a golfing experience to be treasured and enjoyed as often as possible.

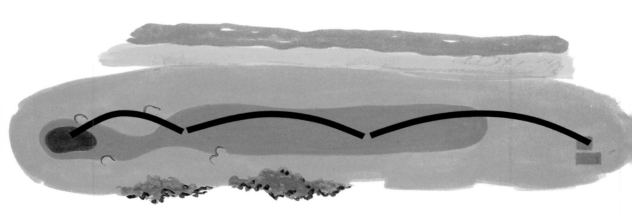

3rd HOLE:
473 yards, par 4

From the medal tee, this is perhaps the most demanding par-four hole on the course. There are two bunkers on the left and one on the right at around the 230 yard mark which threaten the tee shot. And some 70 yards farther on, the hole narrows dramatically, leaving only a thin neck of fairway to thread the ball through.

From this point the hole runs between the sand hills with no fewer than seven more bunkers to be avoided, in order to reach the putting surface in regulation.

The second shot, depending on the weather conditions, can vary between a middle iron and a full-blooded wood. But whatever the club required, the shot must be accurate, to find and hold this small green which is less than 30 yards deep.

GOLFER'S VIEW

With the backdrop of the magnificent Mountains of Mourne, Royal County Down is famous the world over for its magnificent scenery. The fairways, laid out alongside Dundrum Bay, run between giant sand dunes which can funnel a par-four hole into a three-shot monster.

The best policy for the average golfer to adopt when the wind blows hard on this great links course, is to forget about par and simply enjoy the challenge of the course and the magnificent setting.

FACT FILE

Royal County Down has featured among the top twelve courses in the world.

The original course was designed by Old Tom Morris in 1898. It was given permission to style itself as Royal in 1908, the year that Harry Vardon updated the course.

In the final of the 1933 Irish Amateur championship held here, Eric Fiddian twice holed in one — and still lost.

In 1970, Royal County Down saw Michael Bonallack complete a hat-trick of victories in the Amateur championship.

4th HOLE:
217 yards, par 3

Played from the high back tee and into the wind, this monster par three can be as much as a full-blooded driver for the accomplished player and virtually unreachable for the average golfer.

With no fewer than eight bunkers guarding the approach to the green, the ball must be carried all the way to the putting surface, which is both narrow and long. And although there is a small apron immediately in front of the green, any ball which lands well short of this area will need the luck of the Irish to avoid finishing in the sand.

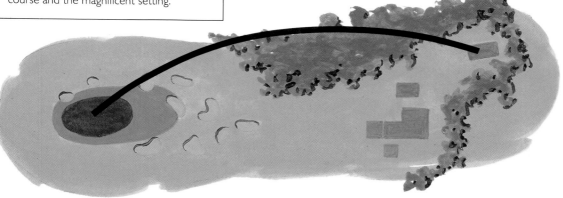

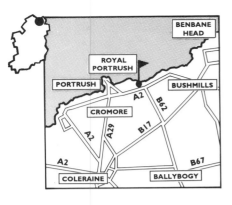

ROYAL PORTRUSH

"Portrush is a course which is not too difficult when the weather is fine. But when the wind starts to blow, you had better come prepared to work to make a decent score."

DAVID STEVENSON: *Professional, Portrush.*

Whenever there is talk about the best golf courses in the world, it is a safe bet that Royal Portrush will be among the first one or two names that are put forward.

Founded in 1888, Portrush became Royal Portrush in 1895, thanks to the patronage of The Prince of Wales, who was later to become King Edward VII. The course originally began in the town of Portrush, with the first hole situated in front of the clubhouse and the first green laid out in front of the old Metropole Hotel. The layout then continued on past The Tavern, which was a favourite spot to stop for refreshments before carrying on with the round. The course then turned back towards the town again and the final green was beside the clubhouse.

The world-famous Giant's Causeway is only a few miles from Portrush and to the west is the River Bann along with the superb links courses at Portstewart and Castle rock; the former being a pre-qualifying course for the 1951 Open, on the only occasion in its history that the

Even on a sunny day the wind can whip up the flag and usually has to be taken into consideration.

The bumpy hillocks and deep traps around many of the greens can easily catch out a wayward approach shot.

championship has ever been played outside mainland Britain.

The eccentric Max Faulkner was the winner on that occasion by two shots from Antonio Cerda. Faulkner was so confident of victory that when he was asked for his autograph prior to playing the final round he signed; "Max Faulkner, Open champion." Faulkner's win at Royal Portrush was to be the last home victory for eighteen years until a young Tony Jacklin took the title at Royal Lytham in 1969.

Many other major international events have been played at Portrush, including the Amateur championship, which was won by Irishman Joe Carr who thrashed American Bob Cochran, eight and seven in the final.

The course gained international status for the first time in 1895 when it staged the British Ladies' championship, won that year by Lady Margaret Scott.

The Dunluce course, which is the more famous of the two courses at Portrush, underwent some major re-design work in the late 1920s which was carried out by Harry Colt, one of the world's leading golf course architects. And when the work was finally completed in 1932, Mr

Colt presented his bill for the sum of £3,200, a fortune in those days.

The only further changes to the Dunluce course took place in 1946 when the club was forced to change the first and eighteenth holes.

The first tee on the Dunluce course is one of the few places on the course where the golfer is sheltered from the wind which often blows in from the Atlantic. However the prevailing left to right breeze often adds to the problems on this hole and with out-of-bounds running all the way down both sides of the fairway, the golfer must give his full attention to the first shot of the round on this testing par-four opening hole.

The course rises and falls as it winds its way between the

huge sand hills and there is rough and heather just waiting to claim any ball that errs from the correct line. After a rather gentle start, the course reveals its true character and the stretch of five holes running from the third to the seventh is among the most demanding on the whole of the course.

However, there is also a more generous side to Portrush, and the course offers the chance to redeem dropped shots by offering birdie opportunities at the final two holes of the first nine. And even when the golf course does appear to be gaining the upper hand, there are always the spectacular views out over the sea and across the lovely Antrim countryside to provide the golfer with another burst of inspiration to rekindle his enthusiasm.

Measuring 6,772 yards, Portrush can be a golfing heaven or a wind-swept hell, depending on the mood of the elements. However the layout is fair, the turf superb and the greens comparatively flat with few hidden borrows. With so much to offer and situated in such a magnificent setting, it is little wonder that Royal Portrush is generally accepted by most profession-als as being among the top twenty courses in the world.

The drive and pitch thirteenth par four, has a slightly raised green.

7th HOLE:
420 yards, par 4
This is perhaps the best par four on the course, The tee shot must be long and straight to hold a fairway that is one of the narrowest on the Dunluce course.

There is a well placed bunker guarding the right side of the fairway and even if this can be avoided, the golfer will still be left with a testing approach shot to an elevated green which has two large bunkers in front of the putting surface just waiting to snare an under-clubbed approach shot.

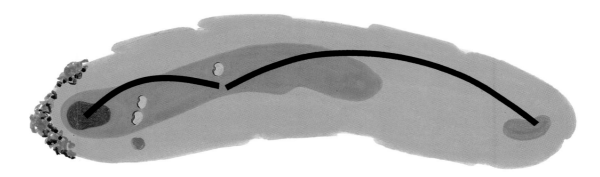

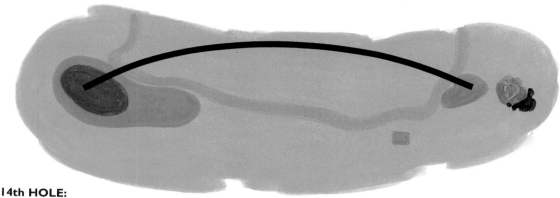

14th HOLE:
205 yards, par 3

Aptly named, 'Calamity', this is one of the most famous and also most frightening short holes in golf. Played from an elevated tee, and often exposed to the full force of the elements, this 'short' hole can require anything between a middle iron and a full hit with a driver, to reach the green.

There are no bunkers around the putting surface, however if the tee shot is short or off line to the right, the ground falls steeply away and the ball will finish at the bottom of a deep ravine from where it will take a great shot to find the green and a miracle to save par.

While the brave may elect to hit straight at the flag by flying the corner of the ravine, a more sensible approach for the higher handicapper would be to try to land the tee shot short and left of the putting surface and hope that the ball will roll on.

GOLFER'S VIEW

The Dunluce course hosted the Open championship in 1951, the only time it has been played in Ireland.

As you would expect with a course which has staged the Open, the layout is demanding, even in calm conditions. And although the opening two holes are not too testing, the next five are extremely difficult and few golfers, regardless of their level of ability, will be able to play this stretch in level par.

The short holes are superb and you will find few to match the fearsome 205-yard fourteenth – aptly named 'Calamity'. Yet despite having many difficult holes, the course is an inspiration to play and offers a wonderful challenge to the average golfer.

17th HOLE:
517 yards, par 5

Once again the golfer is faced with the challenge of hitting a long, straight tee shot to a very narrow fairway, with a well placed bunker on the right and more trouble lurking beyond, waiting to claim a sliced drive.

While a good tee shot can bring the green into range for the long hitters, there are three bunkers strategically placed short of the green to ensure that only a first-class shot will have any chance of reaching the green. For the shorter hitter, a solid three-wood second should finish short of the fairway bunker some 70 yards short of the green leaving a straightforward pitch to a long narrow green which has one bunker on the left and two on the right.

FACT FILE

Portrush is one of the oldest clubs in Ireland and the game was first played here in 1888.

In 1951 Royal Portrush became the only Irish golf club, to date, to host the Open championship which was won by Englishman, Max Faulkner.

Other international championships which have been played over the Dunluce course are; The British Ladies' Open in 1895, won by Lady Margaret Scott. And the British Amateur championship which was won by Joe Carr.

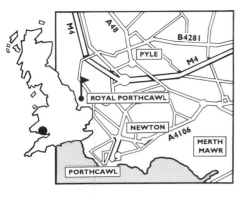

ROYAL PORTHCAWL

"If the first three holes are the most interesting, the finish from the thirteenth in is the sternest stuff."

PETER ALLIS

When a player of the calibre of Ian Woosnam tells you that a golf course is "a fair test for amateurs and professionals alike and that it is one of my favourite courses to play," then you tend to sit up and take notice.

The course Woosie speaks so highly of is Royal Porthcawl in Wales, and national pric'e aside, when you stand on the first tee and take in the magnificent scenery, as the sun reflects off the waters of the Atlantic

Ocean, it is not difficult to understand why Ian Woosnam is such a great admirer of this great links course on the Welsh coast.

One glance at the narrow green ribbons, which the locals refer to as the fairways, winding their way between huge sand dunes pitted with cavernous bunkers, and you quickly realise that this is a driver's course. You don't have to be in the Woosnam league when it comes to length from the tee, but you

had better be straight.

And the fact that there are a number of blind shots and that quite a few of the greens are elevated, only serves to further emphasise the need to hit the ball straight, and also the importance of picking exactly the right club for your approach shots.

Many people say that the par-four ninth at Royal Porthcawl is the finest hole on the course.

A typical links course, Royal Porthcawl offers some of the best golf in Britain.

Stepping onto the first tee, you cannot fail to be impressed by the Gower Peninsula on the right. And on the left, distant yet clearly outlined, is the north Devon coast. Ready for the challenge ahead, a glance at the scorecard might well induce a welcome boost in confidence, due to the fact that at only 326 yards the opening hole at Royal Porthcawl can hardly be described as intimidating.

However before you become too cocky, it might be as well to remember that the last time they experienced what the locals refer to as a "real blow", it took the pro's

shop and Secretary's office along with it. Still it is an ill wind, if you will excuse the pun, and the pro' shop has now been completely rebuilt and is once again well stocked, especially with very necessary golf balls.

Normally played into the prevailing wind, the first hole at Royal Porthcawl can play as benignly as a three wood and a pitch. On the other hand, should that breeze stiffen and you feel tempted to sacrifice accuracy for distance, an off-line hit with a driver will almost certainly bring the fairway bunkers that are well-positioned on both sides of the hole into play.

If the first hole leads you to believe that you are in for an easy passage, the next eight will quickly bring you to your senses, and possibly

your knees, depending on the strength of the wind, two 400-yards-plus par fours are followed by a testing par three which plays just under 300 yards. And unless you can thread your tee shot along the ribbon-thin fairway and avoid a series of fearsome bunkers on the fifth, you will be hard pushed to make your par, let alone entertain any frivolous thoughts you might have harboured about picking up a birdie on this testing par five.

Measuring only 166 yards in length, the par-three seventh hole does offer an obvious birdie opportunity providing, that is, you can avoid the six bunkers which surround the green which is a meagre twenty feet wide. The options are simple, pick the right club, hit the shot perfectly, and you will be putting for a birdie. On the other hand, miss the green and...well we will leave that to your imagination.

The homeward run is every bit as adventurous as the outward nine. Take the twelfth for example. On the card, this 476-yard, par five looks to be a definite birdie opportunity. However, once you discover that the tee shot is blind and requires a long carry over the rough, followed by a second blind shot, it soon becomes more a matter of thinking in terms of a hard-earned par.

As the holes continue to unfold, each with its own, individual character and challenge, it soon becomes clear that, scratch player or rabbit, Royal Portcawl has the power to inspire and frustrate, delight and demoralize, all in the course of playing a single hole.

Yet, as you return to the clubhouse and contemplate your round, you will find that the good shots and lucky

bounces tend to balance out the three putts and lost balls. For although challenging, the course is also fair. Later, as you once again enjoy the superb views from the windows of the warm and friendly clubhouse, you are already devising a strategy that will bring Porthcawl to its knees next time you renew the challenge with this magnificent Welsh course.

Cavernous bunkers such as this one are a feature of Royal Porthcawl.

2nd HOLE:
447 yards, par 4
This long par four runs parallel to the sea and is therefore subject to the full force of the wind, making it very difficult to reach the green in the regulation two shots.

The drive must be flown all of 200 yards in order to reach a hogs-back fairway and even when this is achieved, the golfer is still left with a long second shot to a green which is set hard by the sea.

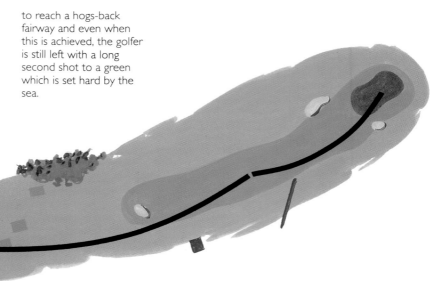

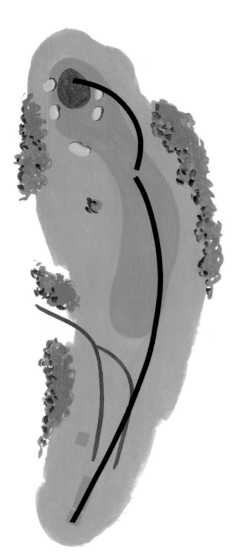

9th HOLE:
371 yards; par 4

This is a classic short par four with the complete hole visible from the tee.

The hole dog-legs to the left and the tee shot must finish on the narrow fairway, in order to set up the best approach to the green, usually played with a medium or short iron.

The green is heavily bunkered, slopes severely from back to front, and is probably the most difficult putting surface on the course to read.

GOLFER'S VIEW

Tight fairways and numerous well-placed bunkers put a premium on straight hitting at the excellent Welsh links course.

Set hard against the waters of the Atlantic Ocean as they sweep around the Gower Peninsula, the course offers spectacular views as far afield as the distant shores of north Devon.

Many of the greens have subtle burrows and are very well bunkered, especially the short holes where the penalties for missing the putting surface can be severe.

On a warm, sunny day with only a slight breeze, the firmness of the seaside fairways can add twenty yards to a good drive and a good touch with the putter can reap rewards on the fast and true greens.

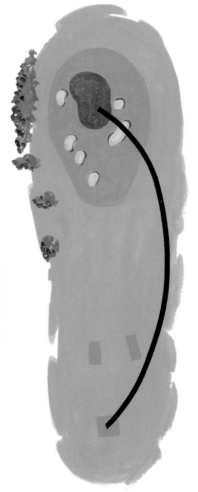

11th HOLE:
187 yards, par 3

This classic short hole plays due south and the green which sits on a shelf on roughly the same level as the tee, is surrounded by seven bunkers.

From the tee, the golfer gets the impression that the hole plays downhill. However this is not in fact the case, but instead an illusion created by the fact that the hole actually plays across a valley.

As the prevailing wind is from left to right, it is important not to let the tee shot drift left into the waiting bunkers.

FACT FILE

Royal Porthcawl first hosted a professional championship in 1932 when the Penfold Tournament was played here.

The British Amateur championship has been played at Porthcawl four times, as well as the Dunlop Masters once, in 1961, many Home Internationals, the Vagliano Trophy and British Ladies' championship.

Percy Allis, father of professional-turned-TV-commentator, Peter, started his career as a professional golfer when he joined Royal Porthcawl as assistant just after World War II had ended.

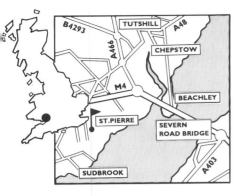

ST. PIERRE

"I wouldn't say it's a difficult course, but it's long."

DARREN TEAR: *Professional, St. Pierre.*

St. Pierre takes its name from the parish of St Pierre – a tiny churchyard and chapel that lies alongside the practice ground of this golf centre.

There are two courses here. The Old Course, a championship eighteen holes that has hosted the old Dunlop Masters and in recent years, the Epson Grand Prix of Europe. The New Course evolved from an initial nine-hole designed by Ken Brown.

Bill Cox extended them into the 5,672 yards, eighteen holes it is today. With a whimsical way all of its own it has earned the nickname 'The Wee Nasty!' perhaps because of the alarming rate at which golf balls disappear into the ditches that are features of the fourth, fifth, sixth and fourteenth holes. These are the holes that, according to Darren Tear are the good holes.

You can't hit a driver at the dog-leg-right fourth because the ditch is within driving distance, so you have to play a three wood or an iron off

The country club at St.Pierre (RIGHT) offers non-golfers a wide range of sport and leisure facilities.

The tenth hole at St. Pierre – a not-too-hard, par four.

the tee. And as the entrance to the green is very narrow it is difficult to get up in two.

The ditch is right in front of the green at the fifth so you have to use a five iron to carry the ball all the way to the putting surface.

The sixth is a 433-yard par four with out-of-bounds down the right. To make sure they don't land in it, most players aim to the left – and land up in the ditch there!

The ditch runs round the edge of the tree-encircled green at the par-five fifteenth.

The rest of the course,

according to the club professional, is quite easy. And on a beautiful spring day when the daffodils are in bloom it is also quite beautiful.

The three star holes of the Old Course are discussed in the diagrams. These are the first hole, a 576-yard par five: the fifteenth, a par-four 375 yarder: and the 237-yard, par-three eighteenth.

The fairways on the Old Course are fairly wide, the greens are well protected and there are a lot of big trees. The eleven-acre lake comes

into play at the tenth, fifteenth, seventeenth and eighteenth holes.

In 1987, Jeff Hawkes fought back against Sam Torrance from three down with four to play to reach the last hole all square. He pulled his tee shot against the out-of-bounds wall while Torrance left his just short of the green. But Hawkes' backhand second shot from an almost impossible lie hit the flagstick and came to rest four feet past. Torrance chipped up short and missed his putt. Hawkes holed out for a par

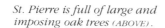

St. Pierre is full of large and imposing oak trees (ABOVE).

Jose Maria Olazabal looks on while Ian Woosnam tries to hole out at the third during the 1990 Epson Grand Prix.

three and the match.

In the next round, Hawkes dispensed with Seve Ballesteros. In the final he lost to Mats Lanner on the same eighteenth green where he

1st HOLE, 576 yards, par 5

The first hole is a very long par five. During the Epson Grand Prix, there's out-of-bounds on the right-hand side of the fairway. The professionals can get to the green in two, but they are two very good hits. Most amateurs are lucky to get down to the green in four.

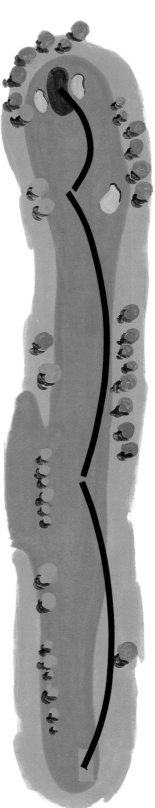

GOLFER'S VIEW

St. Pierre, situated a few miles from the Severn Bridge, offers a wonderful setting for golf. Although the course is long and testing the fairways are usually generously wide.

Over the past few years there has been a programme to improve the course and several alterations have created a more demanding layout.

Tree-lined fairways and well-manicured greens are a feature of the course and the luxury country club offers excellent accommodation and leisure facilities.

From the front tees, St. Pierre is short enough to offer the amateur several good birdie opportunities. However, be prepared to work hard for your par at the famous par-three closing hole where the tee shot must be played over a lake.

had devastated Torrance. The game is never over until the last ball is putted.

At either of the St. Pierre courses when you tee off at the first you will have some memorable golf ahead of you until you, too, putt out at the eighteenth.

FACT FILE

Opened in 1962 and designed by Ken Cotton, the two courses at St. Pierre are regarded as being among Britain's finest.

The land on which the course is built was once the site of the manor house where the crown jewels were stored during part of the Hundred Years War.

There are plans to floodlight St Pierre so that it can be played after dark.

Among the important tournaments played at St. Pierre have been the Dunlop Masters, the Curtis Cup matches against the United States and, in recent years, the Epson Grand Prix match-play tournament.

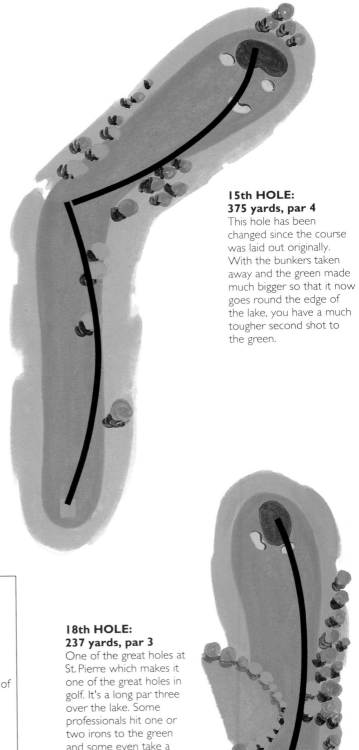

15th HOLE: 375 yards, par 4

This hole has been changed since the course was laid out originally. With the bunkers taken away and the green made much bigger so that it now goes round the edge of the lake, you have a much tougher second shot to the green.

18th HOLE: 237 yards, par 3

One of the great holes at St. Pierre which makes it one of the great holes in golf. It's a long par three over the lake. Some professionals hit one or two irons to the green and some even take a wood out. A three wood or a driver is the club most amateurs go for, but sometimes they just can't reach it at all with one shot. A four at this hole is not bad at all.

ALL ABOUT GOLF

*How to choose the equipment you
will need to play the game.
How to behave on the golf course.
The Rules explained.
A glossary of golfing terms from
address to yellow stake.*

GETTING STARTED

There's no need to fork out hundreds of pounds simply to play golf. Here are your basic needs.

Golf is a game you can start to learn as soon as you can walk and a sport you can continue to play as long as you can stand up.

Because of the effective handicapping system, beginners can compete on level terms with experienced players in a variety of competitions or merely for 50 pence and a lot of enjoyment.

If you want to play golf you will have an estimated fifty million friends around the world who share your sport and with whom you will have a great deal in common.

Having made the decision to take up the game, don't be tempted to rush to your local sports shop and spend a small fortune on a full set of clubs and expensive clothes endorsed by one of the big names. Before spending money on equipment, the best way to make a start in golf is to visit a driving range or public course where the game can be tried with hired clubs and wearing a pair of inexpensive trainers.

In this way it is possible to try out the game and test two or three types of club before making a final choice. Most golf professionals have a selection of second-hand clubs for sale and it is usually possible to take these to the practice ground before making a decision. This is not so easy with new clubs, but an increasing number of trial clubs are to be found in

The basic equipment necessary to enjoy the game need not cost a tiny fortune. With a half-set of good quality second-hand clubs, this player has kitted himself out for well under £200.

pro shops which does at least give the opportunity to try before you buy.

Over the past twenty years a great deal of research and development has gone into developing clubs aimed at making the game easier for the golfer who lacks the perfection of Nick Faldo, Seve Ballesteros and Ian Woosnam. These clubs have come to be known as 'game improvement'

clubs and as this soubriquet suggests a player can get a good result even from a shot which is not hit exactly off the middle of the club. This has been achieved by spreading the weight of the clubhead around the perimeter of the clubface rather than having it concentrated behind the centre of the face.

It is a line of research led by the makers of Ping golf clubs and subsequently followed by every clubmaker. The 'sweet spot' in the centre of the clubface, from which the best shots are hit, has been enlarged from about the size of a thumbnail to an area more like the dimensions of a standard golf ball.

The result is a much greater success rate for golfers whose swings do not always return the clubhead to the ball with pin-point accuracy. At least 90 per cent of golfers around the world would benefit from using clubs designed in this way. Many inexpensive models are now available and there is now a growing number of second-hand sets on the market. Among the clubs in the 'game improvement' range are the Mizuno Domino, the Wilson GE1200, Slazenger XTC, Titleist DTR, Spalding Topflite, McGregor CGI 800, Ram Lazer, Lynx Parallax and Dunlop Max 357. The beginner would be well advised to chose from the 'game improvement' range and leave the traditional 'blade clubs' which offer slightly more feel to the professionals and amateur golfers who have reached a reasonably high standard.

How the club looks to the player when he sets it behind the ball, is also important, and some golfers believe that the traditional shaped clubs are more pleasing to the eye. But traditional blade clubs are not so forgiving as the 'game improvement' models and require the ball to be struck flush from the middle of the club to produce consistently good, accurate shots.

It is not necessary to buy a full set of fourteen clubs in order to get started. Many experienced golfers carry only a half-set for normal, fun games, taking out the full set only for competition.

An ideal set for beginners would be a three-wood rather than a driver which can be difficult to use and best added later, four-, six- and eight-irons, wedge, sand wedge and putter.

If you decide to start with a part set of new clubs, be sure to check that the other clubs in the set are still available from the manufacturers in case you wish to make up a full set later.

The main sources of golf clubs and other equipment are High Street sports shops, the sports sections of large department stores, specialist golf shops, golf supermarkets and the golf professional at your local private or public course. You don't have to be a member of a golf club to buy equipment at the professional shop at the most convenient course.

Specialist golf shops and golf supermarkets offer a better selection than general sports shops and department stores, and at better prices, but as there is not a large number of them in the country a visit to one can mean a long journey for those who do not live in the south-east, the Midlands or close to one of the big cities.

Golf professionals find it difficult to match the low prices of the golf super-markets, but they usually

In game-improving clubs, the weight of the clubface is spread around the perimeter of the clubface (BELOW) rather than being concentrated in the middle as in traditional clubs and the sweet spot is about the size of a golf ball (BOTTOM).

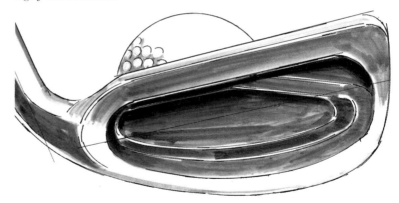

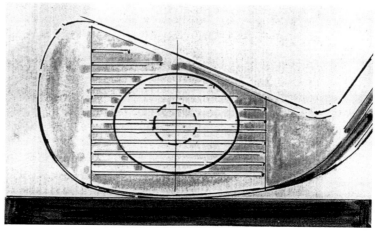

stock a good range at realistic prices. They usually have a practice ground where different clubs can be tried out. Do not be afraid to ask to do this before buying a club.

Professionals also have the experience to give advice on the clubs best suited to a customer's ability and physique. Many will adjust clubs to suit a player's requirements. And most will have the facility to repair damaged clubs.

Many specialist golf shops and professionals carry a large selection of second-hand woods, wedges and putters, clubs which are very much a personal preference. Such selections offer the beginner (and more experienced players) the chance to find clubs that suit both their games and their pockets.

Second-hand clubs often have worn grips. Good grips are essential if you want to play reasonably well, so it is well worth the price of having damaged grips replaced. If you can't afford to have all the clubs re-gripped at the same time, have half the clubs done one month and the other half the following month.

Expect to pay between £90 and £120 for a half set of good quality, second-hand clubs, about £100 for a half set of cheaper quality new clubs. A full set of good quality, second-hand ones cost from £140-£180, and the same number of cheaper quality, new clubs between £130 and £200. You can also find special deals—three woods, nine irons, a putter and a bag for around £200.

Your golf bag
You could pay £700 for a hand-crafted, leather bag of such enormous proportions that in times of hardship it

A good bag is an excellent investment: if you care for it properly, it could well last you all your playing days.

would house your entire family. There are many light-weight bags on the market costing from as little as £25. A good quality, eight-inch trolley bag can usually be obtained for less than £100.

Your bag should have a full-length pocket for an extra sweater or rain jacket. Some of the cheaper bags are not very well balanced and have short, inadequate straps. This can be a constant source of irritation, so make your selection very carefully.

Clothes
Your sweater and waterproof jacket should be quite loose: too tight and they will constrain your swing. Natural fibres are best, especially in hot weather, as they absorb perspiration unlike most man-made ones which can make you feel sticky and extremely uncomfortable.

Not long ago, all golf shoes were fitted with spikes but a modern development has been towards lightweight shoes with rubber pimples or ridges on the soles to give the necessary grip. One of the benefits is that you can step straight from the car on to the first tee, but they can lose much of their effective grip in wet conditions particularly if grass or mud gets packed into the indentations on the sole. In dry conditions trainers or tennis shoes can be perfectly adequate.

Moulded rubber spiked shoes, which are completely waterproof, are cheap to buy and effective in winter, but they are bad for the feet at warmer times of the year and are not recommended for regular wear. They cost around £20.

Good quality spikes or rubber-soled shoes are more expensive, costing between £30 and £40.

Avoid second-hand shoes.

Spiked golf shoes give better grip in damp conditions than shoes with rubber pimples or ridges on the soles.

Golf gloves

A golf glove will prevent the club from slipping in your hand. Suede-effect gloves cost around £3. All-weather synthetic ones start at £7.50. A leather glove will cost £10 or more.

Golf balls

Despite the fact that all golf balls look the same, there are tremendous differences in their construction and materials and it is very important that you get the one best suited to your individual requirements.

At £2 or more each, it would be crazy for a newcomer to golf to choose a ball favoured by the professionals. While these give the pro greater control, they have a skin so thin that one slight miss makes them unusable.

Tournament professionals will use a new ball every two or three holes. The ball they use will probably be of three-piece construction—a central core wrapped round with hundreds of yards of thin, stretched rubber and covered with a thin layer of balata. Leave these to the professionals or low handicap amateurs. Other three-piece wound balls have a Surlyn cover which is far more durable and cost from £1.60. But most amateur golfers will

Your golf glove should be as tight a fit as possible.

get more distance and much longer life from the two-piece balls – a solid core with a Surlyn cover – which cost from £1.30.

Slightly imperfect golf balls are sold off cheaply by manufacturers and are known as X-outs because the name of the ball is scored out with a row of Xs. Most are rejected because of a slight paint or cover imperfection but they are good value for people just starting the game. A new imperfect will cost around £1. However, you cannot use them in official competitions because they do not conform to R&A specifications. Cheapest of all are the lost and founds which most professional shops sell for around 50 pence.

Handicaps

The handicapping system allows all amateurs to play on an equal footing. Essentially, when two players with different handicaps play against each other, the player with the lower handicap sacrifices strokes to the other player. The number of strokes sacrificed depends on the difference between the two handicaps and the course over which they are playing. Handicapping can never be an exact science even in the golfing sense, never mind adjustments for hangovers and bad backs. The system now in use has been devised and refined to make it as likely as possible to contest a close match.

In order to establish a fair system of handicapping it is first necessary to apply some form of measuring system to the 1700-plus golf courses over which the game is played in Britain alone. This course rating is known as the Standard Scratch Score, the score which an on-form scratch player (a player with a zero handicap) is expected to achieve. The initial guide to the SSS is given by the total length of the course— between 6601 and 6800 yards giving an SSS of 72 for instance. Then a number of other factors which may increase or decrease the SSS are taken into consideration— the size of the greens, width of fairways, amount of bunkering, nearness of out-of-bounds areas and whether the course is either exposed to the wind or sheltered.

The handicaps of all players are based on the SSS of their home course and because the difficulty of that course has been reflected in its SSS, golfers from all parts of the country should have

X-outs may be imperfect but they are ideal for beginners whose lack of club control may cause them to damage the ball when they hit it.

handicaps which indicate their ability to play anywhere.

It is worth noting that the SSS is an overall course rating, not a total of individual hole assessments. Each hole is given a par figure, again based initially on length but adjusted for difficulty. A par-three hole may be any length up to a maximum of 250 yards, a par-four between 220-440 yards, and anything over 440 yards may be a par-five. In this way a narrow, 460-yard hole played uphill into the prevailing wind to a well-protected green may be given a par-five rating, while a wide, open, downhill 480-yard hole could be classed par-four. The total par figure and the SSS will not necessarily be the same.

Measurements of holes are taken from a distance-point six feet from the back of the medal tee to the centre of the green. Dog-leg holes are measured down the centre-line of the fairway. Men's back medal tees should be indicated by white tee boxes, men's forward medal tees by yellow boxes and ladies' tees by red boxes.

Only members of clubs affiliated to the National Council of Golf Unions can be given handicaps. In the first instance three cards must be marked and properly signed by a club member to qualify for an initial handicap. Any hole scores of more than two over par will be reduced to two over by the handicap committee and the best of these three scores will decide the handicap which will be equivalent to the number of strokes difference between the actual score and the SSS. Thus a player returning an adjusted score of 91 over a course with an SSS of 68 would be given an initial

handicap of 23.

Handicaps are split into four categories – under 5; 6-12; 13-20; and 21-28. In most cases individual golf clubs are responsible for the handicaps of their players in the upper three categories, but the Golf Union will ratify all handicaps in category one.

Although handicap committees have the authority to adjust handicaps based on ample evidence of a general standard of play, adjustments are normally made only on performances in club competitions. When all scores are recorded, they are averaged out to arrive at a Competition Standard Scratch. Anyone achieving that score or two strokes above it will not have their handicaps adjusted. Anyone more than two strokes above that score will have their handicaps increased by 0.1 of a shot throughout all four categories.

Any players with scores below the Competition Standard Scratch will have their handicaps reduced. In category one the reduction is 0.1 of a stroke for every

stroke below CSS. Category-two players are reduced by 0.2 for every shot below CSS, category-three players by 0.3 and category-four by 0.4.

Players exact handicaps are kept in a register which lists every competitive score. Handicaps are rounded up. A player with an exact handicap of 10.4 would have a playing handicap of 10, but if he was three shots above the CSS in his next competition his exact handicap would increase to 10.5 and his playing handicap would go up to eleven.

Many clubs increase handicaps at the end of each month, but any reduction in handicap comes into effect immediately.

Ladies break their handicap categories into silver and bronze divisions. The silver category consists of category A with handicaps up to three, B is from four to six, and C 7-18. The bronze division is D, 19-29 and E, 30-36. The ladies require four cards before a handicap is given and their current handicaps are based on an average of their best recent scores.

Considerate players mark their opponent's card as they make their way to the next tee, not on the green. Doing so does not cause frustrating delays to the players waiting to play their approach shots.

MANNERS MAKE THE GOLFER

Manners on the golf course are not a way of making golf an elite or 'snobby' game. They are a means of speeding up play, ensuring safety and showing respect to others.

Knowing how to behave on the golf course and being aware of what is expected of you by your fellow golfers are as important to developing your enjoyment of the game as improving your swing. You will get more pleasure and satisfaction from the game if you play in an acceptable manner and are always aware of the pleasure of others.

Manners on the golf course are not a way of making golf an elite or 'snobby' game. They are a means of speeding up play, ensuring safety and showing respect to others.

When you play with more experienced golfers, make a point of watching how they behave. Hopefully, you will see that they always stand quietly when someone else is playing, and pay attention to the flight of everyone's golf ball, not just their own, in case a player loses sight of his ball and it becomes lost.

They will move briskly between shots, not bellow to each other across the width of the fairway, always play in the correct order, and not go striding after the ball before their partners play.

In short, they will be good golfing company, as mindful of others as they are of their own progress. Golf is a game of introspection but it is also essential that we all be aware of other people on the course and treat them as we ourselves would wish to be treated by other players.

Golfers should always be very tolerant of new players—after all, every golfer has been a starter at one time. If your manners on the course match your enthusiasm you will be readily accepted in this marvellous game.

Care of the course

There are three ways in which every golfer damages a golf course—taking divots with iron clubs from the fairways, disturbing the sand in bunkers and landing a high shot on the green. In each case it takes only a few seconds to put matters right and leave the course as nearly as possible in perfect condition. You should never be careless in trying to leave the course in good condition. There is nothing worse than playing well in an important competition and finding your ball at the bottom of a huge footprint in a bunker or an enormous divot mark in the fairway. If you give a little thought to your fellow competitors, hopefully they will do the same for you.

When a player is about to play a shot, his companions should be as quiet and as still as possible so that he is not distracted.

Bunkers: After playing from a bunker, a player should fill up and smooth over any holes and footprints made by him. If there is a rake near a bunker, use it. Try to rake the sand evenly after you play your shot. If you simply pull the sand behind you, this can lead to an uneven distribution of sand and, in extreme cases, leave only a thin layer of sand in certain areas of the bunker. If there is no rake to hand, a sideways sweeping movement with your foot, especially if you are wearing spiked shoes will do almost as good a job. And you can tidy up with the head of your club, trying to leave the sand as smooth as you possibly can.

Divots: Divots are normally wedge-shaped, thin at the back, deep at the front. Whenever possible, players should always replace their divots. Fit them in like a jigsaw back into the hole you

have created, treading them down firmly and, in anything but very dry conditions, they will grow back in place.

Use your foot or, if there is one, a rake, to smooth over holes and footprints after you have played a bunker shot.

If a divot is replaced as carefully as possible, the grass should grow back in place.

Pitch marks are caused by the ball landing on the green. Considerate golfers always make sure they carry a suitable repairer in their pockets.

Greens: Care should be taken not to cause damage to the surface around the hole while either putting or tending the flagstick. When tending the flag, avoid standing too close to the hole. This helps prevent the area around the cup becoming excessively damaged by the spikes on your shoes.

Pitch-marks can be repaired with a tee peg, pushing it into the earth round the edge of the indentation and lifting the depressed soil back into place. Finish off by tapping it smooth with the head of your putter or your foot. Specially-designed, two- and three-pronged pitch-mark repairers are available from most professionals' shops: some courses provide them free.

Consideration to other golfers

The player who wins either the previous hole in stroke-play or who has the lowest score in matchplay has the 'honour' at the next hole and should be permitted to play before his opponent or fellow competitors.

When another golfer is about to play no one should talk, move or stand close to or directly behind him from the tee or on the fairway, or directly in front on the green. The only exception to standing directly behind a person in play would be if he was playing directly into the sun. He might then ask one of his partners to stand behind him in order to follow the flight of the ball.

On every shot, a player should position himself and his equipment so that they cannot be seen by the person in play. On the tee, that position is ideally directly opposite the player and far enough away to be out of his field of vision as he stands over the ball.

Standing behind the person in play's back can sometimes lead to a nasty bump on the head or even worse.

Avoid standing behind the player looking down the line of the shot as this can be very unsettling. And on sunny days make sure that your shadow does not fall over the ball or close to it.

Stillness and silence are the key words when another person is in play.

It is in the interests of all golfers to play your shots without undue delay.

When playing in a group, the golfer farthest from the hole should always play first regardless of where the ball has actually landed.

Wait until the players in front of you are well out of reach before you play.

Three players who know how to behave on the green. The one tending the flagstick has the edge of the flag in his hand to stop it flapping about and has positioned himself so that his shadow is out of the putting line. The other player is lining up his putt without distracting the person putting, so speeding up the game.

Green behaviour

On and around the green, keep well clear of the line of a player's putt. You are not allowed to stand on any extension of that line, even if you are on the far side of the green. Keep shadows away from the putting line and the hole. Be particularly careful of this when standing on the line of the putts of other players.

If it is a windy day, hold the flag against the flagstick to stop it fluttering about and when you lay the pin on the green, roll it over a couple of times to prevent the flag from flapping destractingly.

It is acceptable to line up putts while another player is putting out providing this does not disturb him.

Always walk carefully on the green and avoid spiking-up the surface, especially around the hole.

Priority on the Course

If there are no special local rules in force, two-ball matches should have precedence over three- or four-ball games and should be entitled to pass if they are being held up.

If any match fails to keep its place on the course and loses more than one clear hole on the match in front, it should allow the match following to

play through at the first chance.

A golfer playing alone has no standing on the course and should give way to any other match.

Safety

Before you make a swing, either from the fairway or the tee, make sure that there is no one standing close to you or in a position where they could be struck by your club or the ball.

On some golf courses you may find a notice asking golfers to refrain from making practice swings on the tee. In this instance, the request is made not so much in the interests of safety but in order to protect the teeing area from excessive wear. Whatever the reason, these signs should always be adhered to, especially if you are a visitor to the club.

Speeding up play

Be ready to hit as soon as it is your turn to play and remember that it is in the interests of all golfers to play without delay.

If you are marking a card, do not do it on the green. Do it as you wait to hit your drive at the next hole.

Study the line of your putt while the first player in your group is preparing to play

provided this does not disturb the person putting.

Always leave your bag or trolley near to the route of the next tee. Do not leave it at the front opening of the green as this causes delay in retrieving it while the match behind is waiting to play.

If the match in front is holding you up, do not drive into them in frustration. Ask if you can play through or ask them politely to keep in closer touch with the game in front of them. If they are keeping up with the general pace of the entire field, there is nothing more they or your group can do. Be aware of what is going on behind you.

If you are looking for a lost ball and the group behind you is ready to play, call them through. The same applies if you have lost touch with the match in front. If a fast-moving two-ball catches up with your four-ball, invite them to play through. This can be done very quickly if your four-ball drives off the next tee and then asks the two-ball to play on. They can complete the hole as you and your friends walk slowly towards your drives.

Do not take longer than the five minutes allocated when searching for a lost ball.

RULES OF GOLF

*Designed to give players a broad view of how
to proceed in various situations.*

We are not attempting to cover all eventualities and recommend that every golfer should carry a copy of the rules of the game in their golf bags not because they constantly want to nitpick, but because even in the friendliest game a situation can arise which neither player has come across before. A quick look at the relevant rules should quickly settle any points at issue. Rule books are available free of charge through most golf clubs. Local rules relating to out-of-bounds areas, roads, paths and obstructions are printed on the back of every club's scorecard and should be checked before starting play.

The first written rules were set down in 1744 and were a set of thirteen basic and easily-learned guidelines for playing the game. At first glance, the present rules of golf are frighteningly complex, running to 36 definitions, 42 rules and more than 300 sub-sections. The rules are complex because golf is played over a wide variety of terrain—through trees and bushes, round and over rivers, lakes and streams, past fences and walls and around buildings. Not surprisingly, the vast majority of players never come to terms with them all which have one thing in common—they are all based on common sense and fair play.

In the broadest sense, the ball should be played from where it comes to rest. If this is clearly impossible because it is at the bottom of a lake or river, or in the middle of a bush, then there is provision to drop another ball clear of the offending obstacle at the expense of a penalty stroke.

To drop the ball correctly, the player must stand erect, hold the ball at shoulder height and at arm's-length and then drop it. When the ball is dropped, it must be as close as possible to the original spot where the ball lay, but not nearer the hole, except when a Rule permits or requires it to be dropped elsewhere.

At professional events and at amateur club championships when the captain traditionally accompanies the match as referee, competitors can ask the official for an instant ruling in case of any doubt. This facility is obviously not available at ordinary club level, which is why you should always have a copy of the rule book in your bag.

If a situation cannot be resolved on course there are procedures that should be followed. In match-play any dispute between opponents must be reported to the club committee as soon as the match is completed and a decision will be made. In

*A dropped ball that touches a player, caddie or a
piece of equipment must be redropped without penalty.*

stroke-play, where competitors mark a card with their hole-by-hole scores, there is a provision in the rules to cover any uncertainty. A player who is doubtful about how to cope with a situation can announce to his fellow competitor that he will play a second ball in which he believes to be the correct manner, while also completing the hole with his original ball. A record of both scores must be kept and the player must report the incident to the committee before returning his score-card. A decision will be made by the committee about which score should stand.

One of the most frequently used rules is that relating to balls lost or out-of-bounds. In either case, the procedure is the same: another ball must be played from the same spot as the original ball and there is an additional penalty incurred of one stroke.

If there is some doubt about whether the original ball has been lost or has finished out-of-bounds, a provisional ball may be played from the same spot in order to save time. The player must state at the time that he is playing a

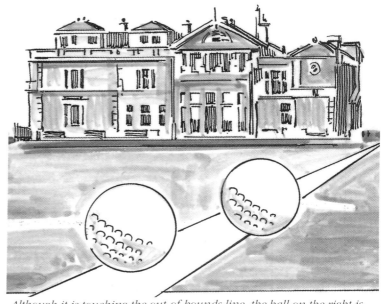

Although it is touching the out-of-bounds line, the ball on the right is still in play. The ball on the left is out of bounds.

provisional ball and may continue to play that ball until he has reached the point where it is established that the original ball is lost or has landed out-of-bounds.

A one-stroke penalty also applies to the provisional ball. Commentators are often heard to say that a competitor is 'playing three off the tee.' Where the player has hit the original drive out-of-bounds, this original stroke counts, plus a penalty stroke. His next stroke with the new ball is therefore his third.

The rule book defines out-of-bounds as ground on which play is prohibited. If defined by stakes or a fence, the inside point of the stakes or fence determines the boundary. When defined by a line, the line itself is out-of-bounds. The out-of-bounds line extends vertically upwards and downwards. A ball is out-of-bounds when all of it lies out-of-bounds. A player may stand out-of-bounds to play a ball lying within bounds.

Penalty strokes are also

If a player declares a ball unplayable he can drop it within two club-lengths from the spot where the ball was unplayable, but it must be no nearer the hole.

When repositioning an unplayable ball, you can go back as far as you want but you must keep the point at which the ball originally lay between yourself and the hole.

incurred by a player who hits a ball into an unplayable lie (unless the problem is caused by any of the abnormal situations we deal with later). The player himself is the sole judge of whether a ball is unplayable. Faced with a situation where it may be possible to hit the ball with the likelihood that it would finish in even greater trouble, the player may quite properly decide to declare the ball unplayable and drop it under penalty of one stroke in a more accessible position. The Rules of Golf allow three ways to deal with unplayable lies: playing another shot as near as possible to the spot from which the unplayable

ball was last played; dropping the ball within two club-lengths, but not nearer the hole; and dropping the ball behind the point where it lay, keeping that point directly between the hole and the spot on which the ball is dropped. In the last option there is no limit on how far back you may go.

If you are dropping the ball within two club-lengths, you measure from the exact spot where the ball came to rest, not from the edge of the bush or tree which is causing the problem. The ball must not be moved until you have measured the requisite club-lengths. (You can use your driver for measuring.) Mark the distance with a tee peg stuck in the ground and only then may you lift the ball.

It is vital that you drop the ball correctly or further penalties could follow. Only the player can make the drop, not his caddie or partner. You must stand erect, hold the ball out at shoulder height and at arm's-length. If the ball touches you, your partner, your caddies or your equipment before or after it hits the ground, it must be re-dropped without penalty.

If you are dropping the ball

within two club-lengths, the ball must strike the ground within that area, even if it subsequently rolls outside. The ball must be redropped, without penalty, if it rolls into a hazard, or rolls out of a hazard if being dropped within it. If it rolls on to a putting green, out-of-bounds, nearer the hole or more than two club-lengths from where it first struck the ground, you must drop it again. If relief is being taken from an immovable obstruction, abnormal ground conditions or the wrong putting green and the ball rolls into these same conditions when dropped, it must be redropped without incurring a penalty stroke.

If, when it is redropped, the ball again rolls outside the specified area it must be placed as near as it is possible to do so on the spot where it first hit the ground when it was re-dropped.

If, in the process of dropping a ball, you suffer one of those twists of fate where it disappears down a rabbit hole or rolls into a lake and the ball cannot be retrieved, another ball may be correctly dropped without a penalty stroke.

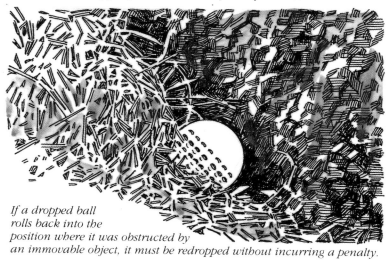

If a dropped ball rolls back into the position where it was obstructed by an immovable object, it must be redropped without incurring a penalty.

Should you take the unplayable-ball option of returning the ball to the spot from which the last stroke was played, the ball must be dropped on the fairway, in the rough, or in a hazard as close as possible to the spot from which it was last played. If the previous stroke was played from the tee, it may be played from anywhere within the teeing area and may be teed up.

If there is reason to believe that a ball is lost (other than in a water hazard) or out-of-bounds, a player is allowed to save time by playing a provisional ball from the same spot – teeing the ball through the ball up on the tee or dropping it through the green. The intention to play this provisional ball must be clearly stated or it immediately becomes the ball in play under the normal stroke and distance penalty.

You may continue to play the provisional ball until you reach the point where the original ball is likely to be. If the original ball cannot be found after the permitted five-minute searching time, or if it has gone out-of-bounds, the hole can be completed with the provisional ball—counting all strokes played plus one penalty stroke. If the original ball is found it must be played or declared unplayable.

There are certain situations where the rules allow the player to remove the ball from problem areas without incurring a penalty. These are areas where the normal nature of the ground has been changed and it is important to know what they are.

Casual Water is any temporary accumulation of water on the course, including

Players are allowed five minutes to search for a lost ball. If the ball is still lost, the hole is completed with the provisional ball, incurring one penalty stroke.

snow and ice, that does not form part of a water hazard. If water begins to ooze out of the ground as the player takes his stand, the ball may be moved without penalty. If the ball is on dry ground, but the player's stance is affected by casual water, it may also be moved without penalty.

As in all cases where a ball is to be dropped, when dropping because of casual water, the ball must never be dropped closer to the hole than where it originally lay. In the case of casual water, it must be dropped within one club-length of the nearest point which avoids the water. If a ball lands in a bunker afflicted with casual water, it may be dropped within the bunker with no penalty, or outside it at the expense of a one-shot penalty. On a putting green, a ball may be lifted and placed at the nearest point which avoids the water.

Ground Under Repair is any area of the course on which work is being, or has been carried out and which the committee has marked by a line on the ground or by stakes and ropes and designated GUR. A free drop may be taken within one club-length of the nearest point of relief from all GUR. Abandoned, piled-up grass cuttings are not ground under repair unless marked as such. But any hole obviously cut by a greenkeeper or material left for removal is deemed to be ground under repair and does not need to be marked as such. If a ball is seen to enter ground under repair or casual water and cannot be found, a new ball may be dropped without penalty within one club-length of the point where the ball crossed the margin of the area.

Other instances where a player can move his ball and

drop it within one club-length are where the ball lies in a hole, cast or burrow made by a burrowing animal, reptile or bird, or where the offending condition interferes with his swing: and when a ball is embedded in its own pitch-mark in a closely-mown area, closely-mown being defined as any areas of the course including paths through the rough, which have been cut to fairway height or less.

When a ball finishes on any putting green other than that of the hole being played, it must be lifted and dropped within one club-length of the nearest point of relief, but not nearer the hole. Even if the two greens are very close together, separated only be a closely-cut fringe, the ball may not be putted from one surface to the other.

Only on the putting surface are sand and loose soil considered loose impediments.

Abandoned, piled-up grass cuttings are not ground under repair unless specially designated as such.

Obstructions are defined as either movable or immovable objects and are essentially anything artificial which interferes with play, apart from walls, fences, stakes and objects which define out-of-bounds areas, any part of an immovable object which is itself out-of-bounds, or any construction declared by the club as an integral part of the course. Artificial roads and paths are held to be immovable obstructions with the exception of the famous road which crosses the eighteenth fairways at St. Andrews. It is considered an integral part of the course and any ball coming to rest on its surface has to be played as it lies – it may not be moved.

Movable obstructions such as newspapers and beer cans should be lifted clear. If the ball moves while this is being done, it must be replaced on its original spot, but there is

Under the Rules of Golf, loose impediments should not be removed from bunkers although local rules may permit stones to be removed.

ball moves while a loose impediment is being removed there is a one-stroke penalty and the ball must be replaced. If the ball is moved while removing a loose impediment on the putting green there is no penalty and the ball should be replaced. Sand and loose soil are loose impediments on the putting green but nowhere else.

The Rules of Golf do not allow loose impediments to be removed when the ball is in a bunker, but many clubs have taken advantage of their ability under local rules to allow stones to be removed before playing a bunker shot to avoid injuries or damages to the club. Any such local rules will appear on the back of the scorecard.

no penalty. If the ball lies on top of such an obstruction, the offending object is removed and the ball put without incurring a penalty in its original place.

When a ball lies in or on an immovable obstruction or so close to it that it interferes with the player's stance or swing, relief without penalty may be gained by dropping the ball within one club-length of the nearest point (without crossing over, through or under the obstruction) which avoids the interference but which is not nearer the hole. The fact that an immovable obstruction blocks a player's line to the green is not interference. This rule is designed only to allow the player enough room to swing the club without unnec-essary interference, not to give him a clear sight of the green.

Loose impediments are things you would encounter naturally on a golf course. They are defined as 'natural objects' such as stones, twigs, branches and the like, dung, worms and insects and casts or heaps made by them, provided they are not fixed or growing, are not solidly embedded and do not adhere to the ball. Snow and ice can be treated as casual water or loose impediments at the option of the player. Loose impediments may be moved in the same way as movable obstructions with one significant distinction. If the

Players may now hold the flagstick with one hand while they putt with the other, as long as the flagstick has been removed and the ball does not strike it.

GLOSSARY

Address The correct position of feet, body and club as the player prepares to hit the ball.

Advice A player cannot give advice to anyone but his partner in competition. He can only seek advice from his partner or either of their caddies.

Albatross A very rare bird. Each hole on every golf course is given a par score of three, four or five, depending on its length. It is the score a good player should record, taking two puts on every green. An albatross is a score of three under par—holing in one at a par four or in two at a par five.

Amateur A golfer who plays the game as a non-remunerative or non-profit-making sport. Limits are set on the value of prizes which can be accepted as an amateur. For events of two rounds or less, the limit is a prize or voucher of £110 retail value. For events of more than two rounds, the limit is £170.

Balata Thin cover on top-quality golf balls, giving professionals greater spin and control. It cuts very easily and balata-covered golf balls are not recommended for the average amateur. Many professionals will use a new ball after every three holes.

Ball marker A small plastic disc or coin placed behind the ball to mark its position on the green if it is lifted either to avoid a player's line or to be cleaned.

Bogey An expression in British golf which has now been replaced by the word 'par'. In American golf bogey means a score of one over par, double-bogey, two over par and so on.

Bunker The most prolific hazard in golf. On the original links courses they were simply areas where the top soil had worn away to reveal the sand underneath. Swirling wind and the efforts of thousands of golfers gradually made them deeper and deeper. Bunkers are known in America as sand traps.

Caddies The name is believed to have originated from the French, *cadet*, traditional bag-carriers, the best of whom have an intimate knowledge of many courses and strike up a close relationship with their professionals.

Carbon fibre One of the new materials used for golf-club shafts instead of steel.

Ball marker

Casual Water Any accumulation of rain or flood water on the course. The ball may be moved from casual water without penalty.

Chip Short shot played from close to the green when there are no obstacles between the player and the hole. The ball is played on a low trajectory and runs most of the way.

Concede Giving your opponent his next stroke in match-play. This is usually done when a ball has been played to within inches of the hole. A player may also concede a hole or a match. Once a concession has been made it cannot be withdrawn or declined.

Curtis Cup Biennial match between teams of eight ladies representing Britain and the United States. The matches are played alternately in the British Isles and America and decided by three foursomes and six singles matches on each of two days.

Delay The rules stipulate penalties for undue delay playing a hole or between holes.

Divot The piece of turf sliced out by the clubhead as the ball is played from the fairway. As a courtesy to those playing behind and in order to encourage the grass to regrow, the divot should be replaced and firmly trodden into position.

Draw A controlled shot where the ball moves slightly from right to left in the air. In its exaggerated form a draw becomes a hook.

Featherie ball

Driving range Practice facilities normally situated in large population areas. Balls are hit into the open from artificial turf under a protective roof so that practice can be continued in bad weather and at night. The number of driving ranges in Britain is increasing. In Japan, where land available for golf courses is severely limited, driving ranges are extremely popular and many of them are two or three tiers high.

Dropping There are many circumstances covered by the Rules of Golf where a ball may be lifted from an unplayable situation and dropped in another position. When a ball is being dropped under the Rules, the player must stand erect, facing his target and drop it from shoulder height at arm's length.

Eagle A score of two under par at any hole – most commonly a three at a par-five hole.

Embedded ball A ball embedded in its own pitch-mark on any closely-mown area may be lifted, cleaned and dropped without penalty. A closely-mown area means any area of the course, including paths through the rough, cut to fairway height or less.

Fade A shot in which the ball moves slightly in the air from left to right (for right handers). A controlled form of slice.

Featherie An early form of golf ball made by stuffing a top hat full of feathers into a leather cover. Only half-a-dozen of these balls could be produced in a day by a skilled ball-maker and they were therefore very expensive.

Foursome A form of play where two players take alternate shots with the same ball.

Golf foundation Non-profit-making entity which encourages junior golf by arranging group coaching for thousands of youngsters and staging national and international events.

Graphite One of the modern developments of golf-shaft technology replacing steel shafts.

Grooves Indentations cut into the face of iron clubs to impart backspin and a greater degree of control over the flight of the ball. The form of these groves is closely regulated by the Rules of golf.

Ground under repair Any area of a golf course which is being treated or repaired, often marked with white lines and a sign which will usually say 'GUR'. The ball may be lifted and dropped from these areas at the closest point out-side and not nearer the hole.

Gutta percha A rubber-like substance from which golf balls were made between 1848 and the end of the nineteenth century. Known as 'gutties', they were made by clamping a lump of heated gutta percha in a mould.

Heel The part of the clubface close to the point at which it joins the shaft.

Hooded Describes the position of the clubface if it is turned to aim left of the target.

Hook A shot which bends significantly from right to left in the air.

Interlock A popular form of grip in which the little finger of the right hand entwines with the forefinger of the left hand.

Knickers The American name given to the modern version of plus-four trousers much favoured by earlier golfers and now seeing something of a revival led by professionals Rodger Davis and Payne Stewart.

Knickers

Lie The angle between the head and the shaft of a golf club. The greater the angle the flatter the lie. A flat lie means that the golfer can stand slightly farther away from the ball and swing on a flatter plane, more around the body. A smaller angle means a more upright lie, allowing the golfer to stand closer to the ball and swing on a more upright plane. Generally, flat lies suit shorter golfers while the tall player will get better results from an upright lie. The word 'lie' also describes the position of the ball on the course – from a good lie in the fairway to a buried lie in bunker.

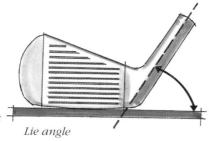

Lie angle

Local rules Within the framework of the Rules of Golf, each club can define its own areas which are out-of-bounds, decide whether immovable obstructions are an integral part of the course, allow stones to be removed from bunkers and so on. Local rules are printed on the back of the scorecard.

Loft The effective angle of the clubface as it hits the ball. Sets of clubs are designed with increasing amounts of loft as the club numbers increase and the length of the shaft reduces. Thus the two-iron has little loft and a long shaft, while the nine-iron has a lot of loft but a short shaft. The amount of loft on a club can be altered in the way the shot is played – particularly by keeping the hands ahead of the clubface as the ball is struck, thus reducing the effective loft and keeping the ball low. This type of punch shot can be very effective against a strong wind.

Loose impediments Natural objects which can be

removed if they lie close to the ball or on a putting line. Leaves, twigs, stones and worms come into this category.

Marker Fellow competitor who marks your scorecard and authenticates it at the end of the round. An independent marker who is not a competitor may be appointed by club committees or tournament-organisers. Such a marker is responsible only for recording scores: he is not a referee.

Match-play Where the winner is decided by the number of holes won rather than the number of strokes taken in a round.

Obstructions Essentially, anything artificial which encroaches on the golfing area, such as surfaced roads and greenkeepers' sheds. But check the scorecard to see if they have been made an integral part of the course. Movable obstructions are artificial items such as beer cans, newspapers and bottles which can be removed without penalty.

Open Championship The official title of the great event played in Britain every year. For clarification abroad, it is now usually referred to as 'The British Open', but when it first started in 1860 there were no others with which to confuse it.

Pitch High-flying approach shot designed to carry all the way to the green and stop quickly.

Pitch-mark Indentation in the surface of the green caused by the ball on landing. The depression should be raised and tapped smoothly by each player.

Pull A shot which flies left of the target.

Pull hook A shot which starts left and hooks farther away to that side.

Royal and Ancient Club of Saint Andrews The club founded in 1754 which eventually became responsible for the Rules of Golf and runs the Open Championship.

Ryder Cup Trophy first presented in 1927 for competition between teams of British and American professionals by Samuel Ryder who made a fortune from selling packets of seeds for one penny. It is now played for by teams representing Europe and the United States.

The Ryder Cup

Sand wedge

Sand wedge Club specifically designed for playing out of bunkers. It has a great deal of loft and a broad, rounded sole to slide through the sand.

Shank Golf's unmentionable shot. Usually caused by the downswing path of the club travelling from out to in, coupled with the player's weight moving forward to the toes. The ball strikes the neck, or hosel of the club instead of the face and flies off at right angles to the intended line of flight.

Slice A shot which bends from left to right in the air. Usually a high shot lacking in any distance.

Slow play One of the curses of the modern game. Many professionals out at the head of a field still cannot complete a round of golf in two-and-a-half to three hours – a time that was considered perfectly normal not so long ago. Rounds can now take as long as six hours.

Stroke-play Form of competition based on the total number of strokes played – as opposed to match-play where each hole is won or lost.

Tee markers The area within which the ball must be played from the tee is defined by two markers. The outer edges of these markers indicate the front and sides of the area to be used and the ball may be played anywhere in the rectangle two club-lengths from the edge of the markers. A player may stand outside the markers to play a ball within the correct area.

Through the green This expression is used a great deal within the Rules of golf and indicates the entire area of the course with the exception of the tee and green of the hole being played and all hazards on the course.

Two piece The most popular ball used by club golfers throughout the world. It is a solid piece of resilient material with a cover, as opposed to the traditionally-made, three-piece ball which has a central core wrapped around with dozens of yards of rubber and then an outer cover.

United States Golf Association The American equivalent of The Royal and Ancient Golf Club, responsible for staging the US Open and Amateur Championships. Also responsible for administering the rules of golf in the United States and Mexico. For many years the R&A and the USGA have worked together on a uniform set of rules which are applicable world-wide.

Walker Cup A contest every two years between amateur teams from the United States and Great Britain and Ireland. Play alternates between the two sides of the Atlantic and consists of four foursomes

The Walker Cup

and eight single matches on each of two days. The trophy, presented by G. H. Walker, is officially The United States Golf Association International Challenge Trophy.

Winter Rules Clubs may apply a special rule during winter months when ground conditions are difficult. A ball lying on any closely-mown area of the course may be lifted, cleaned and placed within six inches, but not nearer the hole, without penalty.

Yellow Stake The margins of water hazards on a golf course are marked by yellow stakes or lines. The stakes themselves are within the hazard. If a ball is lost in a water hazard another ball may be dropped under a penalty of one stroke, behind the hazard, keeping the point where the ball crossed the margin of the hazard between the ball and the hole. Red stakes or lines denote the margin of lateral water hazards behind which it is not permissible to drop a ball. The rule allows a ball to be dropped within two club-lengths to either side, but not nearer the hole.

COURSE DIRECTORY

The following pages list the pick of the Private and Public golf courses of England, Scotland, Ireland and Wales along with other useful information to help you discover new and exciting places to play golf; some distant, others perhaps only a short journey from your home.
The section begins with an excellent new course open to members of the public, and finishes with a look at a private club that has been hailed as a success in its first season.

GUIDE TO VISITORS' CODE.
* With general restrictions (e.g: only open to visitors on weekdays)

** No major restrictions

*** No visitors (e.g: Unless as guests of members)

H-Handicap certificate required or letter of introduction from home club.

FEES- Price in brackets refers to weekends and bank holidays.
The noted fees are up to date at the time of publication. However it is advisable to contact in advance the club you wish to visit to check on the current green fee.
Where there are no brackets, this often means the club is not open to unaccompanied visitors at weekends. Where no fees are listed, the course is not usually open to unaccompanied visitors. We recommend that whatever course you want to play, telephone first to check availability.

CHESFIELD DOWNS

The Family Golf Centre, close to Stevenage, offers excellent on- and off-course facilities to golfers and their non-playing families.

There are many clubs today that remain bastions of upper-class male chauvinism – with prospective members facing enormous subscriptions and scrupulous vetting, their wives tolerated on certain days of the week and certainly not in the smoking room!

Thankfully there are others, the majority, where a warm welcome awaits anyone willing to pay the green fees. Chesfield Downs, near Stevenage in Hertfordshire belongs to this group. Golf is the main attraction but the managers here want to promote the feeling that there is more to golf than hitting a ball from tee to green. It's a course where all the family are welcome either to play over the eighteen-hole course, or the nine-hole, par-three links, practise in the 300-yard, 25-bay floodlit driving range or relax in the coffee shop and bars. And there's even a creche for those who are not yet able to handle even the shortest cut-down club!

But back to the golf! Although it is miles from the sea, The Family Golf Centre at Chesfield Downs has been designed to give it an open, links feel. There are few trees and little thick rough: the turf is tough and doesn't cut up easily. Even the wildest hitter is unlikely to lose many balls at this course.

At 6,630 yards, it is longer than the average par-71 course. A good piece of advice to those playing here for the first time is to use the course guide! The undulating terrain, coupled with a lack of landmarks and definition make it difficult to judge length. There is often broken ground between the ball and the green and it is easy to find that a good shot finishes short of target because distance has been underestimated. One player who knows the course

well gives newcomers this tip: take one more club than you think on longer approaches to the green. The greens are evenly paced and receptive, yet with many having more than one tier, they have the potential to offer a variety of pin positions. The greens on the front nine are generally smaller than those coming home, but they have more severe borrows.

The premium at Chesfield is on accurate irons and fairway wood shots. And although tee

The driving range at Chesfield Downs is the ideal place to work on your swing.

shots are not too demanding, on most of the par-four holes (there are eleven of them) anything other than a good, solid drive makes it difficult to reach the green in regulation. There are no big carries, the landing areas are generous and a ball that drifts off the fairways will not be frustrated by difficult rough.

As in every course, the real key to conquering Chesfield is accuracy to the tee. Thinking golfers will use the many sidehill slopes here to their advantage. Although a mishit drive will be penalized, players here need not feel threatened to hit a long, straight tee-shot or be damned. From the fairway there is only one blind shot, the second at the par-five sixteenth: the only blind tee shot is the one at the par-four thirteenth hole.

Good golfers use the slopes to thread long-iron approach shots through the narrow well-bunkered entrances to the greens which have some cunning borrows. Delicate chips, and pitches are needed by those who miss the putting surface and land amidst the gentle mounds that surround the greens.

Yardage counts for little on a windy day: the 581-yard par-five fifth will play well over 600 yards into the prevailing wind, but because the layout of the course changes direction sixteen times, players find that they never settle into a routine here.

The second hole is the most difficult – 419 yards long into the prevailing wind with water running down most of the right and out-of-bounds to the left. Tee shots should be aimed to the left of centre so that the left-to-right slope runs the ball back into the middle of the fairway which is by far the best position from which to attack the green.

Water is a feature of five other holes on the course, especially the third which one pro has rather understatedly described as 'picturesque'.

Among the other testing holes are the 439-yard eleventh where a good faded drive is needed to clear the

The undulating terrain and absence of landmarks fool many golfers into thinking that the course is easy. A few holes into the round will soon change their minds.

bunkers protecting the corner of the dog-leg fairway, and the par-four fifteenth which is ranked the second most difficult hole. 417 yards long, it usually plays downwind, and water and out-of-bounds demand an accurate drive to achieve par.

The sixth and seventh are the only par-four holes where even after a short drive the green can be reached with a middle iron. The others are tests for even the best golfers.

For those who don't feel up to the challenge of eighteen holes, the par-27 nine-hole, course is great fun, encapsulating in its 927 yards all the fun and challenge of golf for all the family.

Good food and wine are on the menu at the spacious restaurant at Chesfield Downs.

ENGLAND

AVON

ENTRY HILL.
Entry Hill, Bath
Tel: (0225) 834248
Holes: 9 4206 yds
V'trs: *
Fees: 18 £5.20/9 £3.30

BEDFORDSHIRE

MOWSBURY
Kimbolton Road, Bedford
Tel: (0234) 771042
Holes: 18 6514 yds
V'trs: *
Fees: £4 (£6)

STOCKWOOD PARK
London Rd, Stockwood Park,
Luton
Tel: (0582) 413704
Holes: 18 5567 yds
V'trs: *
Fees: £3.40 (£5.10)

TILSWORTH
Dunstable Rd, Tilsworth,
Dunstable
Tel: (0525) 210721/210722
Holes: 9 2773 yds
V'trs: **
Fees: £3 (£4)

WYBOSTON LAKES
Wyboston Lakes, Wyboston
Tel: (0480) 212501
Holes: 18 5721 yds
V'trs: *
Fees: £7 (£10)

BERKSHIRE

DOWNSHIRE
Easthampstead Park,
Wokingham
Tel: (0344) 424066
Holes: 18 6382 yds
V'trs: **
Fees: S-£6.50, W- £4.50

HAWTHORN HILL
Drift Road, Hawthorn Hill,
Maidenhead
Tel: (628) 771030/75588
Holes: 18 6212 yds
V'trs: *
Fees: £7.20 (£8.20)

HURST
Sandford Lane, Hurst,
Wokingham
Tel: (0734) 345143
Holes: 9 3015 yds
V'trs: *
Fees: S-£2.50, W-£1.65

LAVENDER PARK
Swinley Road, Ascot
Tel: (0344) 884074
Holes: 9 1104 yds
V'trs: **
Fees: £3.10

BUCKINGHAMSHIRE

ABBEY HILL
Monks Way, Two Mile Ash,
Milton Keynes
Tel: (0908) 536845
Holes: 18 6193 yds
V'trs: *
Fees: On enquiry

FARNHAM PARK
Park Road, Stoke Poges, Slough
Tel: (02814) 3332
Holes: 18 5847 yds
V'trs: *
Fees: £4.80 (£7)

WINDMILL HILL
Tattenhoe Lane, Bletchley,
Milton Keynes
Tel: (0908) 648149
Holes: 18 6773 yds
V'trs: **
Fees: £3.75 (£5.30)

CAMBRIDGESHIRE

ORTON MEADOWS
Ham Lane, Peterborough
Tel: (0733) 237478
Holes: 18 5800 yds
V'trs: **
Fees: £5 (£7.50)

THORPE WOOD
Nene Parkway, Peterborough
Tel: (0733) 267701
Holes: 18 7086 yds
V'trs: **
Fees: £5 (£7.50)

CHANNEL ISLANDS

ST CLEMENTS
St Clements, Jersey
Tel: (0534) 21938
Holes: 9 3972 yds
V'trs: *
Fees: £8

WESTERN GOLF RANGE
The Mount, Val de la Mare, St
Quens, Jersey
Tel: (0534) 82787
Holes: 12 (Par 3)
V'trs: **
Fees: £3 (£3.25)

CHESHIRE

ELLESMERE PORT
Chester Road, Hooton, South
Wirral
Tel: (051) 339 7502
Holes: 18 6432 yds
V'trs: *
Fees: £2.90 (£3.60)

KNIGHTS GRANGE
Grange Lane, Winsford
Tel: (06065) 52780
Holes: 9 6240 yds
V'trs: *
Fees: 18 £2.10 (£2.80),
9 £1.60 (£2.10)

MALKINS BANK
Malkins Bank, Sandbach
Tel: (0270) 765931
Holes: 18 6071 yds
V'trs: **
Fees: £10

QUEEN'S PARK
Queen's Park Gardens, Crewe
Tel: (0270) 666724
Holes: 9 5370 yds
V'trs: **
Fees: £2.50 (£3)

WALTON HALL
Warrington Road, Higher
Walton, Warrington
Tel: (0925) 63061
Holes: 18 6843 yds
V'trs: **
Fees: £3.65 (£4.50)

WIDNES MUNICIPAL
Dundalk Road, Widnes
Tel: (051) 424 65241
Holes: 18 5612 yds
V'trs: **
Fees: £2.70 (£3.35)

CLEVELAND

**MIDDLESBROUGH
MUNICIPAL**
Ladgate Lane, Middlesbrough
Tel: (0642) 315361
Holes: 18 6314 yds
V'trs: *
Fees: £3.75 (£5)

CUMBRIA

STONEYHOLM
St Aidan's Road, Carlisle
Tel: (0228) 34856
Holes: 18 6000 yds
V'trs: **
Fees: £3.90

DERBYSHIRE

ALLESTREE PARK
Allestree Hall, Allestree, Derby
Tel: (0332) 550616
Holes: 18 5749 yds
V'trs: *
Fees: £3.50 (£4.60)

**CHESTERFIELD
MUNICIPAL**
Murray House, Crow Lane,
Chesterfield
Tel: (0246) 273887
Holes: 18 6013 yds
V'trs: **
Fees: £3.50 (£4.50)

DERBY
Shakespeare Street, Sinfin,
Derby
Tel: (0332) 766462
Holes: 18 6144 yds
V'trs: **
Fees: £3.50 (£4.50)

ILKESTON
Peewit West End Drive, Ilkeston
Tel: (0602) 304550
Holes: 9 4116 yds
V'trs: **
Fees: £4.

DORSET

CHRISTCHURCH
Iford Bridge, Barrack Road,
Christchurch
Tel: (0202) 473817
Holes: 9 4824 yds
V'trs: **
Fees: £3.40 (£3.90)

MEYRICK PARK
Bournemouth
Tel: (0202) 290871
Holes: 18 5878 yds
V'trs: *
Fees: £6.50 (£7.50)

QUEEN'S PARK
Queen's Park, South Drive
Bournemouth
Tel: (0202) 36198
Holes: 18 6505 yds
V'trs: *
Fees: £7.

DURHAM

AYCLIFFE
School Lane, Newton Aycliffe
Tel: (0325) 310820
Holes: 9 6054 yds
V'trs: **
Fees: £2.20 (£3.30)

HOBSON MUNICIPAL
Hobson, nr Bunopfield,
Newcastle-upon-Tyne
Tel: (0207) 71605
Holes: 18 6502 yds
V'trs: **
Fees: £4.50 (£6)

ROSEBERRY GRANGE
Grange Villa, Chester-Le-Street
Tel: (091) 370 0660
Holes: 18 5628 yds
V'trs: **
Fees: £4 (£5)

STRESSHOLME
Snipe Lane, Darlington
Tel: (0325) 461002
Holes: 18 6511 yds
V'trs: **
Fees: £5 (£6)

ESSEX

BASILDON
Clayhill Lane, Sparrow's Hearn,
Kingswood, Basildon
Tel: (0268) 533532
Holes: 18 6120 yds
V'trs: **
Fees: £5.25 (£10)

BELFAIRS
Eastwood Road North, Leigh-
on-Sea
Tel: (0702) 520202
Holes: 18 5871 yds
V'trs: *
Fees: £6 (£9)

**BELHUS PARK
MUNICIPAL**
Belhus Park, South Ockendon
Tel: (0708) 854260
Holes: 18 5450 yds
V'trs: **
Fees: £3.95 (£6)

BUNSAY DOWNS
Little Baddow Road, Woodham
Walter, nr Maldon
Tel: (024 541) 2648/2369
Holes: 9 2913 yds
V'trs: *
Fees: 18 £6.50 (£7), 9 £5
(£5.50)

CHINGFORD
158 Station Road, Chingford,
London
Tel: (081) 529 5708
Holes: 18 6136 yds
V'trs: **
Fees: £7

FAIRLOP WATERS
Forest Road, Barkingside, Ilford
Tel: (081) 500 1881
Holes: 18 6288 yds
V'trs: **
Fees: £3.75 (£6)

HAINAULT FOREST
Chigwell Row, Hainault Forest
Tel: (081) 500 2131
Holes: No 1 18 5754 yds
No 2 18 6600 yds
V'trs: **
Fees: £5 (£7)

HARTSWOOD
King George's Playing Fields, Brentwood
Tel: (0277) 218714
Holes: 18 6238 yds
V'trs: **
Fees: £5 (£7.50)

HAVERING
Risebridge Chase, Lower Bedfords Road, Romford
Tel: (0708) 414290
Holes: 18 6252 yds, 9 hole Par 3
V'trs: *
Fees: £2.95 (£4.50)

ROYAL EPPING FOREST
Forest Approach, Station Road, Chingford, London
Tel: (081) 529 2708
Holes: 18 6220 yds
V'trs: **
Fees: £4.50 (£6.50)

GLOUCESTERSHIRE

CLEVE HILL
Cleve Hill, nr Cheltenham
Tel: (024 267) 2592
Holes: 18 6444 yds
V'trs: *
Fees: £5 (£6)

HAMPSHIRE

DIBDEN
Main Road, Dibden, Southampton
Tel: (0703) 845596
Holes: 18 6206 yds
V'trs: **
Fees: £4.30 (£6.30)

FLEMING PARK
Fleming Park, Eastleigh
Tel: (0703) 612797
Holes: 18 4436 yds
V'trs: **
Fees: £3.85 (£5.95)

GREAT SALTERNS
Portsmouth Golf Centre, Eastern Road, Portsmouth
Tel: (0705) 664549
Holes: 18 5970 yds
V'trs: **
Fees: £5

PORTSMOUTH
Crookhorn Lane, Widley, Portsmouth
Tel: (0705) 372210
Holes: 18 6259 yds
V'trs: **
Fees: £6.40

SOUTHAMPTON
Golf Course Road, Bassett, Southampton
Tel: (0703) 768407
Holes: 18 6218 yds, 9 2391 yds
V'trs: **
Fees: 18 £4.20 (£6), 9 £2.10 (£3)

SOUTHWOOD
Iveley Road, Farnborough
Tel: (0252) 548700
Holes: 18 5553 yds
V'trs: **
Fees: £8

HEREFORD & WORCS

PITCHEROAK
Plymouth Road, Redditch
Tel: (0527) 41054
Holes: 9 4584 yds
V'trs: *
Fees: £2.80 (£3.50)

HERTFORDSHIRE

BATCHWOOD HALL
Batchwood Hall, St Albans
Tel: (0727) 33349
Holes: 18 6465 yds
V'trs: **
Fees: £5 (£6)

CHESHUNT PARK
Park Lane, Cheshunt
Tel: (0992) 24009
Holes: 18 6608 yds
V'trs: **
Fees: £4.50 (£6)

FAMILY GOLF CENTRE
Jacks Hill, Graveley
Tel: (0462) 482929
Holes: 18 6585 yds
V'trs: **
Fees: £10 (£18.50)

LITTLE HAY
Box Lane, Bovingdon, Hemel Hempstead
Tel: (0442) 833798
Holes: 18 6610 yds
V'trs: *
Fees: £4.40 (£6.40)

PANSHANGER
Old Herns Lane, Welwyn Garden City
Tel: (0707) 339507
Holes: 18 6626 mts
V'trs: **
Fees: £5.50 (£6)

RICKMANSWORTH
Moor Lane, Rickmansworth
Tel: (0923) 775278
Holes: 18 4412 yds
V'trs: **
Fees: £4.40 (£6.30)

STEVENAGE
Aston Lane, Stevenage
Tel: (043 888) 4 24
Holes: 18 645 1 yds
V'trs: **
Fees: £4.50 (£6)

HUMBERSIDE

BOOTHFERRY
Spaldington Lane, Spaldington, Howden, Goole
Tel: (0430) 430364
Holes: 18 6593 yds
V'trs: *
Fees: £4 (£7)

KINGSWAY
Kingsway, Scunthorpe
Tel: (0724) 840945
Holes: 9 1915 yds
V'trs: **
Fees: £1.40 (£1.80)

NORMANBY HALL
Normanby Park, Scunthorpe
Tel: (0724) 720226
Holes: 18 6548 yds
V'trs: *
Fees: £5.50 (£7)

SPRINGHEAD PARK
Willerby Road, Hull
Tel: (0482) 656309
Holes: 18 6439 yds
V'trs: **
Fees: £2.85 (£4)

SUTTON PARK
Salthouse Road, Hull
Tel: (0482) 711450
Holes: 18 6251 yds
V'trs: **
Fees: £2.85 (£4)

ISLE OF MAN

DOUGLAS MUNICIPAL
Pulrose Park, Douglas
Tel: (0624) 75952
Holes: 18 6080 yds
V'trs: **
Fees: £5

PORT ST MARY
Kallow Road, Port St Mary
Tel: (0624) 834932
Holes: 9 2711 yds
V'trs: **
Fees: £3

KENT

BECKENHAM PLACE PARK
Beckenham Hill Road, Beckenham
Tel: (081) 585 374
Holes: 18 5722 yds
V'trs: *
Fees: £5.90 (£8.40)

BROMLEY
Magpie Hall Lane, Bromley
Tel: (081) 462 7014
Holes: 9 5538 yds
V'trs: **
Fees: £1.70 (£2.40)

COBTREE MANOR PARK
Chatham Road, Boxley, Maidstone
Tel: (0622) 53276
Holes: 18 5716 yds
V'trs: *
Fees: £5 (£7.50)

DARENTH VALLEY
Statin Road, Shoreham, nr Sevenoaks
Tel: (09592) 2922
Holes: 18 6356 yds
V'trs: *
Fees: £6.50 (£9)

DEANGATE RIDGE
Hoo, Rochester
Tel: (0634) 251180
Holes: 18 6300 yds
V'trs: **
Fees: £3.30 (£4.65)

HIGH ELMS *High Elms Road, Downe, Orpington*
Tel: (0689) 58175
Holes: 18 6210 yds
V'trs: **
Fees: £4.50 (£6.80)

LEEDS CASTLE
Leeds Castle, nr Maidstone
Tel: (0622) 886467
Holes: 9 2910 yds
V'trs: *
Fees: £6.95 (9 holes)

LULLINGSTONE PARK
Parkgate Road, Chelsfield, nr Orpington
Tel: (0959) 34542
Holes: 18/9
V'trs: *
Fees: 18 £7.50, 9 £4.25

LANCASHIRE

ALT
Park Road, West Southport
Tel: (0704) 30435/35268
Holes: 18 6939 yds
V'trs: **
Fees: £2.40 (£3)

BLACKPOOL PARK
North Park Drive, Blackpool
Tel: (0253) 31004
Holes: 18 6192 yds
V'trs: **
Fees: £4 (£5)

DUXBURY PARK
Duxbury Hall Road, Duxbury Park, Chorley
Tel: (025 72) 65380
Holes: 18 6270 yds
V'trs: **
Fees: £3 (£4)

MARSDEN PARK
Townhouse Road, Nelson
Tel: (0282) 67525
Holes: 18 5806 yds
V'trs: **
Fees: £3.85 (£4.95)

TOWNELEY
Towneley Park, Todmorden Road, Burnley
Tel: (0282) 38473
Holes: 18 5840 yds
V'trs: **
Fees: £2.95 (£3.40)

LEICESTERSHIRE

ENDERBY
Mill Lane, Enderby, Leicester
Tel: (0533) 849388
Holes: 9 4356 yds
V'trs: **
Fees: £2.25 (£2.75)

HUMBERSTONE HEIGHTS
Gipsy Lane, Leicester
Tel: (0533) 764674
Holes: 18 6444 yds
V'trs: **
Fees: £3.50 (£4.50)

LEICESTER FOREST CENTRE
Desford
Tel: (0455) 824800
Holes: 18 6111 yds
V'trs: **
Fees: £8 (£12)

OADBY
Leicester Road Racecourse, Oadby, Leicester
Tel: (0533) 709052
Holes: 18 6228 yds
V'trs: **
Fees: £3 (£4)

WESTERN PARK
Scuadmore Road, Leicester
Tel: (0533) 861424
Holes: 18 5700 yds
V'trs: **
Fees: £6 (£7.50)

MANCHESTER (GREASTER)

ALTRINCHAM MUNICIPAL
Stockport Road, Timperley, Altrincham
Tel: (061) 928 0761
Holes: 18 6204 yds
V'trs: **
Fees: £3 (£4.50)

BEACON PARK
Beacon Lane, Dalton, Up Holland, Wigan
Tel: (0695) 622700
Holes: 18 5927 yds
V'trs: **
Fees: £2.95 (£3.95)

BOLTON MUNICIPAL
Links Road, Chorley New Road, Bolton
Tel: (0204) 42336
Holes: 18 6012 yds
V'trs: *
Fees: £3 (£4)

BRACKLEY MUNICIPAL
Bullows Road, Little Hulton
Tel: (061) 790 6076
Holes: 9 3003 yds
V'trs: U
Fees: £2.30 (£3)

HAIGH HALL
Haigh Hall Country Park, Haigh, Wigan
Tel: (0942) 831107
Holes: 18 6423 yds
V'trs: **
Fees: £3 (£5)

HEATON PARK
Heaton Park, Prestwich, Manchester
Tel: (061) 798 0295
Holes: 18 5849 yds
V'trs: **
Fees: £4 (£6)

SPRINGFIELD PARK
Marland, Rochdale
Tel: (0706) 49801
Holes: 18 5209 yds
V'trs: **
Fees: £3.20 (£3.20)

WILLIAM WROE
Pennybridge Lane, Flixton, Manchester
Tel: (061) 748 8680
Holes: 18 4395 yds
V'trs: *
Fees: £3 (£4.50)

MERSEYSIDE

ALLERTON PARK
Allerton Road, Liverpool
Tel: (051) 428 1046
Holes: 18 5084 yds
V'trs: **
Fees: £2.70

ARROW PARK
Arrow Park, Woodchurch, Birkenhead, Wirral
Tel: (051) 677 1527
Holes: 18 6377 yds
V'trs: **
Fees: £3.25

BOWRING
Bowring Park, Roby Road, Huyton
Tel: (051) 489 1901
Holes: 9 5592 yds
V'trs: **
Fees: £2.70

BRACKENWOOD
Brackenwood Park, Bebington, Wirral
Tel: (051) 608 3093
Holes: 18 6131 yds
V'trs: **
Fees: £3.20

HOYLAKE MUNICIPAL
Carr Lane, Hoylake, Wirrall
Tel: (051) 632 2956
Holes: 18 6330 yds
V'trs: * H
Fees: £3.20.

LIVERPOOL MUNICIPAL
Ingoe Lane, Kirkby, nr Liverpool
Tel: (051) 546 5435
Holes: 18 6571 yds
V'trs: *
Fees: £2.20 (£2.20)

ST HELENS
St Helens, Lancs
Tel: (0744) 813149
Holes: 18 5941 yds
V'trs: **
Fees: £2.10

SOUTHPORT MUNICIPAL
Park Road, Southport
Tel: (0704) 35286
Holes: 18 6253 yds
V'trs: **
Fees: £3.50 (£5)

WARREN
Grove Road, Wallasey, Wirral
Tel: (051) 639 5730
Holes: 9 5914 yds
V'trs: **
Fees: £3

MIDDLESEX

AIRLINKS
Southall Lane, Hounslow
Tel: (081) 561 1418
Holes: 18 5883 yds
V'trs: *
Fees: £5.50 (£7.50)

BRENT VALLEY
Church Road, Hanwell, London
Tel: (081) 567 1287
Holes: 18 5426 yds
V'trs: **
Fees: £4 (£5.50)

HAREFIELD PLACE
The Drive, Harefield Place, Uxbridge
Tel: (0895) 37287
Holes: 18 5711 yds
V'trs: **
Fees: £4.50 (£7)

HASTE HILL
The Drive, Northwood
Tel: (092 74) 22877
Holes: 18 5794 yds
V'trs: **
Fees: £3.50 (£5.50)

HORSENDEN HILL
Woodland Rise, Greenford
Tel: (081) 902 4555
Holes: 9 3264 yds
V'trs: **
Fees: £2.30 (£3.50)

HOUNSLOW HEATH
Staines Road, Hounslow
Tel: (081) 5 70 5271
Holes: 18 5820 yds
V'trs: *
Fees: £4 (£5)

LIME TREES PARK
Ruislip Road, Northolt
Tel: (081) 845 3180
Holes: 9 5789 yds
V'trs: **
Fees: On enquiry

PERIVALE PARK
Ruislip Road, Greenford
Tel: (081) 575 8655
Holes: 9 5296 yds
V'trs: **
Fees: £3.50 (£4.50)

PICKETTS LOCK
Picketts Lock Lane, Edmonton, London
Tel: (081) 803 3611
Holes: 9 2496 yds
V'trs: **
Fees: £2.50 (£3)

RUISLIP
Ickenham Road, Ruislip
Tel: (0895) 638835
Holes: 18 5235 yds
V'trs: **
Fees: £4.50 (£7)

TRENT PARK
Bramley Road, Southgate, London
Tel: (081) 366 7432
Holes: 18 6008 yds
V'trs: *
Fees: £4.50 (£6)

TWICKENHAM
Staines Road, Twickenham
Tel: (081) 979 1698
Holes: 9 604 yds
V'trs: **
Fees: £3 (£4)

WHITEWEBBS
Syon Lane, Isleworth
Tel: (081) 847 0685
Holes: 18 6242 yds
V'trs: **
Fees: £12 (£17)

NORTHAMPTONSHIRE

DELAPRE
Eagle Drive, Nene Valley Way, Northampton
Tel: (0604) 64036
Holes: 18 6293 yds
2 x 9 hole Par 3 courses
V'trs: **
Fees: £3.75 (£4.75)

PRIORS HALL
Corby (nr Weldon)
Tel: (0536) 60756
Holes: 18 6677 yds
V'trs: **
Fees: £2.80 (£4.30)

NORTHUMBERLAND

BEDLINGTONSHIRE
Acorn Bank, Bedlington
Tel: (0670) 822087
Holes: 18 6224 mts
V'trs: **
Fees: £4.50 (£6)

MAGDALENE FIELDS
Magdalene Fields, Berwick-upon-Tweed
Tel: (0289) 306384
Holes: 18 6551 yds
V'trs: **
Fees: £6.25

TYNEDALE
The Links, Warkworth, Morpeth
Tel: (0665) 711596
Holes: 9 5706 yds
V'trs: **
Fees: £6 (£10)

NOTTINGHAMSHIRE

BULWELL FOREST
Hucknall Road, Bulwell, Nottingham
Tel: (0602) 278008
Holes: 18 5746 yds
V'trs: **
Fees: £3.20

EDWALTON
Edwalton, Nottingham
Tel: (0602) 234775
Holes: 9 3336 yards
9 hole Par 3 course
V'trs: **
Fees: £2.30 (£2.80)

KILTON FOREST
Blyth Road, Worksop
Tel: (0909) 486563
Holes: 18 6569 yds
V'trs: **
Fees: £4.50 (£5.50)

MANSFIELD WOODHOUSE
Mansfield Woodhouse
Tel: (0623) 23521
Holes: 9 2411 yds
V'trs: **
Fees: £2

NOTTINGHAM CITY
Lawton Drive, Bulwell,
Nottingham
Tel: (0602) 272767
Holes: 18 6218 yds
V'trs: *
Fees: £3.75 (£4)

OXFORDSHIRE

CHERWELL EDGE
Chacombe, Banbury
Tel: (0295) 711591
Holes: 18 5925 yds
V'trs: *
Fees: £3.80 (£4.90)

SHROPSHIRE

MEOLE BRACE
Meole Brace, Shrewsbury
Tel: (0743) 64050
Holes: 9 2915 yds
V'trs: **
Fees: £2.50 (£3.20)

SOMERSET

VIVARY PARK
Taunton
Tel: (0823) 333875
Holes: 18 4620 yds
V'trs: *
Fees: £5.25

STAFFORDSHIRE

GOLDENHILL
Mobberley Road, Goldenhill,
Stoke-on-Trent
Tel: (0782) 784715
Holes: 18 5957 yds
V'trs: *
Fees: On enquiry

NEWCASTLE MUNICIPAL
Keele Road, Newcastle-under-
Lyme
Tel: (0782) 627596
Holes: 18 5822 mts
V'trs: *
Fees: £2.75 (£3.15)

PARK HALL
Hulme Road, Weston Coyney,
Stoke-on-Trent
Tel: (0782) 599584
Holes: 18 2335 yds
V'trs: *
Fees: £2.70 (£3.20)

TAMWORTH
Eagle Drive, Amington,
Tamworth
Tel: (0827) 53850
Holes: 18 6695 yds
V'trs: **
Fees: £3.35

SUFFOLK

CRETINGHAM
Grove Farm, Cretingham,
Woodbridge
Tel: (072882) 275
Holes: 9 1955 yds
V'trs: **
Fees: £5 (£6)

SURREY

ADDINGTON COURT
Featherbed Lane, Addington,
Croydon
Tel: (081) 657 0271
Holes: Old 18 5577 yds
New 18 5513 yds
Lower 9 1812 yds
V'trs: **
Fees: Old £6,
New £5.25,
9 hole £3.50

CHESSINGTON
Garrison Lane, Chessington
Tel: (081) 391 0948
Holes: 9 1400 yds
V'trs: *
Fees: £9 holes—£2.50 (3)

COULSDEN COURT
Coulsden
Tel: (081) 660 0468
Holes: 18 6030 yds
V'trs: *
Fees: £5 (£7.25)

FARNHAM PARK
Farnham
Tel: (0252) 715216
Holes: 9 1163 yds
V'trs: **
Fees: £1.80 (£2.10)

GOAL FARM
Goal Road, Pirbright
Tel: (048 67) 3183/3205
Holes: 9 1273 yds
V'trs: *
Fees: 18 £3.80 (£4.20) 9 £2
(£2.50)

HOEBRIDGE
The Club House, Old Woking
Road, Old Woking
Tel: (0483) 722611
Holes: 18 6587 yds
V'trs: *
Fees: 18 hole—£8.50 Inter—£5
Par 3—£4.50

MOORE PLACE
Portsmouth Road, Esher
Tel: (0372) 63533
Holes: 9 3512 yds
V'trs: **
Fees: £3.50 (£4.50)

OAKS SPORTS CENTRE
Woodmansterne Road,
Carshalton
Tel: (081) 643 8363
Holes: 18 5975 yds
9 1590 yds
V'trs: **
Fees: 18 £5.20 (£7)
9 £2.50 (£3)

RICHMOND PARK
Roehampton Gate, Richmond
Park, London
Tel: (081) 876 3205/1795
Holes: Dukes 18 5940 yds
Princes 18 5969 yds
V'trs: **
Fees: £5.50 (£8)

SANDOWN PARK
More Lane, Esher
Tel: (0372) 63340
Holes: 9 5658 yds
9 hole Par 3
V'trs: **
Fees: £2.80 (3.75)

SHILLINGLEE PARK
Chiddingfold, Godalming
Tel: (0428) 53237
Holes: 9 2400 yds
V'trs: **
Fees: £11.50 (£13.50)

WINDLEMERE
Windlesham Road, West End,.
Woking
Tel: (0276) 858727
Holes: 9 5346 yds
V'trs: **
Fees: £4 (£4.80)

SUSSEX (EAST)

HASTINGS
Beauport Park, Battle Road, St
Leonards-on-Sea
Tel: (0424) 52981
Holes: 18 6248 yds
V'trs: *
Fees: £6.50 (£8)

HOLLINGBURY PARK
Ditching Road, Brighton
Tel: (0273) 500086
Holes: 18 6415 yds
V'trs: **
Fees: £8 (£10)

HORAM PARK
Chiddingly Road, Horam
Tel: (04353) 3477
Holes: 9 5688 yds
V'trs: *
Fees: £12.50 (£14)
9 holes £6.50 (£7)

PAXHILL PARK
Eastmascalls Lane, Lindfield
Tel: (0444) 484467
Holes: 18 6186 yds
V'trs: *
Fees: £15 (£20)

SEAFORD HEAD
Southdown Road, Seaford
Tel: (0323) 890139
Holes: 18 5812 yds
V'trs: **
Fees: £6 (£7.50)

WATERHALL
Devils Dyke Road, Brighton
Tel: (0273) 508658
Holes: 18 5775 yds
V'trs: **
Fees: £8 (£10)

SUSSEX (WEST)

HILL BARN
Hill Barn Lane, Worthing
Tel: (0903) 37301
Holes: 18 6224 yds
V'trs: **
Fees: £7 (£8)

TILGATE
Titmus Drive, Tilgate, Crawley
Tel: (0293) 545411
Holes: 18 6359 yds
V'trs: *
Fees: £6.50 (£9.50)

WEST CHILTINGTON
Broadford Bridge Road, W
Chiltington
Tel: (07983) 2115
Holes: 18 5969 yds
V'trs: **
Fees: £8.50 (£12)

TYNE & WEAR

WALLSEND
Bigges Main, Wallsend
Tel: (091) 262 4231
Holes: 18 6608 yds
V'trs: **
Fees: £6.50 (£8)

WARWICKSHIRE

**CITY OF COVENTRY
(BRANDON WOOD)**
Brandon Lane, Coventry
Tel: (0203) 543141
Holes: 18 65 30 yds
V'trs: **
Fees: £5 (£6.50)

NEWBOLD COMYN
Newbold Terrace Ezst,
Leamington Spa
Tel: (0926) 421157
Holes: 18 6221 yds
V'trs: *
Fees: £3.40 (£4.40)

WARWICK
Warwick Racecourse, Warwick
Tel: (0926) 491284
Holes: 9 2682 yds
V'trs: *
Fees: £2 (£2.50)

WEST MIDLANDS

THE BELFRY
Wishaw
Tel: (0675) 70301
Holes: Brabazon 18 6975 yds
Derby 18 6127 yds
V'trs: **
Fees: £35 (£38)

BOLDMERE
Monmouth Drive, Birmingham,
Sutton Coldfield
Tel: (021) 354 3379
Holes: 18 4463 yds
V'trs: **
Fees: £3.90 (£4.60)

BRAND HALL
Heron Road, Oldbury, Warley
Tel: (021) 552 2195
Holes: 18 5813 yds
V'trs: *
Fees: £3

COCKS MOOR WOODS
Alcester Road, South Kings
Heath, Birmingham
Tel: (021) 444 3584
Holes: 18 5742 yds
V'trs: **
Fees: £3.90 (£4.60)

HARBORNE CHURCH FARM
Vicarage Road, Harborne,
Birmingham
Tel: (021) 427 1204
Holes: 9 4514 yds
V'trs: **
Fees: £3.20 (£4) 18 holes
£1.70 (£2.10) 9 holes

HATCHFORD BROOK
Coventry Road, Sheldon,
Birmingham
Tel: (021) 743 9821
Holes: 18 6164 yds
V'trs: **
Fees: £3.90 (£4.60)

HILLTOP
Park Lane, Handsworth, Birmingham
Tel: (021) 554 4463
Holes: 18 6114 yds
V'trs: ••
Fees: £3.90 (£4.60)

HIMLEY HALL
Himley Hall Park, Dudley
Tel: (0902) 895206
Holes: 9 3090 yds
V'trs: •
Fees: 18 holes £3.50 (£4)
9 holes £2.20 (£2.70)

LICKEY HILLS
Rednal, Birmingham
Tel: (021) 453 3159
Holes: 18 6010 yds
V'trs: ••
Fees: £2 (£2)

PYPE HAYES
Eachelhurst Road, Walmley, Sutton Coldfield
Tel: (021) 351 10141
Holes: 18 5811 yds
V'trs: ••
Fees: £4

WARLEY
Lightwoods Hill, Warley
Tel: (021) 429 2440
Holes: 9 2606 yds
V'trs: ••
Fees: £3.20 (£4)

WILTSHIRE

BROOM MANOR
Pipers Way, Swindon
Tel: (0793) 532403
Holes: 18 6359 yds
9 2745 yds
V'trs: ••
Fees: 18 £4.95 (£5.25)
9 £2.85 (£3.15)

YORKSHIRE

BARNSLEY
Wakefield Road, Staincross, Barnsley
Tel: (0226) 3829054
Holes: 18 6048 yds
V'trs: ••
Fees: £3.25 (£4.40)

BEAUCHIEF MUNICIPAL
Abbey Lane, Sheffield
Tel: (0742) 367274/620040
Holes: 18 5428 yds
V'trs: ••
Fees: £4.50 (£4.50)

BIRLEY WOOD
Birley Lane, Sheffield
Tel: (0742) 390099
Holes: 18 6275 yds
V'trs: ••
Fees: £3.50 (£5)

CONCORDE PARK
Shiregreen Lane, Sheffield
Tel: (0742) 570274/570053
Holes: 18 4321 yds
V'trs: ••
Fees: £4.50

CROOKHILL PARK
Conisborough, nr Doncaster
Tel: (0709) 862979
Holes: 18 5846 yds
V'trs: ••
Fees: £4

GRANGE PARK
Upper Wortley Road, Kimberworth, Rotherham
Tel: (0709) 559497
Holes: 18 6461 yds
V'trs: ••
Fees: £2.75 (£3.60)

TINSLEY PARK
Darnall, Sheffield
Tel: (0742) 560237
Holes: 18 6045 yds
V'trs: ••
Fees: £4.50

WOMBWELL HILLIES
Wentworth View, Wombwell, Barnsley
Tel: (0226) 754433
Holes: 18 6686 yds
V'trs: ••
Fees: £25 (£30)

BINGLEY (ST IVES)
St Ives Estate, Bingley
Tel: (0274) 562506
Holes: 18 6466 yds
V'trs: •
Fees: £5 (£8.50)

BRADLEY PARK
Bradley Road, Huddersfield
Tel: (0484) 539988
Holes: 18 6202 yds
9 Par 3
V'trs: ••
Fees: £4.25 (£5.50)

CITY OF WAKEFIELD
Lupset Park, Horbury Road, Wakefield
Tel: (0924) 360282
Holes: 18 6405 yds
V'trs: •
Fees: £3.60 (£5.80)

GOTTS PARK
Armley Ridge Road, Armley, Leeds
Tel: (0532) 636600
Holes: 18 4960 yds
V'trs: ••
Fees: £3.75 (£4.10)

MIDDLETON PARK
Ring Road, Beeston Park, Middleton, Leeds
Tel: (0532) 709506
Holes: 18 5233 yds
V'trs: ••
Fees: £3.70

PONTEFRACT PARK
Park Road, Pontefract
Tel: (0977) 702799
Holes: 18 4068 yds
V'trs: ••
Fees: £2.50 (£3.60)

ROUNDHAY
Park Lane, Leeds
Tel: (0532) 661686
Holes: 9 5166 yds
V'trs: ••
Fees: £3.70 (£4.10)

TEMPLE NEWSAM
Temple Newsam Road, Halton, Leeds
Tel: (0532) 647362
Holes: 18 6448 yds, Lady Dorothy Wood 18 6029 yds
V'trs: •
Fees: £3.50 (£4)

WHITWOOD
Altofts Lane, Whitwood, Castleford
Tel: (0977) 512835
Holes: 9 6176 yds
V'trs: •
Fees: On enquiry

WALES

GWENT

CAERLEON
Broadway, Caerleon
Tel: (0633) 420342
Holes: 9 3095 yds
V'trs: ••
Fees: £6

ISLE OF ANGLESEY

LLANGEFNI
Llangefni
Tel: (0248) 722193
Holes: 9 1467 yds
V'trs: ••
Fees: £3 (£4)

SCOTLAND

BORDER REGION

BERWICKSHIRE

LAUDER
Lauder
Tel: (05782) 409
Holes: 9 6002 yds
V'trs: ••
Fees: £3.50 (£4)

PEEBLESSHIRE

PEEBLES
Kirkland Street, Peebles
Tel: (0721) 20197
Holes: 18 6137 yds
V'trs: ••
Fees: £6.50 (£9)

SELKIRKSHIRE

GALASHIELS
Ladhope Recreation Ground, Galashiels
Tel: (0896) 3724
Holes: 18 5309 yds
V'trs: ••
Fees: £4.20 (£4.70)

CENTRAL REGION

STIRLINGSHIRE

GRANGEMOUTH
Polmonthill, Grangemouth
Tel: (0324) 714355
Holes: 18 6527 yds
V'trs: ••
Fees: £4 (£5)

FIFE REGION

FIFE

BALGOVE
St Andrews
Tel: (0334) 75757
Holes: 9 beginners course
V'trs: ••
Fees: £2

BALLINGRY
Lochore Meadows Country Park, Crosshill, Lochgelly
Tel: (0592) 860086
Holes: 9 6482 yds
V'trs: ••
Fees: £3.10 (£4.10)

DUNNIKIER PARK
Dunnikier Way, Kirkcaldy
Tel: (0592) 216599
Holes: 18 6601 yds
V'trs: ••
Fees: £3 (£4.15)

EDEN COURSE
St Andrews
Tel: (0334) 74296
Holes: 18 6400 yds
V'trs: ••
Fees: £9 (unlimited play on Eden, Jubilee and New Courses)

FALKLAND
The Myre, Falkland
Tel: (0337) 57404
Holes: 9 2500 yds
V'trs: ••
Fees: £4 (£6)

GLENROTHES
*Golf Course Road, Glenrothes
KY6 2LA1*
Tel: (0592) 758686/658678
Holes: 18 6444 yds
V'trs: ••
Fees: £3 (£4.15)

JUBILEE COURSE
St Andrews
Tel: (0334) 73938
Holes: 18 5 246 yds
V'trs: ••
Fees: £10 (unlimited play over
Jubilee, Eden and New
Courses)

KINGHORN
Macduff Cres, Kinghorn
Tel: (0592) 890345
Holes: 18 5246 yds
V'trs: ••
Fees: £2.80 (£3.95)

LEVEN
North Links, Leven
Tel: (0333) 27057
Holes: 18 5600 yds
V'trs: •
Fees: £3 (£4)

NEW COURSE
St Andrews
Tel: (0334) 73938
Holes: 18 6604 yds
V'trs: ••
Fees: £11

OLD COURSE
St Andrews
Tel: (0334) 73393
Holes: 18 6566 yds
V'trs: • H
Fees: £22.50

GRAMPIAN REGION

ABERDEENSHIRE

AUCHMILL
Provost Rust Drive, Aberdeen
Tel: (0224) 714577
Holes: 9 2538 mts
V'trs: ••
Fees: £2.30

BALNAGASK
St Fitticks Road, Aberdeen
Tel: (0224) 876407
Holes: 18 5468 mts
V'trs: ••
Fees: £4.60

HAZLEHEAD
Hazlehead, Aberdeen
Tel: (0224) 321830
Holes: 18 5763 mts
18 5303 mts
9 hole
V'trs: ••
Fees: £4.60

INVERALLOCHY
Inverallochy, nr Fraserburgh
Tel: (034 65) 2324
Holes: 18 5137 yds
V'trs: ••
Fees: £4 (£5)

KING'S LINKS
Gold Road, Aberdeen
Tel: (0224) 641577
Holes: 18 5839 mts
V'trs: ••
Fees: £4.60

AUCHENBLAE
Auchenblae
Tel: (056 12) 407
Holes: 9 2174 yds
V'trs: •
Fees: £4 (£6)

CAITHNESS

THURSO
Newlands of Greise, Thurso
Tel: (0847) 63807
Holes: 18 5818 yds
V'trs: ••
Fees: £4 (£5)

INVERNESS

SKEABOST
Skeabost Bridge, Isle of Skye
Tel: (047 032) 202
Holes: 9 3224 yds
V'trs: ••
Fees: £3

TORVEAN
Glenurquhart Road, Inverness
Tel: (0463) 237543/225651
Holes: 18 5784 yds
V'trs: ••
Fees: £6 (£7)

SUTHERLAND

DURNESS
Balnakeil, Durness
Tel: (097 181) 364
Holes: 9 5468 yds
V'trs: ••
Fees: £5

LOTHIAN

EAST LOTHIAN

BURGH LINKS
East Links, North Berwick
Tel: (0620) 2726
Holes: 18 6079 yds
V'trs: ••
Fees: On enquiry

HADDINGTON
Amisfield Park, Haddington
Tel: (062 082) 2727
Holes: 18 6280 yds
V'trs: •
Fees: £6.25 (£8)

WINTERFIELD
Back Road, Dunbar
Tel: (0368) 63562
Holes: 18 5053 yds
V'trs: •
Fees: On enquiry

MIDLOTHIAN

BRAIDHILLS No 1
Edinburgh
Tel: (031) 447 8205
Holes: 18 5239 yds
V'trs: ••
Fees: On enquiry

BRAIDHILLS No 2
Edinburgh
Tel: (031) 447 8205
Holes: 18 4832 yds
V'trs: ••
Fees: On enquiry

CARRICK KNOWE
Glendevon Park, Edinburgh
Tel: (031) 337 1096
Holes: 18 6299 yds
V'trs: ••
Fees: £3.50

CRAIGENTINNY
Edinburgh
Tel: (031) 554 7501
Holes: 18 5418 yds
V'trs: ••
Fees: £3.50

PORTOBELLO
*Stanley Street, Portobello,
Edinburgh*
Tel: (031) 669 4361
Holes: 9 2419 yds
V'trs: ••
Fees: £1.75

SILVERKNOWES
*Silverknowes, Parkway,
Edinburgh*
Tel: (031) 336 3843
Holes: 18 6210 yds
V'trs: ••
Fees: On enquiry
•

WEST LOTHIAN

POLMEMMET
By Whitburn, West Lothian
Tel: (0501) 43905
Holes: 9 2967 mts
V'trs: ••
Fees: £1.60 (£2)

ARGYLL

COLONSAY
Isle of Colonsay
Tel: (09512) 316
Holes: 18 4775 yds
V'trs: ••
Fees: On enquiry

AYRSHIRE

ANNANHILL
Irvine Road, Kilmarnock
Tel: (0563) 21644
Holes: 18 6270 yds
V'trs: •
Fees: £3.75 (£8.75)

AUCHENHARVIE
*Moor Park Road, West Brewery
Park, Saltcoats*
Tel: (0292) 603103
Holes: 9 5800 yds
V'trs: ••
Fees: £3.50 (£5)

BELLEISLE
Ayr
Tel: (0292) 41314
Holes: 18 6545 yds
V'trs: • H
Fees: £6.60 (£9.20)

CAPRINGTON
*Kilmarnock Municipal, Ayr
Road, Kilmarnock*
Tel: (0563) 21915
Holes: 18 5460 yds
V'trs: ••
Fees: On request

DALMILLING
*Westwood Avenue, Whitletts,
Ayr*
Tel: (0292) 63893
Holes: 18 5401 yds
V'trs: ••
Fees: £3.50 (£4.30)

GIRVAN
Golf Course Road, Girvan
Tel: (0465) 4272
Holes: 18 5095 yds
V'trs: ••
Fees: £4.40 (£5.60)

IRVIN RAVENSPARK
Irvine
Tel: (0294) 76467
Holes: 18 6496 yds
V'trs: ••
Fees: £3 (£5)

MAYBOLE
Memorial Park, Maybole
Tel: (0292) 281511
Holes: 9 2635 yds
V'trs: ••
Fees: £5 (£5.80)

SEAFIELD
Ayr
Tel: (0292) 41314
Holes: 18 5457 yds
V'trs: ••
Fees: £7

TROON MUNICIPAL
Harling Drive, Troon
Tel: (0292) 312464
Holes: Lochgreen 18 6687 yds
Darley 18 6327 yds
Fullarton 18 4784 yds
V'trs: •
Fees: On request

DUNBARTONSHIRE

CLYDEBANK MUNICIPAL
*Overtoun Road, Dalmuir,
Clydebank*
Tel: (041) 952 6372
Holes: 18 5349 yds
V'trs: ••
Fees: £3

CUMBERNAULD
*Palaacerigg Country Park,
Cumbernauld G67 3HU*
Tel: (0236) 734969
Holes: 18 6412 yds
V'trs: ••
Fees: £5 (£9)

LANARKSHIRE

ALEXANDRA PARK
*Sannox Gardens, Alexandra
Parade, Glasgow*
Tel: (041) 556 3711
Holes: 9 1968 yds
V'trs: **
Fees: £1.10 (£1.40)

BIGGAR
*Public Park, Broughton Road,
Biggar*
Tel: (0899) 20618
Holes: 18 5416 yds
V'trs: **
Fees: £5 (£7.50)

COATBRIDGE
Townhead Road, Coatbridge
Tel: (0236) 21492
Holes: 18 6020 yds
V'trs: **
Fees: £1.75

DEACONSBANK
Glasgow
Tel: (041) 638 7044
Holes: 18 4800 yds
V'trs: **
Fees: £3.75 (£5.50)

HOLLANDBUSH
*Acre Tophead, Lesmahagow by
Coalburn*
Tel: (0555) 893646
Holes: 18 6110 yds
V'trs: **
Fees: £4 (£6)

KING'S PARK
*Croftpark Avenue, Froftfoot,
Glasgow*
Tel: (041) 637 5871
Holes: 9 2010 yds
V'trs: **
Fees: £1.20

KNIGHTSWOOD
Lincoln Avenue, Glasgow
Tel: (041) 9059 2131
Holes: 9 2736 yds
V'trs: **
Fees: £1.50

LARKHALL
Burnhead Road, Larkhall
Tel: (0698) 881113
Holes: 9 6764 yds
V'trs: *
Fees: On enquiry

LETHAMHILL
Cumbernauld Road, Glasgow
Tel: (041) 770 6220
Holes: 18 5946 yds
V'trs: **
Fees: £2.50 (£3)

LINN PARK
Simshill Road, Glasgow
Tel: (041) 637 5871
Holes: 18 4592 yds
V'trs: **
Fees: £2.70 (£3)

LITTLEHILL
*Auchinairn Road, Bishopbriggs,
Glasgow*
Tel: (041) 772 1916
Holes: 18 6228 yds
V'trs: **
Fees: £1.80 (£2.40)

RUCHILL
*Brassey Street, Maryhill,
Glasgow*
Tel: (041) 946 7676
Holes: 9 2240 yds
V'trs: **
Fees: £1.20

STRATHCLYDE PARK
Mote Hill, Hamilton
Tel: (0698) 459201
Holes: 9 6294 yds
V'trs: *
Fees: £1.20

TORRANCE HOUSE
Strathaven Road, East Kilbride
Tel: (035 52) 33451
Holes: 18 6403 yds
V'trs: **
Fees: £4.50

ANGUS

ARBROATH
Elliot, by Arbroath
Tel: (0241) 75837
Holes: 18 6078 yds
V'trs: **
Fees: £5 (£7)

BUDDON LINKS
*Carnoustie Golf Links, Links
Parade, Carnoustie*
Tel: (0241) 53249
Holes: 18 5732 yds
V'trs: **
Fees: £5

BURNSIDE
*Carnoustie Golf Links, Links
Parade, Carnoustie*
Tel: (0241) 53249
Holes: 18 6020 yds
V'trs: *
Fees: £10

CAIRD PARK
Dundee
Tel: (0382) 459438
Holes: 18 6303 yds
V'trs: **
Fees: On enquiry

CAIRD PARK
*City of Dundee Parks Dept, 353
Clepington Road, Dundee*
Tel: (0382) 23141 (Ext 141)
Holes: Yellow 9 1692 yds
Red 9 1983 yds
V'trs: **
Fees: On enquiry

CAMPERDOWN
Camperdown Park, Dundee
Tel: (0382) 623398
Holes: 18 6561 yds
V'trs: **
Fees: £6.50 (£7.50)

**CARNOUSTIE
CHAMPIONSHIP**
Links Parade, Carnoustie
Tel: (0241) 53249
Holes: 18 6936 yds
V'trs: * H
Fees: £22

MONTROSE
Traill Drive, Montrose
Tel: (0674) 72634
Holes: Medal 18 6451 yds
Broomfield 18 4815 yds
V'trs: **
Fees: Medal £8.50 (£10)
Broomfield £6 (£7.50)

PERTHSHIRE

DALMUNZIE
Glenshee, Blairgowrie
Tel: (025 085) 226
Holes: 9 2035 yds
V'trs: **
Fees: 9 holes £3

NORTH INCH
*c/o Perth & Kinross District
Council, 3 High Street, Perth*
Tel: (0738) 39911
Holes: 18 4340 mts
V'trs: **
Fees: £2.70 (£4.90)

IRELAND

CO ARMAGH

CRAIGAVON
*Golf/Ski Centre, Turmoyra
Lane, Silverwood, Lurgan,
Craigavon*
Tel: (0762) 6606
Holes: 18 6496 yds
V'trs: **
Fees: On enquiry

BELFAST

**BALLYEARL GOLF
CENTRE**
*585 Doagh Road,
Newtonabbey*
Tel: (02313) 48287
Holes: 9 2362 yds Par 3
V'trs: **
Fees: £2 (£2.75)

GILNAHIRK
Upepr Bramel Road, Belfast
Tel: (0232) 448477
Holes: 9 2699 mts
V'trs: **
Fees: £2 (£2.50)

CO CLARE

DRUMOLAND CASTLE
Newmarket-on-Fergus
Tel: (061) 71144
Holes: 18 6098 yds
V'trs: **
Fees: £10

KILRUSH
Lahinch
Tel: (065) 81408
Holes: 18 6699 yds
V'trs: **
Fees: £15 (£18) Castle £10

CO DONEGAL

BUNCRANA
Buncrana
Holes: 9 2020 yds
V'trs: **
Fees: On enquiry

DUNFRANAGHY
Dunfanaghy
Tel: (074) 36335
Holes: 18 5600 yds
V'trs: **
Fees: £7 (£8)

CO DOWN

KILKEEL
Mourne Park, Ballyardle, Kilkeel
Tel: (06937) 62296
Holes: 9 6000 yds
V'trs: **
Fees: £8

CO DUBLIN

CORBALLIS
Donabate
Tel: (0001) 436346
Holes: 18 4 971 yds
V'trs: **
Fees: £6

DEER PARK
Howth
Tel: (0001) 322624
Holes: 18 6647 yds
V'trs: **
Fees: £8

KILTERNAN HOTEL
Kilternan
Tel: (0001) 955559
Holes: 18 5413 yds
V'trs: **
Fees: £7

CO MAYO

BALLINROBE
Ballinrobe, Claremorris
Tel: (092) 41448
Holes: 9 5690 yds
V'trs: *
Fees: £5

MULRANY
Mulrany, Westport
Tel: (098) 36185
Holes: 9 6380 yds
V'trs: **
Fees: £3

ENGLAND

AVON

BATH
Sham Castle, North Road, Bath
Tel: (0225) 466953
Holes: 18 6369 yds
V'trs: **H
Fees: £12 (£15)

BRISTOL & CLIFTON
Beggar Bush Lane, Failand, nr Clifton, Bristol
Tel: (0272) 393031
Holes: 18 6294 yds
V'trs: * H
Fees: On enquiry

CHIPPING SODBURY
The Common, Chipping Sodbury, Bristol
Tel: (0454) 314087
Holes: New 18 6912 yds, Old 9 6194 yds
V'trs: *
Fees: New £8 (£10), Old £2.50

CLEVEDON
Castle Road, Clevedon
Tel: (0272) 874704
Holes: 18 5887 yds
V'trs: * H
Fees: £12 (£15)

FILTON
Golf Course Lane, Bristol
Tel: (0272) 694158
Holes: 18 6277 yds
V'trs: *
Fees: £14

FOSSEWAY
Charlton Lane, Midsomer Norton, Bath
Tel: (0761) 412214
Holes: 9 4148 yds
V'trs: *
Fees: £8 (£9)

HENBURY
Westbury-on-Trym, Bristol
Tel: (0272) 503121
Holes: 18 6039 yds
V'trs: * H
Fees: £15

KNOWLE
Fairway, Knowle, Brislington, Bristol
Tel: (0272) 779193
Holes: 18 6016 yds
V'trs: * H
Fees: £12 (£15)

LANSDOWN
Lansdown, Bath
Tel: (0225) 420242
Holes: 18 6267 yds
V'trs: * H
Fees: £14

LONG ASHTON
Long Ashton, Bristol
Tel: (0272) 392265
Holes: 18 6051 yds
V'trs: * H
Fees: £15 (£18)

MANGOTSFIELD
Carsons Road, Mangotsfield, Bristol
Tel: (0272) 565501
Holes: 18 5297 yds
V'trs: **
Fees: £7 (£10)

SALTFORD
Golf Club Lane, Saltford
Tel: (0225) 872043
Holes: 18 6081 yds
V'trs: **
Fees: £14 (£16)

SHIREHAMPTON PARK
Park Hill, Shirehampton, Bristol
Tel: (0272) 822488
Holes: 18 5493 yds
V'trs: *
Fees: £13

TRACY PARK
Tracy Park, Bath Road, Wick, nr Bristol
Tel: (027 582) 3521
Holes: 27 Avon 6834 yds, Cotswold 6203 yds
V'trs: *
Fees: £12 (£15)

WESTON-SUPER-MARE
Uphill Road, Weston-Super-mare
Tel: (0934) 633360
Holes: 18 6308 yds
V'trs: **
Fees: £14 (£18)

WORLEBURY
Monks Hill, Weston-Super-Mare
Tel: (0934) 418473
Holes: 18 5921 yds
V'trs: **
Fees: £11 (£17)

BEDFORDSHIRE

ASPLEY GUISE & WOBURN SANDS
West Hill, Aspley Guise, Milton Keynes
Tel: (0908) 582974
Holes: 18 6248 yds
V'trs: * H
Fees: £13

BEADLOW MANOR HOTEL
Beadlow, Shefford
Tel: (0525) 61292
Holes: 18 6238 yds, 9 6042 yds
V'trs: ** H
Fees: On enquiry

BEDFORD & COUNTY
Green Lane, Clapham, Bedford
Tel: (0234) 59189
Holes: 18 6347 yds
V'trs: *
Fees: £15

BEDFORDSHIRE
Bromham Road, Biddenham, Bedford
Tel: (0234) 53653
Holes: 18 6185 yds
V'trs: *
Fees: On enquiry

COLWORTH
Unilever Reesearch, Sharnbrook, Bedford
Tel: (0234) 222654
Holes: 9 2500 yds
V'trs: ***

DUNSTABLE DOWNS
Whipsnade Road, Dunstable
Tel: (0582) 662806
Holes: 18 6184 yds
V'trs: * H
Fees: On enquiry

GRIFFIN
c/o 3 Hillcrest Avenue, Luton
Tel: (0582) 415573
Holes: 9 5354 yds
V'trs: *
Fees: £3 (£5)

JOHN O'GAUNT
Sutton Park, Sandy, Biggleswade
Tel: (0767) 260094
Holes: John O'Gaunt 18 6513 yards, Carthagena 18 5 869 yds
V'trs: ** H
Fees: £25 (£40)

LEIGHTON BUZZARD
Plantation Road, Leighton Buzzard
Tel: (0525) 372143
Holes: 18 5366 yds
V'trs: *
Fees: £15

MILLBROOK
Millbrook, Ampthill
Tel: (0525) 402269
Holes: 18 6473 yds
V'trs: *
Fees: £10 (£15)

RAF HENLOW
RAF Henlow, Henlow
Tel: (0462) 815016
Holes: 9 5616 yds
V'trs: ***

SOUTH BEDS
Warden Hill, Luton
Tel: (0582) 591209
Holes: 18 6342 yds, 9 4954 yds
V'trs: * H
Fees: 18 £14, (£18), 9 £7 (£10)

STOCKWOOD PARK
London Rd, Stockwood Park, Luton
Tel: (0582) 413704
Holes: 18 5567 yds
V'trs: *
Fees: £3.40 (£5.10)

TILSWORTH
Dunstable Road, Tilsworth, Dunstable
Tel: (0525) 210721/210722
Holes: 9 2773 yds
V'trs: **
Fees: £3 (£4)

BERKSHIRE

BEARWOOD
Mole Road, Sindlesham
Tel: (0734) 760643
Holes: 9 2814 yds
V'trs: * H
Fees: 18 £12, 9 £7

BERKSHIRE
Swinley Road, Ascot
Tel: (0990) 21469
Holes: Red 18 6356 yds, Blue 18 6258 yds
V'trs: *
Fees: On enquiry

CALCOT PARK
Calcot, nr Reading
Tel: (0734) 427797
Holes: 18 6283 yds
V'trs: *
Fees: £18

DATCHET
Buccleuch Road, Datchet
Tel: (0753) 42755
Holes: 9 5978 yds
V'trs: *
Fees: £12

DONNINGTON VALLEY
Oxford Road, Donnington, Newbury
Tel: (0635) 32488
Holes: 18 4033 yds
V'trs: **
Fees: On enquiry

DOWNSHIRE
Easthampstead Park, Wokingham
Tel: (0344) 424066
Holes: 18 6382 yds
V'trs: **
Fees: Summer £6.50, Winter £4.50

EAST BERKSHIRE
Ravenswood Ave, Crowthorne
Tel: (0344) 774112
Holes: 18 6315 yds
V'trs: * H
Fees: £24

ETON COLLEGE
Eton College, Windsor
Tel: (0753) 866461
Holes: 9 3560 yds
V'trs: ***

GORING & STREATLEY
Rectory Road, Streatley-on-Thames
Tel: (0491) 873715
Holes: 18 6266 yds
V'trs: *
Fees: £18

HAWTHORN HILL
Drift Road, Hawthorn Hill, Maidenhead
Tel: (0628) 771030/75588
Holes: 18 6212 yds
V'trs: *
Fees: £7.20 (£8.70)

HURST
Sandford Lane, Hurst, Wokingham
Tel: (0734) 345143
Holes: 9 3015 yds
V'trs: *
Fees: £2.50

LAVENDER PARK
Swinley Road, Ascot
Tel: (0344) 884074
Holes: 9 1104 yds
V'trs: **
Fees: £3.10

MAIDENHEAD
Shopperhangers Road, Maidenhead
Tel: (0628) 24067
Holes: 18 6360 yds
V'trs: *
Fees: £15

MILL RIDE
Mill Ride, North Ascot
Tel: (0344) 890433
Holes: 9 6601 yds
V'trs: ***

NEWBURY & CROOKHAM
Bury's Bank Road, Greenham Common, Newbury
Tel: (0635) 31201
Holes: 18 5880 yds
V'trs: * H
Fees: £15

READING
Kidmore End Road, Emmer Green, Reading
Tel: (0734) 476115
Holes: 18 6204 yds
V'trs: *
Fees: £19

ROYAL ASCOT
Winkfield Road, Ascot
Tel: (0990) 24656
Holes: 18 5709 yds
V'trs: *
Fees: £12

SONNING
Sonning-on-Thames
Tel: (0734) 692910
Holes: 18 6345 yds
V'trs: *
Fees: On enquiry

SWINLEY FOREST
Coronation Road, Ascot
Tel: (0990) 20197
Holes: 18 6001 yds
V'trs: ***

TEMPLE
Henley Road, Hurley, Maidenhead
Tel: (062 882) 4254
Holes: 18 6206 yds
V'trs: *
Fees: £25

WEST BERKSHIRE
Chaddleworth, Newbury
Tel: (04882) 8857
Holes: 18 7053 yds
V'trs: **
Fees: £15 (£20)

WINTER HILL
Grange Lane, Cookham
Tel: (062 85) 27610
Holes: 18 6408 yds
V'trs: *
Fees: £15.

BUCKINGHAMSHIRE

BEACONSFIELD
Beaconsfield
Tel: (0494) 676616
Holes: 18 6469 yds
V'trs: * H
Fees: £20

BUCKINGHAM
Tingewick Road, Buckingham
Tel: (0280) 815210
Holes: 18 6082 yds
V'trs: *
Fees: £18

BURNHAM BEECHES
Burnham, Slough
Tel: (0628) 661661
Holes: 18 6415 yds
V'trs: *
Fees: £18

CHARTRIDGE PARK
Marand Grange, Chartridge, Chesham
Tel: (0494) 775919
Holes: 9 3550 yds
V'trs: *
Fees: £10

CHESHAM & LEY HILL
Ley Hill, Chesham
Tel: (0494) 784541
Holes: 9 5240 yds
V'trs: *
Fees: £12

CHILTERN FOREST
Aston Hill, Halton, Aylesbury
Tel: (0296) 630899
Holes: 9 6038 yds
V'trs: *
Fees: £10

DENHAM
Tilehouse Lane, Denham
Tel: (0895) 832801
Holes: 18 6439 yds
V'trs: * H
Fees: £14

ELLESBOROUGH
Butlers Cross, nr Aylesbury
Tel: (0296) 623126
Holes: 18 6310 yds
V'trs: * H
Fees: On enquiry

FARNHAM PARK
Park Road, Stoke Poges, Slough
Tel: (028 14) 3332
Holes: 18 5847 yds
V'trs: *
Fees: £4.80 (£7)

FLACKWELL HEATH
High Wycombe
Tel: (062 85) 23017
Holes: 18 6150 yds
V'trs: * H
Fees: £19

GERRARDS CROSS
Chalfont Park, Gerrards Cross
Tel: (0753) 885300
Holes: 18 6295 yds
V'trs: * H
Fees: £23

HAREWOOD DOWNS
Cokes Lane, Chalfont St Giles
Tel: (0494) 64102
Holes: 18 5958 yds
V'trs: * H
Fees: On enquiry

HAZLEMERE
Penn Road, Hazlemere, High Wycombe
Tel: (0494) 718298
Holes: 18 6039 yds
V'trs: *
Fees: £14 (£18)

IVER
Hollow Hill Lane, Iver
Tel: (0753) 655615
Holes: 9 3107 yds
V'trs: **
Fees: 18 £5.60 (£8)
9 £3.60 (4.60)

IVINGHOE
Wellcroft, Ivinghoe, nr Leighton Buzzard
Tel: (0296) 667696
Holes: 9 4508 yds
V'trs: **
Fees: 18 £4.50 (£6)
36 £5.50 (£7)

LITTLE CHALFONT
Lodge Lane, Little Chalfont, nr Amersham
Tel: (024 04) 2942
Holes: 9 5852 yds
V'trs: *
Fees: £7 (£9)

STOKE POGES
Park Road, Stoke Poges
Tel: (0753) 23609
Holes: 18 6654 yds
V'trs: * H
Fees: £8 (£14)

STOWE
Stowe, Buckingham
Tel: (0280) 813650
Holes: 9 4573 yds
V'trs: *
Fees: £5

WESTON TURVILLE
New Road, Weston Turville, nr Aylesbury
Tel: (0296) 25949
Holes: 18 6100 yds
V'trs: *
Fees: £8 (£10)

WEXHAM VALLEY
Wexham Street, Wexham, nr Slough
Tel: (028 16) 663425
Holes: Wexham 18 5836 yds
Old Grange 9 2383 yds
V'trs: **
Fees: 18 £5.60 (£8)
9 £3.60 (£4.60)

WHITELEAF
Whiteleaf, Aylesbury
Tel: (084 44) 5472
Holes: 9 2756 yds
V'trs: *
Fees: 18 £15

WOBURN
Bow Brickhill, Milton Keynes
Tel: (0908) 647987
Holes: Dukes 18 6940 yds
Duchess 18 6641 yds
V'trs: * H
Fees: On enquiry

CAMBRIDGESHIRE

ABBOTSLEY
Eynesbury Hardwicke, St Neots
Tel: (0480) 215153
Holes: 18 6150 yds
V'trs: *
Fees: £8 (£13)

CAMBRIDGESHIRE MOAT HOUSE HOTEL
Bar Hill, Cambridge
Tel: (0954) 780098
Holes: 18 6734 yds
V'trs: * H
Fees: £18 (£25)

ELY CITY
Cambridge Road, Ely
Tel: (0353) 2751
Holes: 18 6686 yds
V'trs: ** H
Fees: £14 (£20)

GIRTON
Dodford Lane, Cambridge
Tel: (0223) 276169
Holes: 18 6085 yds
V'trs: *
Fees: £14

GOG MAGOG
Shelford Bottom, Cambridge
Tel: (0223) 246058
Holes: Old 18 6386 yds
New 9 5833 yds
V'trs: *
Fees: Old-£20, New-£10

MARCH
Frogs Abbey, Grange Road, Knights End, March
Tel: (0354) 52364
Holes: 9 6278 yds
V'trs: * H
Fees: £7

PETERBOROUGH MILTON
Milton Ferry, Peterborough
Tel: (0733) 380793
Holes: 18 6431 yds
V'trs: *
Fees: £18

RAMSEY
4 Abbey Terrace, Ramsey, Huntingdon
Tel: (0487) 813573
Holes: 18 6145 yds
V'trs: * H
Fees: £15

ST IVES (HUNTS)
St Ives, Huntingdon
Tel: (0480) 66067
Holes: 9 6100 yds
V'trs: *
Fees: £10 (£15)

ST NEOTS
Crosshall Road, St Neots
Tel: (0480) 76513
Holes: 18 6027 yds
V'trs: * H
Fees: £15

CHANNEL ISLANDS

ALDERNEY
Route des Carrières, Alderney
Tel: (048 182) 2835
Holes: 9 2528 yds
V'trs: **
Fees: £8 (£10)

LA MOYE
La Moye, St Brelade
Tel: (0534) 43130
Holes: 18 6741 yds
V'trs: * H
Fees: £22 (£25)

ROYAL GUERNSEY
L'Ancresse, Guernsey
Tel: (0481) 45070
Holes: 18 6206 yds
V'trs: * H
Fees: £10.50

ROYAL JERSEY
Grouville, Jersey
Tel: (0534) 52234
Holes: 18 6023 yds
V'trs: * H
Fees: £22 (£30)

CHESHIRE

ALDERLEY EDGE
Brook Lane, Aldlerley Edge
Tel: (0625) 584493
Holes: 9 5836 yds
V'trs: ** H
Fees: £10 (£13)

ASTBURY
Peel Lane, Astbury, nr Congleton
Tel: (0260) 272772
Holes: 18 6269 yds
V'trs: * H
Fees: £12

AVRO
British Aerospace, Woodford
Tel: (061) 439 5050
Holes: 9 5735 yds
V'trs: ***

BIRCHWOOD
Kelvin Close, Birchwood, Warrington
Tel: (0925) 818819
Holes: 18 6808 yds
V'trs: **
Fees: £11 (£15)

BRAMHALL
Ladythorn Road, Bramhall, Stockport
Tel: (061) 439 1171
Holes: 18 6300 yds
V'trs: *
Fees: £15 (£20)

CHESTER
Curzon Park, Chester
Tel: (0244) 671185
Holes: 18 6487 yds
V'trs: ** H
Fees: £15 (£20)

CONGLETON
Biddulph Road, Congleton
Tel: (0260) 271083
Holes: 9 5704 yds
V'trs: **
Fees: On enquiry

CREWE
Fields Road, Haslington, Crewe
Tel: (0270) 585032
Holes: 18 6181 yds
V'trs: *
Fees: £13

DELAMERE FOREST
Station Road, Delamere, Northwich
Tel: (0606) 883307
Holes: 18 6305 yds
V'trs: *
Fees: £15 (£20)

EATON
Eaton Park, Eccleston, Chester
Tel: (0244) 680170
Holes: 18 6446 yds
V'trs: * H
Fees: On enquiry

HELSBY
Tower's Lane, Helsby, Warrington
Tel: 18 6204 yds
Holes: 18 6204 yds
V'trs: *
Fees: £10

KNUTSFORD
Mereheath Lane, Knitsford
Tel: (0565) 3355
Holes: 9 6288 yds
V'trs: *
Fees: £10 (£15)

LYMM
Whitbarrow Road, Lymm
Tel: (092 575) 5054
Holes: 18 6304 yds
V'trs: ** H
Fees: £11 (£13)

MACCLESFIELD
The Hollins, Macclesfield
Tel: (0625) 616952
Holes: 12 6184 yds
V'trs: * H
Fees: £10

MERE
Mere, Knutsford
Tel: (0565) 830219
Holes: 18 6849 yds
V'trs: * H
Fees: £30

NEW MILLS
Shaw Marsh, New Mills
Tel: (0663) 46161
Holes: 9 5924 yds
V'trs: *
Fees: £6

OAKLANDS
Forest Road, Tarporley
Tel: (0829) 733884
Holes: 18 6473 yds
V'trs: * H
Fees: £21

POULTON PARK
Dig Lane, Cinnamon Brow
Tel: (0925) 828220
Holes: 9 mts 4918
V'trs: *
Fees: £8 (£10)

PRESTBURY
Macclesfield Road, Prestbury, Macclesfield
Tel: (0625) 828242
Holes: 18 6359 yds
V'trs: * H
Fees: £20

ROMILEY
Goosehouse Green, Romiley, Stockport
Tel: (061) 430 7122
Holes: 18 6335 yds
V'trs: **
Fees: £11 (£16)

RUNCORN
Clifton Road, Runcorn
Tel: (0928) 564791
Holes: 18 6035 yds
V'trs: * H
Fees: £10 (£12)

SANDBACH
Middlewich Road, Sandbach
Tel: (0270) 762117
Holes: 9 5614 yds
V'trs: *
Fees: £10

SANDIWAY
Sandiway
Tel: (0606) 8831809
Holes: 18 6435 yds
V'trs: * H
Fees: £20 (£25)

STOCKPORT
Offerton Road, offerton, Stockport
Tel: (061) 427 2421
Holes: 18 6319 yds
V'trs: **
Fees: £15 (£20)

THE TYTHERINGTON
Macclesfield
Tel: (0625) 617622
Holes: 18 6737 yds
V'trs: **
Fees: £16 (£20)

UPTON-BY-CHESTER
Upton Lane, Chester
Tel: (0244) 381183
Holes: 18 5875 yds
V'trs: *
Fees: £13 (£15)

VICARS CROSS
Vicars Cross, Chester
Tel: (0244) 335174
Holes: 18 5857 *
V'trs: *
Fees: £15

WARRINGTON
Hill Warren, Appleton
Tel: (0925) 65431
Holes: 18 6305 yds
V'trs: **
Fees: £9.50 (£14)

WIDNES
Highfield Road, Widnes
Tel: (051) 424 2995
Holes: 18 5719 yds
V'trs: *
Fees: £10 (£12)

WILMSLOW
Great Warford, Mobberley, Knutsford
Tel: (056 587) 3620)
Holes: 18 6500 yds
V'trs: *   Fees: On enquiry

CLEVELAND

BILLINGHAM
Sandy Lane, Billingham
Tel: (0642) 557060
Holes: 18 6430 yds
V'trs: * H Fees: £12

CASTLE END & PET'ERLEE
Castle End, Hartlepool
Tel: (0429) 836689
Holes: 18 6297 yds
V'trs: **
Fees: £10 (£16)

CLEVELAND
Queen Street, Redcar
Tel: (0642) 483462
Holes: 18 6707 yds
V'trs: *
Fees: £10 (£15)

EAGLESCLIFFE
Yarm Road, Eaglescliffe, Stockton-on-Tees
Tel: (0642) 780588
Holes: 18 6275 yds
V'trs: ** H
Fees: £11 (£15)

HARTLEPOOL
Hart Warren, Hartlepool
Tel: (0429) 267473
Holes: 18 6215 yds
V'trs: *
Fees: £12 (£20)

MIDDLESBROUGH
Brass Castle Lane, Middlesbrough
Tel: (0642) 311766
Holes: 18 5582 mts
V'trs: **
Fees: £12.50 (£15)

SALTBURN
Hob Hill, Saltburn-by-the-Sea
Tel: (0287) 24653
Holes: 18 5846 yds
V'trs: ** Fees: £8 (£10)

SEATON CAREW
Tees Road, Hartlepool
Tel: (0429) 266249
Holes: Old 6604 yds
Brabazon 6802 yds
V'trs: **
Fees: £16 (£20)

TEES-SIDE
Acklam Road, Thornaby
Tel: (0642) 673822
Holes: 18 6472 yds
V'trs: *   Fees: £8 (£12)

WILTON
Wilton, Redcar
Tel: (0642) 465265
Holes: 18 6104 yds
V'trs: *   Fees: £10

CORNWALL

BUDE & NORTH CORNWALL
Burn View, Bude
Tel: (0288) 352006
Holes: 18 6202 yds
V'trs: *   Fees: £9

BUDOCK VEAN HOTEL
Falmouth
Tel: (0326) 250288
Holes: 9 5007 yds
V'trs: H **
Fees: £7 (£9)

CAPE CORNWALL
Penzance
Tel: (0736) 788611
Holes: 18 5665 yds
V'trs: * H
Fees: £15

CARLYON BAY
Carlyon Bay, St Austell
Tel: (072 681) 4228
Holes: 18 6510 yds
V'trs: **
Fees: £8.50 (£10)

CULDROSE
Royal Naval Air Station, Culdrose
Tel: (0326) 574121 (Ext 7113)
Holes: 9 6412 yds
V'trs: ***

FALMOUTH
Swanpool Road, Falmouth
Tel: (0326) 316229
Holes: 18 5581 yds
V'trs: **
Fees: £10 (£10)

ISLES OF SCILLY
St Mary's, Isles of Scilly
Tel: (0720) 22692
Holes: 9 5974 yds
V'trs: *
Fees: £7

LAUNCESTON
St Stephen, Launceston
Tel: (0566) 3442
Holes: 18 6374 yds
V'trs: **
Fees: £10 (£12)

LOOE
Bin Down, nr Looe
Tel: (05034) 239
Holes: 18 5940 yds
V'trs: **
Fees: £10 (£12)

MULLION
Cury Helston
Tel: (0326) 241176
Holes: 18 5610 yds
V'trs: * H
Fees: £12

NEWQUAY
Tower Road, Newquay
Tel: (0637) 874830
Holes: 18 6140 yds
V'trs: * H
Fees: £12 (£15)

PERRANPORTH
Budnick Hill, Perranporth
Tel: (0872) 572317
Holes: 18 6208 yds
V'trs: ***

PRAA SANDS
*Praa Sands, Germoe Cross
Roads, Penzance*
Tel: (0736) 763445
Holes: 9 4036 yds
V'trs: *
Fees: £6

ST AUSTELL
Tregongeeves, St Austell
Tel: (0726) 68621
Holes: 18 5981 yds
V'trs: *
Fees: £9 (£12)

ST ENODOC
Rock, Wadebridge
Tel: (020 886) 2402
Holes: Church 18 6207 yds,
Holywell 18 4165 yds
V'trs: Main course *
Short course **
Fees: Church £15
Holywell £9

ST MELLION
St Mellion, nr Saltash
Tel: (0579) 50724
Holes: Old 18 5927 yds
Jack Nicklaus 18 6626 yds
V'trs: *
Fees: On enquiry

TEHIDY PARK
Camborne
Tel: (0209) 842914
Holes: 18 6241 yds
V'trs: H
Fees: £12 (£16)

**TREGENNA CASTLE
HOTEL**
St Ives
Tel: (0736) 795254 (Ext 121)
Holes: 18 3645 yds
V'trs: **
Fees: £8 (£9)

TREVOSE
Constantine Bay, Padstow
Tel: (0841) 520261
Holes: 18 6608 yds
V'trs: *
Fees: On enquiry

TRURO
Treliske, Truro
Tel: (0872) 76595
Holes: 18 5347 yds
V'trs: **
Fees: £12 (£15)

WEST CORNWALL
Lelant, St Ives
Tel: (0736) 753177
Holes: 18 5854 yds
V'trs: ** H
Fees: £10 (£14)

WHITSAND BAY HOTEL
Portwrinkle, Torpoint
Tel: (0503) 30778
Holes: 18 5512 yds
V'trs: ** H
Fees: £10 (£12)

CUMBRIA

Alston Moor
The Hermitage, Alston
Tel: (0498) 81675
Holes: 9 5880 yds
V'trs: *
Fees: £4 (£5)

APPLEBY
Appleby
Tel: (076 83) 51432
Holes: 18 5914 yds
V'trs: *
Fees: £8 (£10)

BARROW
*Rakesmoor Lane, Hawcoat,
Barrow-in-Furness*
Tel: (0229) 23121
Holes: 18 6209 yds
V'trs: **
Fees: £8 (£8)

**BRAMPTON (TALKIN
TARN)**
Brampton
Tel: (069 77) 2000
Holes: 18 6420 yds
V'trs: **
Fees: £7 (£9)

CARLISLE
Aglionby, Carlisle
Tel: (0228) 5 13241
Holes: 18 6278 yds
V'trs: **
Fees: £15 (£20)

COCKERMOUTH
Embleton, Cockermouth
Tel: (059 681) 223
Holes: 18 5496 yds
V'trs: *
Fees: £6 (£8)

THE DUNNERHOLME
Askam-in-Furness
Tel: (0229) 62675
Holes: 10 6101 yds
V'trs: **
Fees: £6 (£8)

FURNESS
*Walney Island, Barrow-in-
Furness*
Tel: (0229) 41232
Holes: 18 6363 yds
V'trs: *
Fees: £10 (£10)

GRANGE FELL
*Cartmel Road, Grange-over-
Sands*
Tel: (05395) 32536
Holes: 9 4826 mts
V'trs: **
Fees: £8 (£10)

GRANGE-OVER-SANDS
*Meathop Road, Grange-over-
Sands*
Tel: (05395) 33180
Holes: 18 5660 yds
V'trs: **
Fees: £9 (£12)

KENDAL
The Heights, Kendal
Tel: (0539) 723499
Holes: 18 5550 yds
V'trs: ** H
Fees: £9 (£12.50)

KESWICK
Threlkeld Hall, nr Keswick
Tel: (07687) 83324
Holes: 18 6175 yds
V'trs: **
Fees: £10 (£12)

KIRKBY LONSDALE
*Casterton Road, Kirkby
Lonsdale*
Tel: (0468) 72085
Holes: 9 4058yds
V'trs: **
Fees: £3

MARYPORT
Bankend, Maryport
Tel: (0900) 812605
Holes: 18 6272 yds
V'trs: **
Fees: £6 (£8)

PENRITH
Salkeld Road, Penrith
Tel: (0768) 62217
Holes: 18 6026 yds
V'trs: * H
Fees: £10 (£12)

ST BEES
*Rhoda Grove, Rheda,
Frizington*
Tel: (0946) 812105
Holes: 9 5082 yds
V'trs: **
Fees: £5 (£6)

SEASCALE
The Banks, Seascale
Tel: (094 67) 28202/28800
Holes: 18 6416 yds
V'trs: **
Fees: £10 (£12)

SEDBERGH
The Riggs, Sedbergh
Tel: (0587) 20993
Holes: 9 2067 yds
V'trs: **
Fees: £2

SILECROFT
Silecroft, Millom
Tel: (0229) 774250
Holes: 9 5712 yds
V'trs: *
Fees: £5

SILLOTH-ON-SOLWAY
Silloth, nr Carlisle
Tel: (0965) 31179
Holes: 18 6343 yds
V'trs: ** H
Fees: £11

ULVERSTON
Bardsea Park, Ulverston
Tel: (0229) 52806
Holes: 18 6122 yds
V'trs: **
Fees: £14 (£18)

WINDERMERE
Cleabarrow, Windermere
Tel: (096 62) 3550
Holes: 18 5006 yds
V'trs: ** H
Fees: £15 (£20)

WORKINGTON
Branthwaite Road, Workington
Tel: (0900) 603460
Holes: 18 6252 yds
V'trs: ** H
Fees: £10 (£15)

DERBYSHIRE

ALFRETON
Oakerthorpe, Alfreton
Tel: (0773) 832070
Holes: 9 5064 yds
V'trs: *
Fees: £6.50 (£8)

ASHBOURNE
Clifton, Ashbourne
Tel: (0335) 42078
Holes: 9 5388 yds
V'trs: *
Fees: £6 (£8)

BAKEWELL
Station Road, Bakewell
Tel: (0629) 812307
Holes: 9 5240 yds
V'trs: *
Fees: £6 (£10)

BLUE CIRCLE
Cement Works, Hope
Tel: (0433) 20317
Holes: 9 5252 yds
V'trs: ***

**BREADSALL PRIORY
HOTEL**
Moor Road, Morley, Derby
Tel: (0332) 834425
Fees: 18 6402 yds
V'trs: *
Fees: £18 (£20)

BUXTON HIGH PEAK
Townend, Buxton
Tel: (0298) 23112
Holes: 18 5954 yds
V'trs: **
Fees: £10 (£12)

CAVENDISH
Gadley Lane, Buxton
Tel: (0298) 25052
Holes: 18 5833 yds
V'trs: *
Fees: £14 (£16)

CHAPEL-EN-LE-FRITH
*The Cockyard, Manchester
Road, Chapel-en-le-Frith,
Stockport*
Tel: (0298) 812118
Holes: 18 6089 yds
V'trs: **
Fees: £10 (£15)

CHESTERFIELD
Walton, Chesterfield
Tel: (0246) 276297
Holes: 18 6326 yds
V'trs: *
Fees: £15

CHEVIN
Duffield, Derby
Tel: (0332) 841112
Holes: 18 6057 yds
V'trs: *
Fees: £15

EREWASH VALLEY
Stanton-by-Dale, nr Ilkeston
Tel: (0602) 324667
Holes: 18 6487 yds
V'trs: *
Fees: £12 (£16)

GLOSSOP & DISTRICT
Sheffield Road, Glossop
Tel: (045 74) 3117
Holes: 11 5716 yds
V'trs: **
Fees: £6 (£7)

HALLOWES
Dronfield, Sheffield
Tel: (0246) 411196
Holes: 18 6342 yds
V'trs: *
Fees: £7

HORSLEY
Lodge Farm, Smowley Mill Road, Horsley
Tel: (0332) 780838
Holes: 18 6402 yds
V'trs: * H
Fees: £10

KEDLESTON PARK
Kedleston, Derby
Tel: (0332) 841685
Holes: 18 6643 yds
V'trs: **
Fees: £20 (£25)

MATLOCK
Chesterfield Road, Matlock
Tel: (0629) 584934
Holes: 18 5989 yds
V'trs: *
Fees: £15

MICKLEOVER
Uttoxeter Road, Mickleover
Tel: (0332) 578662
Holes: 18 5708 yds
V'trs: *
Fees: £12 (£14)

ORMONDE FIELDS
Nottingham Road, Codnor, Ripley
Tel: (0773) 42987
Holes: 18 5812 yds
V'trs: £5 (£7)

PASTURES
Pastures Hospital, Mickleover
Tel: (0332) 513921 (Ext 348)
Holes: 9 5005 yds
V'trs: ***

SHIRLAND
Lower Delves, Shirland
Tel: (0773) 834935
Holes: 18 5948 yds
V'trs: **
Fees: £8 (£12)

SICKLEHOLME
Bamford, Sheffield
Tel: (0433) 51306
Holes: 18 6064 yds
V'trs: *
Fees: £15 (£20)

STANEDGE
Walton Hay Farm, nr Chesterfield
Tel: (0246) 566156
Holes: 9 4867 yds
V'trs: *
Fees: £7

DEVON

AXE CLIFF
Squires Lane, Axmouth, Seaton
Tel: (0297) 20499
Holes: 18 5111 yds
V'trs: ** H
Fees: £10

BIGBURY
Bigbury, Kingsbridge
Tel: (05 48) 810412
Holes: 18 6076 yds
V'trs: * H
Fees: £12

CHULMLEIGH
Leigh Road, Chulmleigh
Tel: (0769) 80519
Holes: 18 1440 yds (Par 3)
V'trs: **
Fees: £3

CHURSTON
Churston, Brixham
Tel: (0803) 842894
Holes: 18 6201 yds
V'trs: *
Fees: £16 (£20)

CULLOMPTON
Padbrooke Park, Cullompton
Tel: (0884) 38286
Holes: 9 3065 yds
V'trs: * H
Fees: On enquiry

DOWNES CREDITON
Hookway, Crediton
Tel: (036 32) 4864
Holes: 18 5868 yds
V'trs: **
Fees: £12 (£15)

EAST DEVON
North View Road, Budleigh Salterton
Tel: (039 54) 5195
Holes: 18 6214 yds
V'trs: ** H
Fees: £20 (£25)

ELFORDLEIGH HOTEL
Elfordleigh, Plympton, Plymouth
Tel: (0752) 345071
Holes: 9 5759 yds
V'trs: *
Fees: £12 (£12)

EXETER
Countess Wear, Exeter
Tel: (039 287) 5028
Holes: 18 6061 yds
V'trs: *
Fees: £15

HARDWICK
Tavistock Hamlets, Tavistock
Tel: (0822) 612746
Holes: 18 4800 yds
V'trs: *
Fees: £12 (£14)

HOLSWORTHY
Kilatree, Holsworthy
Tel: (0409) 253177
Holes: 18 6012 yds
V'trs: *
Fees: £7

HONITON
Middlehills, Honiton
Tel: (0404) 2943
Holes: 18 5931 yds
V'trs: *
Fees: £14 (£17)

ILFRACOMBE
Hele Bay, Ilfracombe
Tel: (0271) 63328
Holes: 18 5857 yds
V'trs: * H
Fees: £10

MANOR HOUSE HOTEL
Moretonhampstead
Tel: (0647) 40355
Holes: 18 6016 yds
V'trs: **
Fees: £12 (£15)

NEWTON ABBOT (STOVER)
Newton Abbot
Tel: (0626) 62078
Holes: 18 5852 yds
V'trs: ** H
Fees: £15

OKEHAMPTON
Okehampton
Tel: (0837) 53541
Holes: 18 5300 yds
V'trs: **
Fees: On enquiry

ROYAL NORTH DEVON
Golf Links Road, Westward Ho!
Tel: (023 72) 477598
Holes: 18 6644 yds
V'trs: On enquiry
Fees: £14 (£18)

SAUNTON
Saunton, nr Braunton
Tel: (0271) 812013
Holes: East 18 6703 yds
West 18 6322 yds
V'trs: ** H
Fees: £17 (£19)

SIDMOUTH
Cotmaton Road, Sidmouth
Tel: (0395) 516407
Holes: 18 5188 yds
V'trs: **
Fees: £10 (£12)

STADDON HEIGHTS
Plymstock, Plymouth
Tel: (0752) 492630
Holes: 18 5861 yds
V'trs: * H
Fees: £9 (£12)

TAVISTOCK
Down Road, Tavistock
Tel: (0822) 612316
Holes: 18 6250 yds
V'trs: **
Fees: £12 (£15)

TEIGNMOUTH
Teignmouth
Tel: (062 67) 72894
Holes: 18 6142 yds
V'trs: * H
Fees: £15 (£20)

THURLESTONE
Thurlestone, nr Kingsbridge
Tel: (0548) 560715
Holes: 18 6337 yds
V'trs: *
Fees: £15

TIVERTON
Post Hill, Tiverton
Tel: (084) 254836
Holes: 6263 yds
V'trs: * H
Fees: On enquiry

TORQUAY
Petitor Road, St Marychurch, Torquay
Tel: (0803) 329113
Holes: 18 6192 yds
V'trs: ** H
Fees: £15 (£17)

TORRINGTON
Weare Trees, Torrington
Tel: (0805) 22229
Holes: 9 4418 yds
V'trs: *
Fees: £8 (£10)

WARREN
Dawlish
Tel: (0626) 864002
Holes: 18 5968 yds
V'trs: **
Fees: £10 (£12)

WRANGATON (SOUTH DEVON)
Wrangaton, South Brent
Tel: (0364) 73229
Holes: 9 5790 yds
V'trs: *
Fees: £10 (£15)

YELVERTON
Golf Links Road, Yelverton
Tel: (0822) 853593
Holes: 18 6288 yds
V'trs: ** H
Fees: £10 (£12)

DORSET

ASHLEY WOOD
Tarrant Rawston, Blandford Forum
Tel: (0258) 452253
Holes: 9 6227 yds
V'trs: *
Fees: £10 (£12)

BRIDPORT & WEST DORSET
East Cliff, West Bay, Bridport
Tel: (0308) 421491
Holes: 18 5246 yds
V'trs: *
Fees: £10 (£15)

BROADSTONE
Wentworth Drive, Station Approach, Broadstone
Tel: (0202) 692835
Holes: 18 6183 yds
V'trs: * H
Fees: £18

CAME DOWN
Came Down, Dorchester
Tel: (030 581) 2670
Holes: 18 6224 yds
V'trs: * H
Fees: £12.50 (£16)

CANFORD SCHOOL
Canford School, Wimborne
Tel: (0202) 841254
Holes: 9 5918 yds
V'trs: *
Fees: £5

EAST DORSET
Hyde, Wareham
Tel: (0929) 471574
Holes: 18 6146 yds
V'trs: *
Fees: £10 (£12)

FERNDOWN
119 Golf Links Road, Ferndown
Tel: (0202) 837825
Holes: 18 6442 yds
9 5604 yds
V'trs: * H
Fees: Old £25, New £15

HALSTOCK
Common Lane, halstock
Tel: (0936) 89689
Holes: 9 2083 yds
V'trs: **
Fees: £4.50

HIGHCLIFFE CASTLE
107 Lymington Road,
Highcliffe-on-Sea, Christchurch
Tel: (042 52) 6640
Holes: 18 4655 yds
V'trs: * H
Fees: £11 (£15)

ISLE OF PURBECK
Studland
Tel: (092 944) 354
Holes: 18 6283 yds
9 2022 yds
V'trs: ** H
Fees: 18 £16 (£18), 9 £8

KNIGHTON HEATH
Francis Avenue, West Howe,
Bournemouth
Tel: (0202) 578275
Holes: 18 6206 yds
V'trs: * H
Fees: On enquiry

LYME REGIS
Timber Hill, Lyme Regis
Tel: (029 74) 3822
Holes: 18 6262 yds
V'trs: * H
Fees: £15 (£18)

PARKSTONE
Links Road, Parkstone, Poole
Tel: (0202) 708092
Holes: 18 6250 yds
V'trs: * H
Fees: £20 (£25)

SHERBORNE
Clatcombe, Sherborne
Tel: (0935) 812274
Holes: 18 5949 yds
V'trs: ** H
Fees: £12 (£15)

WAREHAM
Sandford Road, Wareham
Tel: (0929) 554147
Holes: 18 5332 yds
V'trs: *
Fees: £10

WEYMOUTH
Weymouth
Tel: (0305) 773997
Holes: 18 5980 metres
V'trs: ** H
Fees: £10 (£13)

DURHAM

BARNARD CASTLE
Harmire Road, Barnard Castle
Tel: (0833) 31980
Holes: 18 5838 yds
V'trs: **
Fees: £10 (£15)

BEAMISH PARK
Beamish, Stanley
Tel: (091) 370 1984
Holes: 18 6205 yds
V'trs: *
Fees: £11

BISHOP AUCKLAND
High Plains, Bishop Auckland
Tel: (0388) 661618
Holes: 18 6420 yds
V'trs: ** H
Fees: £12 (£15)

BLACKWELL GRANGE
Briar Close, Blackwell,
Darlington
Tel: (0325) 462088
Holes: 18 5621 yds
V'trs: *
Fees: £10 (£12)

BRANCEPETH CASTLE
Brancepeth Village, Durham
Tel: (091) 378 0183
Holes: 18 6415 yds
V'trs: *
Fees: £16 (£20)

CHESTER-LE-STREET
Lumley Park, Chester-le-Street
Tel: (091) 388 01157
Holes: 18 6054 yds
V'trs: * H
Fees: £10 (£15)

CONSETT & DISTRICT
Elmfield Road, Consett
Tel: (0207) 580210
Holes: 18 6001 yds
V'trs: **
Fees: £8 (£12)

CROOK
Low Job's Hill, Crook
Tel: (0388) 762429
Holes: 18 6075 yds
V'trs: **
Fees: £6 (£7)

DARLINGTON
Haughton Grange, Darlington
Tel: (0325) 462955
Holes: 18 6272 yds
V'trs: *
Fees: £10 (£12)

DINSDALE SPA
Middleton St George,
Darlington
Tel: (0325) 332515
Holes: 18 6078 yds
V'trs: *
Fees: £10

DURHAM CITY
Littleburn, Langley Moor
Tel: (091) 378 0029
Holes: 18 6211 yds
V'trs: *
Fees: £8 (£12)

MOUNT OSWALD
South Road, Durham City
Tel: (091) 386 7527
Holes: 18 6009 yds
V'trs: **
Fees: £5.50 (£6.50)

SEAHAM
Dawdon, Seaham
Tel: (091) 581 2354
Holes: 18 5972 yds
V'trs: **
Fees: £6 (£12)

SOUTH MOOR
The Middles, Craghead, Stanley
Tel: (0207) 232848
Holes: 18 6445 yds
V'trs: **
Fees: On enquiry

WOODHAM
Burnhill Way, Newton Aycliffe
Tel: (0325) 320574
Holes: 18 6727 yds
V'trs: *
Fees: £7 (£10)

ESSEX

ABRIDGE
Epping Lane, Stapleford
Tawney
Tel: (04028) 333
Holes: 18 6703 yds
V'trs: * H
Fees: £17

BALLARDS GORE
Gore Road, Canewdon,
Rochford
Tel: (0702) 258924
Holes: 18 7062 yds
V'trs: *
Fees: £14

BENTLEY
Ongar Road, Brentwood
Tel: (0277) 373179
Holes: 18 6709 yds
V'trs: *
Fees: £15

BIRCH GROVE
Layer Road, Colchester
Tel: (0206) 34276
Holes: 9 4108 yds
V'trs: *
Fees: £6 (£8)

BOYCE HILL
Vicarage Hill, Benfleet
Tel: (0268) 752565
Holes: 18 5882 yds
V'trs: *
Fees: £15

BRAINTREE
Kings Lane, Stisted, Braintree
Tel: (0376) 43465
Holes: 18 6026 yds
V'trs: * H
Fees: £14 (£17.50)

BURNHAM-ON-CROUCH
Creeksea, Burnham-on-Crouch,
Tel: (0621) 782282
Holes: 9 5866 yds
V'trs: *
Fees: £12

CANONS BROOK
Elizabeth Way, Harlow
Tel: (0279) 418357
Holes: 18 6745 yds
V'trs: *
Fees: £15

CASTLE POINT
Canvey Island
Tel: (0268) 510830
Holes: 18 5627 yds
V'trs: **
Fees: On enquiry

CHANNELS
Belsteads Farm Lane, Little
Waltham, Chelmsford
Tel: (0245) 441056
Holes: 18 6033 yds
V'trs: *
Fees: £8.75

CHELMSFORD
Widford, Chelmsford
Tel: (0245) 257079
Holes: 18 5912 yds
V'trs: * H
Fees: On enquiry

CHIGWELL
High Road, Chigwell
Tel: (081) 500 2384
Holes: 18 6279 yds
V'trs: * H
Fees: £20

CLACTON
West Road, Clacton-on-Sea
Tel: (0255) 424331
Holes: 18 6243 yds
V'trs: *
Fees: £12 (£18)

COLCHESTER
Braiswick, Colchester
Tel: (0206) 85392
Holes: 18 6319 yds
V'trs: * H
Fees: £12

FORRESTER PARK
Beckingham Road, Great
Totham, Maldon
Tel: (0621) 891406
Holes: 18 6073 yds
V'trs: *
Fees: £10 (£14)

FRINTON
The Esplanade, Frinton-on-Sea
Tel: (0255) 671618
Holes: 18 6259 yds
V'trs: * H
Fees: £18, 9 – £6

HARWICH & DOVERCOURT
Parkeston Road, Harwich
Tel: (0256) 3616
Holes: 9 2931 yds
V'trs: **
Fees: On enquiry

ILFORD
Wanstead Park Road, Ilford
Tel: (081) 554 0094
Holes: 18 5702 yds
V'trs: *
Fees: £8 (£10)

LANGDON HILLS
Lower Dunton Road, Boltham
Tel: (0268) 548061
Holes: 18
9
V'trs: * H
Fees: On enquiry

MALDON
Beeleigh Langford, Maldon
Tel: (0621) 53212
Holes: 9 6197 yds
V'trs: *
Fees: £7 (£8)

MARYLANDS
Harold Park, Romford
Tel: (040 23) 46466
Holes: 18 6351 yds
V'trs: * H
Fees: £16 (£25)

ORSETT
Brentwood Road, Orsett
Tel: (0375) 891797
Holes: 18 6614 yds
V'trs: * H
Fees: £20

PIPPS HIOLL
*Aquatels Recreation Centre,
Cranes Farm Road, Basildon*
Tel: (0268) 23456
Holes: 9 2829 yds
V'trs: **
Fees: On enquiry

QUIETWATERS
*Colchester Road, Tolleshunt
D'Arcy, nr Maldon*
Tel: (0621) 860576
Holes: 18 6204 yds
V'trs: *
Fees: On enquiry

ROCHFORD HUNDRED
Rochford
Tel: (0702) 544302
Holes: 18 6256 yds
V'trs: *
Fees: On enquiry

ROMFORD
*Heath Drive, Gidea Park,
Romford*
Tel: (0708) 49393
Holes: 18 6377 yds
V'trs: * H
Fees: £13

SAFFRON WALDEN
Windmill Hill, Saffron Walden
Tel: (0799) 27728
Holes: 18 6608 yds
V'trs: * H
Fees: £20

SKIPS
*Horsemanside, Tysea Hill,
Stapleford Abbots*
Tel: (040 23) 48234
Holes: 18 6146 yds
V'trs: ***

STAPLEFORD ABBOTS
*Horsmanside, Tysea Hill,
Stapleford Abbots*
Tel: (04023) 81278
Holes: 18 6500 yds
9 1200 yds
V'trs: *
Fees: £28 (£30)

STOKE BY NAYLAND
*Keepers Lane, Leavenheath,
Colchester*
Tel: (0206) 262769
Holes: Gainsborough 18 6516
yds
Constable 18 6544 yds
V'trs: * H
Fees: £15 (£18)

THEYDON BOIS
Theydon Bois, Epping
Tel: (037 881) 2460
Holes: 18 5472 yds
V'trs: *
Fees: £16 (£24)

THORNDON PARK
Ingrave, Brentwood
Tel: (0277) 810736
Holes: 18 6455 yds
V'trs: * H
Fees: £20

THORPE HALL
*Thorpe Hall Avenue, Thorpe
Bay*
Tel: (0702) 588195
Holes: 18 6286 yds
V'trs: * H
Fees: On enquiry

THREE RIVERS
*Stow Road, Purleigh, nr
Chelmsford*
Tel: (0621) 828631
Holes: 18 6609 yds
9 1071 yds par 3
V'trs: *
Fees: £12

TOWERLANDS
Panfield Road, Braintree
Tel: (0376) 26802
Holes: 9 2703 yds
V'trs: *
Fees: 18 holes-£6.50 (£9)
9 holes-£5

UPMINSTER
114 Hall Lane, Upminster
Tel: (040 22) 20000
Holes: 18 5951 yds
V'trs: *
Fees: £16

WANSTEAD
Wanstead, London
Tel: (081) 989 9876
Holes: 18 6262 yds
V'trs: * H
Fees: £17.50

WARLEY PARK
*Magpie Lane, Little Warley,
Brentwood*
Tel: (0277) 212552
Holes: 18 6261 yds,
9 3166 yds
V'trs: *
Fees: £15

WARREN
Woodham Walter, Maldon
Tel: (024 541) 4662
Holes: 18 6211 yds
V'trs: * H
Fees: £14

WEST ESSEX
*Bury Road, Stewardstonebury,
Chingford, London*
Tel: (081) 529 4367
Holes: 18 6317 yds
V'trs: * H
Fees: £15

WOODFORD
*2 Sunset Avenue, Woodford
Green*
Tel: (081) 504 4254
Holes: 9 5806 yds
V'trs: *
Fees: £9

BROADWAY
*Willersey Hill, Broadway,
Worcs*
Tel: (0386) 853275
Holes: 18 6211 yds
V'trs: * H
Fees: £16 (£19)

CIRENCESTER
Cheltenham Road, Cirencester
Tel: (0285) 656124
Holes: 18 6021 yds
V'trs: * H
Fees: £18 (£25)

COTSWOLD EDGE
*Upper Rushmire, Wotton-
under-Edge*
Tel: (0453) 844398
Holes: 18 6170 yds
V'trs: *
Fees: £10 (£10)

COTSWOLD HILLS
Ullenwood, nr Cheltenham
Tel: (0242) 515263
Holes: 18 6716 yds
V'trs: ** H
Fees: £17 (£22)

FOREST OF DEAN
Lords Hill, Coleford
Tel: (0594) 33689
Holes: 18 5519 yds
V'trs: **
Fees: £10 (£15)

GLOUCESTERSHIRE
HOTEL
Matson Lane, Gloucester
Tel: (0452) 411331
Holes: 18 6127 yds
9 1980 yds
V'trs: **
Fees: £14 (£18)

LILLEY BROOK
*Cirencester Road, Charlton
Kings, Cheltenham*
Tel: (0242) 525201
Holes: 18 6226 yds
V'trs: ** H
Fees: £20

LYDNEY
Lydney
Tel: (0594) 842614
Holes: 9 5382 yds
V'trs: *
Fees: £8

MINCHINHAMPTON
Minchinhampton, Stroud
Tel: (045 383) 3860
Holes: Old 18 6295 yds
New 18 6675 yds
V'trs: *
Fees: Old £8 (£10)
New £15 (£20)

PAINSWICK
Painswick, nr Stroud
Tel: (0452) 812130
Holes: 18 4780 yds
V'trs: *
Fees: £6 (£8)

STINCHCOMBE HILL
Stinchcombe Hill, Dursley
Tel: (0453) 543878
Holes: 18 5723 yds
V'trs: *
Fees: £12 (£14)

TEWKESBURY PARK
HOTEL
*Lincoln Green Lane,
Tewkesbury*
Tel: (0684) 294892
Holes: 18 6533 yds
V'trs: * H
Fees: £18 (£22)

WESTONBIRT
Westonbirt, Tetbury
Tel: (045 383) 3860
Holes: 9 4504 yds
V'trs: **
Fees: £5

ALRESFORD
Cheriton Road, Alresford
Tel: (0962) 733998
Holes: 12 6038 yds
V'trs: * H
Fees: £10.50

ALTON
Old Odiham Road, Alton
Tel: (0420) 86518
Holes: 9 5744 yds
V'trs: *
Fees: £8 (£12)

AMPFIELD PAR THREE
*Winchester Road, Ampfield, nr
Romsey*
Tel: (0794) 68750
Holes: 18 2478 yds
V'trs: * H
Fees: £5 (£10)

ANDOVER
51 Winchester Road, Andover
Tel: (0264) 24151
Holes: 9 5933 yds
V'trs: *
Fees: £10 (£20)

ARMY GOLF CLUB
Laffan's Road, Aldershot
Tel: (0252) 547232
Holes: 18 6579 yds
V'trs: * H
Fees: £16

BARTON-ON-SEA
Marine Drive, Barton-on-Sea
Tel: (0425) 611210
Holes: 18 5565 yds
V'trs: * H
Fees: £18 (£21)

BASINGSTOKE
Kempshott Park, Basingstoke
Tel: (0256) 51332
Holes: 18 6309 yds
V'trs: * H
Fees: £14

BASINGSTOKE
HOSPITALS
Aldermaston Road, Basingstoke
Tel: (0256) 20347
Holes: 9 5480 yds
V'trs: *
Fees: £6.50 (£9)

BISHOPSWOOD
*Bishopswood Lane, Tadey,
Basingstoke*
Tel: (0734) 815213
Holes: 9 6474 yds
V'trs: *
Fees: £8

BLACKMOOR
Whitehill Bordon
Tel: (04203) 2345
Holes: 18 6213 yds
V'trs: * H
Fees: £15

BRAMSHAW
Brook, Lyndhurst
Tel: (0703) 813434
Holes: Forest 18 5753 yds
Manor 18 6257 yds
V'trs: *
Fees: On enquiry

BROCKENHURST MANOR
Sway Road, Brockenhurst
Tel: (0590) 23092
Holes: 18 6222 yds
V'trs: * H
Fees: £20 (£30)

BURLEY
Burley, Ringwood
Tel: (04253) 2431
Holes: 9 3126 yds
V'trs: **
Fees: £10 (£10)

CORHAMPTON
Sheeps Pond Lane, Droxford, Southampton
Tel: (0489) 877638
Holes: 18 6088 yds
V'trs: * H
Fees: £11

DUNWOOD MANOR
Shootash Hill, Romsey
Tel: (0794) 40663
Holes: 18 6004 yds
V'trs: *
Fees: £10 (£15)

FLEETLANDS
Fareham Road, Gosport
Tel (0705) 822351
Holes: 9 4775 yds
V'trs: ***

GOSPORT & STOKES BAY
Military Road, Fort Road, Haslar, Gosport
Tel: (0705) 581625
Holes: 9 5668 yds
V'trs: *
Fees: £8

HARTLEY WINTNEY
London Road, Hartley Wintney, nr Basingstoke
Tel: (025 126) 3779
Holes: 9 6096 yds
V'trs: *
Fees: £10 (£18)

HAYLING
Ferry Road, Hayling Island
Tel: (0705) 464491
Holes: 18 6489 yds
V'trs: * H
Fees: On enquiry

HOCKLEY
Twyford, nr Winchester
Tel: (0962) 713678
Holes: 18 6279 yds
V'trs: *
Fees: £17 (£21)

LECKFORD & LONGSTOCK
Leckford, Stockbridge
Tel: (0264) 810710
Holes: 9 3251 yds
V'trs: ***

LEE-ON-SOLENT
Brune Lane, Lee-on-Solent
Tel: (0705) 551181
Holes: 18 5991 yds
V'trs: * H
Fees: £14

LIPHOOK
Liphook
Tel: (0428) 723271
Holes: 18 6207 yds
V'trs: * H
Fees: £15 (£25)

MEON VALLEY HOTEL
Sandy Lane, Shedfield, Southampton
Tel: (0329) 833455
Holes: 18 6519 yds
V'trs: ** U
Fees: £18 (£22)

NEW FOREST
Southampton Road, Lyndhurst
Tel: (042 128) 2450/2752
Holes: 18 6748 yds
V'trs: *
Fees: £10 (£12)

NORTH HANTS
Minley Road, Fleet
Tel: (0252) 616655
Holes: 18 6257 yds
V'trs: * H
Fees: £15

OLD THORNS HOTEL
London Kosaido Company Ltd, Longmoor Road, Liphoiok
Tel: (0428) 724555
Holes: 18 6447 yds
V'trs: **
Fees: £18 (£28)

PETERSFIELD
Heath Road, Petersfield
Tel: (0730) 67732
Holes: 18 5720 yds
V'trs: *
Fees: £12 (£18)

ROMSEY
Nursling, Southampton
Tel: (0703) 736673
Holes: 18 5752 yds
V'trs: * H
Fees: £12

ROWLANDS CASTLE
Links Lane, Rowlands Castle
Tel: (0705) 412785
Holes: 18 6627 yds
V'trs: *
Fees: £16 (£20)

ROYAL WINCHESTER
Sarum Road, Winchester
Tel: (0962) 62473
Holes: 18 6218 yds
V'trs: * H
Fees: £20

SANDFORD SPRINGS
Wolverton, Basingstoke
Tel: (0635) 297883
Holes: 18 6064 yds
V'trs: *
Fees: £15

SOUTHWICK PARK
Pinsley Drive, Southwick
Tel: (0705) 380442
Holes: 18 5855 yds
V'trs: *
Fees: On enquiry

STONEHAM
Bassett, Southampton
Tel: (0703) 768397
Holes: 18 6310 yds
V'trs: *
Fees: £18

TIDWORTH GARRISON
Tidworth
Tel: (0980) 42393
Holes: 18 5990 yds
V'trs: *
Fees: £15 (£18)

TILNEY PARK
Rotherwick, Basingstoke
Tel: (0256) 762079
Holes: 18 6108 yds
V'trs: * H
Fees: £13 (£20)

WATERLOOVILLE
Cherry Tree Ave, Cowplain, Portsmouth
Tel: (0705) 256911
Holes: 18 6647 yds
V'trs: *
Fees: £14

HEREFORD & WORCS

ABBEY PARK
Bordesley Lodge Farm, Dagnell End Road, Redditch, Worcs
Tel: (0527) 63918
Holes: 18 6398 yds
V'trs: *
Fees: £4.50 (£5.50)

BELMONT HOUSE
Belmont, Hereford
Tel: (0432) 277445
Holes: 18 6448 yds
V'trs: **
Fees: On enquiry

BLACKWELL
Blackwell, nr Bromsgrove
Tel: (021) 445 3113
Holes: 18 6202 yds
V'trs: *
Fees: £18

CHURCHILL & BLAKEDOWN
Churchill Lane, Blakedown, nr Kidderminster
Tel: (0562) 700200
Holes: 9 5399 yds
V'trs: *
Fees: £7.50

DROITWICH
Ford Lane, Droitwich
Tel: (0905) 770207
Holes: 18 6040 yds
V'trs: *
Fees: £16.50

EVESHAM
Craycombe Links, Fladbury, Pershore, Worcs
Tel: (0386) 860395
Holes: 9 6415 yds
V'trs: *
Fees: £10

HABBERLEY
Trimpley Road, Kidderminster
Tel: (0562) 745756
Holes: 9 5440 yds
V'trs: *
Fees: £7

HEREFORDSHIRE
Raven's Causeway, Wormsley, nr Hereford
Tel: (0432) 71465
Holes: 18 6069 yds
V'trs: **
Fees: £8 (£10)

KIDDERMINSTER
Russell Road, Kidderminster
Tel: (0562) 740090
Holes: 18 6223 yds
V'trs: *
Fees: £18

KING'S NORTON
Brockhill Lane, Weatheroak
Tel: (0564) 822822
Holes: 18 6754 yds, 9 3290 yds
V'trs: *
Fees: £20

KINGTON
Bradnor Hill, Kington
Tel: (0497) 820542
Holes: 18 5840 yds
V'trs: *
Fees: £10 (£14)

LEOMINSTER
Ford Bridge, Leominster
Tel: (0568) 2863
Holes: 9 5249 yds
V'trs: * H
Fees: £10 (£13)

LITLE LAKES
Lye Head, Bewdley
Tel: (0299) 266385
Holes: 9 6247 yds
V'trs: *
Fees: £10

PITCHEROAK
Plymouth Road, Redditch
Tel: (0527) 41054
Holes: 9 4584 yds
V'trs: **
Fees: £2.80 (£3.50)

REDDITCH
Lower Grinsty, Green Lane, Callow Hill, Redditch
Tel: (0527) 46372
Holes: 18 6671 yds
V'trs: *
Fees: £15

ROSS-ON-WYE
Two Park, Gorsley, Ross-on-Wye
Tel: (098 982) 439
Holes: 18 6500 yds
V'trs: *
Fees: £16 (£20)

TOLLADINE
The Fairway, Tolladine Road, Worcester
Tel: (0905) 21074
Holes: 9 5174 yds
V'trs: *
Fees: £10

WORCESTER
Boughton Park, Worcester
Tel: (0905) 422044
Holes: 18 5946 yds
V'trs: *
Fees: £18

WORCESTERSHIRE
Wood Farm, Malvern Hills
Tel: (0684) 564428
Holes: 18 6449 yds
V'trs: * H
Fees: £12 (£15)

HERTFORDSHIRE

ALDENHAM
Radlett Road, Aldenham, nr
Watford
Tel: (0923) 85 7889
Holes: 18 6500 yds
V'trs: **
Fees: £8 (£15)

ARKLEY
Rowley Green Road, Barnet
Tel: (081) 449 8473
Holes: 9 6045 yds
V'trs: *
Fees: £12

ASHRIDGE
Little Gaddesden, Berkhamsted
Tel: (044 284) 2307
Holes: 18 6508 yds
V'trs: *
Fees: On enquiry

BERKHAMSTED
The Common, Berkhamsted
Tel: (0442) 865851
Holes: 18 6605 yds
V'trs: * H
Fees: On enquiry

BISHOP'S STORTFORD
Dunmow Road, Bishop's
Stortford
Tel: (0279) 651324
Holes: 18 6440 yds
V'trs: *
Fees: £15

BOXMOOR
18 Box Lane, Hemel
Hempstead
Tel: (0442) 42434
Holes: 9 4854 yds
V'trs: *
Fees: £5

BRICKENDON GRANGE
Brickendon, nr Hertford
Tel: (099 286) 218
Holes: 18 6325 yds
V'trs: *
Fees: On enquiry

BROOKMANS PARK
Brookmans Park, Hatfield
Tel: (0707) 52468
Holes: 18 6454 yds
V'trs: * H
Fees: £15

BUSHEY
High Street, Bushey
Tel: (081) 950 2215
Holes: 9 3000 yds
V'trs: *
Fees: 18 £9 (£12)
9 £5 (£7)

BUSHEY HALL
Bushey Hall Drive, Bushey
Tel: (0923) 222253
Holes: 18 6099 yds
V'trs: * H
Fees: On enquiry

CHADWELL SPRINGS
Hertford Road, Ware
Tel: (0920) 462075
Holes: 9 3021 yds
V'trs: *
Fees: £12

CHORLEYWOOD
Common Road, Chorleywood
Tel: (092 78) 2009
Holes: 9 2838 yds
V'trs: *
Fees: £8 (£10)

DYRHAM PARK
Galley Lane, Barnet
Tel: (081) 440 3904
Holes: 18 6369 yds
V'trs: ***

EAST HERTS
Hamels Park, Buntingford
Tel: (0920) 821922
Holes: 18 6449 yds
V'trs: * H
Fees: On enquiry

ELSTREE
Watling Street, Elstree
Tel: (081) 2075680
Holes: 18 6100 yds
V'trs: **
Fees: On enquiry

HADLEY WOOD
Beech Hill, Hadley Wood,
Barnet
Tel: (081) 449 3285
Holes: 18 6473 yds
V'trs: * H
Fees: On enquiry

HANBURY MANOR
Sundridge, nr Ware
Tel: (0920) 487722
Holes: 18 6922 yds
V'trs: * H
Fees: £20

HARPENDEN
Hammonds End, Harpenden
Tel: (0582) 767124
Holes: 18 6363 yds
V'trs: *
Fees: £15

HARPENDEN COMMON
East Common, Harpenden
Tel: (0582) 460655
Holes: 18 5651 yds
V'trs: * H
Fees: £11

HARTSBOURNE
Hartsbourne Avenue, Bushey
Heath
Tel: (081) 950 2836
Holes: 18 6305 yds
9 5432 yds
V'trs: **

HATFIELD LONDON
Bedwell Park, Essendon,
Hatfield
Tel: (0707) 42624
Holes: 18 6878 yds
V'trs: *
Fees: £9 (£18)

KNEBWORTH
Deards End Lane, Knebworth
Tel: (0438) 812757
Holes: 18 6428 yds
V'trs: * H
Fees: On enquiry

LETCHWORTH
Letchworth
Tel: (0462) 682713
Holes: 18 6057 yds
V'trs: *
Fees: £16

MID HERTS
Gustard Wood,
Wheathampstead
Tel: (058 283) 2788
Holes: 18 6060 yds
V'trs: * H
Fees: On enquiry

MOOR PARK
Rickmansworth
Tel: (0923) 773146
Holes: High 18 6903 yds
West 18 5823 yds
V'trs: * H
Fees: On enquiry

OLD FOLD MANOR
Hadley Green, Barnet
Tel: (081) 440 7488
Holes: 18 6473 yds
V'trs: * H
Fees: £18

PORTERS PARK
Shenley Hill, Radlett
Tel: (0923) 854366
Holes: 18 6313 yds
V'trs: * H
Fees: £22

POTTERS BAR
Darkes Lane, Potters Bar
Tel: (0707) 52987
Holes: 18 6273 yds
V'trs: * H
Fees: On enquiry

REDBOURN
Kinsbourne Green Lane,
Redbourne, nr St Albans
Tel: (0582) 793493
Holes: 18 6407 yds
9 1361 yds
V'trs: **
Fees: 18 £7.50 (£9)
9 £3 (4.50)

ROYSTON
Baldock Road, Royston
Tel: (0763) 243476
Holes: 18 6032 yds
V'trs: *
Fees: £15

SANDY LODGE
Northwood, Middlesex
Tel: (092 74) 25321
Holes: 18 6340 yds
V'trs: * H
Fees: £18

SOUTH HERTS
Totteridge Lane, London
Tel: (081) 445 4633
Holes: 18 6470 yds
9 1581 yds
V'trs: * H
Fees: On enquiry

VERULAM
London Road, St Albans
Tel: (0727) 61401
Holes: 18 6432 yds
V'trs: *
Fees: £14

WELWYN GARDEN CITY
Mannicotts, High Oaks Road,
Welwyn Garden City
Tel: (0707) 325525
Holes: 18 6100 yds
V'trs: * H
Fees: £16 (£25)

WEST HERTS
Cassiobury Park, Watford
Tel: (0923) 220352
Holes: 18 6488 yds
V'trs: * H
Fees: £12.50

WHIPSNADE PARK
Studham Lane, Dagnall
Tel: (044284) 2330
Holes: 18 6812 yds
V'trs: *
Fees: £15

HUMBERSIDE

BEVERLEY & EAST RIDING
The Westwood, Beverley
Tel: (0482) 869519
Holes: 18 6164 yds
V'trs: *
Fees: £6.50 (£9)

BRIDLINGTON
Belvedere Road, Bridlington
Tel: (0262) 674721
Holes: 18 6330 yds
V'trs: *
Fees: £10 (£15)

BROUGH
Brough
Tel: (0482) 667483
Holes: 18 6183 yds
V'trs: *
Fees: £15

CAVE CASTLE HOTEL
South Cave, N Humberside
Tel: (0403) 422245
Holes: 18 6851 yds
V'trs: **
Fees: On enquiry

CLEETHORPES
Kings Road, Cleethorpes
Tel: (0472) 814060
Holes: 18 6015 yds
V'trs: *
Fees: £10 (£13)

DRIFFIELD
Sunderlandwick, Driffield
Tel: (0377) 43116
Holes: 9 62276 yds
V'trs: **
Fees: £6 (£10)

FLAMBOROUGH HEAD
Lighthouse Road, Flamborough,
Bridlington
Tel: (0262) 850333
Holes: 18 5438 yds
V'trs: **
Fees: £7 (£9)

GATSTEAD PARK
Longdales Lane, Coniston, Hull
Tel: (0482) 811121
Holes: 18 6534 yds
V'trs: * H
Fees: £6 (£9)

GRIMSBY
Littlecoates Road, Grimsby
Tel: (0472) 356981
Holes: 18 6068 yds
V'trs: *
Fees: £12.50 (£15)

HAINSWORTH PARK
Brandesburton, Driffield
Tel: (0964) 542362
Holes: 9 5360 yds
V'trs: *
Fees: £5 (£7.50)

HESSLE
Westfield Road, Cottingham
Tel: (0482) 650190
Holes: 18 6638 yds
V'trs: *
Fees: £13 (£20)

HOLME HALL
*Holme Lane, Bottesford,
Scunthorpe*
Tel: (0724) 851816
Holes: 18 6475 yds
V'trs: * H
Fees: £8

HORNSEA
Rolston Road, Hornsea
Tel: (0964) 534989
Holes: 18 6461 yds
V'trs: *
Fees: £13 (£18)

HULL
The Hall, 27 Packman Lane
Tel: (0482) 653074
Holes: 18 6242 yds
V'trs: *
Fees: £15

IMMINGHAM
*Church Lane, Immingham,
Grimsby*
Tel: (0469) 75493
Holes: 18 5809 yds
V'trs: *
Fees: £8 (£12)

SCUNTHORPE
*Ashby Decoy, Burringham
Road, Scunthorpe*
Tel: (0724) 868972
Holes: 18 6281 yds
V'trs: *
Fees: £12

WITHERNSEA
Chestnut Avenue, Withernsea
Tel: (0964) 612258
Holes: 9 5112 yds
V'trs: *
Fees: £5 (£5)

ISLE OF MAN

CASTLETOWN
Derbyhaven
Tel: (0624) 822125
Holes: 18 6716 yds
V'trs: *
Fees: £7 (£8)

HOWSTRAKE
Groundle Road, Onchan
Tel: (0624) 20430
Holes: 18 5367 yds
V'trs: **
Fees: £5 (£7)

PEEL
Rheast Lane, Peel
Tel: (062 484) 2227
Holes: 18 5914 yds
V'trs: *
Fees: £8 (£10)

RAMSEY
Brookfield Road
Tel: (0624) 813365/812244
Holes: 18 6019 yds
V'trs: ** H
Fees: £8 (£10)

ROWANY
Port Erin
Tel: (0624) 8341089
Holes: 18 5840 yds
V'trs: **
Fees: £8 (£9)

ISLE OF WIGHT

COWES
Crossfield Avenue, Cowes
Tel: (0983) 292303
Holes: 9 5880 yds
V'trs: * H
Fees: £10

FRESHWATER BAY
Afton Down, Freshwater
Tel: (0983) 752955
Holes: 18 5662 yds
V'trs: **
Fees: £12 (£14)

NEWPORT IW
*St George's Down, nr Shide,
Newport*
Tel: (0983) 52507
Holes: 9 5704 yds
V'trs: *
Fees: £10

OSBORNE
Club House, East Cowes
Tel: (0983) 295649
Holes: 9 6286 yds
V'trs: *
Fees: £12

RYDE
Ryde House Park, Ryde
Tel: (0983) 62088
Holes: 9 5220 yds
V'trs: **
Fees: £10 (£12.50)

SHANKLIN &
SANDOWN
Fairway Lake, Sandown
Tel: (0983) 404424
Holes: 18 6000 yds
V'trs: *
Fees: £16 (£18)

VENTNOR
Steephill Down Road, Ventnor
Tel: (0983) 853326
Holes: 9 5772 yds
V'trs: **
Fees: £6 (£7)

KENT

AQUARIUS
*Marmora Road, Hono Oak,
London*
Tel: (081) 693 1626
Holes: 9 5034 yds
V'trs: *
Fees: On enquiry

ASHFORD
Sandyhurst Lane, Ashford
Tel: (0233) 629644
Holes: 18 6246 yds
V'trs: * H
Fees: £16 (£20)

BARNEHURST
*Mayplace Road, East
Barnehurst*
Tel: (0322) 51205
Holes: 9 5320 yds
V'trs: *
Fees: £3.60 (£5.70)

BEARSTED
*Ware Street, Bearsted, nr
Maidstone*
Tel: (0622) 38024
Holes: 18 6253 yds
V'trs: * H
Fees: £14

BEXLEY HEATH
Mount Road, Bexley Heath
Tel: (081) 303 6951
Holes: 9 5239 yds
V'trs: * H
Fees: £8

BROOME PARK
Barham, nr Canterbury
Tel: (0227) 831701
Holes: 18 6610 yds
V'trs: * H
Fees: £15 (£17)

CANTERBURY
Scotland Hills, Canterbury
Tel: (0227) 462865
Holes: 18 6245 yds
V'trs: *
Fees: £16 (£22)

CHERRY LODGE
*Jail Lane, Biggin Hill, nr
Westerham*
Tel: (0959) 72989
Holes: 18 6908 yds
V'trs: *
Fees: £18

CHESTFIELD
(WHITSTABE)
*103 Chestfield Road,
Whitstable*
Tel: (022 779) 3563
Holes: 18 6126 yds
V'trs: * H
Fees: On enquiry

CHISLEHURST
Camden Place, Chislehurst
Tel: (081) 467 6798
Holes: 18 5123 yds
V'trs: * H
Fees: £20

CORINTHIAN
*Gay Dawn Farm, Fawkham, nr
Dartford*
Tel: (04747) 7559
Holes: 9 3118 yds
V'trs: *
Fees: £7.50

CRANBROOK
Benenden Road, Cranbrook
Tel: (0580) 712934
Holes: 18 6128 yds
V'trs: **
Fees: £8 (£11)

CRAY VALLEY
*Sandy Lane, St Paul's Cray,
Orpington*
Tel: (0689) 37909
Holes: 18 5624 yds
V'trs: * H
Fees: £6 (£10)

DARTFORD
Dartford Heath, Dartford
Tel: (0322) 26409
Holes: 18 5914 yds
V'trs: * H
Fees: £20

EDENBRIDGE
*Crouch House Road,
Edenbridge*
Tel: (0732) 865202
Holes: 18 6604 yds
V'trs: *
Fees: £10 (£12)

ELTHAM WARREN
*Clubhouse, Bexley Road,
Eltham, London*
Tel: (081) 850 1166
Holes: 9 5840 yds
V'trs: * H
Fees: £14

FAVERSHAM
Belmont Park, Faversham
Tel: (079 589) 275
Holes: 18 6021 yds
V'trs: * H
Fees: £16

GILLINGHAM
Woodlands Road, Gillingham
Tel: (0634) 55862
Holes: 18 5911 yds
V'trs: * H
Fees: £11

HAWKHURST
High Street, Hawkhurst
Tel: (0580) 753600
Holes: 9 57669 yds
V'trs: *
Fees: £10 (£14)

HERNE BAY
Eddington, Herne Bay
Tel: (0227) 374727
Holes: 18 5466 yds
V'trs: * H
Fees: £12 (£16.50)

HOLTYE
Holtye, Cowden
Tel: (034 286) 635
Holes: 9 52590 yds
V'trs: *
Fees: On enquiry

HYTHE IMPERIAL
Prince's Parade, Hythe
Tel: (0303) 67441
Holes: 9 5533 yds
V'trs: ** H
Fees: £10 (£15)

KNOLE PARK
Seal Hollow Road, Sevenoaks
Tel: (0732) 452709
Holes: 18 6249 yds
V'trs: * H
Fees: £16

LAMBERHURST
Church Road, Lamberhurst
Tel: (0892) 890552
Holes: 18 6257 yds
V'trs: * H
Fees: £20 (£25)

LANGLEY PARK
Barnfield Wood Road, Beckenham
Tel: (081) 650 1663
Holes: 18 6488 yds
V'trs: * H
Fees: £20

LITTLESTONE
Littlestone, New Romney TN28 8RB
Tel: (0679) 62231
Holes: 18 6417 yds
9 3996 yds
V'trs: * H
Fees: On enquiry

MID KENT
Singlewell Road, Gravesend
Tel: (0474) 332810
Holes: 18 6206 yds
V'trs: * H
Fees: On enquiry

NEVILLE
Benhall Mill Road, Tunbridge Wells
Tel: (0892) 32941
Holes: 18 6336 yds
V'trs: * H
Fees: £18

NORTH FORELAND
Kingsgate, Broadstairs, Thanet
Tel: (0843) 69628
Holes: 18 6374 yds
V'trs: * H
Fees: £13 (£17)

POULT WOOD
Poult Wood, Higham Lane, Tonbridge
Tel: (0732) 364039
Holes: 18 5569 yds
V'trs: **
Fees: £4.75 (£7)

PRINCE'S
Sandwich Bay, Sandwich
Tel: (0304) 613797
Holes: 27 holes (3x9) 6238-6497 yds
V'trs: *
Fees: £25 (£32)

ROCHESTER & COBHAM PARK
Park Pale, by Rochester
Tel: (047 482) 3658
Holes: 18 6467 yds
V'trs: * H
Fees: £18

ROYAL BLACKHEATH
Court Road, Eltham, London
Tel: (081) 850 1763
Holes: 18 6209 yds
V'trs: * H
Fees: £25

ROYAL CINQUE PORTS
Golf Road, Deal
Tel: (0304) 374170
Holes: 18 6744 yds
V'trs: * H
Fees: On enquiry

ROYAL ST GEORGE'S
Sandwich
Tel: (0304) 615236
Holes: 18 6534 yds
V'trs: * H
Fees: £25

RUXLEY
Sandy Lane, St Pau's Cray, Orpington
Tel: (0689) 71490
Holes: 18 5017 yds
V'trs: *
Fees: £7 (£9)

ST AUGUSTINES
Cottington Road, Cliffsend, Ramsgate
Tel: (0843) 590222
Holes: 18 5138 yds
V'trs: * H
Fees: £15 (£17)

SENE VALLEY FOLKESTONE & HYTHE
Sene, Folkestone
Tel: (0303) 68514
Holes: 18 6287 yds
V'trs: * H
Fees: £25

SHEERNESS
Power Station Road, Sheerness
Tel: (0795) 662585
Holes: 18 6500 yds
V'trs: *
Fees: £10 (£12)

SHOOTER'S HILL
Lowood, Eaglesfield Road, London
Tel: (081) 854 0073
Holes: 18 5736 yds
V'trs: * H
Fees: £18

SHORTLANDS
Meadow Road, Shortlands, Bromley
Tel: (081) 460 2471
Holes: 9 5261 yds
V'trs: ***

SIDCUP
Hurst Road, Sidcup
Tel: (081) 300 2864
Holes: 9 5692 yds
V'trs: * H
Fees: £10

SITTINGBOURNE & MILTON
Wormdale, Newington, Sittingbourne
Tel: (0795) 842775
Holes: 18 6121 yds
V'trs: * H
Fees: £13

SUNDRIDGE PARK
Garden Lane, Bromley
Tel: (081) 460 5540
Holes: East 18 64109 yds
West 18 6027 yds
V'trs: * H
Fees: £25

TENTERDEN
Woodchurch Road, Tenterden
Tel: (058 06) 3987
Holes: 9 5141 yds
V'trs: *
Fees: On enquiry

TUDOR PARK
Ashford Road, Bearsted, Maidstone
Tel: (0622) 34334
Holes: 18 6000 yds
V'trs: * H
Fees: On enquiry

TUNBRIDGE WELLS
Langton Road, Tunbridge Wells
Tel: (0892) 41386
Holes: 9 4684 yds
V'trs: *
Fees: £15

WALMER & KINGSDOWN
The Leas, Kingsdown, Deal
Tel: (0304) 363017
Holes: 18 6451 yds
V'trs: *
Fees: £15 (£17)

WEST KENT
West Hill, Downe, Orpington
Tel: (0689) 56863
Holes: 18 6369 yds
V'trs: * H
Fees: £17.50

WEST MALLING
Addington, nr Maidstone
Tel: (0732) 844785
Holes: Spitfire 18 6142 yds
Hurricane 18 62409 yds
V'trs: * H
Fees: £14 (£16)

WESTGATE & BIRCHINGTON
176 Canterbury Road, Westgate-on-Sea
Tel: (0843) 31115
Holes: 18 4926 yds
V'trs: * H
Fees: £10 (£12)

WHITSTABLE & SEASALTER
Collingwood Road, Whitstable
Tel: (0227) 272020
Holes: 9 5284 yds
V'trs: * H
Fees: £10 (£12)

WILDERNESSE
Seal, Sevenoaks
Tel: (0732) 61527
Holes: 18 6478 yds
V'trs: * H
Fees: £18.50 (£27.50)

WOODLANDS MANOR
Woodlands, Sevenoaks
Holes: 18 5858 yds
V'trs: * H
Fees: £9 (£15)

WROTHAM HEATH
Seven Mile Lane Comp, Sevenoaks
Tel: (0732) 883854
Holes: 9 5823 yds
V'trs: *
Fees: £12

ACCRINGTON & DISTRICT
West End, Oswaldtwistle, Accrington
Tel: (0254) 31091
Holes: 18 5954 yds
V'trs: **
Fees: £8.50 (£11)

ASHTON & LEA
Tudor Ave, off Blackpool Road, Lea, nr Preston
Tel: (0772) 720374
Holes: 18 6289 yds
V'trs: **
Fees: £12.50 (£17)

BACUP
Maden Road, Bacup
Tel: (0706) 873170
Holes: 9 5656 yds
V'trs: **
Fees: £6 (£7)

BAXENDEN & DISTRICT
Top o' th' Meadow, Baxenden, nr Accrington
Tel: (0254) 34555
Holes: 9 5740 yds
V'trs: **
Fees: £4 (£5)

BLACKBURN
Beardwood Brow, Blackburn
Tel: (0254) 55942
Holes: 18 6100 yds
V'trs: * H
Fees: £12 (£15)

BLACKPOOL NORTH SHORE
Devonshire Road, Blackpool
Tel: (0253) 54640
Holes: 18 6443 yds
V'trs: *
Fees: £14 (£16)

BURNLEY
Glen View, Burnley
Tel: (0282) 55266
Holes: 18 5891 yds
V'trs: **
Fees: £11 (£12)

CHORLEY
Hall o' th' Hill Heath, Charnock
Tel: (0257) 481245
Holes: 18 6277 yds
V'trs: * H
Fees: On enquiry

CLITHEROE
Whalley Road, Clitheroe
Tel: (0200) 24242
Holes: 18 6045 yds
V'trs: **
Fees: £15 (£18)

COLNE
Law Farm, Skipton Old Road, Colne
Tel: (0282) 863391
Holes: 9 5961 yds
V'trs: **
Fees: £8 (£10)

DARWEN
Winter Hill, Darwen
Tel: (0254) 776370
Holes: 18 5752 yds
V'trs: **
Fees: £10 (£15)

DEAN WOOD
Laford Lane, Up Holland,
Skelmersdale
Tel: (0695) 622980
Holes: 18 6129 yds
V'trs: *
Fees: £13.50 (£17.50)

FAIRHAVEN
Lytham Hall Park, Ansdel,
Lytham St Annes FY8 4JU
Tel: (0253) 736976
Holes: 18 6883 yds
V'trs: *
Fees: £15 (£20)

FISHWICK HALL
Glenluce Drive, Farringdon
Park, Preston
Tel: (0772) 7958709
Holes: 18 6028 yds
V'trs: *
Fees: £12 (£18)

FLEETWOOD
Golf House, Princes Way,
Fleetwood
Tel: (039 17) 3661
Holes: 18 6723 yds
V'trs: **
Fees: £14 (£16)

GREAT HARWOOD
Harwood Bar, Great Harwood
Tel: (0254) 886728
Holes: 9 6413 yds
V'trs: **
Fees: £7 (£8)

GREEN HAWORTH
Green Haworth, Accrington
Tel: (0254) 37580
Holes: 9 5470 yds
V'trs: *
Fees: £5 (£6)

HEYSHAM
Tramacar Park, Middleton
Road, Heysham, Morecambe
Tel: (0524) 52000
Holes: 18 6224 yds
V'trs: **
Fees: £10 (£18)

HINDLEY HALL
Hall Lane, Hindley, Wigan
Tel: (0942) 55991
Holes: 18 5840 yds
V'trs: * H
Fees: £13 (£18)

**INGEL GOLF & SQUASH
CLUB**
Tanterton Hall Road, Ingol,
Preston
Tel: (0772) 734556
Holes: 18 6345 yds
V'trs: **
Fees: £8 (£10)

KNOTT END
Wyreside, Knott End on Sea,
Blackpool
Tel: (0253) 811365
Holes: 18 5351 mts
V'trs: *
Fees: £18

LANCASTER
Ashton Hall, Ashton-with-
Stodday, nr Lancaster
Tel: (0524) 751802
Holes: 18 6465 yds
V'trs: * H
Fees: £18

LANSIL
Caton Road, Lancaster
Tel: (0524) 39269
Holes: 9 5608 yds
V'trs: *
Fees: £4 (£6)

LEYLAND
Wigan Road, Leyland
Tel: (0772) 423425
Holes: 18 6123 yds
V'trs: *
Fees: £13

LOBDEN
Whitworth, nr Rochdale
Tel: (0706) 343228
Holes: 9 5770 yds
V'trs: **
Fees: £5 (£6.50)

LONGRIDGE
Fell Barn, Jeffrey Hill,
Longridge, nr Preston
Tel: (0772) 783291
Holes: 18 5726 yds
V'trs: **
Fees: £10 (£12)

LYTHAM (GREEN DRIVE)
Ballam Road, Lytham
Tel: (0253) 737379
Holes: 18 6159 yds
V'trs: *
Fees: £16.50 (£20)

MORECAMBE
Bare, Morecambe
Tel: (0524) 415596
Holes: 18 5766 yds
V'trs: ** H
Fees: £10 (£14)

NELSON
Kings Causeway, Brierfield,
Nelson
Tel: (0282) 67000
Holes: 18 5967 yds
V'trs: *
Fees: £10 (£12)

ORMSKIRK
Cranes Lane, Lathom, Ormskirk
Tel: (0695) 572112
Holes: 18 6350 yds
V'trs: * H
Fees: £20 (£25)

PENWORTHAM
Blundell Lane, Penwortham,
Preston
Tel: (0772) 742345
Holes: 18 5915 yds
V'trs: *
Fees: £15 (£18)

PLEASINGTON
Nr Blackburn
Tel: (0254) 201630
Holes: 18 6445 yds
V'trs: ** H
Fees: £15 (£20)

POULTON-LE-FYLDE
Myrtle Farm, Breck Road,
Poulton, nr Blackpool
Tel: (0253) 892444
Holes: 9 2979 yds
V'trs: ** H
Fees: £2.50 (£3.50)

PRESTON
Fulwood Hall Lane, Fulwood,
Preston
Tel: (0772) 700022
Holes: 18 6249 yds
V'trs: ** H
Fees: £15 (£20)

RISHTON
Fachill Links, Hawthorn Drive,
Rishton
Tel: (0254) 884442
Holes: 9 6199 yds
V'trs: *
Fees: £6

ROSSENDALE
Ewood Lane, Head Haslingden,
Rossendale
Tel: (0706) 213616
Holes: 18 6262 yds
V'trs: *
Fees: £11 (£14)

**ROYAL LYTHAM & ST
ANNES**
Links Gate, Lytham St Annes
Tel: (0253) 720094
Holes: 18 6673 yds
V'trs: * H
Fees: £30

ST ANNES OLD LINKS
Highbury Road, Lytham St
Annes
Tel: (0253) 722432
Holes: 18 6647 yds
V'trs: *
Fees: £20 (£23)

SHAW HILL
Whittle-le-Woods, Chorley
Tel: (025 72) 79222
Holes: 18 6467 yds
V'trs: *
Fees: £17

SILVERDALE
Red Bridge Lane, Silverdale,
Carnforth
Tel: (0524) 701300
Holes: 9 5288 yds
V'trs: *
Fees: £6 (£10)

TURTON
Towneley Park, Todmorden
Road, Burnley
Tel: (0204) 852235
Holes: 9 5805 yds
V'trs: *
Fees: £6

WHALLEY
Long Leese Barn, Clerkhill,
Whalley, nr Blackburn
Tel: (025 482) 2236
Holes: 9 5953 yds
V'trs: *
Fees: £5 (£8)

WILPSHIRE
72 Whalley Road, Wilpshire,
Blackburn
Tel: (0254) 249558
Holes: 18 5911 yds
V'trs: *
Fees: £13 (£17)

BIRSTALL
Station Road, Birstall, Leicester
Tel: (0533) 675245
Holes: 18 6203 yds
V'trs: *
Fees: £15

CHARNWOOD FOREST
Breakback Road, Woodhouse
Eaves, Loughborough
Tel: (0509) 890259
Holes: 9 5960 yds
V'trs: ** H
Fees: £12 (£15)

COSBY
Chapel Lane, off Broughton
Road, Cosby, nr Leicester
Tel: (0533) 848275
Holes: 18 6277 yds
V'trs: * H
Fees: £15

GLEN GORSE
Glen Road, Oadby, Leicester
Tel: (0533) 713748
Holes: 18 6641 yds
V'trs: *
Fees: £14

HINCKLEY
Leicester Road, Hinckley
Tel: (0455) 615014
Holes: 18 6462 yds
V'trs: *
Fees: £15

KIBWORTH
Weir Road, Kibworth
Beachamp, Leicester
Tel: (053 753) 792283
Holes: 18 6282 yds
V'trs: *
Fees: £12

KIRBY MUXLOE
Station Road, Kirby Muxloe, nr
Leicester
Tel: (0533) 392813
Holes: 18 6303 yds
V'trs: * H
Fees: £12.50

LEICESTERSHIRE
Evington Lane, Leicester
Tel: (0533) 736730
Holes: 18 6330 yds
V'trs: ** H
Fees: £17 (£20)

LINGDALE
Joe Moores Lane, Woodhouse
Eaves, Loughborough
Tel: (0509) 890684
Holes: 9 6114 yds
V'trs: **
Fees: £9 (£12)

LONGCLIFFE
Nanpantan, Loughborough
Tel: (0509) 231450
Holes: 18 6551 yds
V'trs: *
Fees: £17

LUFFENHAM HEATH
Ketton, Stamford, Lincs
Tel: (0780) 720298
Holes: 18 6254 yds
V'trs: **
Fees: £22 (£28)

LUTTERWORTH
Lutterworth, Leicester
Tel: (045 55) 2532
Holes: 18 5570 yds
V'trs: *
Fees: £10

MARKET HARBOROUGH
Oxendon Road, Market Harborough
Tel: (0858) 63684
Holes: 9 6080 yds
V'trs: *
Fees: £18

MELTON MOWBRAY
Waltham Rd, Thorpe Arnold, Melton Mowbray
Tel: (0665) 62118
Holes: 9 6200 yds
V'trs: *
Fees: £9 (£12)

RAF NORTH LUFFENHAM
RAF North Luffenham, Oakham
Tel: (0780) 720041 (Ext 273/240)
Holes: 9 6006 yds
V'trs: *
Fees: £4.50 (£5.50)

ROTHLEY PARK
Westfield Lane, Rothley, Leicester
Tel: (0533) 303023
Holes: 18 6487 yds
V'trs: **
Fees: £20 (£25)

SCRAPTOFT
Beeby Road, Scraptoft, Leicester
Tel: (0533) 449138
Holes: 18 6166 yds
V'trs: *
Fees: £12 (£16)

ULLESTHORPE COURT
Erolesworth Road, Ullesthorpe, Lutterworth
Tel: (0455) 209150
Holes: 18 6540 yds
V'trs: **
Fees: £11.50

WHETSTONE
Cambridge Road, Cosby, Leicester
Tel: (0533) 861424
Holes: 18 5700 yds
V'trs: **
Fees: £6 (£7.50)

WILLESLEY PARK
Measham Road, Ashby-de-la-Zouch
Tel: (0530) 414820
Holes: 18 6310 yds
V'trs: * H
Fees: £20 (£25)

LINCOLNSHIRE

BELTON PARK
Belton Lane, Londonthorpe Road, Grantham
Tel: (0476) 63911
Holes: 27 Brownlow 6412 yds
Ancaster 6109 yds
Belmont 5857 yds
V'trs: *
Fees: £13 (£16)
27/36 £18 (£20)

BLANKNEY
Blankney, Lincoln
Tel: (0526) 20202
Holes: 18 6402 yds
V'trs: *
Fees: £12 (£20)

BOSTON
Cowbridge, Horncastle Road, Boston
Tel: (0205) 62306
Holes: 18 5825 yds
V'trs: **
Fees: £10 (£15)

BURGHLEY PARK
St Martin's, Stamford
Tel: (0780) 62100
Holes: 18 6133 yds
V'trs: * H
Fees: £15

CANWICK PARK
Canwick Park, Washingborough Road, Lincoln
Tel: (0522) 536870
Holes: 18 6257 yds
V'trs: *
Fees: £8 (£12)

CARHOLME
Lincoln
Tel: (0522) 33263
Holes: 18 6086 yds
V'trs: **
Fees: On enquiry

ELSHAM
Barton Road, Elsham, nr Brigg
Tel: (0652) 680432
Holes: 18 6411 yds
V'trs: *
Fees: £15

GAINSBOROUGH
Thonock, Gainsborough
Tel: (0427) 613088
Holes: 18 6527 yds
V'trs: * H
Fees: £12

HORNCASTLE
West Ashby, nr Horncastle
Tel: (0507) 526800
Holes: 18 5782 yds
V'trs: *
Fees: £10

LINCOLN
Lincoln
Tel: (042 771) 273
Holes: 18 6400 yds
V'trs: * H
Fees: £14

BELTON WOODS
nr Grantham
Tel: (0476) 593200
Holes: 18 Wellington 6875 yds
18 Lancaster 7021 yds
V'trs: * H
Fees: £15 (£20)

LOUTH
Crowtree Lane, Louth
Tel: (0507) 604648
Holes: 18 6477 yds
V'trs: **
Fees: £10 (£12)

MARKET RASEN
Legsby Road, Market Rasen
Tel: (0673) 842416
Holes: 18 6043 yds
V'trs: * H
Fees: £10

MILLFIELD
Laughterton, Lincoln
Tel: (042 771) 255
Holes: 18 5583 yds
V'trs: *
Fees: £3

NORTH SHORE
North Shore Road, Skegness
Tel: (0754) 4822
Holes: 18 6134 yds
V'trs: ** H
Fees: £17 (£22)

RAF WADDINGTON
Waddington, Lincoln
Tel: (0522) 720271
Holes: 18 5223 yds
V'trs: On enquiry
Fees: £2

SANDILANDS
Sandilands, Sutton-on-Sea
Tel: (0521) 41600
Holes: 18 5995 yds
V'trs: **
Fees: £8 (£10)

SEACROFT
Seacroft, Skegness
Tel: (0754) 69624
Holes: 18 6478 yds
V'trs: *
Fees: £15 (£20)

SLEAFORD
South Rauceby, Sleaford
Tel: (052 98) 644
Holes: 18 6443 yds
V'trs: ** H
Fees: £12 (£20)

SPALDING
Surfleet, Spalding
Tel: (077 585) 474
Holes: 18 5807 yds
V'trs: ** H
Fees: On enquiry

STOKE ROCHFORD
Great North Road, nr Grantham
Tel: (047 683) 218
Holes: 18 6204 yds
V'trs: *
Fees: On enquiry

SUTTON BRIDGE
New Road, Sutton Bridge
Tel: (0406) 350323
Holes: 9 58094 yds
V'trs: *
Fees: £12

WOODHALL SPA
Woodhall Spa
Tel: (0526) 52511
Holes: 18 6866 yds
V'trs: **
Fees: £12 (£14.50)

WOODTHORPE HALL
Woodthorpe, Alford
Tel: (0507) 450294
Holes: 9 1990 yds
V'trs: *
Fees: £4.50

MANCHESTER (GREATER)

ASHTON-ON-MERSEY
Church Lane, Sale, Cheshire
Tel: (061) 973 3727
Holes: 9 3073 yds
V'trs: **
Fees: £8

ASHTON-UNDER-LYNE
Gorsey Way, Hurst, Ashton-under-Lyne
Tel: (061) 330 2095
Holes: 18 6209 yds
V'trs: *
Fees: £11

BLACKLEY
Victoria Avenue, East Manchester
Tel: (061) 643 3912
Holes: 18 6235 yds
V'trs: *
Fees: £8

BOLTON
Lostock Park, Bolton
Tel: (0204) 43073
Holes: 18 6215 yds
V'trs: **
Fees: £15 (£20)

BOLTON OLD LINKS
Chorley Old Road, Montserrat, Bolton
Tel: (0204) 43089
Holes: 18 6406 yds
V'trs: * H
Fees: £15 (£20)

BRAMALL PARK
Manor Road, bramhall, Stockport
Tel: (061) 485 2205
Holes: 18 6214 yds
V'trs: * H
Fees: £15 (£20)

BREIGHTMET
Red Bridge, Ainsworth, nr Boton
Tel: (0204) 27381
Holes: 9 6146 yds
V'trs: *
Fees: £8 (£10)

BROOKDALE
Woodhouses, Failsworth
Tel: (061) 681 2655
Holes: 18 6040 yds
V'trs: *
Fees: £8 (£12)

BURY
Unsworth Hall, Blackford Bridge, Bury
Tel: (061) 766 2213
Holes: 18 5961 yds
V'trs: **
Fees: £12 (£15)

CASTLE HAWK
Heywood Road, Castleton, Rochdale
Tel: (0706) 40841
Holes: 27 3160 yds
V'trs: **
Fees: £3 (£4)

CHEADLE
Shiers Drive, Cheadle
Tel: (061) 428 2160/9878
Holes: 9 5006 yds
V'trs: * H
Fees: £8 (£10)

CHORLTON-CUM-HARDY
Barlow Hall, Manchester
Tel: (061) 881 9911
Holes: 18 6003 mts
V'trs: **
Fees: £12 (£15)

CROMPTON & ROYTON
High Barn, Royton, Oldham
Tel: (061) 624 2154
Holes: 18 6212 yds
V'trs: *
Fees: £9 (£12)

DAVENPORT
Middlewood Road, Poynton, Stockport
Tel: (0625) 877319
Holes: 18 6066 yds
V'trs: *
Fees: £12 (£18)

DAVYHULME PARK
Gleneagles Road, Davyhulme, Manchester
Tel: (061) 748 3931
Holes: 18 6237 yds
V'trs: *
Fees: £9.50 (£11.50)

DEANE
Off Junction Road, Deane, Bolton
Tel: (0204) 61944
Holes: 18 5583 yds
V'trs: *
Fees: £10

DENTON
Manchester Road, Denton
Tel: (061) 336 2070
Holes: 18 6290 yds
V'trs: *
Fees: £7

DIDSBURY
Ford Lane, Northenden, Manchester
Tel: (061) 998 2811
Holes: 18 6273 yds
V'trs: *
Fees: £10 (£12)

DISLEY
Stanley Hall Lane, Disley, Stockport
Tel: (0663) 62884
Holes: 18 6015 yds
V'trs: *
Fees: £10 (£12)

DUKINFIELD
Yew Tree Lane, Dukinfield
Tel: (061) 338 2340
Holes: 16 5544 yds
V'trs: *
Fees: £6

DUNHAM FOREST
Oldfield Lane, Altrincham
Tel: (061) 928 2727
Holes: 18 6636 yds
V'trs: *
Fees: £16 (£20)

DUNSCAR
Longworth Lane, Bromley Cross, Bolton
Tel: (0204) 592992
Holes: 18 5968 yds
V'trs: *
Fees: £12.50 (£15)

ELLESMERE
Old Clough Lane, Worsley
Tel: (061) 790 8591
Holes: 18 5957 yds
V'trs: *
Fees: £9 (£12)

FAIRFIELD
Booth Road, Audenshaw, Manchester
Tel: (061) 370 22921
Holes: 18 5664 yds
V'trs: *
Fees: £9 (£10)

FLIXTON
Church Road, Flixton, Manchester
Tel: (061) 748 2116
Holes: 9 6410 yds
V'trs: *
Fees: £10

GATHURST
Miles Lane, Shevington, nr Wigan
Tel: (025 75) 4909
Holes: 9 6308 yds
V'trs: *
Fees: £10

GATLEY
Waterfall Farm, Styal Road, Heald Green, Cheadle
Tel: (061) 437 2830
Holes: 9 5934 yds
V'trs: *
Fees: £10

GREAT LEVER & FARNWORTH
Lever Edge Lane, Bolton
Tel: (0204) 62582
Holes: 18 5859 yds
V'trs: **
Fees: £9 (£12.50)

GREENMOUNT
Greenmount, nr Bury
Tel: (020 488) 3712
Holes: 9 4920 yds
V'trs: *
Fees: £6

HALE
Rappax Road, Hale
Tel: (061) 980 4225
Holes: 9 5780 yds
V'trs: *
Fees: £10

HARWOOD
"Springfield" Roading Brook Road, Bolton
Tel: (0204) 398472
Holes: 9 5960 yds
V'trs: *
Fees: £10

HAZEL GROVE
Club House, Hazel Grove, nr Stockport
Tel: (061) 483 7272
Holes: 18 6300 yds
V'trs: *
Fees: £15 (£20)

HEATON MOOR
Heaton Mersey, Stockport
Tel: (061) 432 0846
Holes: 18 5876 yds
V'trs: *
Fees: £10 (£14)

HORWICH
Victoria Road, Horwich
Tel: (0204) 6969870
Holes: 9 5404 yds
V'trs: ***

HOULDSWORTH (LEVENSHULME)
Wingate House, Higher Levenshulme, Manchester
Tel: (061) 224 4571
Holes: 18 6078 yds
V'trs: *
Fees: £6 (£8)

LEIGH
Kenyon Hall, Culcheth, Warrington
Tel: (092 576) 2013
Holes: 18 5853 yds
V'trs: ** H
Fees: £11 (£16)

LOWES PARK
Hill Top, Walmersley, Bury
Tel: (061) 764 1231
Holes: 9 6043 yds
V'trs: **
Fees: £7 (£8)

MANCHESTER GC LTD
Hopwood Cottage, Rochdale Road, Middleton, Manchester
Tel: (061) 643 2638
Holes: 18 6450 yds
V'trs: * H
Fees: £13

MARPLE
Hawk Green, Marple, Stockport
Tel: (061) 427 0690
Holes: 18 5506 yds
V'trs: *
Fees: £7.50

MELLOR & TOWNSCLIFFE
Tarden, Gibb Lane, Mellor, nr Stockport
Tel: (061) 427 2208/5759
Holes: 18 5939 yds
V'trs: *
Fees: £10 (£15)

NORTH MANCHESTER
Rhodes House, Manchester Old Road, Middleton, Manchester
Tel: (061) 643 7094
Holes: 18 6542 yds
V'trs: **
Fees: £14 (£15)

NORTHEND
Palatine Road, Manchester
Tel: (061) 998 3386
Holes: 18 6435 yds
V'trs: **
Fees: £13.50 (£17)

OLDHAM
Lees New Road, Oldham
Tel: (061) 624 8346
Holes: 18 5045 yds
V'trs: *
Fees: £8 (£10)

PIKE FOLD
Cooper Lane, Victoria Avenue, Blackley, Manchester
Tel: (061) 740 1136
Holes: 9 5789 yds
V'trs: *
Fees: £5

PRESTWICH
Hilton Lane, Prestwich
Tel: (061) 773 2544
Holes: 18 4522 yds
V'trs: * H
Fees: £10 (£12)

REDDISH VALE
Southcliffe, Reddish, Stockport
Tel: (061) 480 3824
Holes: 18 6086 yds
V'trs: *
Fees: £12

RINGWAY
Hale Mount, Hale Barns, Altrincham
Tel: (061) 904 8432
Holes: 18 6494 yds
V'trs: *
Fees: £18 (£22)

ROCHDALE
Edenfield Road, Bagslate, Rochdale
Tel: (0706) 522104
Holes: 18 6002 yds
V'trs: **
Fees: £11 (£14)

SADDLEWORTH
Uppermill, nr Oldham, Lancs
Tel: (04577) 3653)
Holes: 18 5976 yds
V'trs: **
Fees: £8 (£10.50)

SALE
Sale Lodge, Golf Road, Sale
Tel: (061) 973 1730
Holes: 18 6351 yds
V'trs: **
Fees: £12 (£18)

STAMFORD
Oakfield House, Huddersfield Road, Stalybridge
Tel: (04575) 4829
Holes: 18 5524 yds
V'trs: *
Fees: £8 (£12.50)

STAND
The Dales, Ashbourne Grove, Whitefield, Manchester
Tel: (061) 766 2214
Holes: 18 6411 yds
V'trs: **
Fees: £10 (£14)

SWINTON PARK
East Lancashire Road, Swinton, Manchester
Tel: (061) 794 1785 8077
Holes: 18 6675 yds
V'trs: *
Fees: £12

TUNSHILL
Club House, Kiln Lane, Milnrow, nr Rochdale
Tel: (0706) 861982
Holes: 9 5812 yds
V'trs: *
Fees: £6 (£6.50)

WALMERSLEY
Garretts Close, Walmersley, Bury
Tel: (061) 764 1429
Holes: 9 5588 mtrs
V'trs: *
Fees: £6

WERNETH
Green Lane Garden Suburb, Oldham
Tel: (061) 624 1190
Holes: 18 5363 yds
V'trs: *
Fees: £10

WERNETH LOW
Gee Cross, Hyde, Tameside
Tel: (061) 358 6908
Holes: 9 5734 yds
V'trs: *
Fees: £8.50 (£13.50)

WESTHOUGHTON
Long Island, Westhoughton, Bolton
Tel: (0942) 811085
Holes: 9 5834 yds
V'trs: *
Fees: £8

WHITEFIELD
Higher Lane, Whitefield, Manchester
Tel: (061) 766 3096
Holes: 18 6041
18 5714 yds
V'trs: *
Fees: £11.50 (£17)

WHITTAKER
Littleborough
Tel: (0706) 78310
Holes: 9 5576 yds
V'trs: *
Fees: £6 (£8)

WIGAN
Arley Hall, Haigh, Wigan
Tel: (0257) 421360
Holes: 9 6058 yds
V'trs: **
Fees: £10 (£12)

WITHINGTON
243 Palatine Road, West Didsbury
Tel: (061) 445 4861
Holes: 18 6410 yds
V'trs: *
Fees: £12 (£15)

WORSLEY
Stableford Avenue, Monton Green, Eccles, Manchester
Tel: (061) 789 4202
Holes: 18 6217 yds
V'trs: * H
Fees: £12

MERSEYSIDE

ASHTON-IN-MAKERFIE-LD
Garswood Park, Liverpool Road, Ashton-in-Makerfield
Tel: (0942) 724229
Holes: 18 6120 yds
V'trs: *
Fees: £7

BIDSTON
Scoresby Road, Leasowe, Moreton
Tel: (051) 638 6650
Holes: 18 6207 yds
V'trs: *
Fees: £7.50 (£12)

BOOTLE
Dunnings Bridge Road, Litherland
Tel: (051) 928 1371
Holes: 18 6362 yds
V'trs: **
Fees: £2.55 (£3.75)

BROMBOROUGH
Raby Hall Road, Bromborough
Tel: (051) 334 4499
Holes: 18 6650 yds
V'trs: *
Fees: £12 (£15)

CALDY
Links Hey Road, Caldy, Wirral
Tel: (051) 625 1818
Holes: 18 6675 yds
V'trs: *
Fees: £20

CHILDWALL
Naylor's Road, Gateacre, Liverpool
Tel: (051) 487 9871
Holes: 18 6425 yds
V'trs: *
Fees: £10.50 (£16)

EASTHAM LODGE
Ferry Road, Eastham, Wirral
Tel: (051) 327 3008
Holes: 15 5826 yds
V'trs: *
Fees: £11

FORMBY
Golf Road, Formby, Liverpool
Tel: (070 48) 73090
Holes: 18 6871 yds
V'trs: * H
Fees: £30 (£35)

FORMBY LADIES
Formby, Liverpool
Tel: (070 48) 73090
Holes: 18 5426 yds
V'trs: **
Fees: £19 (£22)

GRANGE PARK
Toll Bar, Prescot Road, St Helens
Tel: (0744) 28785
Holes: 18 6480 yds
V'trs: * H
Fees: £15 (£21.50)

HAYDOCK PARK
Golborne Park, Rob Lane, Newton-le-Willows
Tel: (0925) 226944
Holes: 18 6014 yds
V'trs: * H
Fees: £15

HESKETH
Cockle Dick's Lane, Cambridge Road, Southport
Tel: (0704) 30050
Holes: 18 6478 yds
V'trs: *
Fees: £15 (£20)

HESWALL
Cottage Lane, Gayton Heswall, Wirral
Tel: (051) 342 7431
Holes: 18 6472 yds
V'trs: *
Fees: £16 (£20)

HILLSIDE
Hastings Road, Southport
Tel: (0704) 68360
Holes: 18 6850 yds
V'trs: *
Fees: £25 (£30)

HUYTON & PRESCOT
Hurst Park, Huyton
Tel: (051) 489 2022
Holes: 18 5738 yds
V'trs: *
Fees: £12 (£15)

LEASOWE
Leasowe Road, Moreton, Wirral
Tel: (051) 677 5460
Holes: 18 6204 yds
V'trs: *
Fees: £10 (£12)

LEE PARK
Childwall Valley Road, Gateacre, Liverpool
Tel: (051) 487 9861
Holes: 18 6204 yds
V'trs: **
Fees: On enquiry

PRENTON
Golf Links Road, Prenton, Birkenhead
Tel: (051) 608 1636
Holes: 18 6411 yds
V'trs: *
Fees: £15 (£18)

ROYAL BIRKDALE
Waterloo Road, Birkdale, Southport
Tel: (0704) 68857
Holes: 18 6703 yds
V'trs: * H
Fees: £30 (£45)

ROYAL LIVERPOOL
Meols Drive, Hoylake
Tel: (051) 632 5868
Holes: 18 6804 yds
V'trs: * H
Fees: £25 (£30)

SOUTHPORT & AINSDALE
Bradshaws Lane, Ainsdale, Southport
Tel: (0704) 77316
Holes: 18 6612 yds
V'trs: *
Fees: £20

SOUTHPORT OLD LINKS
Moss Lane, Southport
Tel: (0704) 24294/28207
Holes: 9 6486 yds
V'trs: *
Fees: £10 (£15)

WALLASEY
Bayswater Road, Wallasey
Tel: (051) 639 3888
Holes: 18 6607 yds
V'trs: **
Fees: £18 (£20)

WEST DERBY
Yew Tree Lane, Liverpool
Tel: (051) 228 5478
Holes: 187 6322 yds
V'trs: **
Fees: £12 (£16)

WEST LANCASHIRE
Blundellsands, Crosby, Liverpool
Tel: (051) 924 5662
Holes: 18 6756 yds
V'trs: **
Fees: £14 (£17)

WIRRAL LADIES
93 Bidstone Road, Birkenhead, Wirral I43 6TS
Tel: (051) 652 2468
Holes: 18 4966 yds ladies 18 5170 yds men
V'trs: *
Fees: £12

WOOLTON
Doe Park, Speke Road, Woolton, Liverpool
Tel: (051) 486 1601
Holes: 18 5706 yds
V'trs: **
Fees: £13 (£19)

MIDDLESEX

ASHFORD MANOR
Fordbridge Road, Ashford
Tel: (0784) 255940
Holes: 18 6372 yds
V'trs: **
Fees: £20 (£25)

BUSH HILL PARK
Bush Hill, Winchmore Hill, London
Tel: (081) 360 4103
Holes: 18 5809 yds
V'trs: **
Fees: £14

CREWS HILL
Cattlegate Road, Crews Hill, Enfield
Tel: (081) 366 7422
Holes: 18 6208 yds
V'trs: * H
Fees: On enquiry

EALING
Perivale Lane, Greenford
Tel: (081) 997 2559
Holes: 18 6216 yds
V'trs: *
Fees: On enquiry

ENFIELD
Old Park Road South, Enfield
Tel: (081) 386 4492
Holes: 18 6137 yds
V'trs: * H
Fees: £16

FINCHLEY
Nether Court, Frith Lane, London
Tel: (081) 346 5086
Holes: 18 6411 yds
V'trs: *
Fees: £20 (£25)

FULWELL
Hampton Hill
Tel: (081) 977 3844
Holes: 18 6490 yds
V'trs: * H
Fees: £15 (£20)

GRIM'S DYKE
Oxhey Lane, Hatch End, Pinner
Tel: (081) 428 7484
Holes: 18 5600 yds
V'trs: * H
Fees: £25 (£30)

HAMPSTEAD
Winnington Road, London
Tel: (081) 455 7089
Holes: 9 5812 yds
V'trs: * H
Fees: £15 (£20)

HARROW SCHOOL
Harrow-on-the-Hill
Tel: (081) 869 1214
Holes: 9 1775 yds
V'trs: ***

HENDON
Off Sanders Lane, Devonshire
Road, London
Tel: (081) 346 8990
Holes: 18 6241 yds
V'trs: *
Fees: £18 (£30)

HIGHGATE
Denewood Road, Highgate,
London
Tel: (081) 340 5 467
Holes: 18 5964 yds
V'trs: *
Fees: £16

HILLINGDON
18 Dorset Way, Hillingdon,
Uxbridge
Tel: (0895) 51980
Holes: 9 5459 yds
V'trs: * H
Fees: £15

HOLIDAY INN
Stockley Road, West Drayton
Tel: (0895) 444232
Holes: 9 3800 yds
V'trs: **
Fees: £3 (£3.50)

MILL HILL
100 Barnet Way, Mill Hill,
London
Tel: (081) 959 7261
Holes: 18 6309 yds
V'trs: *
Fees: £16 (£25)

MUSWELL HILL
Rhodes Avenue, Wood Green,
London
Tel: (081) 888 8046
Holes: 18 6474 yds
V'trs: **
Fees: £23 (£30)

NORTH MIDDLESEX
The Manor House, Friern Barnet
Lane, London
Tel: (081) 445 3060
Holes: 18 5611 yds
V'trs: * H
Fees: £15 (£22)

NORTHWOOD
Rickmansworth Road,
Northwood
Tel: (092 74) 20112
Holes: 18 6493 yds
V'trs: * H
Fees: £20

PERIVALE PARK
Ruislip Road, Greenford
Tel: (081) 575 8655
Holes: 90 5296 yds
V'trs: **
Fees: £3.50 (£4.50)

PINNER HILL
Pinner Hill
Tel: (0981) 866 2109
Holes: 18 6293 yds
V'trs: * H
Fees: On enquiry

STANMORE
Gordon Avenue, Stanmore
Tel: (081) 95 4 2646
Holes: 18 5881 yds
V'trs: * H
Fees: £15 (£6)

STRAWBERRY HILL
Wellesley Road, Twickenham
Tel: (081) 892 2082
Holes: 9 2381 yds
V'trs: * H
Fees: £8

SUDBURY
Bridgewater Road, Wembley
Tel: (081) 902 7910
Holes: 18 6282 yds
V'trs: * H
Fees: £20 (£30)]

WEST MIDDLESEX
Greenford Road, Southall
Tel: (081) 574 1800
Holes: 18 6242 yds
V'trs: **
Fees: £9.50 (£16)

WYKE GREEN
Syon Lane, Isleworth
Tel: (081) 847 0685
Holes: 18 6242 yds
V'trs: **
Fees: £12 (£17)

NORFOLK

BARNHAM BROOM HOTEL
Barnham Broom, Norwich
Tel: (060 545) 393
Holes: Valley 18 6470 yds
Hill 18 6628 yds
V'trs: * H
Fees: £20

BAWBURGH
Long lane, Bawburgh
Tel: (0603) 746390
Holes: 9 5278 yds
V'trs: *
Fees: 18 £10 (£12.50), 9 £6

COSTESSEY PARK
Costessey Park, Costessey,
Norwich
Tel: (0603) 747085
Holes: 18 5853 yds
V'trs: *
Fees: £10 (£12)

DEREHAM
Quebech Road, Dereham
Tel: (0362) 695631
Holes: 9 6225 yds
V'trs: * H
Fees: £12.50

EATON
Newmarket Road, Norwich
Tel: (0603) 52478
Holes: 18 6135 yds
V'trs: * H
Fees: £14 (£18)

FAKENHAM
Fakenham
Tel: (0328) 3534
Holes: 9 5879 yds
V'trs: *
Fees: £8 (£11)

FELTWELL
Thor Ave, off Wilton Road,
Feltwell
Tel: (0466) 7328035
Holes: 9 6260 yds
V'trs: **
Fees: £7 (£10)

GORLESTON
Warren Road, Gorleston, Gt
Yarmouth
Tel: (0493) 662103
Holes: 18 64000 yds
V'trs: ** H
Fees: £12 (£14)

GRANARY HOTEL
Little Dunham, King's Lynn
Tel: (0362) 694383
Holes: 9 2023 yds
V'trs: **
Fees: On enquiry

GREAT YARMOUTH & CAISTER
Beach House, Caister-on-Sea,
Gt Yarmouth
Tel: (0493) 720421
Holes: 18 6284 yds
V'trs: *
Fees: £8 (£10)

HUNSTANTON
Hunstanton
Tel: (048 53) 2751
Holes: 18 6670 yds
V'trs: *
Fees: £20 (£25)

KING'S LYNN
Castle Rising, King's Lynn
Tel: (055 387) 655
Holes: 18 6646 yds
V'trs: * H
Fees: £14 (£20)

LINKS COUNTRY PARK HOTEL
West Runton, Cromer
Tel: (026 375) 691
Holes: 9 4814 yds
V'trs: **
Fees: £12 (£14)

MUNDESLEY
Links Road, Mundesley
Tel: (0263) 720279
Holes: 9 5410 yds
V'trs: *
Fees: £10 (£16)

RAF MARHAM
RAF Marham, King's Lynn
Tel: (0760) 337261 (Ext 604)
Holes: 9 5 244 yds
V'trs: *
Fees: £5 (£7)

ROYAL CROMER
Overstrand Road, Cromer
Tel: (0263) 512267
Holes: 18 6508 yds
V'trs: * H
Fees: £18 (£22)

ROYAL NORWICH
Drayton High Road, Hellesdon,
Norwich
Tel: (0603) 504459
Holes: 18 6603 yds
V'trs: *
Fees: £15

ROYAL WEST NORFOLK
Brancaster, King's Lynn
Tel: (0485) 210616
Holes: 18 6428 yds
V'trs: *
Fees: £20 (£25)

RYSTON PARK
Ely Road, Denver, Downham
Market
Tel: (0366) 382133
Holes: 9 6292 yds
V'trs: *
Fees: £15

SHERINGHAM
Sheringham
Tel: (0263) 822980
Holes: 18 6464 yds
V'trs: * H
Fees: £20 (£25)

SPROWSTON PARK
Wroxham Road, Sprowston,
Norwich
Tel: (0603) 410657
Holes: 18 5985 yds
V'trs: * H
Fees: On enquiry

SWAFFHAM
Cley Road, Swaffham
Tel: (036) 621284
Holes: 9 6252 yds
V'trs: *
Fees: £12

THETFORD
Brandon Road, Thetford
Tel: (0842) 752662
Holes: 18 6879 yds
V'trs: *
Fees: £15 (£20)

NORTHAMPTONSHIRE

COLD ASHBY
Cold Ashby, nr Northampton
Tel: (0604) 740099
Holes: 18 5957 yds
V'trs: *
Fees: £10 (£12)

COLLINGTREE
Windingbrook Lane, North-
ampton
Tel: (0604) 701202
Holes: 18 6821 yds
V'trs: * H
Fees: £35 (£40)

DAVENTRY & DISTRICT
Norton Road, Daventry
Tel: (0327) 702829
Holes: 9 2871 yds
V'trs: *
Fees: £4.50 (£5.50)

KETTERING
Headlands, Kettering
Tel: (0536) 81014
Holes: 18 6035 yds
V'trs: *
Fees: £12

KINGSTHORPE
Kingsley Road, Northampton
Tel: (0604) 719602
Holes: 18 6006 yds
V'trs: * H
Fees: £18

NORTHAMPTON
Kettering Road, Northampton
Tel: (0604)] 714897
Holes: 18 6002 yds
V'trs: *
Fees: £18

NORTHAMPTONSHIRE COUNTY
Church Brampton, Northampton
Tel: (0604) 842226
Holes: 18 6503 yds
V'trs: * H
Fees: £13 (£15)

OUNDLE
Oundle
Tel: (0832) 273267
Holes: 18 5506 yds
V'trs: *
Fees: £12 (£15)

RUSHDEN
Kimbolton Road, Chelveston, Wellingborough
Tel: (0933) 312581
Holes: 9 6381 yds
V'trs: *
Fees: £12

STAVERTON PARK
Staverton, nr Daventry
Tel: (0327) 705 506
Holes: 18 6634 yds
V'trs: ** H
Fees: £12.50 (£19.50)

WAVENDON
Lower End Road, Wavendon, Milton Keynes
Tel: (0908) 281811
Holes: 18 5361 yds
9 2848 yds
V'trs: *
Fees: £8 (£10) £3 (£4)

WELLINGBOROUGH
Harrowden Hall, Great Harrowden, Wellingboroiugh
Tel: (0933) 678752
Holes: 18 6620 yds
V'trs: * H
Fees: £20

WOODLANDS VALE
Farthingstone, nr Towcester
Tel: (032 736) 291
Holes: 18 6330 yds
V'trs: **
Fees: £9 (£12)

NORTHUMBERLAND

ALLENDALE
Thornley Gate, Allendale, Hexham
Tel: (091) 267 5875
Holes: 9 4410 yds
V'trs: **
Fees: £3 (£4)

ALNMOUTH
Foxton Hall, Alnmouth
Tel: (0665) 820231
Holes: 18 6414 yds
V'trs: **
Fees: £11 (£14)

ALNMOUTH VILLAGE
Marine Road, Alnmouth
Tel: (0665) 830370
Holes: 9 6020 yds
V'trs: **
Fees: £6 (£10)

ALNWICK
Swansfield Park, Alnwick
Tel: (0665) 602632
Holes: 9 5387 yds
V'trs: **
Fees: £6

ARCOT HALL
Dudley, Cramlington
Tel: (091) 236 2147
Holes: 18 6389 yds
V'trs: *
Fees: £14 (£18)

BAMBURGH CASTLE
Bamburgh
Tel: (066 84) 378
Holes: 18 5465 yds
V'trs: *
Fees: £12

BELLINGHAM
Bellingham
Tel: (0660) 20530
Holes: 9 5226 yds
V'trs: **
Fees: £6 (£7.50)

BERWICK-UPON-TWEED
Goswick Beal, Berwick-upon-Tweed
Tel: (0289) 87380
Holes: 18 6425 yds
V'trs: *
Fees: £9 (£12)

BLYTH
New Delaval, Blyth
Tel: (0670) 356514
Holes: 18 6498 yds
V'trs: *
Fees: £8

DUNSTANBURGH CASTE
Embleton
Tel: (066 576) 562
Holes: 18 6357 yds
V'trs: **
Fees: £8 (£11)

HALTWHISTLE
Greenhead, nr Haltwhistle
Tel: (069) 72367
Holes: 12 5968 yds
V'trs: **
Fees: £5 (£5)

HEXHAM
Spital Park, Hexham
Tel: (0434) 602057/604904
Holes: 18 6272 yds
V'trs: **
Fees: £8 (£11)

MORPETH
The Common, Morpeth
Tel: (0670) 512065
Holes: 18 6215 yds
V'trs: ** H
Fees: £6.50 (£8)

NEWBIGGIN-BY-THE-SEA
Newbiggin-by-the-Sea
Tel: (0670) 817833
Holes: 18 6540 yds
V'trs: *
Fees: £5.50 (£7.50)

PONTELAND
Bell Villas, Ponteland, Newcastle-upon-Tyne
Tel: (0661) 22689
Holes: 18 6512 yds
V'trs: *
Fees: £10

PRUDHOE
Eastwood Park, Prudhoe-on-Tyne
Tel: (0661) 36188
Holes: 18 5812 yds
V'trs: *
Fees: £7 (£8)

ROTHBURY
Old Race Course, Rothbury, Morpeth
Tel: (0669) 21271
Holes: 9 5560 yds
V'trs: *
Fees: £3.50 (£6)

SEAHOUSES
Beadnell Road, Seahouses
Tel: (0665) 720794
Holes: 18 5374 yds
V'trs: **
Fees: £8 (£10.50)

SLALEY HALL
Slaley, Hexham
Tel: (0434) 673691
Holes: 18 6994 yds
V'trs: ** H
Fees: £25

STOCKSFIELD
New Ridley
Tel: (0661) 843041
Holes: 18 5594 yds
V'trs: **
Fees: £10 (£15)

WARKWORTH
The Links, Warkworth, Morpeth
Tel: (0665) 711596
Holes: 9 5817 yds
V'trs: **
Fees: £6 (£10)

WOOLER
Doddington, Wooler
Tel: (0668) 81956
Holes: 9 6353 yds
V'trs: **
Fees: £4

NOTTINGHAMSHIRE

BEESTON FIELDS
Beeston, Nottingham
Tel: (0602) 257503
Holes: 18 6404 yds
V'trs: **
Fees: £15 (£17)

CHILWELL MANOR
Meadow Lane, Chilwell, Nottingham
Tel: (0602) 258993
Holes: 18 6379 yds
18 5438 yds
V'trs: *
Fees: £9

COXMOOR
Coxmoor Road, Sutton-in-Ashfield
Tel: (0623) 559906
Holes: 18 6501 yds
V'trs: * H
Fees: £16 (£20)

MANSFIELD WOODHOUSE
Mansfield Woodhouse
Tel: (09623) 23521
Holes: 9 2411 yds
V'trs: **
Fees: £2

MAPPERLEY
Central Avenue, Plains Road, Mapperley, Nottingham
Tel: (0602) 202227
Holes: 18 6224 yds
V'trs: **
Fees: £9 (£11)

NEWARK
Kelwick, Coddington, Newark
Tel: (0636 84) 492
Holes: 18 6486 yds
V'trs: *
Fees: £10 (£15)

NOTTS
Hollingwell, Kirby-in-Ashfield
Tel: (0623) 753087
Holes: 18 7020 yds
V'trs: * H
Fees: On enquiry

OXTON
Oaks Lane, Oxton
Tel: (0602) 653545
Holes: 18 6600 yds
9 3300 yds
V'trs: *
Fees: £7.50 (£9)

RADCLIFFE-ON-TRENT
Dewberry Lane, Cropwell Road, Radcliffe-on-Trent
Tel: (0602)] 332396
Holes: 18 6423 yds
V'trs: ** H
Fees: £14 (£18)

RETFORD
Brecks Road, Ordsall, Retford
Tel: (0777) 703733
Holes: 9 6230 yds
V'trs: *
Fees: £4 (£6)

RUDDINGTON GRANGE
Wilford Road, Ruddington, Nottingham
Tel: (0602) 211951
Holes: 18 6467 yds
V'trs: * H
Fees: £15 (£18)

RUSHCLIFFE
East Leake, nr Nottingham
Tel: (050 982) 2701
Holes: 18 6090 yds
V'trs: ***

SERLBY PARK
Serlby, Doncaster, S Yorks
Tel: (0777) 818268
Holes: 9 5370yds
V'trs: ***
SHERWOOD FOREST
Eakring Road, Mansfield
Tel: (0623) 27403
Holes: 18 6710 yds
V'trs: **
Fees: £15 (£20)
STANTON-ON-THE-WOLDS
Stanton Lane, Keyworth
Tel: (060 77) 2044/ 2390
Holes: 18 6437 yds
V'trs: *
Fees: £13 (£15)
WOLLATON PARK
Nottingham
Tel: (0602) 784834
Holes: 18 6494 yds
V'trs: **
Fees: £11 (£17)
WORKSOP
Windmill Lane, Worksop
Tel: (0909) 477732
Holes: 18 6851 yds
V'trs: * H
Fees: £13 (£16)

OXFORDSHIRE

BADGEMORE PARK
Henley-on-Thames
Tel: (0491) 547175
Holes: 18 6112 yds
V'trs: *
Fees: £18
BURFORD
Burford
Tel: (099 382) 2344
Holes: 18 6405 yds
V'trs: * H
Fees: On enquiry
CHESTERTON
Chesterton, nr Bicester
Tel: (0869) 242023
Holes: 18 6224 yds
V'trs: * H
Fees: £10 (£15)
CHIPPING NORTON
Southcombe, Chipping Norton
Tel: (0608) 3356
Holes: 18 6280 yds
V'trs: *
Fees: £14
FRILFORD HEATH
Frilford Heath, Abingdon
Tel: (0865) 390887
Holes: 18 6768 yds
V'trs: *H
Fees: £22 (£30)
HENLEY
Harpsden, Henley-on-Thames
Tel: (0491) 575710
Holes: 18 6329 yds
V'trs: * H
Fees: £18
HUNTERCOMBE
Nuffield, Henley-on-Thames
Tel: (0491) 641241
Holes: 18 6261 yds
V'trs: * H
Fees: £23

NORTH OXFORD
Banbury Road, Oxford
Tel: (0865) 53977
Holes: 18 5805 yds
V'trs: **
Fees: £18 (£25)
RAF BENSON
Royal Air Force, Benson
Tel: (0491) 37766
Holes: 9 4395 yds
V'trs: *
Fees: On enquiry
SOUTHFIELD
Hill Top Road, Oxford
Tel: (0865) 244258
Holes: 18 6230 yds
V'trs: * H
Fees: £16
TADMARTON HEATH
Wigginton, Banbury
Tel: (0608) 730047
Holes: 18 5917 yds
V'trs: * H
Fees: £18

SHROPSHIRE

BRIDGNORTH
Stanley Lane, Bridgnorth
Tel: (07462) 2045
Holes: 18 6638 yds
V'trs: **
Fees: £12.50 (£18)
CHURCH STRETTON
Trevor Hill, Church Stretton
Tel: (0694) 722281
Holes: 18 5008 yds
V'trs: * H
Fees: £7 (£11)
HAWKSTONE PARK
Weston-under-Redcastle, nr Shrewsbury
Tel: (093924) 209
Holes: Hawkstone 18 6465 yds
Weston 18 5368 yds
V'trs: *
Fees: Hawkstone £13 (£16)
Weston £8.50 (£9.50)
HILL VALLEY
Terrick Road, Whitchurch
Tel: (0948) 3032
Holes: 18 6050 yds
9 5016 yds
9 hole Par 3 course
V'trs: **
Fees: £11 (£15) 9 holes—£7
Par 3 course—£3
LILLESHALL HALL
Abbey Road, Lilleshall, nr Newport
Tel: (0952) 604104
Holes: 18 5861 yds
V'trs: *
Fees: £12.50
LLANYMYNECH
Pant, nr Oswestry
Tel: (0691) 830879
Holes: 18 6114 yds
V'trs: *
Fees: £10 (£15)

LUDLOW
Bromfield, nr Ludlow
Tel: (058 477) 366
Holes: 18 6240 yds
V'trs: **
Fees: £8 (£10)
MARKET DRAYTON
Sutton, Market Drayton
Tel: (0630) 2266
Holes: 18 6225 yds
V'trs: *
Fees: £10
OSWESTRY
Aston Park, Oswestry
Tel: (069 188) 448
Holes: 18 6038 yds
V'trs: *H
Fees: £10 (£14)
SHIFNAL
Decker Hill, Shifnal
Tel: (0952) 460457
Holes: 18 6422 yds
V'trs: *
Fees: On enquiry
SHREWSBURY
Condover, Shrewsbury
Tel: (074 372) 3751
Holes: 18 6212 yds
V'trs: **
Fees: £12 (£18)
TELFORD HOTEL
Great Hay, Sutton Hill, Telford
Tel: (0952) 586052
Holes: 18 6766 yds
V'trs: **
Fees: £16 (£20)
WREKIN
Wellington, Telford
Tel: (0952) 244032
Holes: 18 5657 yds
V'trs: *
Fees: £10 (£12)

SOMERSET

BREAN
Coast Road, Brean
Tel: (027 875) 570
Holes: 18 5711 yds
V'trs: *
Fees: £6.50 (£10.50)
BURNHAM & BERROW
St Christopher's Way, Burnham-on-Sea
Tel: (0278) 784545
Holes: 18 6547 yds
9 6550 yds
V'trs: * H
Fees: £18 (£25)
ENMORE PARK
Enmore, Bridgwater
Tel: (027 867) 519
Holes: 18 6443 yds
V'trs: *
Fees: £14 (£17)
KINGWESTON
Somerton
Tel: (0458) 53921
Holes: 9 5416 yds
V'trs: ***
MENDIP
Gurney Slade, Bath
Tel: (0749) 840793
Holes: 18 5982 yds
V'trs: * H
Fees: £12 (£20)

MINEHEAD & WEST SOMERSET
Warren Road, Minehead
Tel: (0643) 4378
Holes: 18 6130 yds
V'trs: *
Fees: £12 (£15)
TAUNTON & PICKERIDGE
Corfe, Taunton
Tel: (082 342) 790
Holes: 18 5927 yds
V'trs: ** H
Fees: On enquiry
WELLS
East Horrington Road, Wells
Tel: (0749) 72868
Holes: 18 5354 yds
V'trs: * H
Fees: £8 (£10)
WINDWHISTLE
Cricket St Thomas, Chard
Tel: (046 030) 231
Holes: 12 6055 yds
V'trs: *
Fees: On enquiry
YEOVIL
Sherborne Road, Yeovil
Tel: (0935) 73763
Holes: 18 6144 yds
V'trs: * H
Fees: £12 (£14)

STAFFORDSHIRE

ALSAGER
Audley Road, Alsager, Stoke-on-Trent
Tel: (0270) 877432
Holes: 18 6192 yds
V'trs: *
Fees: £10
BARLASTON
Meaford Road, Barlaston, Stone
Tel: (078 139) 2795
Holes: 18 5800 yds
V'trs: **
Fees: £9 (£12)
BEAU DESERT
Hazel Slade, Cannock
Tel: (054 38) 2492
Holes: 18 6279 yds
V'trs: *
Fees: £20
BRANSTON
Burton Road, Branston, Burton-on-Trent
Tel: (0283) 53207
Holes: 18 6480 yds
V'trs: *
Fees: £10 (£12)
BROCTON HALL
Brocton, Stafford
Tel: (0785) 661485
Holes: 18 6095 yds
V'trs: * H
Fees: £15 (£17)
BURSLEM
Wood Farm, High Lane, Stoke-on-Trent
Tel: (0782) 837704
Holes: 11 5527 yds
V'trs: *
Fees: £7

BURTON-ON-TRENT
43 Ashby Road, East Burton
Tel: (0283) 62240
Holes: 18 6555 yds
V'trs: * H
Fees: £9 (£13)

CRAYTHORNE GOLF CENTRE
Craythorne Road, Stretton, Burton-on-Trent
Tel: (0283) 33745
Holes: 18 5230 yds
9 hole course
V'trs: *
Fees: £7 (£9)

DRAYTON PARK
Drayton Park, Tamworth
Tel: (0827) 251478
Holes: 18 6414 yds
V'trs: * H
Fees: £18

GREENWAY HALL
Stockton Brook, Stoke-on-Trent
Tel: (0782) 503158
Holes: 18 5676 yds
V'trs: *
Fees: On enquiry

INGESTRE PARK
nr Stafford
Tel: (0889) 270061
Holes: 18 6334 yds
V'trs: *
Fees: £15

LAKESIDE
Rugeley Power Station, Rugeley
Tel: (08894) 3181
Holes: 9 4768 yds
V'trs: ***

LEEK
Big Birchall, Leek
Tel: (0538) 384767/385889
Holes: 18 6240 yds
V'trs: * H
Fees: £18 (£24)

NEWCASTLE-UNDER-LYME
Whitmore Road, Newcastle-under-Lyme
Tel: (0782) 618526
Holes: 18 6450 yds
V'trs: *
Fees: £10

ONNELEY
Onneley, nr Crewe, Cheshire
Tel: (0782) 750577
Holes: 9 5584 yds
V'trs: *
Fees: £10

STAFFORD CASTLE
Newport Road, Stafford
Tel: (0785) 223821
Holes: 9 6562 yds
V'trs: *
Fees: £7 (£10)

STONE
Filleybrooks, Stone
Tel: (0785) 813103
Holes: 9 6299 yds
V'trs: *
Fees: £10

TRENTHAM
14 Barlaston Old Road, Trentham, Stoke-on-Trent
Tel: (0782) 657309
Holes: 18 6644 yds
V'trs: * H
Fees: £15 (£18)

TRENTHAM PARK
Trentham Park, Stoke-on-Trent
Tel: (0782) 642245
Holes: 18 6403 yds
V'trs: **
Fees: £15 (£17)

UTTOXETER
Wood Lane, Uttoxeter
Tel: (0889) 564884
Holes: 18 5695 yds
V'trs: *
Fees: £10 (£15)

WESTWOOD
Newcastle Road, Walbridge, Leek
Tel: (0538) 383060
Holes: 13 4766 yds
V'trs: * H
Fees: £8

WHITTINGTON BARRACKS
Tamworth Road, Lichfield
Tel: (0543) 432261
Holes: 18 6457 yds
V'trs: * H
Fees: £18

WOLSTANTON
Dimsdale Old Hall, Newcastle
Tel: (0782) 622718
Holes: 18 5807 yds
V'trs: *
Fees: £8

SUFFOLK

ALDERBURGH
Aldeburgh
Tel: (0728) 453309
Holes: 18 6330 yds
V'trs: * H
Fees: On enquiry

BECCLES
The Common, Beccles
Tel: (0502) 712244
Holes: 9 2696 yds
V'trs: *
Fees: £6 (£7)

BUNGAY & WAVELEY VALLEY
Bungay
Tel: (0986) 2337
Holes: 18 5944 yds
V'trs: *
Fees: £12

BURY ST EDMUNDS
Tut Hill, Bury St Edmunds
Tel: (0284) 755978
Holes: 18 6615 yds
V'trs: * H
Fees: £12.50 (£16)

DISS
Stuston Common, Diss
Tel: (0379) 644399
Holes: 9 5900 yds
V'trs: *
Fees: £10

FELIXSTOWE FERRY
Ferry Road, Felixstowe
Tel: (0395) 283975
Holes: 18 6308 yds
V'trs: * H
Fees: £15 (£18)

FLEMPTON
Bury St Edmunds
Tel: (028 484) 291
Holes: 9 6704 yds
V'trs: * H
Fees: £15

FORNHAM PARK
Fornham St Martin, Bury St Edmunds
Tel: (0284) 63426
Holes: 6212 yds
V'trs: **
Fees: £8.50 (£12.50)

HAVERHILL
Coupals Road, Haverhill
Tel: (0440) 712628
Holes: 9 5707 yds
V'trs: **
Fees: £10 (£15)

IPSWICH (PURDIS HEATH)
Purdis Heath, Ipswich
Tel: (0473) 724017
Holes: 18 6405 yds
9 1950 yds
V'trs: * H
Fees: 18 £14 (£16)
9 £7 (£9)

NEWMARKET LINKS
Cambridge Road, Newmarket
Tel: (0638) 662395
Holes: 18 6402 yds
V'trs: * H
Fees: £15 (£20)

NEWTON GREEN
Newton Green, Sudbury
Tel: (0787) 77501
Holes: 9 5488 yds
V'trs: *
Fees: £10

ROOKERY PARK
Carlton Colville, Lowestoft
Tel: (0502) 515103
Holes: 18 6649 yds
V'trs: *
Fees: £12 (£14)

ROYAL WORLINGTON & NEWMARKET
Worlington, Bury St Edmunds
Tel: (0638) 715224
Holes: 9 6218 yds
V'trs: *
Fees: £18.50

RUSHMERE
Rushmere Heath, Ipswich
Tel: (0473) 728076
Holes: 18 6287 yds
V'trs: *
Fees: On enquiry

SOUTHWOLD
The Common, Southwold
Tel: (0502) 723790
Holes: 9 6001 yds
V'trs: *
Fees: On enquiry

STOWMARKET
Lower Road, Onehouse, Stowmarket
Tel: (044 93) 392
Holes: 18 6119 yds
V'trs: * H
Fees: £10 (£16.50)

THORPENESS HOTEL
Thorpeness
Tel: (0728) 452524
Holes: 18 6208 yds
V'trs: **
Fees: £15 (£25)

WALDRINGFIELD HEATH
Newbourne Road, Waldringfield, Woodbridge
Tel: (0473) 36768
Holes: 18 5837 yds
V'trs: *
Fees: On enquiry

WARREN HEATH
Bucklesham Road, Ipswich
Tel: (0473) 726821
Holes: 9 3162 yds
V'trs: **
Fees: £2.50

WOODBRIDGE
Bromeswell Heath, nr Woodbridge
Tel: (039 43) 3213
Holes: 18 6314 yds
9 2243 yds
V'trs: * H
Fees: £15

SURREY

THE ADDINGTON
Shirley Church Road, Croydon
Tel: (081) 777 1701
Holes: 18 6242 yds
V'trs: ** H
Fees: On enquiry

ADDINGTON PALACE
Gravel Hill, Addington, Croydon
Tel: (081) 654 1786
Holes: 18 6410 yds
V'trs: * H
Fees: £22

BANSTEAD DOWNS
Burdon Lane, Belmont, Sutton
Tel: (081) 642 6884
Holes: 18 6169 yds
V'trs: * H
Fees: £20

BARROWS HILL
Longcross, Chertsey
Tel: (0932) 848117
Holes: 18 3090 yds
V'trs: ***

BETCHWORTH PARK
Reigate Road, Dorking
Tel: (0306) 884334
Holes: 18 6266 yds
V'trs: *
Fees: £20 (£27)

BRAMLEY
Bramley, nr Guildford
Tel: (0483) 893685
Holes: 18 5966 yds
V'trs: *
Fees: £15

BURHILL
Walton-on-Thames
Tel: (0932) 221729
Holes: 18 6224 yds
V'trs: * H
Fees: On enquiry

CAMBERLEY HEATH
Golf Drive, Camberley
Tel: (0276) 27905
Holes: 18 6402 yds
V'trs: * H
Fees: £17

CHIPSTEAD
How Lane, Chipstead, Coulsdon
Tel: (0737) 554939
Holes: 18 5450 yds
V'trs: *
Fees: £20

COOMBE HILL
Kingston Hill
Tel: (081) 949 3713
Holes: 18 6286 yds
V'trs: * H
Fees: On enquiry

COOMBE HILL
*George Road, Kingston Hill,
Kingston-upon-Thames*
Tel: (081) 942 6764
Holes: 18 5210 yds
V'trs: * H
Fees: £20

CROHAM HURST
Croham Road, South Croydon
Tel: (081) 657 7705
Holes: 18 6274 yds
V'trs: * H
Fees: £21

CRONDALL
*Oak Park, Heath Lane,
Crondall, nr Farnham*
Tel: (0252) 850066
Holes: 18 6278 yds
V'trs: **
Fees: £12 (£17)

CUDDINGTON
Banstead Road, Banstead
Tel: (081) 3903 0952
Holes: 18 6352 yds
V'trs: * H
Fees: £24

DORKING
Chart Park, Dorking
Tel: (0306) 889786
Holes: 9 5106 yds
V'trs: *
Fees: £10

DRIFT
The Drift, East Horsley
Tel: (048 65) 4772
Holes: 18 6414 yds
V'trs: **
Fees: £120 (£13)

**DULWICH & SYDENHAM
HILL**
*Grange Lane, College Road,
London*
Tel: (081) 693 8491
Holes: 18 6051 yds
V'trs: * H
Fees: £16

EFFINGHAM
*Effingham Crossroads,
Effingham*
Tel: (0372) 52606
Holes: 18 6488 yds
V'trs: * H
Fees: £25

EPSOM
Longdown Lane, South Epsom
Tel: (037 27) 41867
Holes: 18 5607 yds
V'trs: *
Fees: £10 (£12.50)

FARNHAM
The Sands, Farnham
Tel: (025 18) 2198
Holes: 18 6313 yds
V'trs: * H
Fees: £18

FERNFELL
Barhatch Lane, Cranleigh
Tel: (0483) 277188
Holes: 18 5 258 yds
V'trs: *
Fees: £12 (£15)

FOXHILLS
Stonehill Road, Ottershaw
Tel: (093 287) 3961
Holes: 18 6880 yds
18 6747 yds
V'trs: **
Fees: £22

GATTON MANOR HOTEL
Ockley, nr Dorking
Tel: (030 679) 557
Holes: 18 6903 yds
V'trs: *
Fees: £9 (£11)

GUILDFORD
*High Path Road, Merrow,
Guildford*
Tel: (0483) 66765
Holes: 18 6080 yds
V'trs: *
Fees: £20

HANKLEY COMMON
Tilford, Farnham
Tel: (025 125) 3761
Holes: 18 6418 yds
V'trs: * H
Fees: £20

HINDHEAD
Churt Road, Hindhead
Tel: (042 873) 4458
Holes: 18 6357 yds
V'trs: * H
Fees: £22 (£27)

HOME PARK
*Hampton Wick, Kingston-upon-
Thames*
Tel: (081) 977 265 8
Holes: 18 6519 yds
V'trs: **
Fees: £10.50 (£18)

KINGSWOOD
*Sandy Lane, Kingswood,
Tadworth*
Tel: (0737) 832334
Holes: 18 6855 yds
V'trs: ** H
Fees: £25 (£30)

LALEHAM
Laleham Reach, Chertsey
Tel: (093 28) 62877
Holes: 18 6203 yds
V'trs: *
Fees: £17

LEATHERHEAD
Kingston Road, Letherhead
Tel: (037 284) 3966
Holes: 18 6060 yds
V'trs: *
Fees: £27.50 (£32.50)

LIMPSFIELD CHART
Limpsfield
Tel: (0883) 723405
Holes: 9 5718 yds
V'trs: *
Fees: On enquiry

LINGFIELD PARK
Racecourse Road, Lingfield
Tel: (0342) 832659
Holes: 18 6500 yds
V'trs: *
Fees: £15 (£20)

LONDON SCOTTISH
*Windmill Enclosure, Wimbledon
Common, London*
Tel: (081) 789 1207
Holes: 18 5486 yds
V'trs: *
Fees: £6

MALDEN (1926)
Traps Lane, New Malden
Tel: (081) 942 6009
Holes: 18 6201 yds
V'trs: *
Fees: £19.50 (£25)

MITCHAM
*Carshalton Road, Mitcham
Junction*
Tel: (081) 640 4280
Holes: 18 5931 yds
V'trs: *
Fees: £8 (£8)

NEW ZEALAND
*Woodham Lane, Woodham,
Weybridge*
Tel: (093 23) 49619
Holes: 18 6012 yds
V'trs: * H
Fees: On enquiry

NORTH DOWNS
Northdown Road, Woldingham
Tel: (0883) 653004
Holes: 18 5787 yds
V'trs: *
Fees: £16

PURLEY DOWNS
106 Purley Downs Road, Purley
Tel: (081) 65 0819
Holes: 18 6243 yds
V'trs: * H
Fees: On enquiry

PUTTENHAM
Puttenham, nr Guildford
Tel: (0483) 810277
Holes: 18 5300 yds
V'trs: * H
Fees: On enquiry

RAC COUNTRY CLUB
Woodcote Park, Epsom
Tel: (0372) 267311
Holes: 18 6672 yds
18 5520 yds
V'trs: ***

REDHILL & REIGATE
*Clarence Lodge, Pendleton
Road, Redhill*
Tel: (0737) 244433
Holes: 18 5238 yds
V'trs: *
Fees: £10 (£12)

REIGATE HEATH
Reigate Heath
Tel: (0737) 242610
Holes: 9 5554 yds
V'trs: *
Fees: On enquiry

RICHMOND
Sudbrook Park, Richmond
Tel: (081) 940 7792
Holes: 18 5965 yds
V'trs: *
Fees: £25

ROEHAMPTON
Roehampton Lane, London
Tel: (081) 876 3858
Holes: 18 6057 yds
V'trs: ***

ROYAL MID-SURREY
Old Deer Park, Richmond
Tel: (081) 940 0459
Holes: Outer 18 6337 yds
Inner 18 5446 yds
V'trs: * H
Fees: £30

ROYAL WIMBLEDON
*29 Camp Road, Wimbledon,
London*
Tel: (081) 946 4606
Holes: 18 6300 yds
V'trs: * H
Fees: £27

ST GEORGE'S HILL
Weybridge
Tel: (0932) 843523
Holes: 18 6492 yds
9 2360 yds
V'trs: **
Fees: £35, 9 £8

SELSDON PARK HOTEL
*Addington Road, Sanderstead,
S Croydon*
Tel: (081) 657 4129
Holes: 18 6402 yds
V'trs: **
Fees: £20

SHIRLEY PARK
Addiscombe Road, Croydon
Tel: (081) 654 8767
Holes: 18 6210 yds
V'trs: *
Fees: £17.50

SILVERMERE
Redhill Road, Cobham
Tel: (0932) 67275
Holes: 18 6333 yds
V'trs: *
Fees: £10 (£14)

SUNNINGDALE
Sunningdale
Tel: (0990) 21681
Holes: Old 18 6586 yds
New 6676 yds
V'trs: * H
Fees: £47

SUNNINGDALE LADIES
Cross Road, Sunningdale
Tel: (0990) 20507
Holes: 18 3622 yds
V'trs: *
Fees: £11 (£13)
Men £14 (£16)

SURBITON
Woodstock Lane, Chessington
Tel: (081) 398 6619
Holes: 18 6211 yds
V'trs: * H
Fees: £20

TANDRIDGE
Oxted
Tel: (0883) 713701
Holes: 18 6250 yds
V'trs: * H
Fees: £21

THAMES DITTON & ESHER
Portsmouth Road, Esher
Tel: (081) 398 1551
Holes: 9 5415 yds
V'trs: *
Fees: £6 (£8)

TYRRELLS WOOD
Leatherhead
Tel: (0372) 375200
Holes: 18 6219 yds
V'trs: * H
Fees: £22 (£30)

WALTON HEATH
Tadworth
Tel: (0737) 812152
Holes: Old 18 6813 yds
New 18 6659 yds
V'trs: * H
Fees: £30

WENTWORTH
Virginia Water
Tel: (0334) 843333
Holes: West 18 6945 yds
East 18 6176 yds
South 18 6979 yds
Executive 9 1902 yds Part 54
V'trs: * H
Fees: On enquiry

WEST BYFLEET
Sheerwater Road, West Byfleet
Tel: (093 23) 46584
Holes: 18 6211 yds
V'trs: * H
Fees: £20

WEST HILL
Brookwood, nr Woking
Tel: (048 67) 3172
Holes: 18 6368 yds
V'trs: * H
Fees: £24

WEST SURREY
Enton Green, nr Godalming
Tel: (048 68) 727
Holes: 18 6247 yds
V'trs: ** H
Fees: £16 (£30)

WIMBLEDON COMMON
19 Camp Road, Wimbledon Common, London
Tel: (081) 9046 0294
Holes: 18 5438 yds
V'trs: *
Fees: £10

WIMBLEDON PARK
Home Park Road, London
Tel: (081) 946 1002/4053
Holes: 18 5465 yds
V'trs: * H
Fees: £20

WOKING
Pond Road, Hook Heath, Woking
Tel: (0483) 769582
Holes: 18 6322 yds
V'trs: * H
Fees: £20

WOODCOTE PARK
Bridle Way, Meadow Hill, Coulsdon
Tel: (081) 668 1843
Holes: 18 6624 yds
V'trs: *
Fees: £20

WORPLESDON
Heath House Road, Woking
Tel: (04867) 3287
Holes: 18 6422 yds
V'trs: * H
Fees: On enquiry

SUSSEX (EAST)

ASHDOWN FOREST HOTEL
Chapel Lane, Forest Row
Tel: (0342 82) 2247
Holes: 18 5510 yds
V'trs: **
Fees: £10 (£12.50)

BRIGHTON & HOVE
Dyke Road, Brighton
Tel: (0273) 556482
Holes: 9 5722 yds
V'trs: *
Fees: £12 (£18)
9 holes—£6

COODEN BEACH
Cooden Beach, nr Bexhill-on-Sea
Tel: (042 43) 3938
Holes: 18 6540 yds
V'trs: **
Fees: £17 (£20)

CROWBOROUGH BEACON
Beacon Road, Crowborough
Tel: (0892) 653877
Holes: 18 6279 yds
V'trs: * H
Fees: £20 (£20)

DALE HILL
Ticehurst, nr Wadhurst
Tel: (0580) 201090
Holes: 18 6055 yds
V'trs: *
Fees: £12.50 (£16.50)

THE DYKE
Dyke Road, Brighton
Tel: (079 156) 260
Holes: 18 6577 yds
V'trs: *
Fees: £14 (£20)

EAST BRIGHTON
Roedean, Brighton
Tel: (0273) 604838
Holes: 18 6337 yds
V'trs: *
Fees: £15 (£20)

EAST SUSSEX NATIONAL
Little Horstead, Uckfield
Tel: (0825) 75577
Holes: East 18 7112 yds
West 18 7072 yds
V'trs: *
Fees: £100 (Hotel guests—£57.50)

EASTBOURNE DOWNS
East Dean Road, Eastbourne
Tel: (0323) 32264
Holes: 18 6635 yds
V'trs: *
Fees: £10 (£12)

HIGHWOODS (BEXHILL)
Ellerslie Lane, Bexhill-on-Sea
Tel: (0424) 212776
Holes: 18 6218 yds
V'trs: * H
Fees: £18 (£22)

LEWES
Chapel Hill, Lewes
Tel: (0273) 473245
Holes: 18 5959 yds
V'trs: **
Fees: £10 (£12)

PAXHILL PARK
Paxhill Park
Tel: (0372) 379592
Holes: 18 xxxx yds
V'trs: z
Fees: £xx

PEACEHAVEN
Brighton Road, Newhaven
Tel: (0273) 512602
Holes: 9 5235 yds
V'trs: *
Fees: On enquiry

PILTDOWN
Uckfield
Tel: (082 572) 2389
Holes: 18 6059 yds
V'trs: * H
Fees: £25 (£25)

ROYAL ASHDOWN FOREST
Chapel Lane, Forest Row, E Grinstead
Tel: (034 282) 2018 (Old);
(034 282) 4866 (New)
Holes: Old 18 6477 yds
New 18 5549 yds
V'trs: On enquiry
Fees: £20 (£25)

ROYAL EASTBOURNE
Paradise Drive, Eastbourne
Tel: (0323) 36986
Holes: 18 6109 yds
9 2147 yds
V'trs: ** H
Fees: 18 £17.50 (£25)
9 £10 (£12)

RYE
Camber, Rye
Tel: (0797) 225218
Holes: 18 6301 yds
9 6625 yds
V'trs: ***

SEAFORD
East Blatchington, Seaford
Tel: (0323) 894160
Holes: 18 6241 yds
V'trs: *
Fees: £20

WEST HOVE
369 Old Shoreham Road, Hove
Tel: (0273) 413494
Holes: 18 6038 yds
V'trs: *
Fees: £7 (£9)

WILLINGDON
Southdown Road, Eastbourne
Tel: (0323) 410984
Holes: 18 6049 yds
V'trs: * H
Fees: £17 (£20)

SUSSEX (WEST)

BOGNOR REGIS
Downview Road, Felpham, Bognor Regis
Tel: (0243) 865209
Holes: 18 6238 yds
V'trs: *
Fees: £16 (£20)

CHARTHAM MANOR
Chartham Manor
Tel: (0492) 534481
Holes: 18 xxxx yds
V'trs: x
Fees: £xx

COPTHORNE
Borers Arm Road, Copthorne
Tel: (0342) 712405
Holes: 18 6505 yds
V'trs: *
Fees: £17 (£30)

COTTESMORE
Buchan Hill, Crawley
Tel: (0293) 35399
Holes: 18 6097 yds
18 5321 yds
V'trs: **
Fees: £14 (£18)

COWDRAY PARK
Midhurst
Tel: (0730) 812091
Holes: 18 6212 yds
V'trs: * H
Fees: £10 (£20)

EFFINGHAM PARK
nr Copthorne
Tel: (0342) 716528
Holes: 9 1749 yds
V'trs: *
Fees: £6 (£7)

GATWICK MANOR
Crawley
Tel: (0293) 24470
Holes: 9 1109 yds
V'trs: **
Fees: On enquiry

GOODWOOD
Goodwood, nr Chichester
Tel: (0243) 774994
Holes: 18 6383 yds
V'trs: * H
Fees: £16 (£25)

HAM MANOR
West Drive, Angmering, nr Littlehampton
Tel: (0903) 783732
Holes: 18 6216 yds
V'trs: * H
Fees: On enquiry

HAYWARDS HEATH
High Beech Lane, Haywards Heath
Tel: (0444) 414866
Holes: 18 6202 yds
V'trs: * H
Fees: £15 (£25)

IFIELD
Rusper Road, Ifield, Crawley
Tel: (0293) 202222/23088
Holes: 18 6314 yds
V'trs: * H
Fees: £15

LITTLEHAMPTON
170 Rope Walk, Littlehampton
Tel: (0903) 716369
Holes: 18 6244 yds
V'trs: *
Fees: £18 (£25)

MANNINGS HEATH
Mannings Heath, Horsham
Tel: (0403) 210332
Holes: 18 6402 yds
V'trs: * H
Fees: £15

PEASE POTTAGE
Horsham Road, Pease Pottage, Crawley
Tel: (0293) 21706
Holes: 9 3511 yds
V'trs: **
Fees: £5 (£7)

PYECOMBE
Pyecombe, Brighton
Tel: (079 18) 5398
Holes: 18 6234 yds
V'trs: *
Fees: £16 (£25)

SELSEY
Golf Links Lane, Selsey
Tel: (0243) 602203
Holes: 9 5932 yds
V'trs: **
Fees: £9 (£12)

WEST SUSSEX
Hurston Lane, Pulborough
Tel: (079 82) 2426
Holes: 18 6156 yds
V'trs: * H
Fees: On enquiry

WORTHING
Links Road, Worthing
Tel: (0903) 60718
Holes: Lower 18 6477 yds
Upper 18 5243 yds
V'trs: *
Fees: £22 (£26)

TYNE & WEAR

BACKWORTH
The Hall, Backworth, Shiremoor, Newcastle-upon-Tyne
Tel: (091) 268 1048
Holes: 9 5930 yds
V'trs: *
Fees: £5 (£6.25)

BIRTLEY (PORTOBELLO)
Portobello Road, Birtley
Tel: (091) 510 2207
Holes: 9 5660 yds
V'trs: *
Fees: £6

BOLDON
Dipe Lane, East Boldon
Tel: (091) 536 5835
Holes: 18 6348 yds
V'trs: **
Fees: £7 (£9)

CITY OF NEWCASTLE
Three Mile Bridge, Great North Road, Gosforth, Newcastle-upon-Tyne
Tel: (091) 285 5481
Holes: 18 6508 yds
V'trs: **
Fees: £9 (£13)

CLOSE HOUSE
Close House, Heddon on the Wall, Newcastle-upon-Tyne
Tel: (0661) 852953
*Holes: 18 5511 yds
V'trs: ***

GARESFIELD
Chopwell
Tel: (0207) 561309
Holes: 18 6196 yds
V'trs: **
Fees: £4.50 (£6)

GOSFORTH
Broadway East, Gosforth, Newcastle-upon-Tyne
Tel: (091) 285 0553
Holes: 18 6030 yds
V'trs: **
Fees: £10 (£15)

GOSFORTH PARK GOLFING COMPLEX
High Gosforth Park, Newcastle 3
Tel: (091) 236 4480/4867
Holes: 187 5807 yds
V'trs: **
Fees: £7.50

HEWORTH
Gingling Gate, Heworth, Gateshead
Tel: (091) 469 2137
Holes: 18 6462 yds
V'trs: *
Fees: £5 (£7.50)

HOUGHTON-LE-SPRING
Copt Hill Links, Houghton-le-Spring
Tel: (091) 584 7421
Holes: 18 6416 yds
V'trs: **
Fees: £8 (£12)

NEWCASTLE UNITED
60 Ponteland Road, Newcastle-upon-Tyne
Tel: (091) 286 9998
Holes: 18 6484 yds
V'trs: *
Fees: £6 (£8)

NORTHUMBERLAND
High Gosforth Park, Newcastle-upon-Tyne
Tel: (091) 236 2009
Holes: 18 6629 yds
V'trs: * H
Fees: £17.50

RAVENSWORTH
Mossheaps, Wrekenton, Gateshead
Tel: (0991) 487 6014/2843
Holes: 18 5872 yds
V'trs: **
Fees: £8 (£12)

RYTON
nr Stanners, Clara Vale
Tel: (091) 413 3737
Holes: 18 6300 yds
V'trs: *
Fees: £8 (£10)

SOUTH SHIELDS
Cleadon Hills, South Shields
Tel: (091) 456 0110
Holes: 18 6264 yds
V'trs: *
Fees: £10 (£15)

TYNEMOUTH
Spital Dene, Tynemouth, North Shields
Tel: (091) 258 0728
Holes: 18 6403 yds
V'trs: *
Fees: £10 (£12)

TYNESIDE
Westfield Lane, Ryton
Tel: (091) 413 2177
Holes: 18 6055 yds
V'trs: *
Fees: £10 (£16)

WASHINGTON
Stone Cellar Road, Washington
Tel: (091) 417 8346
Holes: 18 6604 yds
V'trs: **
Fees: £4.35 (£6)

WEARSIDE
Coxgreen, Sunderland
Tel: (091) 534 4269
Holes: 18 6315 yds
V'trs: * H
Fees: £7 (£10)

WESTERHOPE
Whorlton Grange, Westerhope, Newcastle-upon-Tyne
Tel: (091) 286 0594
Holes: 18 6407 yds
V'trs: **
Fees: £9

WHICKHAM
Hollinside Park, Whickham, Newcastle-upon-Tyne
Tel: (091) 488 8591
Holes: 18 6129 yds
V'trs: **
Fees: £10 (£15)

WHITBURN
Lizard Lane, South Shields
Tel: (091) 529 4210
Holes: 18 6046 yds
V'trs: **
Fees: £7.50 (£12)

WHITLEY BAY
Claremount Road, Whitley Bay
Tel: (091) 252 0180
Holes: 18 6614 yds
V'trs: *
Fees: £10

WARWICKSHIRE

ATHERSTONE
The Outwoods, Atherstone
Tel: (0827) 713110
Holes: 18 6239 yds
V'trs: * H
Fees: £10

KENILWORTH
Crew Lane, Kenilworth
Tel: (0926) 512732
Holes: 18 6408 yds
V'trs: **
Fees: £11 (£15)

LADBROOK PARK
Poolhead Lane, Tamworth-in-Arden, Solihull
Tel: (05644) 2581
Holes: 18 6407 yds
V'trs: * H
Fees: On enquiry

LEAMINGTON & COUNTY
Golf Lane, Whitnash, leamington Spa
Tel: (0926) 428014
Holes: 18 6430 yds
V'trs: **
Fees: £12 (£18)

MAXSTOKE PARK
Castle Lane, Coleshill, Birmingham
Tel: (0675) 621518
Holes: 18 6460 yds
V'trs: *
Fees: £14

NEWBOLD COMYN
Newbold Terrace East, Leamington Spa
Tel: (0926) 411157
Holes: 18 6221 yds
V'trs: *
Fees: £3.40 (£4.40)

NUNEATON
Golf Drive, Whitestone, Nuneaton
Tel: (0203) 340201
Holes: 18 6412 yds
V'trs: * H
Fees: £12

PURLEY CHASE
Pipers Lane, Ridge Lane, nr Nuneaton
Tel: (0203) 395348
Holes: 18 6604 yds
V'trs: *
Fees: £10 (£15)

RUGBY
Clifton Road, Rugby
Tel: (0788) 75134
Holes: 18 5 457 yds
V'trs: *
Fees: £12

STRATFORD OAKS
Bealey Road, Snitterfield, Stratford-upon-Avon
Tel: (0789) 731571
Holes: 18 6121 yds
V'trs: *
Fees: On enquiry

STRATFORD-ON-AVON
Tiddington Road, Stratford-on-Avon
Tel: (0789) 205677
Holes: 18 6309 yds
V'trs: **
Fees: On enquiry

WELCOMBE HOTEL
Warwick Road, Stratford-on-Avon CV37 0NR
Tel: (0789) 299012
Holes: 18 6202 yds
V'trs: * H
Fees: £20 (£25)

WEST MIDLANDS

BLOXWICH
Stafford Road, Bloxwich
Tel: (0922) 476889
Holes: 18 6277 yds
V'trs: *
Fees: £14

CALDERFIELDS
Aldridge Road, Walsall
Tel: (0922) 32243
Holes: 18 6636 yds
V'trs: **
Fees: £8 (£10)

COCKS MOOR WOODS
Alcester Road, South King's Heath, Birmingham
Tel: (021) 444 3584
Holes: 18 5742 yds
V'trs: **
Fees: £3.90 (£4.60)

COPT HEATH
1220 Warwick Road, Knowle, Solihull
Tel: (0564) 772650
Holes: 18 6504 yds
V'trs: * H
Fees: £20

COVENTRY
Finham Park, Coventry
Tel: (0203) 411123 411298
Holes: 18 6613 yds
V'trs: * H
Fees: £17.50

COVENTRY HEARSALL
Beechwood Avenue, Coventry
Tel: (0203) 713156
Holes: 18 5963 yds
V'trs: *
Fees: £14

DARTMOUTH
Vale Street, West Bromwich
Tel: (021) 588 2131
Holes: 18 6060 yds
V'trs: *
Fees: £9

DRUIDS HEATH
Stonnall Road, Aldridge
Tel: (0922) 59523
Holes: 18 6914 yds
V'trs: *
Fees: £12 (£17)

DUDLEY
Turners Hill, Rowley Regis, Warley
Tel: (0384) 54020
Holes: 18 5715 yds
V'trs: *
Fees: £12

EDGBASTON
Church Road, Birmingham
Tel: (021) 454 3226
Holes: 18 6118 yds
V'trs: **
Fees: £20 (£25)

ENVILLE
Highgate Common, Enville, nr Stourbridge
Tel: (0384) 872585
Holes: Highgate 18 6451 yds
Lodge 18 6207 yds
V'trs: * H
Fees: £15

FOREST OF ARDEN
Maxstoke Lane, Meriden, Coventry
Tel: (0676) 22118
Holes: 18 6900 yds
V'trs: **
Fees: £12 (£15)

FULFORD HEATH
Tanners Green Lane, Wythall, Birmingham
Tel: (0564) 0822930
Holes: 18 6256 yds
V'trs: *
Fees: £12

GAY HILL
Hollywood Lane, Birmingham
Tel: (021) 4746001
Holes: 18 6532 yds
V'trs: *
Fees: £18

GRANGE
Copsewood, Coventry
Tel: (0203) 451465
Holes: 9 6002 yds
V'trs: *
Fees: £7

GREAT BARR
Chapel Lane, Birmingham
Tel: (021) 357 5270
Holes: 18 6545 yds
V'trs: * H
Fees: £12 (£15)

HAGLEY
Wassell Grove, Hagley, nr Stourbridge
Tel: (0562) 883701
Holes: 18 6353 yds
V'trs: *
Fees: £3.90 (£4.60)

LITTLE ASTON
Streetly, Sutton Coldfield
Tel: (021) 353 2942
Holes: 18 6724 yds
V'trs: *
Fees: On enquiry

MOOR HALL
Four Oaks, Sutton Coldfield
Tel: (021) 308 5106
Holes: 18 6219 yds
V'trs: *
Fees: £17

MOSELEY
Springfield Road, King's Heath, Birmingham
Tel: (021) 444 2063
Holes: 18 6227 yds
V'trs: H
Fees: £25

NORTH WARWICKSHIRE
Hampton Lane, Meriden, Coventry
Tel: (0676) 22259
Holes: 9 6362 yds
V'trs: *
Fees: £10 (£14)

NORTH WORCESTERSHIRE
Frankley Beeches Road, Northfield, Birmingham
Tel: (021) 475 5721
Holes: 18 5907 yds
V'trs: *
Fees: £10

OLTON
Mirfield Road, Solihull
Tel: (021) 705 7296
Holes: 18 6229 yds
V'trs: *
Fees: £16

OXLEY PARK
Stafford Road, Bushbury, Wolverhampton
Tel: (0902) 25445
Holes: 18 6168 yds
V'trs: **
Fees: £14 (£16)

PATSHULL PARK
Pattingham, Wolverhampton
Tel: (0902) 700342
Holes: 18 6412 yds
V'trs: **
Fees: £17 (£20)

PENN
Penn Common, Wolverhampton
Tel: (0902) 330472
Holes: 18 6465 yds
V'trs: *
Fees: £12

ROBIN HOOD
St Bernards Road, Solihull
Tel: (021) 706 0806
Holes: 189 6609 yds
V'trs: *
Fees: £16

SANDWELL PARK
Birmingham Road, West Bromwich
Tel: (021) 553 4384
Holes: 18 6470 yds
V'trs: *
Fees: £14

SHIRLEY
Stratford Road, Monkspath, Shirley, Solihull
Tel: (021) 745 4979
Holes: 18 6510 yds
V'trs: *
Fees: £15

SOUTH STAFFORDSHIRE
Danescourt Road, Tettenhall, Wolverhampton
Tel: (0902) 754816
Holes: 18 6621 yds
V'trs: *
Fees: £14

SPHINX
Siddeley Avenue, Stoke, Coventry
Tel: (0203) 451361
Holes: 9 4104 yds
V'trs: **
Fees: £3.50

STOURBRIDGE
Worcester Lane, Pedmore, Stourbridge
Tel: (0384) 393129
Holes: 18 6178 yds
V'trs: *
Fees: £15

SUTTON COLDFIELD
Thornhill Road, Sutton Coldfield
Tel: (021) 353 9633
Holes: 18 6541 yds
V'trs: ** H
Fees: £18 (£20)

SWINDON
Bridgnorth Road, Swindon, Dudley
Tel: (0902) 896191
Holes: 18 6042 yds
9 hole Par 3 1135 yds
V'trs: **
Fees: £12 (£18)

WALMLEY (WYLDE GREEN)
Brooks Road, Wylde Green, Sutton Coldfield
Tel: (021) 373 7103
Holes: 18 6537 yds
V'trs: *
Fees: £18

WALSALL
Broadway, Walsall
Tel: (0922) 26766
Holes: 18 6232 yds
V'trs: *
Fees: £12.50 (£18)

WILTSHIRE

BREMHILL PARK
Shrivenham, Swindon
Tel: (0793) 782946
Holes: 18 5889 yds
V'trs: **
Fees: £8 (£10)

BRINKWORTH
Longmans Farm, Brinkworth, Chippenham
Tel: (066 641) 277
Holes: 9 6086 yds
V'trs: **
Fees: £3 (£3.50)

BROOME MANOR
Pipers Way, Swindon
Tel: (0793) 532403
Holes: 18 6359 yds
9 2745 yds
V'trs: *
Fees: 18 hole £4.75 (5.25)
9 hole £2.85 (£3.15)

CHIPPENHAM
Malmesbury Road, Chippenham
Tel: (0249) 655519
Holes: 18 5540 yds
V'trs: * H
Fees: £15 (£18)

HIGH POST
Great Durnford, Salisbury
Tel: (0722) 732190
Holes: 18 6267 yds
V'trs: * H
Fees: £14 (£20)

KINGSDOWN
Kingsdown, Corsham
Tel: (0225) 742634
Holes: 18 6445 yds
V'trs: *
Fees: £15

MARLBOROUGH
The Common, Marlborough
Tel: (0672) 52493
Holes: 18 6440 yds
V'trs: ** H
Fees: £15

NORTH WILTS
Bishop's Cannings, Devizes
Tel: (038 086) 330
Holes: 18 5898 mts
V'trs: **
Fees: £10 (£16)

RAF UPAVON
York Road, Upavon, Pewsey
Tel: (0980) 630787
Holes: 9 5597 yds
V'trs: *
Fees: £8 (£8)

RMCS SHRIVENHAM
RMCS Shrivenham, Swindon
Tel: (0793) 782551 (Ext 2355)
Holes: 9 5206 yds
V'trs: ***

SALISBURY & SOUTH WILTS
Netherhampton, Salisbury
Tel: (0722) 742929
Holes: 18 6130 yds
V'trs: * H
Fees: £13 (£20)

SWINDON
Ogbourne St George, Marlborough, nr Swindon
Tel: (067 284) 287
Holes: 18 6226 yds
V'trs: **
Fees: On enquiry

WEST WILTS
Elm Hill, Warminster
Tel: (0985) 212110
Holes: 18 5701 yds
V'trs: * H
Fees: £15 (£23)

YORKSHIRE (NORTH)

ALDWARK MANOR
Aldwark Manor, Aldwark Alne, York
Tel: (03473) 353
Holes: 9 2569 yds
V'trs: **
Fees: £8 (£14)

AMPLEFORTH COLLEGE
56 High Street, Helmsley, York
Tel: (0439) 70678
Holes: 10 4018 yds
V'trs: *
Fees: £4 (£6)

BEDALE
Leyburn Road, Bedale
Tel: (0677) 22443
Holes: 18 5737 yds
V'trs: **
Fees: £10 (£15)

BENTHAM
Robin Lane, Bentham, Lancaster
Tel: (05242) 61018
Holes: 9 5752 yds
V'trs: **
Fees: £7 (£9)

CATTERICK GARRISON
Leyburn Road, Catterick Garrison
Tel: (0748) 83367
Holes: 18 6336 yds
V'trs: **
Fees: £10 (£15)

CRIMPLE VALLEY
Hookstone Wood Road, Harrogate
Tel: (0423) 883485
Holes: 9 2500 yds
V'trs: **
Fees: £3

EASINGWOLD
Stillington Road, Easingwold, York
Tel: (0347) 21964
Holes: 18 6262 yds
V'trs: **
Fees: £14 (£18)

FILEY
West Ave, Filey
Tel: (0723) 513134
Holes: 18 6030 yds
V'trs: ** H
Fees: £11 (£14)

FULFORD (YORK)
Heslington Lane, York
Tel: (0904) 412882
Holes: 18 6779 yds
V'trs: On enquiry
Fees: £20 (£23)

GANTON
Station Road, Ganton, Scarborough
Tel: (0944) 70260
Holes: 18 6693 yds
V'trs: *
Fees: On enquiry

GHYLL
Ghyll Brow, Barnoldswick, Colne
Tel: (0282) 842466
Holes: 9 5708 yds
V'trs: *
Fees: £6 (£8)

HARROGATE
Forest Lane Head, Harrogate
Tel: (0423) 862547
Holes: 18 6241 yds
V'trs: *
Fees: £18 (£25)

HEWORTH
Muncaster House, Muncastergate, York
Tel: (0904) 422389
Holes: 11 6141 yds
V'trs: *
Fees: £10 (£12)

KIRKBYMOORSIDE
Manor Vale, Kirkbymoorside, York
Tel: (0904) 31525
Holes: 18 6027 yds
V'trs: **
Fees: £10 (£15)

KNARESBOROUGH
Boroughbridge Road, Knaresborough
Tel: (0423) 864865
Holes: 18 6281 yds
V'trs: **
Fees: £10 (£16)

LOFTUS HILL
Boroughbridge Road, Ferresnby, Knaresborough
Tel: (0423) 340731
Holes: 9 5106 yds
V'trs: *
Fees: £8 (£10)

MALTON & NORTON
Welham Park, Norton, Malton
Tel: (0653) 693882
Holes: 18 6401 yds
V'trs: * H
Fees: £11.50 (£15.50)

MASHAM
Burnholme, Swinton Road, Masham, Ripon
Tel: (0765) 89379
Holes: 9 5244 yds
V'trs: *
Fees: £10

OAKDALE
Oakdale, Harrogate
Tel: (0423) 560510
Holes: 18 6456 yds
V'trs: *
Fees: £15 (£20)

PANNAL
Follifoot Road, Pannal, Harrogate
Tel: (0423) 872620
Holes: 18 6659 yds
V'trs: * H
Fees: £17 (£22)

PIKE HILLS
Tadcaster Road, Copmanthorpe, York
Tel: (0904) 708756
Holes: 18 6048 yds
V'trs: * H
Fees: £14

RICHMOND
Bend Hagg, Richmond
Tel: (0748) 2457
Holes: 18 5704 yds
V'trs: **
Fees: £8 (£12)

RIPON CITY
Palace Road, Ripon
Tel: (0765) 700411
Holes: 9 5752 yds
V'trs: *
Fees: £5 (£7)

SCARBOROUGH NORTH CLIFF
North Cliff Avenue, Burniston Road, Scarborough
Tel: (0723) 356920
Holes: 18 6425 yds
V'trs: * H
Fees: £12 (£16)

SCARBOROUGH SOUTH CLIFF
Deepdale Avenue, off Filey Road, Scarborough
Tel: (0723) 365150
Holes: 18 6085 yds
V'trs: ** H
Fees: £11.50 (£15)

SELBY
Mill Lane, Brayton, Selby
Tel: (075 782) 785
Holes: 18 6246 yds
V'trs: * H
Fees: £13

SETTLE
Giggleswick, Settle
Tel: (072 92) 3912
Holes: 9 2276 yds
V'trs: **
Fees: £4 (£5)

SKIPTON
Off NW Bypass, Skipton
Tel: (0756) 3257
Holes: 18 6087 yds
V'trs: *
Fees: £10 (£15)

THIRSK & NORTHALLERTON
Thornton-le-Street, Thirsk
Tel: (0846) 22170
Holes: 9 6257 yds
V'trs: *
Fees: £10

WHITBY
Low Straggleton, Whitby
Tel: (0947) 602719
Holes: 18 5710 yds
V'trs: **
Fees: £10 (£15)

YORK
Lords Moor Lane, Strensall, York
Tel: (0904) 490304
Holes: 18 6285 yds
V'trs: *
Fees: £17 (£21)

YORKSHIRE (SOUTH)

ABBEYDALE
Twentywell Lane, Dore, nr Sheffield
Tel: (0742) 365633
Holes: 18 6419 yds
V'trs: **
Fees: £15 (£20)

AUSTERFIELD PARK
Cross Lane, Austerfield, nr Bawtry, Doncaster
Tel: (0302) 719461
Holes: 18 6284 yds
V'trs: **
Fees: £10 (£12)

DONCASTER
Bawtry Road, Bessacarr, nr Doncaster
Tel: (0302) 868404
Holes: 18 6230 yds
V'trs: * H
Fees: £14 (£17.50)

DONCASTER TOWN MOOR
c/o The Belle Vue Club, Bellevue, Doncaster
Tel: (0302) 535286
Holes: 18 6314 yds
V'trs: *
Fees: £9 (£11)

DORE & TOTLEY
Bradway Road, Bradway, nr Sheffield
Tel: (0742) 366844
Holes: 18 6301 yds
V'trs: *
Fees: £13

HALLAMSHIRE
Sandygate, Sheffield
Tel: (0742) 305222
Holes: 18 6396 yds
V'trs: **
Fees: £17 (£25)

HICKELTON
Hickelton, nr Doncaster
Tel: (0709) 895170
Holes: 18 6403 yds
V'trs: *
Fees: £10 (£15)

HILLSBOROUGH
Worrall Road, Sheffield
Tel: (0742) 332666
Holes: 18 5762 mts
V'trs: **
Fees: £14 (£20)

LEES HALL
Hemsworth Road, Norton, Sheffield
Tel: (0742) 554402
Holes: 18 6137 yds
V'trs: **
Fees: £11.50 (£17.25)

LINDRICK
Lindrick Common, nr Worksop, Notts
Tel: (0909) 475820
Holes: 18 6615 yds
V'trs: *
Fees: £25 (£30)

PHOENIX
Brinsworth, Rotherham
Tel: (0709) 382624
Holes: 18 6170 yds
V'trs: **
Fees: £10 (£14)

RENISHAW PARK
Golf House, Renishaw, Sheffield
Tel: (0246) 435484
Holes: 18 6253 yds
V'trs: **
Fees: £14 (£16)

ROTHERHAM
Thrybergh Park, Rotherham
Tel: (0709) 850480
Holes: 18 6324 yds
V'trs: **
Fees: £17 (£20)

ROUNDWOOD
Green Lane, Rawmarsh, Rotherham
Tel: (0709) 523471
Holes: 9 5646 yds
V'trs: *
Fees: £5 (£7)

SHEFFIELD TRANSPORT DEPT
Meadow Head, Sheffield
Tel: (0742) 373216
Holes: 18 3966 yds
V'trs: ***

SILKSTONE
Field Head, Silkstone, nr Barnsley
Tel: (0226) 790128
Holes: 18 6045 yds
V'trs: *
Fees: £10

SITWELL PARK
Shrogs Wood Road, Rotherham
Tel: (0709) 541046
Holes: 18 6250 yds
V'trs: **
Fees: £12 (£14)

STOCKSBRIDGE & DISTRICT
30 Royd lane, Townend, Deepcar, nr Sheffield
Tel: (0742) 882003
Holes: 15 5055 yds
V'trs: **
Fees: £6 (£7)

TANKERSLEY PARK
High Green, Sheffield
Tel: (0742) 455583
Holes: 18 6241 yds
V'trs: *
Fees: £10 (£12)

THORNE
Kirton Lane, Thorne, Doncaster
Tel: (0405) 812054
Holes: 18 5146 yds
V'trs: ***
Fees: £4 (£5)

WATH-UPON-DEARNE
Abdy Rawmarsh, Rotherham
Tel: (0709) 872149/878677
Holes: 18 5776 yds
V'trs: *
Fees: £10

WHEATLEY
Armthorpe Road, Doncaster
Tel: (0302) 834085
Holes: 18 6345 yds
V'trs: **
Fees: £12 (£16)

YORKSHIRE (WEST)

ALWOODLEY
Wigton Lane, Alwoodley, Leeds
Tel: (0532) 681680
V'trs: **
Fees: £25 (£30)

BAILDON
Moorgate, Baildon, Shipley
Tel: (0274) 595162
Holes: 18 6085 yds
V'trs: *
Fees: £9 (£12)

BEN RHYDDING
High Wood, Ben Rhydding, Ilkley
Tel: (0943) 608759
Holes: 9 4711 yds
V'trs: *
Fees: £5

BRADFORD
Hawksworth Lane, Guiseley, Leeds
Tel: (0943) 73719
Holes: 18 6259 yds
V'trs: *
Fees: On enquiry

BRADFORD MOOR
Scarr Hall, Pollard Lane, Bradford
Tel: (0274) 631163
Holes: 9 5854 yds
V'trs: **
Fees: £7.50 (£8)

BRANSHAW
Branshaw Moor, Oakworth, nr Keighley
Tel: (0535) 43235
Holes: 18 5858 yds
V'trs: *
Fees: £8 (£10)

CALVERLEY
Woodhall Lane, Pudsey
Tel: (0532) 569244
Holes: 18 5348 yards
9 hole course
V'trs: *
Fees: £10, 9 holes £4

CASTLE FIELDS
Rastrick Common, Brighouse
Tel: (0484) 712108
Holes: 6 2406 yds
V'trs: **
Fees: £1.50

CLAYTON
Thornton View Road, Clayton, Bradford
Tel: (0274) 880047
Holes: 9 5515 yds
V'trs: *
Fees: £5 (£8)

CLECKHEATON & DISTRICT
Bradford Road, Cleckheaton
Tel: (0274) 851267
Holes: 18 5994 yds
V'trs: **
Fees: £11 (£17.50)

CROSLAND HEATH
Crosland Heath, Huddersfield
Tel: (0484) 653877
Holes: 18 5961 yds
V'trs: **
Fees: On enquiry

DEWSBURY DISTRICT
The Pinnacle, Mirfield
Tel: (0924) 496030
Holes: 18 6256 yds
V'trs: **
Fees: £9

EAST BIERLEY
South View Road, Bradford
Tel: (0274) 681023
Holes: 9 4692 yds
V'trs: *
Fees: £6 (£8)

ELLAND
Hullen Edge, Elland
Tel: (0422) 374886
Holes: 9 2763 yds
V'trs: **
Fees: £6 (£10)

FERRYBRIDGE 'C'
PO Box 39, Stranglands Lane, Knottingley
Tel: (0977); 84188 (Ext 256)
Holes: 9 5138 yds
V'trs: ***

FULNECK
Pudsey
Tel: (0532) 565191
Holes: 9 5564 yds
V'trs: *
Fees: £6

GARFORTH
Long Lane, Garforth, Leeds
Tel: (0532) 862063
Holes: 18 6327 yds
V'trs: * H
Fees: £14

HALIFAX
Union Lane, Ogden, Halifax
Tel: (0422) 240041
Holes: 18 6038 yds
V'trs: *
Fees: £10 (£15)

HALIFAX BRADLEY HALL
Holywell Green, Halifax
Tel: (0422) 370231
Holes: 18 6213 yds
V'trs: **
Fees: £10 (£15)

HALIFAX WEST END
Highroad Well, Halifax
Tel: (0422) 363293
Holes: 18 6003 yds
V'trs: **
Fees: £8 (£10)

HANGING HEATON
Whitecross Road, Dewsbury
Tel: (0924) 467077
Holes: 9 2868 yds
V'trs: *
Fees: £6 (£8)

HEADINGLEY
Back Church Lane, Adel, Leeds
Tel: (0532) 675100
Holes: 18 6238 yds
V'trs: **
Fees: £15 (£24)

HEADLEY
Headley Lane, Thornton, nr Bradford.
Tel: (0274) 833481
Holes: 9 2457 yds
V'trs: *
Fees: £3 (£6)

HORSFORTH
Layton Rise, Layton Road, Horsforth, Leeds
Tel: (0532) 585200
Holes: 18 6293 yds
V'trs: *
Fees: £14 (£18)

HOWLEY HALL
Scotchman Lane, Morley, Leeds
Tel: (0924) 473852
Holes: 18 6029 yds
V'trs: **
Fees: £12 (£18)

HUDDERSFIELD
Fixby Hall, Lightridge Road, Fixby, Huddersfield
Tel: (0484) 426463
Holes: 18 6402 yds
V'trs: *
Fees: £18.50 (£20)

ILKLEY
Myddleton, Ilkley
Tel: (0943) 607463
Holes: 18 6249 yds
V'trs: **
Fees: £17

KEIGHLEY
Howden Park, Utley, Keighley
Tel: (0535) 665370
Holes: 18 6134 yds
V'trs: *
Fees: £15

LEEDS
Elmete Road, Roundhay, Leeds
Tel: (0532) 658786
Holes: 18 6096 yds
V'trs: *
Fees: £12.50

LIGHTCLIFFE
Knowle Top Road, Lightcliffe
Tel: (0422) 202459
Holes: 9 5368 mts
V'trs: *
Fees: £10 (£12)

PRIVATE COURSES

LONGLEY PARK
Maple Street, off Somerset
Road, Huddersfield
Tel: (0484) 422304
Holes: 9 5324 yds
V'trs: *
Fees: £6.50 (£8)

LOW LAITHE
Parkmill Lane, Flushdyke, Ossett
Tel: (0924) 74667
Holes: 18 6468 yds
V'trs: *
Fees: £12 (£18)

MARSDEN
Hemplow, Marsden, nr
Huddersfield
Tel: (0484) 844253
Holes: 9 5702 yds
V'trs: *
Fees: £5 (£10)

MELTHAM
Thick Hollins Hall, Meltham,
Huddersfield
Tel: (0484) 851521
Holes: 18 6145 yds
V'trs: **
Fees: £12 (£15)

MOOR ALLERTON
Coal Road, Leeds
Tel: (0532) 665209
Holes: 18 6542 yds
9 3541 yds
V'trs: *
Fees: £21

MOORTOWN
Harrogate Road, Leeds
Tel: (0532) 683636
Holes: 18 6544 yds
V'trs: * H
Fees: £20 (£25)

MOUNT SKIP
Wadsworth, Hebden Bridge
Tel: (0422) 842896
Holes: 9 5114 yds
V'trs: **
Fees: £6

NORMANTON
Snydale Road, Normanton,
Wakefield
Tel: (0924) 220134
Holes: 9 5284 yds
V'trs: *
Fees: £4.50 (£8.50)

NORTHCLIFFE
Highbank Lane, Moorhead,
Shipley
Tel: (0274) 587193
Holes: 18 6065 yds
V'trs: **
Fees: £12 (£17)

OTLEY
West Busk Lane, Otley
Tel: (0943) 463403
Holes: 18 6235 yds
V'trs: **
Fees: £17 (£22)

OUTLANE
Slack Lane, Outlane,
Huddersfield
Tel: (0422) 3374762
Holes: 18 5735 yds
V'trs: **
Fees: £8 (£12)

PAINTHORPE HOUSE
Painthorpe Lane, Crigglestone,
Wakefield
Tel: (0924) 255083
Holes: 9 4008 yds
V'trs: *
Fees: £2 (£4)

PHOENIX PARK
Phoenix Park, Thornbury,
Bradford
Tel: (0274) 667573
Holes: 9 4982 yds
V'trs: *
Fees: £5

**PONTEFRACT &
DISTRICT**
Park Lane, Pontefract
Tel: (0977) 706806
Holes: 18 6227 yds
V'trs: * H
Fees: £12 (£15)

QUEENSBURY
Queensbury, nr Bradford
Tel: (0274) 882155
Holes: 9 5102 yds
V'trs: **
Fees: £6 (£10)

RAWDON
Buckstone Drive, Micklefield
Lane, Rawdon
Tel: (0532) 505017
Holes: 9 5982 yds
V'trs: * H
Fees: £8.50

RIDDLESDEN
Howden Rough, Riddlesden,
Keighley
Tel: (0535) 602148
Holes: 18 4185 yds
V'trs: *
Fees: £4 (£7)

RYBURN
Norland, Sowerby Bridge,
Halifax
Tel: (0422) 831355
Holes: 9 5002 yds
V'trs: **
Fees: £3 (£5)

SAND MOOR
Alwoodley Lane, Leeds
Tel: (0532) 683925
Holes: 18 6423 yds
V'trs: H
Fees: £24

SCARCROFT
Syke Lane, Leeds
Tel: (0532) 892780
Holes: 18 6426 yds
V'trs: *
Fees: £20 (£27.50)

SHIPLEY
Beckfoot Lane, Cottingley
Bridge, Bingley
Tel: (0274) 563212
Holes: 18 6218 yds
V'trs: *
Fees: £15 (£20)

SILSDEN
Brunthwaite, SIlsden, Keighley
Tel: (0535) 52998
Holes: 14 4870 yds
V'trs: *
Fees: £5 (£8)

SOUTH BRADFORD
Pearson Road, Odsal, Bradford
Tel: (0274) 673346
Holes: 9 6004 yds
V'trs: *
Fees: On enquiry

SOUTH LEEDS
Gipsy Lane, Ring Road, Beeston
Tel: (0532) 702598
Holes: 18 5835 yds
V'trs: *
Fees: £10 (£13)

TODMORDEN
Rive Rocks, Cross Stone,
Todmorden
Tel: (070 681) 2986
Holes: 9 5818 yds
V'trs: **
Fees: £6 (£8)

WAKEFIELD
Woodthorpe, Wakefield
Tel: (00924) 255380
Holes: 18 6626 yds
V'trs: **
Fees: £13 (£16)

WEST BOWLING
Newall Hall, Rooley Lane, West
Bowling, Bradford
Tel: (0274) 728036
Holes: 18 5570 yds
V'trs: * H
Fees: £12 (£18)

WEST BRADFORD
Chellow Grange, Haworth
Road, Bradford
Tel: (0274) 542102
Holes: 18 5705 yds
V'trs: *
Fees: £9 (£12)

WETHERBY
Linton Lane, Wetherby
Tel: (0937) 63375
Holes: 18 6235 yds
V'trs: *
Fees: £13 (£16)

WOODHALL HILLS
Calverley, Pudsey
Tel: (0532) 5 63857
Holes: 18 6102 yds
V'trs: *
Fees: £9 (£12)

WOODSOME HALL
Woodsome Hall, Fenay Bridge,
Huddersfield
Tel: (0484) 602971
Holes: 18 6080 yds
V'trs: *
Fees: £16 (£20)

WORTLEY
Hermit Hill Lane, Wortley,
Sheffield
Tel: (0742) 886490
Holes: 18 5983 yds
V'trs: **
Fees: £12 (£18)

WALES

CLWYD

ABERGELE & PENSARN
Ton-y-Goppa Road, Abergele
Tel: (0745) 823813
Holes: 18 6086 yds
V'trs: **
Fees: £12 (£14)

BRYN MORFYDD
The Princess Course,
Llanrhaeadr
Tel: (074 578) 280
Holes: 9 1190 yds
V'trs: **
Fees: £5

DENBIGH
Henllan Road, Denbigh
Tel: (074 571) 4159
Holes: 18 5582 yds
V'trs: *
Fees: £9 (£11)

FLINT
Cornist Park, Flint
Tel: (035 26) 2327
Holes: 9 5829 yds
V'trs: *
Fees: £6

HAWARDEN
Groomsdale Lane, Hawarden,
Deeside
Tel: (0244) 531447
Holes: 9 5620 yds
V'trs: *
Fees: £8

HOLYWELL
Brynford, Holywell
Tel: (0352) 710040
Holes: 10 3117 yds
V'trs: *
Fees: £7 (£9)

MOLD
Pantmywyn, Mold
Tel: (0352) 740318
Holes: 18 5521 yds
V'trs: **
Fees: £8 (£10)

OLD COLWYN
Woodland Avenue, Old
Colwyn
Tel: (0492) 515581
Holes: 9 5268 yds
V'trs: *
Fees: £6 (£7)

OLD PADESWOOD
Station Road, Padeswood
Tel: (0244) 547401
Holes: 18 6728 yds
V'trs: **
Fees: £10

**PADESWOOD &
BUCKLEY**
Station Lane, Padeswood
Tel: (0244) 543636
Holes: 18 5775 yds
V'trs: **
Fees: £10 (£12)

PRESTATYN
Marine Road East, Prestatyn
Tel: (074 56) 45320/88353
Holes: 18 6714 yds
V'trs: **
Fees: £11 (£13)

RHUDDLAN
Rhuddlan, Rhyl
Tel: (0745) 590898
Holes: 18 6473 yds
V'trs: * H
Fees: £14 (£17)

RHYL
Coast Road, Rhyl
Tel: (0745) 35 3171
Holes: 9 6153 yds
V'trs: **
Fees: £8 (£10)

RUTHIN-PWLLGLAS
Ruthin
Tel: (082 42) 2296
Holes: 9 5313 yds
V'trs: **
Fees: £7 (£9)

ST MELYD
Meliden Road, Prestatyn
Tel: (074 56) 88858
Holes: 9 5857 yds
V'trs: *
Fees: £10 (£14)

VALE OF LLANGOLLEN
Holyhead Road, Llangollen
Tel: (0978) 860040
Holes: 18 6661 yds
V'trs: **
Fees: £14 (£18)

WREXHAM
Holt Road, Wrexham
Tel: (0978) 351476
Holes: 18 6078 yds
V'trs: ** H
Fees: On request

DYFED

ABERYSTWYTH
Bryn-y-Mor, Aberystwyth
Tel: (0970) 625103
Holes: 18 5868 yds
V'trs: **
Fees: £8 (£12)

ASHBURNHAM
Cliffe Terrace, Barry Port
Tel: (05546) 3846
Holes: 18 6916 yds
V'trs: ** H
Fees: £16 (£22)

BORTH & YNYSLAS
Borth
Tel: (0970) 871556
Holes: 18 6100 yds
V'trs: **
Fees: £14 (£17)

CARDIGAN
Gwbert-on-Sea
Tel: (0239) 612035
Holes: 18 6207 yds
V'trs: **
Fees: £10 (£14)

CARMARTHEN
Blaenycoed Road, Carmarthen
Tel: (0267) 87214
Holes: 18 6212 yds
V'trs: **
Fees: £11 (£12)

CILGWYN
Llangybi, Lampeter
Tel: (0570 45) 286
Holes: 9 5318 yds
V'trs: **
Fees: £7 (£10)

GLYNHIR
Glynhir Road, Llandybie, Ammanford
Tel: (0269) 851010
Holes: 18 6090 yds
V'trs: **
Fees: Summer £10 (£12)

HAVERFORDWEST
Arnold Down, Haverfordwest
Tel: (0437) 768409
Holes: 18 5945 yds
V'trs: **
Fees: £12 (£14)

MILFORD HAVEN
Hubbertston, Milford Haven
Tel: (06462) 2368
Holes: 18 6071 yds
V'trs: **
Fees: £9

NEWPORT
Newport
Tel: (0239) 820244
Holes: 9 3089 yds
V'trs: **
Fees: £8

ST DAVID'S CITY
Whitesands Bay, St Davids
Tel: (03483) 607
Holes: 9 5695 yds
V'trs: **
Fees: £10

SOUTH PEMBROKESHIRE
Defensible Barracks, Pembroke Dock
Tel: (0646) 683817
Holes: 9 5804 yds
V'trs: **
Fees: £7

TENBY
The Burrows, Tenby
Tel: (0834) 4447
Holes: 18 6450 yds
V'trs: **
Fees: £12 (£15)

GWENT

BLACKWOOD
Cwymgelli, Blackwood
Tel: (0495) 223152
Holes: 9 5304 yds
V'trs: **
Fees: £8 (£10)

GREENMEADOW
Croesyceiliog, Cwmbran
Tel: (06333) 62626
Holes: 15 5593 yds
V'trs: **
Fees: £10 (£12)

LLANWERN
Golf House, Tennyson Ave, Llanwern
Tel: (0633) 415233
Holes: 18 6139 yds
9 5686 yds
V'trs: * H
Fees: £16

MONMOUTH
Leasebrook Lane, Monmouth
Tel: (0600) 2212
Holes: 9 5454 yds
V'trs: **
Fees: £11 (£16)

MONMOUTHSHIRE
Llanfoist, Abergavenny
Tel: (0873) 2532
Holes: 18 6045 yds
V'trs: ** H
Fees: £16 (£22)

NEWPORT
Great Oak, Rogerstone, Newport
Tel: (0633) 893271
Holes: 18 6370 yds
V'trs: *
Fees: £16 (£22)

PONTNEWYDD
Maesgwyn Farm, West Pontnewydd, Cwmbran
Tel: (06333) 2170
Holes: 10 5340 yds
V'trs: *
Fees: £10

PONTYPOOL
Trevethin, Pontypool
Tel: (04955) 55544
Holes: 18 6013 yds
V'trs: **
Fees: £12 (£17)

ROLLS OF MONMOUTH
The Hendre, Monmouth
Tel: (0600)] 5353
Holes: 18 6723 yds
V'trs: **
Fees: £20 (£24)

ST MELLONS
St Mellons, Cardiff
Tel: (0633) 6870101
Holes: 18 6225 yds
V'trs: *
Fees: £16

ST PIERRE
Chepstow
Tel: (02912) 5261
Holes: 18 6700 yds
18 5762 yds
V'trs: * H
Fees: On request

TREDEGAR & RHYMNEY
Tredegar, Rhymney
Tel: (0685) 840732
Holes: 9 5564 yds
V'trs: **
Fees: £6

TREDEGAR PARK
Bassaleg Road, Newport
Tel: (0633) 894517
Holes: 18 6097 yds
V'trs: *
Fees: £14 (£18)

WEST MONMOUTHSHIRE
Pond Road, Nantyglo
Tel: (0495) 310233
Holes: 18 6118 yds
V'trs: **
Fees: On request

GWYNEDD

ABERDOVEY
Aberdovey
Tel: (065 472) 602
Holes: 18 6445 yds
V'trs: **
Fees: £18 (£26)

ABERSOCH
Abersoch
Tel: (075 881) 2622
Holes: 9 5800 yds
V'trs: **
Fees: On request

BALA
Penlan, Bala
Tel: (0678) 520359
Holes: 10 4934 yds
V'trs: *
Fees: £7 (£9)

BALA LAKE
Bala
Tel: (0678) 520344
Holes: 9 3362 yds
V'trs: **
Fees: £8 (£9)

BETWYS-Y-COED
Betws-y-Coed
Tel: (069 02) 556
Holes: 9 2515 yds
V'trs: **
Fees: £8 (£9)

CAERNARFON
Llanfaglan, Caernarfon
Tel: (0286) 3783
Holes: 18 5870 yds
V'trs: **
Fees: £9

CONWY (CAERNARVONSHIRE)
Conwy
Tel: (0492) 593225
Holes: 18 6901 yds
V'trs: *
Fees: £14 (£18)

CRICCIETH
Ednyfed Hill, Criccieth
Tel: (0766) 522154
Holes: 18 5755 yds
V'trs: **
Fees: £6

DOLGELLAU
Pencefn Road, Dolgellau
Tel: (0341) 422603
Holes: 9 4671 yds
V'trs: **
Fees: £8 (£9.50)

FFESTINIOG
Ffestiniog
Tel: (0766) 831829
Holes: 9 5500 yds
V'trs: **
Fees: £5

LLANDUDNO (MAESDU)
Hospital Road, Llandudno
Tel: (0492) 75195
Holes: 18 6513 yds
V'trs: ** H
Fees: £14 (£18)

LLANDUDNO (NORTH WALES)
Bryniau Road, West Shore, Llandudno
Tel: (0492) 76878
Holes: 18 6132 yds
V'trs: **
Fees: £14 (£18)

LLANFAIRFECHAN
Llanerch Road, Llanfairfechan
Tel: (0248) 680144
Holes: 9 3119 yds
V'trs: **
Fees: £6

NEFYN & DISTRICT
Nefyn
Tel: (0758) 720218
Holes: 18 6294 yds
V'trs: * H
Fees: £12 (£14)

PENMAENMAWR
Conway Old Road, Penmaenmawr
Tel: (0492) 623330
Holes: 9 5143 yds
V'trs: **
Fees: £8 (£10)

PORTMADOC
Morfa Bychgan, Porthmadog
Tel: (0766) 513828
Holes: 18 6309 yds
V'trs: **
Fees: £12 (£14)

PWLLHELI
Pwllheli
Tel: (0758) 612520
Holes: 18 6110 yds
V'trs: **
Fees: On request

RHOS-ON-SEA
Pernrhyn Bay, Llandudno
Tel: (0492) 49641
Holes: 18 6064 yds
V'trs: **
Fees: On request

ROYAL ST DAVID'S
Harlech
Tel: (0766) 780857
Holes: 18 6427 yds
V'trs: ** H
Fees: £18 (£22)

ST DEINIOL
Penbryn, Bangor
Tel: (0248) 353098
Holes: 18 5572 yds
V'trs: **
Fees: £8

ISLE OF ANGLESEY

ANGLESEY
Rhosneigr
Tel: (0407) 810703
Holes: 18 6204 yds
V'trs: **
Fees: £8 (£10)

BARON HILL
Beaumaris
Tel: (0248) 810231
Holes: 9 5562 yds
V'trs: *
Fees: £8 (£10)

BULL BAY
Amlwch
Tel: (0407) 831188
Holes: 18 6160 yds
V'trs: *
Fees: £9 (£12)

HOLYHEAD
Trearddur Bay, Holyhead
Tel: (0407) 2022
Holes: 18 6058 yds
V'trs: *
Fees: On request

MID GLAMORGAN

ABERDARE
Abernant, Aberdare
Tel: (0685) 878735
Holes: 18 5875 yds
V'trs: * H
Fees: £10 (£12)

BARGOED
Heolddu, Bargoed
Tel: (0443) 830143
Holes: 18 6233 yds
V'trs: *
Fees: £10

BRYN MEADOWS
The Bryn, Hengoed
Tel: (0495) 221905
Holes: 18 6200 yds
V'trs: **
Fees: £14 (£17)

CAERPHILLY
Mountain Road, Caerphilly
Tel: (0222) 869104
Holes: 14 6063 yds
V'trs: *
Fees: £10

CASTELL HEIGHTS
Blaengwynlais, Caerphilly
Tel: (0222) 886666
Holes: 9 2688 yds
V'trs: **
Fees: £4

CREIGIAU
Creigiau, Cardiff
Tel: (0222) 891909
Holes: 18 5800 yds
V'trs: *
Fees: £10

LLANTRISANT & PONTYCLUN
Talbot Green, Llantrisant
Tel: (0443) 228169
Holes: 12 5712 yds
V'trs: *
Fees: £10

MAESTEG
Mount Pleasant, Maesteg
Tel: (0656) 732037
Holes: 18 5845 yds
V'trs: **
Fees: £10 (£14)

MERTHYR TYDFIL
Cilsanws Mountain, Cefn Coed
Tel: (0685) 723308
Holes: 9 5794 yds
V'trs: **
Fees: £10

MORLAIS CASTLE
Pant, Dowlais, Merthyr Tydfil
Tel: (0685) 722822
Holes: 18 6320 yds
V'trs: *
Fees: £12

MOUNTAIN ASH
Cefnpennar
Tel: (0443) 478770
Holes: 18 5535 yds
V'trs: **
Fees: £12 (£14)

MOUNTAIN LAKES
Blaengwynlais, Caerphilly
Tel: (0220) 886666
Holes: 18 6851 yds
V'trs: * H
Fees: £14 (£17)

PONTYPRIDD
Ty Gwyn Road, Pontypridd
Tel: (0443) 491210
Holes: 18 5650 yds
V'trs: * H
Fees: On request

PYLE & KENFIG
Waun-y-Mer, Kenfig
Tel: (065 671) 772446
Holes: 18 6655 yds
V'trs: *
Fees: £18

RHONDDA
Penrhys, Rhondda
Tel: (0443) 433204
Holes: 18 6428 yds
V'trs: * H
Fees: £10

ROYAL PORTHCAWL
Porthcawl
Tel: (065 671) 6984
Holes: 18 6691 yds
V'trs: * H
Fees: On request

SOUTHERNDOWN
Ewenny, Bridgend
Tel: (0656) 880326
Holes: 18 6705 yds
V'trs: * H
Fees: £20 (£28)

WHITEHALL
The Pavilion, Nelson, Treharris
Tel: (0443) 740245
Holes: 9 5750 yds
V'trs: *
Fees: £8

POWYS

BRECON
Llanfaes, Brecon
Tel: (08974) 2004
Holes: 9 5218 yds
V'trs: **
Fees: £7

BUILTH WELLS
Golf Club Road, Builth Wells
Tel: (0982) 553293
Holes: 18 5376 yds
V'trs: **
Fees: £10 (£12)

CRADOC
Penoyre Park, Cradoc, Brecon
Tel: (0874) 5524
Holes: 18 6234 yds
V'trs: **
Fees: £12 (£16)

KNIGHTON
Little Ffrydd Wood, Knighton
Tel: (0547) 528646
Holes: 9 5320 yds
V'trs: **
Fees: £6 (£8)

LLANDRINDOD
Llandrindod Wells
Tel: (0597) 2010
Holes: 18 5759 yds
V'trs: **
Fees: £8 (£11)

LLANIDLOES (ST IDLOES)
Penrhalt, Llanidloes
Tel: (055 12) 2559
Holes: 9 5210 yds
V'trs: **
Fees: £4 (£6)

MACHYNLLETH
Ffordd Drenewydd, Machynlleth
Tel: (0654) 2000
Holes: 9 5726 yds
V'trs: *
Fees: £8

OLD RECTORY HOTEL
Llangattock, Crickhowell
Tel: (0873) 810373
Holes: 9 1409 yds
V'trs: **
Fees: £7

ST GILES NEWTOWN
Pool Road, Newtown
Tel: (0686) 625844
Holes: 9 5964 yds
V'trs: *
Fees: £7 (£9)

WELSHPOOL
Golfa Hill, Welshpool
Tel: (093 883) 249
Holes: 18 5708 yds
V'trs: **
Fees: £7 (£9)

SOUTH GLAMORGAN

BRYNHILL
Port Road, Colcot, Barry
Tel: (0446) 733660
Holes: 18 6021 yds
V'trs: *
Fees: £15 (£17)

CARDIFF
Sherborne Avenue, Cyncoed
Tel: (0222) 754772
Holes: 18 6014 yds
V'trs: * H
Fees: £22

DINAS POWIS
Dinas Powis
Tel: (0222) 512727
Holes: 18 5377 yds
V'trs: *
Fees: £8 (£10)

GLAMORGANSHIRE
Lavernock Road, Penarth
Tel: (0222) 707401
Holes: 18 6150 yds
V'trs: ** H
Fees: £16 (£21)

LLANISHEN
Cwm Lisvane, Cardiff
Tel: (02212) 755076
Holes: 18 5296 yds
V'trs: * H
Fees: £16

RAF ST ATHAN
Barry
Tel: (0446) 75103
Holes: 9 5957 yds
V'trs: *
Fees: £10 (£12)

RADYR
Radyr, Cardiff
Tel: (0222) 842476
Holes: 18 6031 yds
V'trs: * H
Fees: £12

WENVOE CASTLE
Wenvoe, Cardiff
Tel: (0222) 593649
Holes: 18 6422 yds
V'trs: ** H
Fees: £14 (£16)

WHITCHURCH
Pantmawr Road, Whitchurch
Tel: (0222) 61460
Holes: 18 6245 yds
V'trs: * H
Fees: £16 (£18)

WEST GLAMORGAN

CLYNE
Owls Lodge Lane, Mayals, Swansea
Tel: (0792) 402094
Holes: 18 6312 yds
V'trs: **
Fees: £12 (£17)

FAIRWOOD PARK
Upper Killay, Swansea
Tel: (0792) 299194
Holes: 18 6606 yds
V'trs: **
Fees: £14 (£16)

GLYNNEATH
Penycraig, Glynneath
Tel: (0639) 720452
Holes: 18 5425 yds
V'trs: **
Fees: £7 (£11)

INCO
Clydach, Swansea
Tel: (0792) 844216
Holes: 13 5976 yds
V'trs: **
Fees: £5 (£6)

LANGLAND BAY
Langland Bay, Swansea
Tel: (0792) 366186
Holes: 18 5830 yds
V'trs: **
Fees: £14 (£16)

MORRISTON
Clasemont Road, Morriston, Swansea
Tel: (0792) 772335
Holes: 18 5773 yds
V'trs: * H
Fees: £13 (£20)

NEATH
Cadoxton, Neath
Tel: (0639) 643615
Holes: 18 6500 yds
V'trs: **
Fees: £9 (£13)

PALLEG
Palleg Road, Lower Cwmtwrch, Swansea
Tel: (0639) 842193
Holes: 9 3209 yds
V'trs: **
Fees: £6 (£9)

PENNARD
Southgate Road, Southgate, nr Swansea
Tel: (044 128) 3451
Holes: 18 6268 yds
V'trs: ** H
Fees: £11 (£13)

PONTARDAWE
Cefn Llan, Pontardawe, Swansea
Holes: 18 6061 yds
V'trs: **
Fees: £11 (£18)

SWANSEA BAY
Jersey Marine, Neath
Tel: (0792) 812198/814153
Holes: 18 6302 yds
V'trs: **
Fees: £11 (£13)

SCOTLAND

BORDER REGION

BERWICKSHIRE

DUNS
Hardens Road, Duns
Tel: (0361) 82717
Holes: 9 5826 yds
V'trs: **
Fees: £6 (£6)

EYEMOUTH
Gunsgreen House, Eyemouth
Tel: (08907) 50551
Holes: 9 2369 mts
V'trs: **
Fees: £5

THE HIRSEL
Coldstream
Tel: (0890) 2678
Holes: 9 5680 yds
V'trs: **
Fees: £5 (£7)

PEEBLESSHIRE

INNERLEITHEN
Leithen Water, Leithen Road, Innerleithen
Tel: (0896) 830951
Holes: 9 5829 yds
V'trs: *
Fees: £5 (5)

WEST LINTON
West Linton
Tel: (0968) 60256
Holes: 18 6132 yds
V'trs: **
Fees: £8 (£9)

ROXBURGHSHIRE

HAWICK
Vertish Hill, Hawick
Tel: (0450) 72293
Holes: 18 5929 yds
V'trs: **
Fees: £5 (£8)

JEDBURGH
Dunion Road, Jedburgh
Tel: (0835) 63587
Holes: 9 5492 yds
V'trs: **
Fees: £5 (£6)

KELSO
Berrymoss Racecourse Road, Kelso, Roxburghshire
Tel: (0573) 23009
Holes: 18 6066 yds
V'trs: **
Fees: £5.50 (£6.50)

MELROSE
Dingleton, Melrose
Tel: (089 682) 2855
Holes: 9 5579 yds
V'trs: **
Fees: £5 (£6)

MINTO
Denholm, Hawick
Tel: (0450) 87220
Holes: 18 5460 yds
V'trs: **
Fees: £7 (£8)

ST BOSWELLS
St Boswells
Tel: (0835) 22359
Holes: 9 5250 yds
V'trs: **
Fees: £4 (£5)

SELKIRKSHIRE

SELKIRK
Selkirk
Tel: (0750) 20621
Holes: 9 5560 yds
V'trs: **
Fees: £7

TORWOODLEE
Galashiels
Tel: (0896) 2260
Holes: 9 5800 yds
V'trs: *
Fees: £8 (£10)

CENTRAL REGION

CLACKMANNANSHIRE

ALLOA
Schawpark, Sauchie, Alloa
Tel: (0259) 724476
Holes: 18 6240 yds
V'trs: **
Fees: £7 (£12)

ALVA
Beauclerc Street, Alva
Tel: (0259) 60431
Holes: 9 2407 yds
V'trs: **
Fees: £3.50 (£4.50)

BRAEHEAD
Cambus, Alloa
Tel: (0259) 722078
Holes: 18 6013 yds
V'trs: **
Fees: £8 (£10)

DOLLAR
Brewlands House, Dollar
Tel: (02594) 2400
Holes: 18 5144 yds
V'trs: **
Fees: £5 (£8)

MUCKHART
Muckhart by Dollar
Tel: (025 981) 493
Holes: 18 6112 yds
V'trs: **
Fees: £6 (£9)

TILLICOULTRY
Alva Road, Tillicoultry
Tel: (0259) 50124
Holes: 9 2528 yds
V'trs: **
Fees: £3.50 (£5.50)

TULLIALLAN
Kincardine, by Alloa
Tel: (0259) 30798
Holes: 18 5982 yds
V'trs: **
Fees: £7 (£9)

PRIVATE COURSES

PERTHSHIRE

CALLANDER
Aveland Road, Callander
Tel: (0877) 30975
Holes: 18 5091 yds
V'trs: **
Fees: On enquiry

DUNBLANE NEW
Dunblane
Tel: (0786) 823711
Holes: 18 5878 yds
V'trs: *
Fees: £16 (£20)

KILLIN
Killin
Tel: (05672) 312
Holes: 9 2410 yds
V'trs: **
Fees: £4.50 (£4.50)

STIRLINGSHIRE

BALMORE
Balmore by Torrance
Tel: (0360) 21200240
Holes: 18 5735 yds
V'trs: *
Fees: £15

BONNYBRIDGE
Larbert Road, Bonnybridge
Tel: (0324) 812822
Holes: 9 6058 yds
V'trs: * H
Fees: On enquiry

BRIDGE OF ALLAN
Synnylaw, Bridge of Allan
Tel: (0786) 832332
Holes: 9 4932 yds
V'trs: **
Fees: £5 (£7)

BUCHANAN CASTLE
nr Drymen
Tel: (0360) 60330
Holes: 18 6015 yds
V'trs: *
Fees: On enquiry

CAMPSIE
Crow Road, Lennoxtown
Tel: (0360) 310244
Holes: 18 5517 yds
V'trs: *
Fees: £6

FALKIRK
Stirling Road, Camelon, Falkirk
Tel: (0324) 611061
Holes: 18 6257 yds
V'trs: *
Fees: On enquiry

FALKIRK TRYST
Burnhead Road, Larbert
Tel: (0324) 562091
Holes: 18 6053 yds
V'trs: *
Fees: £9

GLENBERVIE
Stirling Road, Larbert
Tel: (0324) 562725
Holes: 18 6469 yds
V'trs: * H
Fees: £15

GRANGEMOUTH
Polmonthill, Grangemouth
Tel: (0324) 714355
Holes: 18 6527 yds
V'trs: **
Fees: £4 (£5)

POLMONT
Manuelrigg, Maddiston, Falkirk
Tel: (0324) 711277
Holes: 9 3044 yds
V'trs: *
Fees: £3 (£5)

STIRLING
Queen's Road, Stirling
Tel: (0786) 71490
Holes: 18 6409 yds
V'trs: *
Fees: £12 (£22)

STRATHENDRICK
Drymen
Tel: (0360) 40582
Holes: 9 4962 yds
V'trs: ***

DUMFRIES & GALLOWAY

DUMFRIESSHIRE

CRICHTON ROYAL
Dumfries
Holes: 9 3084 yds
V'trs: ***

DUMFRIES & COUNTY
Nunfield, Edinburgh Road, Dumfries
Tel: (0387) 68918
Holes: 18 5928 yds
V'trs: *
Fees: £10 (£12)

DUMFRIES & GALLOWAY
Laurieston Avenue, Maxwelltown, Dumfries
Tel: (0387) 56902
Holes: 18 5782 yds
V'trs: **
Fees: £8 (£11)

LANGHOLM
Langholm
Tel: (0541) 80559
Holes: 9 2872 yds
V'trs: **
Fees: £4 (£4)

LOCHMABEN
Castlehill Gate, Lochmaben
Tel: (03887) 810552
Holes: 9 5304 yds
V'trs: *
Fees: £5

LOCKERBIE
Corrie Road, Lockerbie
Tel: (057 62) 3363
Holes: 18 5418 yds
V'trs: **
Fees: £6

MOFFAT
Coatshill, Moffat
Tel: (0683) 20020
Holes: 18 5218 yds
V'trs: *
Fees: £8 (£11)

POWFOOT
Cummertrees, Annan
Tel: (04617) 327
Holes: 18 6266 yds
V'trs: *
Fees: Summer £10 (£12)

SANQUHAR
Blackaddie Road, Sanquhar
Tel: (0659) 50577
Holes: 9 5630 yds
V'trs: **
Fees: £6 (£8)

SOUTHERNESS
Southerness, Dumfries
Tel: (0387) 88677
Holes: 18 6554 yds
V'trs: **
Fees: On enquiry

THORNHILL
Black Nest, Thornhill
Tel: (0848) 30546
Holes: 18 6011 yds
V'trs: **
Fees: £8 (£10)

KIRKCUDBRIGHTSHIRE

CASTLE DOUGLAS
Abercromby Road, Castle Douglas
Tel: (0556) 2801
Holes: 9 5400 yds
V'trs: **
Fees: £5

COLVEND
Sandyhills, nr Dalbeattie
Tel: (055 663) 398
Holes: 9 2322 yds
V'trs: **
Fees: £5 (£5)

DALBEATTIE
Dalbeattie
Tel: (0556) 611421
Holes: 9 4200 yds
V'trs: **
Fees: £6 (£6)

GATEHOUSE
Gatehouse of Fleet
Tel: (055) 74252
Holes: 9 2398 yds
V'trs: **
Fees: £5.50

KIRKCUDBRIGHT
Stirling Crescent, Kirkcudbright
Tel: (0557) 30542
Holes: 18 5681 yds
V'trs: **
Fees: £7

NEW GALLOWAY
New Galloway
Tel: (0556) 2794
Holes: 9 2509 yds
V'trs: **
Fees: £5 (£5)

WIGTOWNSHIRE

NEWTON STEWART
Kirroughtree Avenue, Minnigaff, Newton Stewart
Tel: (0671) 2172
Holes: 9 5512 yds
V'trs: **
Fees: £5 (£6)

PORTPATRICK DUNSKEY
Golf Course Road, Portpatrick
Tel: (0776) 81273
Holes: 18 5644 yds
9 1442 yds
V'trs: **
Fees: £8 (10)
9 holes £4

ST MEDAN
Port William
Tel: (098 87) 358
Holes: 9 2277 yds
V'trs: **
Fees: £6

STRANRAER
Creachmore, Leswalt, Stranraer
Tel: (0776) 87245
Holes: 18 6300 yds
V'trs: **
Fees: £8 (£10)

WIGTOWN & BLADNOCH
Wigtown
Tel: (098 84) 3354
Holes: 9 2731 yds
V'trs: **
Fees: £6 (£8)

WIGTOWNSHIRE COUNTY
Mains of Park, Glenluce, Newton Stewart
Tel: (058 13) 420
Holes: 18 5715 yds
V'trs: **
Fees: £7 (£9)

FIFE REGION

FIFE

ABERDOUR
Seaside Place, Aberdour
Tel: (0383) 860256
Holes: 18 5469 yds
V'trs: *
Fees: £8 (£11)

ANSTRUTHER
Marsfield Shore Road, Anstruther
Tel: (0333) 310956
Holes: 9 4504 yds
V'trs: **
Fees: On enquiry

AUCHTERDERRAN
Woodend Road, Cardenden
Tel: (0592) 721579
Holes: 9 5400 yds
V'trs: **
Fees: £2.55 (£3.90)

BALBIRNIE PARK
Balbirnie Park, Markinch, Glenrothes
Tel: (0592) 752006
Holes: 18 6210 yds
V'trs: **
Fees: £8 (£10)

BURNTISLAND GOLF HOUSE CLUB
Dodhead, Burntisland
Tel: (0592) 873247
Holes: 18 5897 yds
V'trs: **
Fees: £10 (£13)

CANMORE *Venturefair, Dunfermline*
Tel: (0383) 728416
Holes: 18 5437 yds
V'trs: *
Fees: £7 (£10)

CRAIL GOLFING SOCIETY
Balcomie Clubhouse, Fifeness, Crail
Tel: (0333) 50960
Holes: 18 5720 yds
V'trs: **
Fees: On enquiry

CUPAR
Hilarvitt, Cupar
Tel: (0334) 53549
Holes: 9 5074 yds
V'trs: *
Fees: £4 (£5)

DUNFERMLINE
Pitfirrane, Crossford, Dunfermline
Tel: (0383) 723534
Holes: 18 6217 yds
V'trs: *
Fees: £10

EDEN COURSE
St Andrews
Tel: (0334) 74296
Holes: 18 6400 yds
V'trs: **
Fees: £9 (unlimited play on Eden, Jubilee and New Courses)

FALKLAND
The Myre, Falkland
Tel: (0337) 57404
Holes: 9 2384 mts
V'trs: **
Fees: £4 (£6)

GLENROTHES
Golf Course Road, Glenrothes
Tel: (0592) 758686/758678
Holes: 18 6444 yds
V'trs: **
Fees: £3 (£4.15)

GOLF HOUSE CLUB
Elie, Leven
Tel: (0333) 330955
Holes: 18 6241 yds
9 2277 yds
V'trs: *
Fees: £12 (£16)

KIRKCALDY
Ballwearie Road, Kirkcaldy
Tel: (0592) 260370
Holes: 18 6007 yds
V'trs: **
Fees: £5 (£6)

LADYBANK
Annsmuir, Ladybank
Tel: (0337) 30725
Holes: 18 6617 yds
V'trs: *
Fees: £15 (£18)

LESLIE (FIFE)
Balsillie Laws, Leslie, Glenrothes
Tel: (0592) 741449
Holes: 9 4940 yds
V'trs: **
Fees: £4 (£5)

LEVEL LINKS
Leven
Tel: (0333) 21390
Holes: 18 6434 yds
V'trs: *
Fees: £11 (£14)

LOCHGELLY
Cartmore Road, Lochgelly
Tel: (0592) 780174
Holes: 18 5491 yds
V'trs: **
Fees: £3.50 (£4.75)

LUNDIN
Golf Road, Lundin Links
Tel: (0333) 320051
Holes: 18 6377 yds
V'trs: * H
Fees: £12 (£18)

LUNDIN LADIES
Woodielea Road, Lundin Links
Tel: (0333) 320022
Holes: 9 4730 yds
V'trs: **
Fees: £2.50 (£3.50)

PITREAVIE
Queensferry Road, Dunfermline
Tel: (0383) 723151
Holes: 18 6086 yds
V'trs: *
Fees: £8 (£16)

ST MICHAEL'S
Leuchars
Tel: (033483) 365
Holes: 9 5578 yds
V'trs: *
Fees: £6 (£6)

SALINE
Kinneddar Hill, Saline
Tel: (0383) 852591
Holes: 9 5302 yds
V'trs: *
Fees: £4 (£5)

SCOTSCRAIG
Golf Road, Taylort
Tel: (0382) 552515
Holes: 18 6496 yds
V'trs: *
Fees: On enquiry

THORNTON
Station Road, Thornton
Tel: (0592) 771111
Holes: 18 6175 yds
V'trs: **
Fees: £6 (£9)

ABERDEENSHIRE

ABOYNE
Formaston Park, Aboyne
Tel: (03398) 86469
Holes: 18 5304 yds
V'trs: **
Fees: £8 (£12)

BALLATER
Victoria Road, Ballater
Tel: (03397) 556589
Holes: 18 6106 yds
V'trs: **
Fees: £8 (£10)

BRAEMAR
Cluniebank Road, Braemar
Tel: (03397) 41618
Holes: 18 4916 yds
V'trs: **
Fees: £5 (£6)

CRUDEN BAY
Cruden Bay
Tel: (0779) 812414
Holes: 18 6370 yds
9 4710 yds
V'trs: * H
Fees: £12 (£15)

DEESIDE
Bieldside, Aberdeen
Tel: (0224) 861041
Holes: 18 5972 yds
9 6632 yds
V'trs: * H
Fees: £12 (£15)

DUNECHT HOUSE
Dunecht, Skene
Tel: (0224) 743443
Holes: 9 3135 yds
V'trs: **
Fees: On enquiry

FRASERBURGH
Philorth, Fraserburgh
Tel: (0346) 28287
Holes: 18 6217 yds
V'trs: **
Fees: £7 (£9)

HUNTLY
Huntly
Tel: (0466) 2643
Holes: 18 5399 yds
V'trs: **
Fees: £5 (£8)

INSCH
Golf Terrace, Insch
Tel: (0464) 20363
Holes: 9 5488 yds
V'trs: **
Fees: £4 (£5)

INVERURIE
Blackhall Road, Inverurie
Tel: (0467) 20207
Holes: 18 5096 yds
V'trs: *
Fees: £6 (£8)

KEMNAY
Kemnay
Tel: (0467) 42681
Holes: 9 2751 yds
V'trs: *
Fees: £4 (£5)

KINTORE
Kintore
Tel: (0467) 32631
Holes: 9 2688 yds
V'trs: *
Fees: £4 (£6)

McDONALD
Ellon
Tel: (0358) 22891
Holes: 18 5986 yds
V'trs: **
Fees: On enquiry

MURCAR
Bridge of Don, Aberdeen
Tel: (0224) 704370
Holes: 18 6226 yds
V'trs: *
Fees: £10 (£17)

NEWBURGH-ON-YTHAN
Newburgh
Tel: (03586) 89438
Holes: 9 3202 yds
V'trs: *
Fees: £6 (£8)

OLDMELDRUM
Oldmeldrum
Tel: (06512) 2122
Holes: 9 5 252 yds
V'trs: **
Fees: £3 (£4)

PETERHEAD
Craigewan, Peterhead
Tel: (0779) 72149
Holes: 18 6070 yds
9 2600 yds
V'trs: **
Fees: £5 (£10)

ROYAL ABERDEEN
Balgownie, Bridge of Don, Aberdeen
Tel: (0224) 702221
Holes: 18 6372 yds
18 4066 yds
V'trs: * H
Fees: £18 (£22)

TARLAND
Tarland
Tel: (033 981) 413
Holes: 9 5 812 yds
V'trs: *
Fees: £5 (£7)

TORPHINS
Torphins
Tel: (033 982) 493
Holes: 9 2330 yds
V'trs: **
Fees: £4 (£5)

TURRIFF
Rosehall, Turriff
Tel: (0888) 63025
Holes: 18 6105 yds
V'trs: * H
Fees: £6 (£9)

WESTHILL
Westhill, Skene
Tel: (0224) 740159
Holes: 18 5866 yds
V'trs: *
Fees: £6 (£7)

BANFFSHIRE

BUCKPOOL
Barhill Road, Buckie
Tel: (0542) 32236
Holes: 18 6257 yds
V'trs: ••
Fees: £6 (£8)

CULLEN
The Links, Cullen
Tel: (0542) 40685
Holes: 18 4610 yds
V'trs: ••
Fees: £4 (£4.50)

DUFF HOUSE ROYAL
The Barnyards, Banff
Tel: (026 12) 2062
Holes: 18 6161 yds
V'trs: •
Fees: £6.50 (£9)

DUFFTOWN
Dufftown
Tel: (0340) 20325
Holes: 18 5308 yds
V'trs: ••
Fees: £5 (£6)

KEITH
Fife Park, Keith
Tel: (054 22) 2649
Holes: 18 5811 yds
V'trs: ••
Fees: £4 (£5)

ROYAL TARLAIR
Buchan Street, Macduff
Tel: (0261) 32548/32897
Holes: 18 5866 yds
V'trs: ••
Fees: £5 (£6)

STRATHLENE
Buckie
Tel: (0542) 31798
Holes: 18 5957 yds
V'trs: ••
Fees: £4 (£6)

GRAMPIAN

NEWMACHAR
Swalend, Newmachar
Tel: (06517) 2127
Holes: 18 6605 yds
V'trs: • H
Fees: £12 (£20)

KINCARDINESHIRE

BANCHORY
Kinneskie, Banchory
Tel: (056 12) 407
Holes: 18 5284 yds
V'trs: ••
Fees: £12 (£14)

STONEHAVEN
Cowie, Stonehaven
Tel: (0569) 62124
Holes: 18 5128 yds
V'trs: •
Fees: £10

MORAYSHIRE

ELGIN
Hardhillock, Birnie Road, Elgin
Tel: (0343) 2884
Holes: 18 6401 yds
V'trs: •
Fees: £7.50 (£10)

FORRES
Muiryshade, Forrest
Tel: (0309) 72250
Holes: 18 6141 yds
V'trs: ••
Fees: £7 (£10)

GARMOUTH & KINGSTON
Garmouth, Fochabers
Tel: (034 387) 388
Holes: 18 5637 yds
V'trs: ••
Fees: £4

GRANTOWN
Grantown-on-Spey
Tel: (0479) 2079
Holes: 18 5672 yds
V'trs: ••
Fees: £6 (£7)

HOPEMAN
Hopeman
Tel: (0343) 830578
Holes: 18 5500 yds
V'trs: •
Fees: £5 (£7)

MORAY
Stotfield Road, Lossiemouth
Tel: (034 381) 3330
Holes: Old 18 6643 yds
New 18 6005 yds
V'trs: ••
Fees: Old £7 (£10)
New £5 (£7)

SPEY BAY
c/o Spey Bay Hotel, Spey Bay, Fochabers
Tel: (0343) 820424
Holes: 18 6059 yds
V'trs: ••
Fees: £4.50 (£6)

HIGHLAND REGION

CAITHNESS

Lybster
Main Street, Lybster
Holes: 9 1896 yds
V'trs: ••
Fees: £3

REAY
Reay, by Thurso
Tel: (084 781) 288
Holes: 18 5865 yds
V'trs: ••
Fees: £5

THURSO
Newlands of Geise, Thurso
Tel: (0847) 63807
Holes: 18 5818 yds
V'trs: ••
Fees: £4 (£5)

WICK
Reiss, Wick
Tel: (0955) 2726
Holes: 18 59045 yds
V'trs: ••
Fees: £5 (£6)

INVERNESSHIRE

ABERNETHY
Nethy Bridge
Tel: (047 982) 305
Holes: 9 2484 yds
V'trs: ••
Fees: £5

BOAT-OF-GARTEN
Boat-of-Garten
Tel: (047 983) 282
Holes: 18 5 720 yds
V'trs: ••
Fees: £8 (£10)

CARRBRIDGE
Carrbridge
Tel: (047 984) 674
Holes: 9 2623 yds
V'trs: ••
Fees: £5 (£6)

FORT AUGUSTUS
Markethill, Fort Augustus
Tel: (0320) 6460
Holes: 9 5454 yds
V'trs: •
Fees: £5 (£5)

FORT WILLIAM
North Road, Fort William
Tel: (0397) 4464
Holes: 18 5868 mts
V'trs: ••
Fees: £5

INVERNESS
Culcabock Road, Inverness
Tel: (0463) 231989
Holes: 18 6226 yds
V'trs: •
Fees: £10 (£12)

KINGUSSIE
Gynack Road, Kingussie
Tel: (0540) 661374
Holes: 18 5555 yds
V'trs: ••
Fees: £6

NEWTONMORE
Newtonmore
Tel: (05403) 328
Holes: 18 5880 yds
V'trs: ••
Fees: £7

SCONSER
Between Broadford and Sigachan, Isle of Skye
Tel: (0478) 2277
Holes: 9 4796 yds
V'trs: •
Fees: £4

TRAIGH
Back of Keppoch, Arisaig
Tel: (06875) 262
Holes: 9 2100 yds
V'trs: ••
Fees: £2 (£5)

NAIRNSHIRE
Nairn
Tel: (0667) 5 2787
Holes: 18 6556 yds
9 1918 yds
V'trs: ••
Fees: £15 (£18)

NAIRN DUNBAR
Lochloy Road, Nairn
Tel: (0667) 53964
Holes: 18 6431 yds
V'trs: ••
Fees: £10 (£12)

ROSS & CROMARTY

ALNESS
Ardross Road, Alness
Tel: (0349) 883877
Holes: 9 2436 yds
V'trs: •
Fees: £3 (£4)

FORTROSE & ROSEMARKIE
Ness Road East, Fortrose
Tel: (0381) 20733
Holes: 18 5973 yds
V'trs: ••
Fees: £7.50 (£8)

GAIRLOCH
Gairloch
Tel: (0445) 2407
Holes: 9 1942 yds
V'trs: •
Fees: £4

INVERGORDON
King George Street, Invergordon
Tel: (0349) 852116
Holes: 9 6028 yds
V'trs: ••
Fees: £3 (£4)

LOCHCARRON
Lochcarron, Strathcarron
Tel: (05202) 259
Holes: 9 3470 yds
V'trs: ••
Fees: £3

MUIR OF ORD
Great North Road, Muir of Ord
Tel: (0463) 870601
Holes: 18 5202 yds
V'trs: ••
Fees: £7 (£8)

STRATHPEFFER SPA
Strathpeffer
Tel: (0997) 21219
Holes: 18 4792 yds
V'trs: ••
Fees: £5

TAIN
Tain
Tel: (0862) 2314
Holes: 18 6207 yds
V'trs: ••
Fees: £7 (£8)

TARBAT
Portmahomack
Tel: (0862 87) 236
Holes: 9 2328 yds
V'trs: • H
Fees: £4 (£5)

SUTHERLAND

BONAR-BRIDGE & ARDGAY
Bonar-Bridge, Ardgay
Tel: (054 9082) 248
Holes: 9 4626 yds
V'trs: **
Fees: £4

BRORA
Golf Road, Brora
Tel: (0408) 21417
Holes: 18 6110 yds
V'trs: * H
Fees: £8

GOLSPIE
Ferry Road, Golspie
Tel: (04083) 3266
Holes: 18 5 836 yds
V'trs: **
Fees: £8

HELMSDALE
Helmsdale
Tel: (0943) 12240
Holes: 9
V'trs: **
Fees: £3 (£3)

ROYAL DORNOCH
Golf Road, Dornoch
Tel: (0862) 810902
Holes: C'ship 18 6577 yds
Struie 18 5242 yds
V'trs: **
Fees: On enquiry

EAST LOTHIAN

DUNBAR
East Link, Lothian
Tel: (0368) 62317
Holes: 18 6426 yds
V'trs: *
Fees: £12 (£20)

GIFFORD
Gifford
Tel: (062 081) 267
Holes: 9 6138 yds
V'trs: *
Fees: £5

GULLANE
Gullane
Tel: (0620) 843111
Holes: No 1 18 6491 yds
No 2 18 6127 yds
No 3 18 5035 yds
V'trs: **
Fees: No 1 26 (£35)
No 2 £12 (£15)
No 3 £8 (£10)

THE HONOURABLE COMPANY OF EDINBURGH GOLFERS
Muirfield, Gullane
Tel: (0620) 842123
Holes: 18 6601 yds
V'trs: * H
Fees: £35

KILSPINDIE
Aberlady, Longniddry
Tel: (087 57) 216/358
Holes: 18 4957 mts
V'trs: *
Fees: On enquiry

LONGNIDDRY
Links Road, Longniddry
Tel: (0875) 52228
Holes: 18 6219 yds
V'trs: *
Fees: £14 (£28)

LUFFNESS NEW
Aberlady
Tel: (0620) 843114
Holes: 18 6122 yds
V'trs: *
Fees: On enquiry

MUSSELBURGH
Monktonhall, Musselburgh
Tel: (031) 665 7055
Holes: 18 6623 yds
V'trs: **
Fees: On enquiry

MUSSELBURGH OLD COURSE
Silver Ring Clubhouse, Millhill, Musselburgh
Tel: (031) 665 3711
Holes: 9 5380 yds
V'trs: *
Fees: 18 £2.40

NORTH BEWICK
West L links, Beach Road, North Berwick
Tel: (0620) 3233
Holes: 18 6315 yds
V'trs: ** H
Fees: £12 (£17.50)

ROYAL MUSSELBURGH
Prestongrange House, Prestonpans
Tel: (0875) 810139
Holes: 18 6237 yds
V'trs: *
Fees: £12 (£20)

MIDLOTHIAN

BABERTON
Juniper Green, Edinburgh
Tel: (031) 453 3361
Holes: 18 6098 yds
V'trs: ***

BROOMIEKNOWE
Golf Course Road, Bonnyrigg
Tel: (031) 66 2035
Holes: 18 5754 yds
V'trs: *
Fees: £8 (£10)

BRUNTSFIELD LINKS GOLFING SOCIETY
Barnton Avenue, Davidson's Mains, Edinburgh
Tel: (031) 336 4050
Holes: 18 6407 yds
V'trs: * H
Fees: On enquiry

CRAIGMILLAR PARK
Observatory Road, Edinburgh
Tel: (031) 667 0047
Holes: 18 5846 yds
V'trs: * H
Fees: On enquiry

DALMAHOY
Dalmahoy, Kirknewton, Midlothian
Tel: (031) 333 1436
Holes: East 18 6639 yds
West 18 5212 yds
V'trs: *
Fees: On enquiry

DUDDINGSTON
Duddingston, Edinburgh
Tel: (031) 661 4301
Holes: 18 6647 yds
V'trs: * H
Fees: £12.50

GLENCORSE
Milton Bridge, Penicuik, Midlothian
Tel: (0968) 76481
Holes: 18 5205 yds
V'trs: *
Fees: £8 (£12)

KINGSKNOWE
Lanark Road, Edinburgh
Tel: (031) 441 4030
Holes: 18 5966 yds
V'trs: *
Fees: £7.50

LIBERTON
Glimerton Road, Edinburgh
Tel: (031) 664 1056
Holes: 18 5299 yds
V'trs: *
Fees: £9.50 (£11.50)

LOTHIANBURN
Biggar Road, Edinburgh
Tel: (031) 445 2288
Holes: 18 5750 yds
V'trs: *
Fees: £6 (£7.50)

MERCHANTS OF EDINBURGH
Craighill Gardens, Morningside, Edinburgh
Tel: (031) 447 8709
Holes: 18 4889 yds
V'trs: * H
Fees: £4.50

MORTONHALL
Braid Road, Edinburgh
Tel: (031) 447 5185
Holes: 18 6557 yds
V'trs: * H
Fees: £13 (£16)

MURRAYFIELD
Murrayfield Road, Edinburgh
Tel: (031) 337 34790
Holes: 18 5727 yds
V'trs: * H
Fees: £12

NEWBATTLE
Abbey Road, Eskbank, Dalkeith
Tel: (031) 660 1631
Holes: 18 6012 yds
V'trs: *
Fees: £7.50

PRESTONFIELD
Priestfield Road North, Edinburgh
Tel: (031) 667 8597
Holes: 18 6216 yds
V'trs: *
Fees: £11 (£15)

RATHO PARK
Ratho, Newbridge, Midlothian
Tel: (031) 333 1406
Holes: 18 6028 yds
V'trs: *
Fees: £15 (£25)

RAVELSTON
Ravelston Dykes Road, Edinburgh
Tel: (031) 315 2486
Holes: 9 5332 yds
V'trs: ***

ROYAL BURGESS GOLFING SOCIETY OF EDINBURGH
Whitehouse Road, Barnton, Edinburgh
Tel: (031) 339 6474
Holes: 18 6604 yds
V'trs: * H
Fees: On request

SWANSTON
Swanston Road, Fairmilehead, Edinburgh
Tel: (031) 445 4002
Holes: 18 5024 yds
V'trs: *
Fees: £3.45

TORPHIN HILL
Torphin Road, Edinburgh
Tel: (031) 441 1100
Holes: 18 5025 yds
V'trs: *
Fees: £5 (£8)

TURNHOUSE
Turnhouse Road, Corstorphine, Edinburgh
Tel: (031) 339 7701
Holes: 18 6171 yds
V'trs: ***

WEST LOTHIAN

BATHGATE
Edinburgh Road, Bathgate
Tel: (0506) 630553
Holes: 18 6326 yds
V'trs: **
Fees: £8 (£11)

DEER PARK
Carmondean, Livingston
Tel: (0506) 38843
Holes: 18 6636 yds
V'trs: **
Fees: £5 (£8.50)

DUNDAS PARK
Loch Place, South Queensferry
Tel: (031) 331 1601
Holes: 9 5510 mts
V'trs: ***

GREENBURN
Fauldhouse
Tel: (0501) 70292
Holes: 18 6223 yds
V'trs: **
Fees: £3.30 (£4.40)

HARBURN
West Calder, West Lothian
Tel: (0506) 871582
Holes: 18 5853 yds
V'trs: **
Fees: £6.50 (£8.50)

LINLITHGOW
Braehead, Linlithgow
Tel: (0506) 44356
Holes: 18 5858 yds
V'trs: **
Fees: £6 (£8.50)

NIDDRY CASTLE
Winchburgh
Tel: (0506) 890185
Holes: 9 5476 yds
V'trs: **
Fees: £4 (£6)

PUMPHERSTON
Drumshoreland Road,
Pumpherston
Tel: (0506) 32869
Holes: 9 5154 yds
V'trs: ***

UPHALL
Uphall
Tel: (0506) 856404
Holes: 18 5567 yds
V'trs: **
Fees: £6 (£10)

WEST LOTHIAN
Airngath Hill, by Linlithgow
Tel: (0506) 826030
Holes: 18 6578 yds
V'trs: **
Fees: £7 (£9)

ORKNEY & SHETLAND REGION

ORKNEY & SHETLAND

ORKNEY
Grainbank, Kirkwall, Orkney
Tel: (0856) 2457
Holes: 18 5406 yds
V'trs: **
Fees: £5

SHETLAND
Lewick
Tel: (059 584) 369
Holes: 18 5776 yds
V'trs: **
Fees: £4 (£5)

STROMNESS
Ness, Orkney
Tel: (0856) 850772
Holes: 18 4665 yds
V'trs: **
Fees: £4 (£4)

WESTRAY
Westray, Orkney
Tel: (085 77) 28
Holes: 9 hole course
V'trs: *
Fees: On enquiry

STRATHCLYDE REGION

ARGYLL

BLAIRMORE & STRONE
Strone-by-Dunoon
Tel: (036984) 676
Holes: 9 2122 yds
V'trs: **
Fees: £4 (£4)

CARRADALE
Carradale
Tel: (05833) 387
Holes: 9 2387 yds
V'trs: **
Fees: £3

COWAL
Ardenslate Road, Dunoon
Tel: (0369) 2395
Holes: 18 6251 yds
V'trs: **
Fees: On enquiry

CRAIGNURE
Isle of Mull Hotel, Isle of Mull
Tel: (068 02) 370/351
Holes: 9 4436 mts
V'trs: **
Fees: £5

DUNAVERTY
Southend
Tel: (0586) 83698
Holes: 18 4597 yds
V'trs: **
Fees: £1.10

GLENCRUITTEN
Oban
Tel: (0631) 64115
Holes: 18 4452 yds
V'trs: **
Fees: £6.50 (£8)

INNELLAN
Innellan
Tel: (0369) 3546
Holes: 9 4878 yds
V'trs: **
Fees: £4 (£5)

KYLES OF BUTE
Tighnabruaich
Tel: (0700) 811355
Holes: 9 2389 yds
V'trs: **
Fees: £4

LOCHGILPHEAD
Blarbuie Road, Lochgilphead
Tel: (0546) 2340
Holes: 9 4484 yds
V'trs: **
Fees: £4 (£6)

MACHRIE HOTEL
Port Ellen, Isle of Islay
Tel: (0496) 2310
Holes: 18 6226 yds
V'trs: *
Fees: £15

MACHRIHANISH
Campbeltown, Machrihanish
Tel: (05867) 81277
Holes: 18 6228 yds
V'trs: **
Fees: £10 (£15)

TARBERT
Kilberry Road, Tarbert
Tel: (08802) 565
Holes: 9 4460 yds
V'trs: **
Fees: £4

TOBERMORY
Tobermory, Isle of Mull
Tel: (0688) 2020
Holes: 9 24609 yds
V'trs: **
Fees: £5

VAUL
Scarinish, Isle of Tiree
Tel: (087 92) 344
Holes: 9 3123 yds
V'trs: **
Fees: £3

AYRSHIRE

ARDEER
Greenhead, Stevenston
Tel: (0294) 64542
Holes: 18 6630 yds
V'trs: *
Fees: £14 (£18)

BALLOCHMYLE
Ballochmyle, Mauchline
Tel: (0290) 50469
Holes: 18 6952 yds
V'trs: **
Fees: £12 (£18)

BEITH
Bigholm Road, Beith
Tel: (050 55) 3166
Holes: 9 5648 yds
V'trs: *
Fees: £6

GIRVAN
Golf Course Road, Girvan
Tel: (0465) 4272
Holes: 18 5095 yds
Holes: **
Fees: £5.40 (£6.60)

GLASGOW GAILES
Gailes, Irvine
Tel: (041 942) 8507
Holes: 18 6447 yds
V'trs: * H
Fees: £25

IRVINE
Bogside, Irvine
Tel: (0294) 75626
Holes: 18 6408 yds
V'trs: *
Fees: £16

KILBURNIE PLACE
Largs Road, Kilbirnie
Tel: (0505) 683398
Holes: 18 5411 yds
V'trs: *
Fees: £5 (£10)

KILMARNOCK (BARASSIE)
Hillhouse Road, Barassie
Tel: (0292) 311322
Holes: 18 6473 yds
V'trs: *
Fees: On request

LARGS
Irvine Road, Largs
Tel: (0475) 686192
Holes: 18 6257 yds
V'trs: **
Fees: £14

LOUDON
Galston
Tel: (0563) 820551
Holes: 18 6300 yds
V'trs: *
Fees: £10

PRESTWICK
Links Road, Prestwick
Tel: (0292) 79483
Holes: 18 6631 yds
V'trs: * H
Fees: On enquiry

PRESTWICK ST CUTHBERT
East Road, Prestwick
Tel: (0292) 77101
Holes: 18 6470 yds
V'trs: *
Fees: £15

PRESTWICK ST NICHOLAS
Grangemuir Road, Prestwick
Tel: (0292) 79755
Holes: 18 5926 yds
V'trs: * H
Fees: On request

ROYAL TROON
Craigend Road, Troon
Tel: (0292) 313281
Holes: Old 18 7097 yds
Portland 18 6274 yds
V'trs: * H
Fees: £45 Old and Portland
£20 Portland

SKELMORLIE
Skelmorlie
Tel: (0475) 520152
Holes: 13 5056 yds
V'trs: *
Fees: £8 (£12)

TURNBERRY
Turnberry
Tel: (0655) 31000
Holes: Ailsa 18 69509 yds
Arran 18 6276 yds
V'trs: * H
Fees: On enquiry

WEST KILBRIDE
West Kilbride
Tel: (0294) 823042
Holes: 18 6452 yds
V'trs: *
Fees: On enquiry

WESTERN GAILES
Gailes, Irvine
Tel: (0294) 311649
Holes: 18 6614 yds
V'trs: * H
Fees: £23

BUTE

BRODICK
Brodick, Isle of Arran
Tel: (0770) 2513
Holes: 18 4404 yds
V'trs: **
Fees: £10

BUTE
Kingarth, Isle of Bute
Tel: (070083) 648
Holes: 9 2497 yds
V'trs: **
Fees: £4

CORRIE
Corrie, Isle of Arran
Tel: (077 081) 223
Holes: 9 1948 yds
V'trs: **
Fees: £4

LAMLASH
Lamlash, Isle of Arran
Tel: (07706) 296
Holes: 18 4681 yds
V'trs: **
Fees: £6

LOCHRANZA
Lochranza, Isle of Arran
Tel: (077 083) 273
Holes: 9 1700 yds
V'trs: **
Fees: £2

MACHRIE BAY
Brodick, Isle of Arran
Tel: (077 084) 267
Holes: 9 2082 yds
V'trs: **
Fees: £3

MILLPORT
Millport, Isle of Cumbrae
Tel: (0475) 530311
Holes: 18 5831 yds
V'trs: **
Fees: £7

PORT BANNATYNE
Port Bannatyne, Isle of Bute
Tel: (0700) 2009
Holes: 13 4730 yds
V'trs: **
Fees: £6

ROTHESAY
Canada Hill, Rothesay, Isle of Bute
Tel: (0700) 3554
Holes: 18 5358 yds
V'trs: **
Fees: £10.50

SHISKINE
Blackwaterfoot, Isle of Arran
Tel: (077086) 226
Holes: 12 2990 yds
V'trs: **
Fees: £5.50

WHITING BAY
Whiting Bay, Isle of Arran
Tel: (077 07) 487
Holes: 18 4405 yds
V'trs: **
Fees: £5

DUNBARTONSHIRE

BEARSDEN
Thorn Road, Bearsden
Tel: (041) 942 2351
Holes: 9 5977 yds
V'trs: ***

CARDROSS
Cardross, Dumbarton
Tel: (0389) 841350
Holes: 18 6466 yds
V'trs: *
Fees: £11

CLOBER
Craigton Road, Milngavie, Glasgow
Tel: (041) 956 1685
Holes: 18 5068 yds
V'trs: *
Fees: £8

CLYDEBANK & DISTRICT
Hardgate, Clydebank
Tel: (0389) 73289
Holes: 18 5815 yds
V'trs: * H
Fees: £12

DOUGALSTON
Milngavie, Glasgow
Tel: (041) 956 5750
Holes: 18 6269 yds
V'trs: **
Fees: £7 (£8)

DOUGLAS PARK
Hillfoot, Bearsden
Tel: (041) 942 2220
Holes: 18 5957 yds
V'trs: ***

DULLATUR
Dullatur, Glasgow
Tel: (0236) 723230
Holes: 18 6253 yds
V'trs: *
Fees: £11

DUMBARTON
Broadmeadow, Dumbarton
Tel: (0389) 32830
Holes: 18 5981 yds
V'trs: *
Fees: £9

GLASGOW
Killermont, Bearsden, Glasgow
Tel: (041) 942 8507
Holes: 18 5968 yds
V'trs: ***

HAYSTON
Campsie Road, Kirkintilloch, Glasgow
Tel: (041) 776 0882
Holes: 18 6042 yds
V'trs: * H
Fees: £10

HELENSBURGH
East Abercromby Street, Helensburgh
Tel: (0436) 75505
Holes: 18 6058 yds
V'trs: *
Fees: £12

HILTON PARK
Auldmarroch Estate, Stockiemuir Road, Milngavie
Tel: (041) 956 5125
Holes: Hilton 18 6003 yds
Allander 18 5361 yds
V'trs: *
Fees: On request

KIRKINTILLOCH
Todhill, Campsie Road, Kirkintolloch
Tel: (041) 776 1256
Holes: 18 5269 yds
V'trs: ***

MILNGAVIE
Leighpark, Milngavie
Tel: (041) 956 1619
Holes: 18 5818 yds
V'trs: ***
Fees: On enquiry

VALE OF LEVEN
Northfield Road, Bonhill, Alexandria
Tel: (0389) 52351
Holes: 18 5156 yds
V'trs: *
Fees: £7 (£11)

WINDYHILL
Windyhill, Bearsden
Tel: (041) 942 7157
Holes: 18 6254 yds
V'trs: * H
Fees: £9

LANARKSHIRE

AIRDRIE
Rochsoles, Airdrie
Tel: (0236) 54360
Holes: 18 6004 yds
V'trs: * H
Fees: £12

BELLSHILL
Orbiston, Bellshill
Tel: (0698) 745124
Holes: 18 6607 yds
V'trs: *
Fees: £9 (£12)

BISHOPBRIGGS
Brackenbrae Road, Bishopbriggs, Glasgow
Tel: (041) 772 1810
Holes: 18 6041 yds
V'trs: * H
Fees: £12

BLAIRBETH
Burnside, Rutherglen
Tel: (041) 634 3355
Holes: 18 5448 yds
V'trs: ***

BOTHWELL CASTLE
Blantyre Road, Bothwell
Tel: (0698) 852052
Holes: 18 6240 yds
V'trs: *
Fees: £8

CALDERBRAES
Roundknowe Road, Ruddingston
Tel: (0698) 813425
Holes: 9 5046 yds
V'trs: ***

CAMBUSLANG
Westburn Drive, Cambuslang
Tel: (041) 641 3130
Holes: 9 6072 yds
V'trs: ***

CARLUKE
Hallcraig, Carluke
Tel: (0555) 51053
Holes: 18 5805 yds
V'trs: *
Fees: £6

CARNWATH
Main Street, Carnwath
Tel: (0555) 840251
Holes: 18 5955 yds
V'trs: *
Fees: £10 (£12)

CATHKIN BRAES
Cathkin Road, Rutherglen, Glasgow
Tel: (041) 634 0650
Holes: 18 6266 yds
V'trs: *
Fees: £10

CAWDER
Cadder Road, Bishopbriggs, Glasgow
Tel: (041) 772 5167
Holes: Cawder 18 6295 yds
Keir 18 5877 yds
V'trs: *
Fees: £16.50

COLVILLE PARK
Jerviston Estate, Motherwell
Tel: (0698) 65779
Holes: 18 6265 yds
V'trs: *
Fees: £10

COWGLEN
Barrhead Road, Glasgow
Tel: (041) 649 9401
Holes: 18 6006 yds
V'trs: ***

CROW WOOD
Muirhead, Chryston, Glasgow
Tel: (041) 779 1943
Holes: 18 6249 yds
V'trs: ***

DOUGLAS WATER
Douglas Water, Lanark
Tel: (055 588) 361
Holes: 9 2916 yds
V'trs: **
Fees: £3 (£4)

DRUMPELLIER
Drumpellier Ave, Coatbridge
Tel: (0236) 32971
Holes: 18 6227 yds
V'trs: *
Fees: £12.50

EAST KILBRIDE
Chapelside Road, Nerston, East Kilbride
Tel: (035 52) 22192
Holes: 18 6419 yds
V'trs: *
Fees: £8

EASTER MOFFAT
Plains by Airdrie
Tel: (0236) 843015
Holes: 18 6221 yds
V'trs: *
Fees: £8

HAGGS CASTLE
Dunbreck Road, Dumbreck,
Glasgow
Tel: (041) 427 3355
Holes: 18 6464 yds
V'trs: *
Fees: £14

LANARK
The Moor, Lanark
Tel: (0555) 61456
Holes: 18 6426 yds
9 1562 yds
V'trs: *
Fees: £14 (£20)
9 £2

LEADHILLS
Leadhills, Biggar
Tel: (0659) 74222
Holes: 9 2031 yds
V'trs: **
Fees: £3 (£4)

LENZIE
Crosshill Road, Lenzie
Tel: (041) 77 7748
Holes: 18 5982 yds
V'trs: ***

MOUNT ELLEN
Gartcosh, Glasgow
Tel: (0236) 872277
Holes: 18 5525 yds
V'trs: *
Fees: £6

POLLOK
Barrhead Road, Pollokshaws,
Glasgow
Tel: (041) 632 1080
Holes: 18 6257 yds
V'trs: * H
Fees: £18

SANDYHILLS
Sandyhills Road, Glasgow
Tel: (041) 778 1179
Holes: 18 6253 yds
V'trs: ***

SHOTTS
Blairhead, Benhar Road, Shotts
Tel: (0501) 20431
Holes: 18 6290 yds
V'trs: *
Fees: £8 (£10)

STRATHAVEN
Strathaven
Tel: (0357) 21812
Holes: 18 6226 yds
V'trs: * H
Fees: On enquiry

WISHAW
Cleland Road, Wishaw
Tel: (0698) 372869
Holes: 18 6134 yds
V'trs: *
Fees: £7 (£14)

RENFREWSHIRE

BARSHAW
Barshaw Park, Paisley
Tel: (041) 889 2908
Holes: 18 5703 yds
V'trs: **
Fees: £2.30

BONNYTON
Eaglesham, Glasgow
Tel: (035 53) 2256
Holes: 18 6252 yds
V'trs: * H
Fees: £14

CALDWELL
Caldwell, Uplawmoor
Tel: (050 585) 616
Holes: 18 6046 yds
V'trs: *
Fees: £8

CATHCART CASTLE
Mearns Road, Clarkston
Tel: (041) 638 0082
Holes: 18 5832 yds
V'trs: ***

COCHRANE CASTLE
Craigston, Johnstone
Tel: (0505) 2865
Holes: 18 6226 yds
V'trs: *
Fees: £8

EAST RENFREWSHIRE
Pilmuir, Newton Mearns
Tel: (03555) 206
Holes: 18 6097 yds
V'trs: *
Fees: On enquiry

EASTWOOD
Muirshield, Loganswell, Newton
Mearns, Glasgow
Tel: (03555) 285
Holes: 18 5886 yds
V'trs: ***

ELDERSLIE
Elderslie
Tel: (0505) 23956
Holes: 18 6031 yds
V'trs: ***

ERSKINE
Bishopton
Tel: (0505) 862108
Holes: 18 6287 yds
V'trs: * H
Fees: £11

FERENEZE
Barrhead
Tel: (041) 880 7058
Holes: 18 5821 yds
V'trs: *
Fees: £10

GLEDDOCH
Langbank
Tel: (047 554) 704
Holes: 18 6200 yds
V'trs: *
Fees: £16.50

GOUROCK
Cowal View, Gourock
Tel: (0475) 36834
Holes: 18 6492 yds
V'trs: * H
Fees: On enquiry

GREENOCK
Forsyth Street, Greenock
Tel: (0475) 87236
Holes: 18 5888 yds
9 2149 yds
V'trs: *
Fees: £12 (£15)

KILMACOLM
Kilmacolm
Tel: (050 587) 2695
Holes: 18 5890 yds
V'trs: *
Fees: On enquiry

LOCHWINNOCH
Burnfoot Road, Lochwinnoch
Tel: (0505) 843029
Holes: 18 6223 yds
V'trs: *
Fees: £8 (£10)

OLD RANFURLY
Bridge of Weir
Tel: (0505) 613612
Holes: 18 6089 yds
V'trs: *
Fees: On enquiry

PAISLEY
Braehead, Paisley
Tel: (041) 884 2292
Holes: 18 6424 yds
V'trs: * H
Fees: £8

PORT GLASGOW
Port Glasgow
Tel: (0475) 704181
Holes: 18 5712 yds
V'trs: *
Fees: £8

RALSTON
Ralston, Paisley
Tel: (041) 810 4925
Holes: 18 6100 yds
V'trs: ***

RANFURLY CASTLE
Golf Road, Bridge of Weir
Tel: (0505) 614795
Holes: 18 6284 yds
V'trs: * H
Fees: On enquiry

RENFREW
Blythswood Estate, Inchinnan
Road, Renfrew
Tel: (041) 886 7477
Holes: 18 6818 yds
V'trs: ***

WHINHILL
Beith Road, Greenock
Tel: (0475) 24694
Holes: 18 5454 yds
V'trs: **
Fees: On enquiry

WHITECRAIGS
Ayr Road, Giffnock, Glasgow
Tel: (041) 639 2140
Holes: 18 6230 yds
V'trs: * H
Fees: £16

WILLIAMWOOD
Clarkston Road, Glasgow
Tel: (041) 637 2715
Holes: 18 5878 yds
V'trs: ***

STIRLINGSHIRE

ABERFOYLE
Aberfoyle
Tel: (087 72) 493
Holes: 18 5204 yds
V'trs: **
Fees: £10

KILSYTH LENNOX
Tak-Ma-Doon Road, Kilsyth
Tel: (0236) 822190
Holes: 18 5930 yds
V'trs: *
Fees: £8

TAYSIDE REGION

ANGUS

BRECHIN GOLF &
SQUASH CLUB
Trinity, Brechin
Tel: (03562) 5270
Holes: 18 5267 yds
V'trs: *
Fees: £7 (£8)

DOWNFIELD
Turnberry Avenue, Dundee
Tel: (0382) 89246
Holes: 18 6804 yds
V'trs: *
Fees: £12

EDZELL
High St, Edzell, by Brechin
Tel: (03564) 462
Holes: 18 6299 yds
V'trs: *
Fees: £9 (£11)

FORFAR
Cunninghill, Forfar
Tel: (0307) 65683
Holes: 18 5537 mts
V'trs: **
Fees: £11 (£17)

KIRRIEMUIR
Kirriemuir
Tel: (0575) 73317
Holes: 18 5541 yds
V'trs: *
Fees: £10.50

LETHAM GRANGE
Colliston, Arbroath
Tel: (024) 189377
Holes: 18 6789 yds
V'trs: * H
Fees: £12 (£15)

MONIFIETH GOLF LINKS
Princes Street, Monifieth,
Dundee
Tel: (0382) 532945
Holes: Medal 18 66509 yds
Ashludie 18 5123 yds
V'trs: *
Fees: Medal £10 (11)
Ashludie £8 (£9)

PANMURE
Barry, by Carnoustie
Tel: (0241) 53120
Holes: 18 6317 yds
V'trs: *
Fees: £9

KINROSS-SHIRE

BISHOPSHIRE
Kinnesswood
Tel: (0592) 860379
Holes: 9 2180 yds
V'trs: **
Fees: £2 (£3)

GREEN HOTEL
Beeches Park, Kinross
Tel: (0577) 63467
Holes: 18 6111 yds
V'trs: **
Fees: £9 (£13.50)

KINROSS
Kinross
Tel: (0577) 62237
Holes: 18 6111 yds
V'trs: *
Fees: £14 (£18)

MILNATHORT
South Street, Milnathort
Tel: (0577) 64069
Holes: 9 2959 yds
V'trs: **
Fees: £5 (£6)

PERTHSHIRE

ABERFELDY
Taybridge Road, Aberfeldy
Tel: (0887) 20535
Holes: 9 2733 yds
V'trs: **
Fees: £5

Looking across the Firth of Clyde from the eighth tee of Royal Troon, the Isle of Arran looms in the distance.

ALYTH
Pitcrocknie, Alyth
Tel: (082 83) 2411
Holes: 18 6226 yds
V'trs: **
Fees: £6 (£9)

AUCHTERARDER
Ochil Road, Auchterarder
Tel: (0764) 63711
Holes: 18 5757 yds
V'trs: **
Fees: £7 (£9)

BLAIR ATHOLL
Blair Atholl, Perthshire
Tel: (079 681) 407
Holes: 9 2855 yds
V'trs: **
Fees: £6 (£7)

BLAIRGOWRIE
Rosemount, Blairgowrie
Tel: (0250) 3116
Holes: Rosemount 18 6588 yds
Lansdowne 18 6895 yds
Wee 9 4614 yds
V'trs: * H
Fees: £18 (£27)

COMRIE
Comrie
Tel: (0764) 70544
Holes: 9 2983 yds
V'trs: **
Fees: £5 (£6)

CRAIGIE HILL
Cherrybank, Perth
Tel: (0738) 22644
Holes: 18 5379 yds
V'trs: **
Fees: £8 (£10)

CRIEFF
Perth Road, Crieff
Tel: (0764) 2909
Holes: Ferntower 18 6402 yds
Dornock 9 4772 yds
V'trs: * H
Fees: Ferntower £12 (£15)
Dornock £8 (£9)

DUNKELD & BIRNAM
Fungarth, Dunkeld
Tel: (03502) 524
Holes: 9 4945 yds
V'trs: **
Fees: £6 (£8)

DUNNING
Rollo Park, Dunning
Tel: (076484) 312
Holes: 9 4836 yds
V'trs: *
Fees: £4

GLENALMOND
Trinity College, Glenalmond
Tel: (073 888) 270
Holes: 9 5812 yds
V'trs: ***

GLENEAGLES HOTEL
Gleneagles
Tel: (076 46) 2231
Holes: King's 18 6471 yds
Queen's 18 5965 yds
Prince's 18 4664 yds
Glendevon 18 5719 yds
V'trs: *
Fees: On enquiry

KING JAMES VI
Moncrieffe Island, Perth
Tel: (0738) 32460
Holes: 18 6026 yds
V'trs: **
Fees: £7.50 (£15)

MURRAYSHALL
Murrayshall, New Scone, Perth
Tel: (0738) 52784
Holes: 18 5877 mts
V'trs: *
Fees: £12 (£18)

MUTHILL
Peat Road, Muthill
Tel: (076 481) 523
Holes: 9 2371 yds
V'trs: **
Fees: £4 (£4.50)

PITLOCHRY
Golf Course Road, Pitlochry
Tel: (0796) 2792
Holes: 18 5811 yds
V'trs: **
Fees: £10 (£13)

ROYAL PERTH GOLFING SOCIETY
Atholl Crescent, Perth
Tel: (0738) 22265
Holes: 18 5141 yds
V'trs: *
Fees: On enquiry

ST FILLANS
South Lochearn Road, St Fillans
Tel: (076 485) 312
Holes: 9 5268 yds
V'trs: **
Fees: £5 (£6)

STRATHAY
Tighonoisinn, Grandtully
Tel: (08874) 367
Holes: 9 4082 yds
V'trs: **
Fees: £4 (£5)

TAYMOUTH CASTLE
Kenmore
Tel: (08873) 228
Holes: 18 6066 yds
V'trs: *
Fees: £11 (£14)

WESTERN ISLES REGION

WESTERN ISLES

ASKERNISH
Lochboisdale, South Uist
Holes: 9 5114 yds
V'trs: **
Fees: £2 (£2)

STORNOWAY
Lady Lever Park, Stornoway, Outer Hebrides
Tel: (0851) 2240
Holes: 18 5119 yds
V'trs: *
Fees: £5

IRELAND

CO ANTRIM

BALLYCASTLE
Cushendall Road, Ballycastle
Tel: (02657) 62506
Holes: 18 5882 yds
V'trs: ** H
Fees: £10 (£35)

BALLYCLARE
25 Springvale Road, Ballyclare
Tel: (09603) 42352
Holes: 18 5840 yds
V'trs: *
Fees: £10 (£15)

BALLYMENA
128 Raceview Road, Ballymena
Tel: (0266) 861652
Holes: 18 5168 yds
V'trs: **
Fees: £7 (£9)

BUSHFOOT
Portballintrae, Bushmills
Tel: (02657) 31317
Holes: 9 5572 yds
V'trs: **
Fees: £7 (£20)

CAIRNDHU
192 Coast Road, Ballygally, Larne
Tel: (0574) 83417
Holes: 18 6112 yds
V'trs: **
Fees: £8 (£11)

CARRICKFERGUS
35 North Road, Carrickkfergus
Tel: (09603) 51803
Holes: 18 5769 yds
V'trs: **
Fees: £10 (£28)

CUSHENDALL
21 Shore Road, Cushendall
Tel: (026 67) 73366
Holes: 9 4678 yds
V'trs: *
Fees: £10

DUNMURRY
91 Dunmurry Lane, Dunmurry, Belfast
Tel: (0232) 301179
Holes: 18 6000 yds
V'trs: *
Fees: £9 (£12)

GREENISLAND
156 Upper Road, Greenisland, Carrickfergus
Tel: (0232) 864583
Holes: 9 6200 yds
V'trs: **
Fees: £7 (£10)

LARNE
54 Ferris Bay Road, Island Magee, Larne
Tel: (0574) 82228
Holes: 9 6114 yds
V'trs: *
Fees: £4 (£8)

LISBURN
68 Eglantine Road, Lisburn
Tel: (0846) 677217
Holes: 18 6200 yds
V'trs: *
Fees: £10 (£15)

MASSEREENE
51 Lough Road, Antrim
Tel: (08494) 64074
Holes: 18 6614 yds
V'trs: **
Fees: £10 (£12)

ROYAL PORTRUSH
Dunluce Road, Portrush
Tel: (0265) 823335
Holes: Dunluce 18 6772 yds
Valley 18 6273 yds
V'trs: **
Fees: Dunluce £14 (£20)
Valley £9 (£12)

WHITEHEAD
McCrae's Brae, Whitehead, Carrickfergus
Tel: (09603) 53792
Holes: 18 6426 yds
V'trs: *
Fees: £7.50 (£10)

CO ARMAGH

COUNTY ARMAGH
Newry Road, Armagh
Tel: (0861) 522501
Holes: 18 6184 yds
V'trs: **
Fees: £7 (£10)

LURGAN
The Demesne, Lurgan
Tel: (0762) 322087
Holes: 18 6500 yds
V'trs: **
Fees: £10 (£12)

PORTADOWN
Carrickblacker, Portadown
Tel: (0762) 355356
Holes: 18 6119 yds
V'trs: *
Fees: £6 (£10)

TANDRAGEE
Markethill Road, Tandragee
Tel: (0762) 841761
Holes: 18 6084 yds
V'trs: **
Fees: £7 (£10)

BELFAST

BALMORAL
Lisburn Road, Belfast
Tel: (0232) 667747
Holes: 18 6600 yds
V'trs: **
Fees: £10 (£15)

BELVOIR CASTLE
Newtownbreda, Belfast
Tel: (0232) 646714
Holes: 18 6476 yds
V'trs: **
Fees: £12 (£15)

CLIFTONVILLE
Westland Road, Belfast
Tel: (0232) 744158
Holes: 9 4678 yds
V'trs: **
Fees: On enquiry

FORTWILLIAM
Downview Avenue, Belfast
Tel: (0232) 770980
Holes: 18 5642 yds
V'trs: **
Fees: £9 (£12)

KNOCKBRACKEN
*Ballymaconaghy Road,
Knockbracken, Belfast*
Tel: (0232) 401811
Holes: 18 5312 yds
V'trs: *
Fees: £5 (£7)

MALONE
*Upper Malone Road,
Dunmurry, Belfast*
Tel: (0232) 614917
Holes: 18 6499 yds
V'trs: **
Fees: £10 (£13)

ORMEAU
Ravenhill Road, Belfast
Tel: (0232) 641069
Holes: 9 5308 yds
V'trs: **
Fees: £4 (£5)

SHANDON PARK
Shandon Park, Belfast
Tel: (0232) 797859
Holes: 18 6252 yds
V'trs: *
Fees: £12 (£16)

KNOCK
*Summerfield, Dundonald,
Belfast*
Tel: (02318) 3825
Holes: 18 6500 yds
V'trs: **
Fees: £12 (£16)

CO CARLOW

BORRIS
Deerpark, Borris
Tel: (0503) 73143
Holes: 9 6026 yds
V'trs: **
Fees: £5 (£6)

CARLOW
Oak Park, Carlow
Tel: (0503) 31695
Holes: 18 6347 yds
V'trs: **
Fees: £7 (£10)

CO CAVAN

BELTURBET
Erne Hill, Belturbet
Tel: (049) 22287
Holes: 9 5180 yds
V'trs: **
Fees: £5

BLACKLION
Toam, Blacklion, via Sligo
Tel: (072) 53024
Holes: 9 6200 yds
V'trs: **
Fees: £4 (£10)

CABRA CASTLE
Kingscourt
Tel: (042) 67189
Holes: 9 5800 yds
V'trs: **
Fees: £4

COUNTY CAVAN
Arnmore House, Drumelis
Tel: (049) 31283
Holes: 18 5519 mts
V'trs: **
Fees: £8

VIRGINIA
T Virginia
Tel: (042) 65766
Holes: 9 4600 yds
V'trs: **
Fees: On enquiry

CO CLARE

ENNIS
Drumbiggle Road, Ennis
Tel: (065) 20690
Holes: 18 6000 yds
V'trs: **
Fees: £10

KILKEE
East End, Kilkee
Tel: Kilkee 48
Holes: 9 6185 yds
V'trs: **
Fees: £8 (£25)

LAHINCH
Lahinch
Tel: (065) 81408
Holes: Old 18 6699 yds
Castle 18 5265 yds
V'trs: **
Fees: £15 (£18), Castle £10

SHANNON
Shannon Airport
Tel: (061) 61551
Holes: 18 6854 yds
V'trs: **
Fees: £12

SPANISH POINT
Miltown Malbay
Tel: (065) 84198
Holes: 9 3820 yds
V'trs: **
Fees: £5 (£24)

CO CORK

BANDON
Castlebernard, Bandon
Tel: (023) 42224
Holes: 18 5696 yds
V'trs: **
Fees: £8 (£10)

BANTARY PARK
Donemark, Bantry
Tel: (027) 50579
Holes: 9 6486 yds
V'trs: **
Fees: £7

CHARLEVILLE
Smiths Road, Charleville
Tel: (011) 81257
Holes: 18 6380 yds
V'trs: **
Fees: £6

COBH
Ballywilliam, Cobh
Tel: (021) 812399
Holes: 9 5000 yds
V'trs: **
Fees: £4 (£5)

CORK
Little Island, Cork
Tel: (021) 353037
Holes: 18 6505 yds
V'trs: *
Fees: £15 (£17)

DONERAILE
Doneraile
Tel: (022) 24137
Holes: 9 5528 yds
V'trs: **
Fees: £3

DOUGLAS
Douglas
Tel: (021) 362055
Holes: 18 6184 yds
V'trs: **
Fees: £14 (£18)

DUNMORE
Dunmore, Clonakilty
Tel: (023) 33352
Holes: 9 4464 yds
V'trs: **
Fees: £5

EAST CORK
Gortacue, Midleton
Tel: (021) 631687
Holes: 18 6000 yds
V'trs: **
Fees: £6

FERMOY
Corin, Fermoy
Tel: Fermoy 31472
Holes: 18 6300 yds
V'trs: **
Fees: On enquiry

GLENGARIFF
Glengariff
Tel: (027) 63150
Holes: 9 4328 yds
V'trs: **
Fees: On enquiry

KANTURK
Fairy Hill, Kanturk
Tel: (029) 50534
Holes: 9 5527 yds
V'trs: *
Fees: £5

KINSALE
Ringenane, Belgooly, Kinsale
Tel: (021) 772197
Holes: 9 5332 yds
V'trs: **
Fees: £8

MACROOM
Lackaduve, Macroom
Tel: (026) 41072
Holes: 9 6000 yds
V'trs: **
Fees: £8

MALLOW
Balleyellis, Mallow
Tel: (022) 21145
Holes: 18 6559 yds
V'trs: **
Fees: £10 (£25)

MITCHELSTOWN
Mitchelstown
Tel: (025) 24072
Holes: 9 5500 yds
V'trs: **
Fees: £6

MONKSTOWN
Parkgarriffe, Monkstown
Tel: (021) 841 686
Holes: 18 6100 yds
V'trs: **
Fees: £11 (£12)

MUSKERRY
Carrigrohane
Tel: (021) 385104
Holes: 18 6200 yds
V'trs: *
Fees: £10

SKIBBEREEN
Skibbereen
Tel: (028) 21227
Holes: 9 5774 yds
V'trs: **
Fees: £6

YOUGHAL
Knockaverry, Youghal
Tel: (024) 92787
Holes: 18 6223 yds
V'trs: **
Fees: £11

CO DONEGAL

**BALLYBOFEY &
STRANORLAR**
Ballybofey
Tel: (074) 31093
Holes: 18 5922 yds
V'trs: **
Fees: £6

BALLYLIFFIN
Ballyliffin, Clonmany
Tel: (0787) 76119
Holes: 18 6611 yds
V'trs: **
Fees: £8 (£10)

BUNDORAN
*Great Northern Hotel,
Bundoran*
Tel: (072) 41302
Holes: 18 6328 yds
V'trs: *
Fees: £9 (£10)

DONEGAL
Murvagh
Tel: (073) 34054
Holes: 18 7271 yds
V'trs: **
Fees: £6 (£8)

GREENCASTLE
Via Lifford, Greencastle
Tel: (077) 81013
Holes: 9 5 386 yds
V'trs: **
Fees: £5 (£7)

GWEEDORE
Derrybeg, Letterkenny
Tel: (075) 31140
Holes: 18 6230 yds
V'trs: **
Fees: £5 (£7)

LETTERKENNY
Barnhill, Letterkenny
Tel: (074) 21150
Holes: 18 6299 yds
V'trs: **
Fees: £6

NARIN & PORTNOO
Narin, Portnoo
Tel: (075) 45107
Holes: 18 5950 yds
V'trs: ** H
Fees: £6 (£7)

NORTH WEST
Lisfannon, Fahan
Tel: (077) 61027
Holes: 18 6203 yds
V'trs: **
Fees: £10 (£15)

OTWAY
Saltpans, Rathmullen,
Letterkenny
Tel: (074) 58319
Holes: 9 4134 yds
V'trs: **
Fees: £3

PORTSALON
Portsalon, Letterkenny
Tel: Portsalon 59102
Holes: 18 5844 yds
V'trs: **
Fees: £4

ROSAPENNA
Golf Hotel, Rosapenna
Tel: (074) 55301
Holes: 18 6254 yds
V'trs: **
Fees: On enquiry

CO DOWN

ARDGLASS
Castle Place, Ardglass
Tel: (0396) 841219
Holes: 18 5900 yds
V'trs: **
Fees: £7 (£10)

BANBRIDGE
Huntly Road, Banbridge
Tel: (08206) 22342
Holes: 12 5879 yds
V'trs: **
Fees: £7 (£8)

BANGOR
Broadway, Bangor
Tel: (0247) 462164
Holes: 18 6372 yds
V'trs: *
Fees: £12 (£17)

BRIGHT CASTLE
Coniamstown Road, Bright,
Downpatrick
Tel: (0396) 841319
Holes: 18 6730 yds
V'trs: **
Fees: £4 (£6)

CARNALEA
Station Road, Bangor
Tel: (0247) 270122
Holes: 18 5584 yds
V'trs: *
Fees: £7 (£10)

CLANDEBOYE
Conlig, Newtownards
Tel: (0247) 271750
Holes: 18 6300 yds
18 5,600 yds
V'trs: *
Fees: £15, £12

DONAGHADEE
Warren Road, Donaghadee
Tel: (0237) 882392
Holes: 18 6200 yds
V'trs: *
Fees: £10

DOWNPATRICK
Saul Road, Downpatrick
Tel: (0396) 2152
Holes: 18 6300 yds
V'trs: **
Fees: £10

HELEN'S BAY
Golf Road, Helen's Bay, Bangor
Tel: (0247) 853313
Holes: 9 5676 yds
V'trs: * H
Fees: On enquiry

HOLYWOOD
Nuns Walk, Demesne Road,
Holywood
Tel: (02317) 5503
Holes: 18 5885 yds
V'trs: *
Fees: £15

KIRKISTOWN CASTLE
Main Road, Cloughey,
Newtownards
Tel: (024 77) 71233/71353
Holes: 18 6100 yds
V'trs: *
Fees: £13

MAHEE ISLAND
Comber, Belfast
Tel: (0238) 541234
Holes: 9 2790 yds
V'trs: **
Fees: £10

ROYAL BELFAST
Holywood, Craigavad
Tel: (0232) 428165
Holes: 18 6184 yds
V'trs: * H
Fees: £16

ROYAL COUNTY DOWN
Newcastle
Tel: (03967) 22419
Holes: 18 6968 yds
18 4100 yds
V'trs: On enquiry
Fees: £25

SCRABO
Scrabo Road, Newtownards
Tel: (0247) 812355
Holes: 18 6100 yds
V'trs: **
Fees: £10

THE SPA
Grove Road, Ballynahinch
Tel: (0238) 562365
Holes: 18 6500 yds
V'trs: **
Fees: £10

WARRENPOINT
Dromore Road, Warrenpoint
Tel: (0690 37) 72371
Holes: 18 6100 yds
V'trs: **
Fees: £15

DUBLIN CITY

CARRICKMINES
Carrickmines
Tel: (0001) 9559721
Holes: 18 6044 yds
V'trs: ***

CASTLE
Woodside Drive, Rathfarnham,
Dublin
Tel: (0001) 933444
Holes: 18 6240 yds
V'trs: *
Fees: £13

CLONTARF
Malahide Road, Dublin
Tel: (0001) 310016
Holes: 18 5700 yds
V'trs: **
Fees: £12

EDMONDSTOWN
Rathfarnham, Dublin
Tel: (0001) 934602
Holes: 18 6195 yds
V'trs: **
Fees: £13

ELM PARK
Nutley House, Donnybrook,
Dublin
Tel: (0001) 692650
Holes: 18 5600 yds
V'trs: **
Fees: £18

FOXROCK
Torquay Road, Dublin
Tel: (0001) 893992
Holes: 6000 yds
V'trs: *
Fees: £15

GRANGE
Whitechurch, Rathfarnham,
Dublin
Tel: (0001) 932299
Holes: 18 5800 yds
V'trs: *
Fees: £20

HOWTH
Carrickbrack Road, Sutton,
Dublin
Tel: (0001) 393895
Holes: 18 5900 yds
V'trs: *
Fees: £12

MILLTOWN
Lower Churchtown Road,
Milltown, Dublin
Tel: (0001) 977072
Holes: 18 6000 yds
V'trs: **
Fees: £18 (£26)

RATHFARNHAM
Newtown, Dublin
Tel: (0001) 931201
Holes: 9 6100 yds
V'trs: **
Fees: £10

ROYAL DUBLIN
Bull Island, Dollymount, Dublin
Tel: (0001) 336477
Holes: 18 6858 yds
V'trs: *
Fees: £25 (£35)

ST ANNE'S
North Bull Island, Dollymount,
Dublin
Tel: (0001) 332797
Holes: 6400 yds
V'trs: *
Fees: £15

SLACKSTOWN
Kellystown Road, Rathfarnham,
Dublin
Tel: (0001) 942338
Holes: 18 6500 yds
V'trs: *
Fees: £10

SUTTON
Cush Point, Burrow Road,
Sutton, Dublin
Tel: (0001) 323013
Holes: 9 5522 yds
V'trs: *
Fees: £10

CO DUBLIN

BALBRIGGAN
Blackhall, Balbriggan
Tel: (0001) 412173
Holes: 18 5900 yds
V'trs: *
Fees: £11

BALLINASCORNEY
Ballinascorney, Tallaght
Tel: (0001) 512516
Holes: 9 5 322 yds
V'trs: **
Fees: £8

BEAVERSTOWN
Beaverstown, Donabate
Tel: (01) 436439
Holes: 18 6100 yds
V'trs: **
Fees: £10

BEECH PARK
Johnstown, Rathcoole
Tel: (0001) 580522
Holes: 18 6500 yds
V'trs: **
Fees: £12

DONABATE
Balcarrick, Donabate
Tel: (0001) 436059
Holes: 18 6187 yds
V'trs: *
Fees: On enquiry

DUN LAOGHAIRE
Dun Laoghaire, Eglinton Park,
Dublin
Tel: (0001) 810694
Holes: 18 5800 yds
V'trs: **
Fees: £18

FORREST LITTLE
Cloghran
Tel: (0001) 401183
Holes: 18 6100 yds
V'trs: **
Fees: £15

HERMITAGE
Lucan
Tel: (0001) 268491
Holes: 18 6500 yds
V'trs: *
Fees: £18

THE ISLAND
Corballis, Donabate
Tel: (0001) 436104
Holes: 18 6320 yds
V'trs: *
Fees: £20

KILLINEY
Killiney
Tel: (0001) 851983
Holes: 9 6201 yds
V'trs: **
Fees: £11

LUCAN
Celbridge Road, Lucan
Tel: (0001) 280246
Holes: 9 6000 yds
V'trs: *
Fees: £8

MALAHIDE
Coast Road, Malahide
Tel: (0001) 450248
Holes: 9 5568 yds
V'trs: **
Fees: £8

NEWLANDS
Clondalkin, Dublin
Tel: (01) 593538
Holes: 18 6184 yds
V'trs: **
Fees: £15

PORTMARNOCK
Portmarnock
Tel: (01) 325157
Holes: 27 A 7096 yds
B 7046 yds
C 6596 yds
V'trs: * H
Fees: £35

RUSH
Rush
Tel: (01) 437548
Holes: 9 5800 yds
V'trs: **
Fees: £8

SKERRIES
Skerries
Tel: (01) 490925
Holes: 18 6182 yds
V'trs: **
Fees: £15

SLADE VALLEY
Lynch Park, Brittas
Tel: (01) 582207
Holes: 18 6500 yds
V'trs: *
Fees: £8

WOODBROOK
Bray
Tel: (081) 24799
Holes: 18 6600 yds
V'trs: *
Fees: £16

CO FERMANAGH

ENNISKILLEN
Castlecoole, Enniskillen
Tel: (0365) 25250
Holes: 18 6208 yds
V'trs: **
Fees: £8

CO GALWAY

ATHENRY
Derrydonnel, Oranmore
Tel: (091) 94466
Holes: 9 5448 yds
V'trs: **
Fees: £6

BALLINASLOE
Ballinasloe
Tel: (0905) 42126
Holes: 18 5830 yds
V'trs: **
Fees: £6

CONNEMARA
Aillebrack, Ballyconnelly, nr Clifden
Tel: (095) 23502
Holes: 18 6885 yds
V'trs: * H
Fees: £12

GALWAY
Blackrock, Salthill, Galway
Tel: (091) 23038
Holes: 18 6300 yds
V'trs: **
Fees: £15

GORT
Laughtyshaughnessy, Gort
Tel: (091) 31336
Holes: 9 5300 yds
V'trs: **
Fees: £6

LOUGHREA
Graigue, Loughrea
Tel: (091) 41049
Holes: 9 5578 yds
V'trs: **
Fees: £5

MOUNT BELLEW
Mount Bellew, Ballinasloe
Tel: (0905) 9259
Holes: 9 5564 yds
V'trs: **
Fees: £6

OUGHTERARD
Oughterard
Tel: (091) 82131
Holes: 18 6150 yds
V'trs: **
Fees: £12

PORTMUMNA
Portmumna
Tel: (0509) 41059
Holes: 9 5776 yds
V'trs: **
Fees: £6

TUAM
Barnacurragh, Tuam
Tel: (093) 24354
Holes: 18 6321 yds
V'trs: *
Fees: £8

CO KERRY

BALLYBUNION
Ballybunion
Tel: (068) 27209
Holes: Old 18 6542 yds
New 18 6477 yds
V'trs: **
Fees: £22

CEANN SIBEAL
Ballyferriter, Tralee
Tel: (066) 56255
Holes: 18 6600 yds
V'trs: **
Fees: £12

DOOKS
Glenbeigh
Tel: (066) 68205
Holes: 18 6802 yds
V'trs: * H
Fees: £15

KENMARE
Kenmare
Tel: (064) 41291
Holes: 9 4900 yds
V'trs: **
Fees: £7

KILLARNEY
O'Mahoney's Point, Killarney
Tel: (064) 31615
Holes: Mahoney's Point 6700 yds
Killeen 18 6900 yds
V'trs: ** H
Fees: £20

PARKNASILLA
Parknasilla
Tel: (064) 45172
Holes: 9 4834 yds
V'trs: **
Fees: £8

TRALEE
West Barrow, Ardfert
Tel: (066) 36379
Holes: 18 6800 yds
V'trs: **
Fees: £12 (£14)

WATERVILLE
Ring of Kerry, Waterville
Tel: (0667) 4237
Holes: 18 7184 yds
V'trs: ** H
Fees: £18

CO KILDARE

ATHY
Geraldine, Athy
Tel: (0507) 31729
Holes: 9 6158 yds
V'trs: *
Fees: £4 (£6)

BODENSTOWN
Bodenstown, Sallins
Tel: (045) 97096
Holes: 18 7031 yds
V'trs: **
Fees: £15

CILL DARA
Little Curragh, Kildare Town
Tel: (045) 21433
Holes: 9 6000 yds
V'trs: **
Fees: £4 (£6)

CURRAGH
Curragh
Tel: (045) 41238/41714
Holes: 18 6600 yds
V'trs: *
Fees: £12

KNOCKANALLY
Donadea, North Kildare
Tel: (045) 69322
Holes: 18 6484 yds
V'trs: **
Fees: £8 (£10)

NAAS
Kerdiffstown, Naas
Tel: (045) 97509
Holes: 9 6233 yds
V'trs: **
Fees: £5

CO KILKENNY

CALLAN
Geraldine, Callan
Tel: (056) 25136
Holes: 9 5844 yds
V'trs: **
Fees: £5

CASTLECOMER
Castlecomer
Tel: (056) 41139
Holes: 9 6985 yds
V'trs: **
Fees: £7

KILKENNY
Glendine, Kilkenny
Tel: (056) 61730
Holes: 18 6374 yds
V'trs: **
Fees: £12

CO LAOIS

ABBEY LEIX
Abbey Leix, Portlaoise
Tel: (0502) 31450
Holes: 9 5680 yds
V'trs: **
Fees: £5

HEATH
Portlaoise
Tel: (0502) 46622
Holes: 18 6247 yds
V'trs: **
Fees: £7

MOUNTRATH
Knockanina, Mountrath
Tel: (0502) 32558
Holes: 9 5300 yds
V'trs: **
Fees: £5

PORTARLINGTON
Carryhinch, Portarlington
Tel: (0502) 23115
Holes: 9 5800 yds
V'trs: **
Fees: £6

RATHDOWNEY
Rathdowney, Portlaoise
Tel: (0505) 46170
Holes: 9 6086 yds
V'trs: **
Fees: £5

CO LEITRIM

BALLINAMORE
Ballinamore
Tel: (078) 44346
Holes: 9 5680 yds
V'trs: **
Fees: £4

CARRICK-ON-SHANNON
Woodbrook, Carrick-on-Shannon
Tel: (078) 67015
Holes: 9 5584 yds
V'trs: *
Fees: £5

CO LIMERICK

ADARE MANOR
Adare
Tel: (061) 86204
Holes: 9 5600 yds
V'trs: *
Fees: £10

CASTLETROY
Castletroy, Limerick
Tel: (061) 338283
Holes: 18 6200 yds
V'trs: *
Fees: £10

LIMERICK
Ballyclough, Limerick
Tel: (061) 42492
Holes: 18 5767 yds
V'trs: *
Fees: £12

NEWCASTLE WEST
Newcastle West
Tel: (069) 62015
Holes: 9 5482 yds
V'trs: *
Fees: £6

CO LONDONDERRY

BROWN TROUT
209 Agivey Road, Aghadovey, Coleraine
Tel: (0265) 868209
Holes: 9 2500 yds
V'trs: **
Fees: £5

CASTLEROCK
Circular Road, Castlerock
Tel: (0265) 848314
Holes: 18 6600 yds
9 2600 yds
V'trs: *
Fees: £10 (£20) and £3 (£5)

CITY OF DERRY
Victoria Road, Londonderry
Tel: (05604) 311496
Holes: Prehen 18 6406 yds
Dunhugh 9 4708 yds
V'trs: ** H
Fees: Prehen £6 (18)
Dunhugh £3

KILREA
Drumagarner Road, Kilrea
Tel: (02665) 71397
Holes: 9 4326 yds
V'trs: *
Fees: £5 (£5)

MAYOLA PARK
Shanemullagh, Castledawson, Magherafelt
Tel: (0648) 68830
Holes: 18 6517 yds
V'trs: **
Fees: £8 (£10)

PORTSTEWART
Strand Road, Portstewart
Tel: (026 583) 2601
Holes: Strand 18 6784 yds
Town 18 4733 yds
V'trs: *
Fees: Strand £12 (£17)
Town £4 (£6)

CO LONGFORD

CO LONGFORD
Glack, Dublin Road, Longford
Tel: (043) 46310
Holes: 18 5912 yds
V'trs: **
Fees: On enquiry

CO LOUTH

ARDEE
Townparks, Ardee
Tel: (041) 53227
Holes: 18 5833 yds
V'trs: **
Fees: £8 (£9)

COUNTY LOUTH
Baltray, Drogheda
Tel: (041) 22444
Holes: 18 6978 yds
V'trs: *
Fees: On enquiry

DUNDALK
Blackrock, Dundalk
Tel: (042) 22102
Holes: 18 6615 yds
V'trs: **
Fees: £10 (£12)

GREENORE
Greenore
Tel: (042) 73212
Holes: 18 5800 yds
V'trs: *
Fees: £8 (£10)

CO MAYO

ACHILL ISLAND
Keel, Achill Island
Tel: (098) 43202
Holes: 9 2723 yds
V'trs: ** H
Fees: £3

BALLINA
Mosgrove, Shanaghy, Ballina
Tel: (096) 21050
Holes: 9 5702 yds
V'trs: *
Fees: £5 (£5)

BALLYHAUNIS
Coolaha, Ballyhaunis
Tel: (0907) 30014
Holes: 9 5800 yds
V'trs: *
Fees: £5

BELMULLET
Belmullet, Ballina
Tel: (097) 81093
Holes: 9 2829 yds
V'trs: **
Fees: £3

CASTLEBAR
Rocklands, Castlebar
Tel: (094) 21649
Holes: 18 6109 yds
V'trs: **
Fees: £8

CLAREMORRIS
Claremorris
Tel: (094) 71527
Holes: 9 6454 yds
V'trs: **
Fees: £4

SWINFORD
Brabazon Park, Swinford
Tel: (094) 51378
Holes: 9 5230 yds
V'trs: **
Fees: £5

WESTPORT
Carowholly, Westport
Tel: (098) 25113
Holes: 18 6355 yds
V'trs: **
Fees: £9

CO MEATH

BLACKBUSH
Thornastown, Dunshaughglin
Tel: (01) 250021
Holes: 18 7000 yds
9 2309 yds
V'trs: **
Fees: £5 (£8)

HEADFORT
Kells
Tel: (046) 40639
Holes: 18 6350 yds
V'trs: **
Fees: £8 (£11)

LAYTON & BETTYSTOWN
Bettystown
Tel: (041) 27170
Holes: 18 6254 yds
V'trs: **
Fees: £10 (£15)

ROYAL TARA
Bellinter, Navan
Tel: (046) 25244/25584
Holes: 18 6200 yds
V'trs: **
Fees: £10 (£12)

TRIM
Newtownmoynagh, Trim
Tel: (046) 31463
Holes: 9 6266 yds
V'trs: *
Fees: £8

CO MONAGHAN

CASTLEBLAYNEY
Castleblayney
Tel: (042) 40197
Holes: 9 2678 yds
V'trs: **
Fees: £3 (£4)

CLONES
Scotshouse, Clones
Tel: (049) 56017
Holes: 9 5570 yds
V'trs: *
Fees: £5

NUREMORE
Nuremore, Carrickmacross
Tel: (042) 61438
Holes: 9 6032 yds
V'trs: **
Fees: £5

ROSSMORE
Rossmoare Park, Monaghan
Tel: Monaghan 81316
Holes: 9 5859 yds
V'trs: **
Fees: £4 (£5)

CO OFFALY

BIRR
The Glenns, Birr
Tel: (0509) 20082
Holes: 18 6216 yds
V'trs: *
Fees: £6

EDENDERRY
Kishavanna, Edenderry
Tel: (0405) 310972
Holes: 9 5791 yds
V'trs: **
Fees: £5 (£6)

TULLAMORE
Brookfield, Tullamore
Tel: (0506) 21439
Holes: 18 6314 yds
V'trs: *
Fees: £10

CO ROSCOMMON

ATHLONE
Hodson Bay, Athlone
Tel: (0902) 92073
Holes: 18 6500 yds
V'trs: *
Fees: £10

BALLAGHADERREEN
Ballaghaderreen
Holes: 9 5663 yds
V'trs: *
Fees: £5

BOYLE
Roscommon Road, Boyle
Tel: (079) 62594
Holes: 9 5650 yds
V'trs: **
Fees: £4

CASTLEREA
Clonalis, Castlerea
Tel: (0907) 20068
Holes: 9 5466 yds
V'trs: **
Fees: £3 (£5)

ROSCOMMON
Mote Park, Roscommon
Tel: (0903) 6382
Holes: 9 5657 yds
V'trs: **
Fees: £3

CO SLIGO

BALLYMOTE
Ballymote
Tel: Ballymote 3460
Holes: 9 5032 yds
V'trs: **
Fees: £4

COUNTY SLIGO
Rosses Point
Tel: (071) 77171
Holes: 18 6500 yds
V'trs: *
Fees: £15 (£15)

ENNISCRONE
Enniscrone
Tel: (096) 36297
Holes: 18 6487 yds
V'trs: **
Fees: £7

STRANDHILL
Strandhill
Tel: (071) 68188
Holes: 18 5937 yds
V'trs: *
Fees: £8

CO TIPPERARY

CAHIR PARK
Kilcommon, Cahir
Tel: (052) 41474
Holes: 9 6262 yds
V'trs: *
Fees: £6 (£6)

CARRICK-ON-SUIR
Garravone, Carrick-on-Suir
Tel: (051) 40047
Holes: 9 5948 yds
V'trs: *
Fees: £5

CLONMEL
Mountain Road, Clonmel
Tel: (052) 21138
Holes: 18 6330 yds
V'trs: **
Fees: £6 (£8)

NENAGH
Beechwood, Nenagh
Tel: (067) 33242
Holes: 18 5900 yds
V'trs: **
Fees: £7 (£12)

ROSCREA
Roscrea
Tel: (0505) 21130
Holes: 9 6059 yds
V'trs: **
Fees: £5

TEMPLEMORE
Manna South, Templemore
Tel: Templemore 53
Holes: 9 5442 yds
V'trs: *
Fees: £4 (£5)

THURLES
Turtulla, Thurles
Tel: (0504) 21983/22466
Holes: 18 6400 yds
V'trs: *
Fees: £10

TIPPERARY
Rathanny, Tipperary
Tel: (062) 51119
Holes: 9 6074 yds
V'trs: **
Fees: £6

CO TYRONE

DUNGANNON
Mullaghmore, Dungannon
Tel: (08687) 22098
Holes: 18 5914 yds
V'trs: **
Fees: £7 (£9)

FINTONA
Ecclesville Demesne, Fintona
Tel: (0662) 841480
Holes: 9 5716 yds
V'trs: *
Fees: £5 (£10)

KILLIMOON
Killymoon Road, Cookstown
Tel: (064 87) 63762/62254
Holes: 18 5800 yds
V'trs: **
Fees: £10 (£14)

NEWTOWNSTEWART
Golf Course Road,
Newtownstewart
Tel: (06626) 61466
Holes: 18 5800 yds
V'trs: **
Fees: £6 (£8)

OMAGH
Dublin Road, Omagh
Tel: (0662) 316/41442
Holes: 18 5700 yds
V'trs: **
Fees: £6 (£8)

STRABANE
Ballycolman, Strabane
Tel: (0504) 382271
Holes: 18 5900 yds
V'trs: **
Fees: £6 (£8)

CO WATERFORD

DUNGARVAN
Ballinacourty, Dungarvan
Tel: (058) 41605
Holes: 9 6300 yds
V'trs: **
Fees: £8

LISMORE
Lismore, Ballyin
Tel: (058) 54026
Holes: 9 5600 yds
V'trs: *
Fees: £6

TRAMORE
Tramore
Tel: (051) 86170
Holes: 18 6690 yds
V'trs: **
Fees: £15

WATERFORD
Newrath, Waterford
Tel: (051) 76748
Holes: 18 6800 yds
V'trs: **
Fees: £10

CO WESTMEATH

MOATE
Moate
Tel: (0902) 81271
Holes: 9 5348 yds
V'trs: **
Fees: £5 (£6)

MULLINGAR
Belvedere, Mullingar
Tel: (044) 48366
Holes: 18 6370 yds
V'trs: **
Fees: £10

CO WEXFORD

COURTOWN
Courtown Harbour, Gorey
Tel: (055) 25166
Holes: 18 6398 yds
V'trs: **
Fees: £8 (£11)

ENNISCORTHY
Knockmarshal, Enniscorthy
Tel: (054) 33191
Holes: 18 5803 yds
V'trs: *
Fees: £6 (£8)

NEW ROSS
Tinneranny, New Ross
Tel: (051) 21433
Holes: 9 6300 yds
V'trs: *
Fees: £6 (£8)

ROSSLARE
Strand, Rosslare
Tel: (053) 32113/32238
Holes: 18 6502 yds
V'trs: **
Fees: £10 (£12)

WEXFORD
Mulgannon, Wexford
Tel: (053) 42238
Holes: 18 6109 yds
V'trs: **
Fees: £7 (£8)

CO WICKLOW

ARKLOW
Abbeylands, Arklow
Tel: (0402) 32492
Holes: 18 5770 yds
V'trs: *
Fees: £8 (£9)

BALTINGLASS
Baltinglass
Tel: (0508) 81530
Holes: 9 6070 yds
V'trs: *
Fees: £6 (£8)

BLAINROE
Blainroe
Tel: (0404) 68168
Holes: 18 6681 yds
V'trs: **
Fees: £8 (£14)

BRAY
Ravenswell Road, Bray
Tel: (0001) 862484
Holes: 9 5800 yds
V'trs: *
Fees: £10

COOLLATTIN
Coollattin, Shillelagh
Tel: (055) 29125
Holes: 9 6070 yds
V'trs: **
Fees: £5 (£8)

DELGANY
Delgany
Tel: (0404) 874536
Holes: 18 5249 yds
V'trs: **
Fees: £12 (£15)

GREYSTONES
Greystones
Tel: (0001) 876624
Holes: 18 5800 yds
V'trs: *
Fees: £14 (£17)

OLD CONNA
Ferndale Road, Bray
Tel: (0001) 826055
Holes: 18 6600 yds
V'trs: **
Fees: £14

WICKLOW
Dunbur Road, Wicklow
Tel: (0404) 67379
Holes: 9 5556 yds
V'trs: **
Fees: £7 (£11)

WOODENBRIDGE
Arklow
Tel: (0402) 5202
Holes: 9 6104 yds
V'trs: *
Fees: £10 (£12)

HANBURY MANOR

Opened in 1991 and designed by Jack Nicklaus, Junior, Hanbury Manor has been enthusiastically received by all who have played over it.

Although only in its first season, this superb new course already has links with two British Open champions, Harry Vardon and America's Jack Nicklaus.

The Vardon connection goes back to the 1920s which was when the five-times Open champion, was commissioned to design a nine-hole golf course in the grounds of Hanbury Manor. The house which overlooks this beautiful 200-acre estate, situated some 22 miles north of London, was originally designed in 1890 by Sir Ernest George who was also responsible for designing the famous Claridges Hotel in London.

Over the intervening years, Vardon's nine-hole course slowly disappeared and it was not until work began clearing the land for this exciting new eighteen-hole course, that evidence of the great man's layout was discovered. And it is at this point in the story that Hanbury Manor's second British Open champion connection comes to light.

In 1987 the new owners set out to restore the old house to its former glory and open it as a luxury hotel, featuring a top quality, eighteen-hole golf course. The man given the task of designing the course was Jack Nicklaus, Junior, eldest son of the three-times British Open champion.

BELOW: The thirteenth hole is a challenging par four. Below right: the bunker that guards the green at the par-three fourth hole will gather any ball that is hit too short.

ABOVE AND RIGHT: *It soon becomes clear to visitors to Hanbury Manor that little money has been spared in restoring the house to its former grandeur.*

Hanbury Manor is Jackie's first course in Great Britain and when the design work was completed he said, "Hanbury Manor is blessed with a variety of land features, including significant elevation changes, an impressive stock of hardwoods, as well as lakes and streams. I have designed a course to accommodate a wide range of golfers. I believe it has the ability to tax the skilled player, yet is enjoyable to all."

Jack Nicklaus, Jnr. has certainly made the most of these established features, along with the introduction of some outstanding fairway sculpturing, all of which have combined to give the golf course a remarkably mature appearance in a very short period of time. This feeling of maturity is helped greatly by some magnificent old trees, especially on the back nine, which have been skilfully incorporated into the design of many of the holes.

Although there are fewer trees on the opening nine holes, the changes in elevation and the creative use of water have resulted in the design of several quite spectacular holes, like the par-five ninth, which plays slightly uphill and dog-legs to the right. The green is set into the slopes of what was once an old quarry and this hole is certain to become one of the features of a course which will measure over 7,000 yards from the championship tees.

No expense has been spared in the construction of the course and only the finest grasses have been used for the greens and fairways. Likewise, Hanbury Manor, which has been tastefully extended in the same architectural style as the original building. The hotel offers first class accommodation, a superb leisure centre and a first class restaurant with comprehensive banqueting and conference facilities.

Situated at Thunderbridge, near Ware in Hertfordshire, this superb new facility has all the credentials to become one of the top Golf and Country Clubs of the 90s.

The professional at Hanbury Manor Golf and Country Club is Peter Blaze, who was previously professional at Moor Allerton in Yorkshire for seventeen years. Many fellow professionals are, no doubt, envious of the facilities this new club offers.

Attention to detail is a hallmark at Hanbury Manor as evidenced by this elegant bedroom.

INDEX

Entries in italic refer to illustrations and caption references

Acknowledgements

The photographs in this book were taken by Matthew Harris, Phil Sheldon, and Bob Atkins.
The artwork was prepared by Graham Gaches.
The publishers gratefully acknowledge their contribution.

Front cover picture: Matthew Harris.